SOCIAL STRATIFICATION IN AFRICA

ABOUT THE EDITORS

ARTHUR TUDEN is Professor of Anthropology at the University of Pittsburgh. Managing Editor of the journal *Ethnology* and co-editor of *Political Anthropology* and *Comparative Social Stratification,* Professor Tuden has also written several works on slavery and political change.

LEONARD PLOTNICOV is Associate Professor of Anthropology at the University of Pittsburgh. He is the author of *Strangers to the City: Urban Man in Jos, Nigeria* and co-editor of *Comparative Social Stratification.*

SOCIAL STRATIFICATION IN AFRICA

EDITED BY

ARTHUR TUDEN

AND **LEONARD PLOTNICOV**

THE FREE PRESS, NEW YORK
COLLIER-MACMILLAN LIMITED, LONDON

CONTENTS

Contents

CONTRIBUTORS

JACQUES MAQUET, Professor of Anthropology at Case–Western Reserve University, was educated at the University of Louvain, the University of London and Harvard University. He was head of the Research Center of the Institut pour la Recherche Scientifique en Afrique centrale. His major publications include *The Premise of Inequality in Ruanda; The Sociology of Knowledge.* He has published numerous articles on political sociology and stratification.

RONALD COHEN, Associate Professor of Anthropology and Political Science at Northwestern University, was educated at the University of Toronto and the University of Wisconsin. He has been the chairman of the Committee on African Studies in Canada and assistant editor of *Anthropologica.* His publications include *The Kanuri of Bornu,* and he has co-edited *Reader in Political Anthropology* and *Handbook of Methodology in Cultural Anthropology.*

MELVIN PERLMAN, Assistant Professor of Anthropology at the University of California at Berkeley, was trained at Oxford University. His major publication on East Africa, *Toro Marriage: A Study of Changing Conjugal Institutions in Western Uganda,* is now in press.

AIDAN W. SOUTHALL, born in England, is a Professor of Anthropology at the University of Wisconsin. He has taught at Syracuse University and Makerere University College. Professor Southall was the chairman of the East African Institute of Social Research. Among his numerous publications are *Alur Society* and *Townsmen in the Making;* he edited *Social Change in Modern Africa.*

Contributors

JAMES CLYDE MITCHELL, born in Pietermaritzburgh, South Africa, is Professor of Urban Sociology at the University of Manchester. Previously he held the position of Director of the Rhodes-Livingstone Institute, Vice-Principal, University College of Rhodesia and Nyasaland, and Visiting Professor, S.A.I.S., Johns Hopkins University. He has published *The Yao Village, The Kalela Dance,* and numerous articles on urbanization and social stratification.

PIERRE L. VAN DEN BERGHE, born in Elisabethville, Congo, is Associate Professor of Sociology at the University of Washington. His publications include *Caneville: The Social Structure of a South African Town,* and *South Africa: A Study in Conflict;* he was editor of *Africa, Social Problems of Change and Conflict.* In addition he has published numerous articles on ethnic relations and social stratification in both United States and European journals.

JAMES H. VAUGHAN, Jr. Associate Professor and Chairman of the Department of Anthropology, University of Indiana, was educated at the University of North Carolina and Northwestern University. He is the president of the Central States Anthropological Society. His publications are based on fifteen months of field work among the Marghi of the Cameroons and Nigeria.

ALLAN HOBEN, Assistant Professor of Anthropology at the University of Rochester, was trained at the University of California, Berkeley. Among his publications is the *Land Tenure Among Damot Amhara.*

HERBERT S. LEWIS, Associate Professor of Anthropology at the University of Wisconsin, was trained at Columbia University. Among his publications is *A Galla Monarchy: Jimma Abba Jifar, Ethiopia, 1830–1932.*

LEONARD PLOTNICOV, Chairman and Associate Professor of Anthropology at the University of Pittsburgh, was trained at the University of California at Berkeley. His research has focused on modern urbanization with particular emphasis on West Africa. He is the author of *Strangers to the City: Urban Man in Jos, Nigeria* and co-editor of *Comparative Social Stratification.*

ARTHUR TUDEN is Professor of Anthropology at the University of Pittsburgh. He has been the Managing Editor for the past four years of the journal *Ethnology.* He is the co-editor of *Political Anthropology* and *Comparative Social Stratification.* He has published works on slavery and political change.

Introduction

The appearance of *African Political Systems* in 1940, edited by M. Fortes and E. E. Evans-Pritchard, marked the initiation of a publication style in African studies that has continued through the present and still shows strong indications of maintaining its vitality. The list of volumes that have appeared within this format—each work dealing with a special topic—is impressive and has no counterpart for any other major cultural area of the world.[1] Some may view this plethora of volumes in African ethnology and sociology as the decreasingly profitable mining of a finite research resource and they may therefore ask: Why yet another?

The contributors to the present volume believe that the variety of cultural and social patterns illustrated by African institutions of social stratification indicate the value of pursuing comparative research in this topical area. There are limitations, of course, of which we should be aware. With all of their different forms, African societies do not exhaust the range of types of social stratification phenomena that exist or have

1. The extensiveness of such a list is a tribute not only to the scholars who contributed to this development, but also to the variety and richness of the African cultural heritage. The following compilation includes the major studies: A. R. Radcliffe-Brown and D. Forde, 1950, African Systems of Kinship and Marriage; D. Forde, 1954, African Worlds: Studies in the Cosmological Ideas and Social Values of African Peoples; International African Institute for UNESCO, 1956, Social Implications of Urbanization and Industrialization in Africa South of the Sahara; J. Middleton and D. Tait, 1958, Tribes without Rulers; W. R. Bascom and M. J. Herskovits, 1959, Continuity and Change in African Cultures; P. Bohannan, 1960, African Homicide and Suicide; A. I. Richards, 1960, East African Chiefs: A Study of Political Development in some Uganda and Tanganyika Tribes; A. Southall, 1961, Social

1

existed. Yet the range of variation within Africa is broad enough to justify a theoretical treatment of this continent as a major step toward wider comparisons.

SOCIAL STRATIFICATION

Social stratification is so intrinsic to economic and political institutions that without understanding it one cannot hope to comprehend either the direction and forms of social and cultural changes that occur in Africa or the structure and processes of any complex social system. Nevertheless, scholars have been relatively little interested in stratification as compared with kinship and economic and political organization, as a review of past research in Africa indicates. On another level, one is struck by the disproportionate emphasis on the traditional features of African societies as compared with the study of the processes of change and contemporary developments, although a more recent trend points to a correction of this imbalance. As part of this trend, the present volume seeks not only to provide substantive and theoretical contributions to the neglected but important topic of social stratification, but also to enhance its heuristic value by relating it to the dynamics of social change.

Most ethnographies dealing with traditional conditions are directed toward topical and theoretical interests other than social stratification, and because of the neglect of social stratification as a theoretical concern, the relevant data for Africa are usually presented in the context of other topics, such as political affairs, economic organization, or contemporary urban and national developments. Whether or not these practices reflect a previous lack of interest in the topic or an inadequate theoretical framework to permit its separate treatment, they have resulted in an insufficient and uneven presentation of information required by the scholar singling out social stratification for analysis and comparison. The relative absence of a direct concern with African examples of social inequality makes the attempt to provide a comprehensive picture of social stratification for many groups difficult, and also, because of the omission of crucial or

Change in Modern Africa; P. Bohannan and G. Dalton, 1962, Markets in Africa; J. Middleton and E. H. Winter, 1963, Witchcraft and Sorcery in East Africa; R. F. Gray and P. H. Gulliver, 1964, The Family Estate in Africa: Studies in the Role of Property in Family Structure and Lineage Continuity; M. J. Herskovits and M. Harwitz, 1964, Economic Transition in Africa; J. Vansina et al., 1964, The Historian in Tropical Africa; M. Fortes and G. Dieterlen, 1965, African Systems of Thought; H. Kuper, 1965, Urbanization and Migration in West Africa; R. A. Lystad, 1965, The African World: A Survey of Social Research; J. Goody, 1966, Succession to High Office; H. and L. Kuper, 1966, African Law: Adaptation and Development; I. M. Lewis, 1966, Islam in Tropical Africa; P. C. Lloyd, 1966, The New Elites of Tropical Africa.

sufficiently detailed information, it has hindered the development of fruitful theoretical formulations.

Conceptual confusion has played no small part in the relative weakness of African social stratification studies. Where there has been a specific interest in this topic, the theoretical frameworks and categories of analysis have been so diverse as to render almost impossible an attempt to make comparisons and generalizations. This problem is well illustrated in the literature on the various groups designated as "castes" described for the Sahara, Sudan, Ethiopia, and East Africa. Such concepts as caste, slavery, class, and pluralism have been employed to describe and analyze specific ethnographic contexts, and the attempt to compare the data and situations from diverse societies has often resulted in controversy. The differences of opinion lie primarily in the *definition* of the types of stratification, and secondarily in the concept of social stratification itself. In this regard Africanist scholars bear no special guilt, for these problems of definition and conceptualization are widely shared. Let us bear in mind that not only are the empirical manifestations of social stratification, such as slavery and caste, never exactly comparable between societies, but the theoretical orientations through which they can be analyzed are also quite varied. The scholar dealing with this topic can employ a Marxist, Weberian, Parsonian, functionalist, or other approach, or can even deny the existence of concrete strata as empirical groups. One intended value of a work such as the present volume is to elicit common features from a range of examples so that the generalizations derived may be applied to similar phenomena both within Africa and in societies in other parts of the world. Thus, for example, employing the material in this volume, the reader may compare what has been described as castes in South Africa, Ethiopia, and among the Marghi, and the Rwanda, with those of India, Japan, and elsewhere.

Before we can approach any general agreement on a theoretical framework with which to initiate comparative studies of social stratification, it is necessary to offer a definition of the general phenomenon, to distinguish it from the ubiquitous condition of social ranking, and to indicate where current theories and concepts of these phenomena require modification in order to facilitate their suitable application to the African examples.

The term *social stratification* first of all implies the existence of a structure of layers in a society. Within each layer (stratum) persons are grouped on the basis of status criteria, and the arrangement of these layers (strata) is of a hierarchical order indicating differences of social worth associated with the strata or with the statuses which the strata respectively incorporate. In other words, for a society to be stratified, it must have principles for organizing individuals into hierarchically arranged groups.

Some scholars suggest that all societies are stratified (Parsons, 1954;

Tumin, 1967). This is not so, and the belief that stratification is universal indicates a confusion among stratification, ranking, and individual differences within societies. Ranking—the evaluation of individuals and roles—is universal. But societies composed of ranked social groups that are organized on bases other than kinship statuses or biological factors, like age and sex, are not everywhere the rule.

Some scholars, notably Fallers (1964), hold that stratification is essentially a moral or cultural phenomenon. There may well be a deep-rooted tendency for man to evaluate and rank his fellows in terms of a cultural notion of worth, but this, too, fails to distinguish between ranking and stratification. Not all societies are stratified, although those that are share similar general characteristics with those that are not. All societies have a division of labor, evaluation of statuses, and unequal distribution of rewards and valuables, with the result that some form of social inequality is universal. All human societies rank individuals on such bases as age and sex, and such skills as hunting, curing, dancing, or telling stories; on their capacity to have visions or produce artworks; or on their personal physical attributes of beauty, strength, swiftness, and agility. Both stratified and nonstratified societies have ideological supports justifying these inequalities of social worth, and in all societies individuals associated with political, economic, and religious power are accorded greater respect and deference. Still there are quantitative and qualitative differences between those societies that can be described as stratified and those that lack such social divisions.

The difference between stratified and unstratified societies is not merely one of complexity. To suggest that a stratified society is more complex by virtue of that feature is to reason in a circle, for one must further ask why it is that, all other factors being equal, of two given societies one will be stratified and the other not. Thus, for example, the Nuer had slaves while some Nilotic groups did not. Castes were associated with the Masai and Marghi, yet comparable pastoral and horticultural peoples lacked them. From these African examples alone it is clear that stratification is not solely a function of social complexity, for unless we ignore slavery and caste groups, relatively simple societies can manifest stratification. Above a certain level of internal complexity social stratification is very likely a necessary concomitant, but below that level, social stratification may also appear, although it is usually limited to forms of slavery and caste.

Stratification displays a *distinctive anatomy* that ranking lacks. Essentially it is a structural phenomenon. Only secondarily is it cultural, and then in terms of ideological supports or ways of rationalizing and comprehending the structure. In logical terms, and perhaps chronological terms as well, the social structure holds primacy. Given the structure,

people develop cultural means of organizing it cognitively and evalua-
tively.

Like all other forms of social organization, stratification has structural
and cultural dimensions; the following characteristics appear in all
stratified societies in either rudimentary or easily recognizable forms:

1. Social groups are ranked hierarchically.
2. They are relatively permanent, as viewed by most of the population.
3. They are based upon or intrinsically associated with major social
   institutions (e.g., economic, political, or religious power is differentially allocated).
4. Cultural distinctions and social distance distinguish members of the
   different strata.
5. The cultural criterion for placing individuals into the same stratum
   is based on the similarity of their social statuses. Individuals have a
   sense of identity with others of their own stratum, or at least an
   awareness of their position within the overall hierarchy, because of
   their knowledge of these cultural principles.
6. There is an overarching ideology that articulates the groups and
   provides a rationale for the hierarchical arrangement.

Some forms of stratification are more readily identifiable than
others, but it is difficult to construct an ideal model of a stratified
society, for the comparative data show that the degree to which the
foregoing features apply to any particular society will vary. Even the
basic structural feature of a hierarchical arrangement may show considerable variation—as with the Marghi caste, described by Vaughan in
this volume.

Turning to the example of contemporary South Africa, van den
Berghe points to the scholar's dilemma of attempting to describe the
nature of stratification. If one takes the subjective views of the members
of the society, in terms of their mutual evaluations, one must conclude
that the society lacks a single, coherent system, but consists of many
microsystems which are at best loosely integrated with each other. On
the other hand, if the observer applies his own criteria to achieve an
objective definition of the strata, as most of the contributors here have
done, "the picture becomes much simpler but the universe with which
one endeavors to deal is grotesquely pulled out of shape," as van den
Berghe states.

If the choice of defining criteria is a serious problem, the concept of
system in social stratification equally presents difficulties, although of a
different nature. In order to deal with a system of stratification, in terms of
system, it is insufficient merely to describe particular attributes of strata
or certain aspects of the overall hierarchy, such as changes in the ranking

of strata or the degree of individual mobility. The moment we employ the term *system* we commit ourselves to a consideration of both structure and process. Structure consists of articulating parts in particular designs or patterns. Process, the dynamic counterpart of structure, is *what happens, and how* it happens, as a result of the structure. System also implies that the component units are functionally interrelated in such a manner that the associated processes are normally consistent and repetitive. It is no simple intellectual task to deal, first, with the processes of stratification, then to wed process to structure and, finally, to perform this at the abstract level of society. Yet all of this is required by the concept of system. The success Marx achieved in this task is what makes his theory so admirable, whatever its shortcomings. A model of a system of social stratification is a model at the level of society and requires answers to such questions as what are the number and nature of the strata, what are their relations to one another, and what are the concomitant processes that bear on the society as a total system. We cannot merely talk about the parts without relating these to the whole.

COMPARATIVE IMPLICATIONS

It is not our purpose to refute or defend any of the major theories dealing with social stratification, if any one work indeed could. Rather, we think it is important to indicate how some of the prevalent assumptions regarding the nature and underlying factors of social stratification have failed to utilize comparative data sufficiently. It is also incumbent upon us to point out relevant new data and the implications these raise. We have already touched on this to some extent when noting that stratification may occur in Africa in the absence of complex social organization or even a clear ranking between groups. Similarly it will be observed from the examples included here that slaves do not necessarily form a separate stratum. Present theories, definitions, and conceptual frameworks of social stratification have proven inadequate for dealing with African conditions. For example, models of stratified societies based exclusively on one criterion or another, such as control of the modes of production, political power, or the differential allocation of honor, simply do not apply to most traditional African societies. Within these societies great differences in wealth or control over means of production are absent.

As the latest edition of that outstanding and influential work *Class, Status, and Power* points out, the major problem of current social stratification studies is that of controlled comparisons (Bendix and Lipset, 1966). Control in this context refers to the attempt to determine which societies are sufficiently similar so that the key variables can be regarded as constants. But there is another problem of control which relates to the range of examples with which we are provided. Viewpoints of social stratification and generalizations on the subject have primarily emerged from Western societies, which cover a narrow range of types of stratification. Furthermore, the data on non-Western areas obtained from published sources, and employed in the construction of universal generalizations, have often lacked empirical richness and theoretical cogency, for they were collected by researchers who were not primarily concerned with social stratification. Such factors have inevitably resulted in a distortion of the data for comparative study, and consequently have had serious implications for theoretical development and generalization. Some of the faults are minor, other shortcomings are more critical. For example, studies have consistently emphasized the rigidity of social mobility in traditional societies as opposed to the fluidity within industrial Western societies (Lipset and Bendix, 1959). As the case studies presented here repeatedly show, Africa displays a very different picture of mobility in the traditional systems. Indeed, if rates of mobility among different types of systems could be measured and compared, we think the African rates would be far greater than has been previously assumed. The African examples suggest that the rates of mobility may be better understood, not in terms of industrial societies versus traditional societies, but through the degree of cultural differences and distinctiveness between the strata. For example, in Africa we observe that social mobility is greatest where the cultural differences between the strata are least salient and, conversely, that mobility is most sharply restricted where the distinctive attributes of the hierarchical groups are most pronounced. These concomitant variations point to a further underlying condition that may well be the independent variable—the degree of discrepancy in the rewards offered by political control and economic power. Where the discrepancies are great, the rate of mobility is diminished and the extent of stratum subcultural differences increased.

All stratified societies tend to maintain their basic anatomy. The simplest and most common way this is done is through the application of rules of descent and filiation at birth for the recruitment of new members into the strata. However, a degree of mobility between the strata is also always present. Mobility may be rapid (intragenerational) or slow (intergenerational), and great or little in terms of the percentage of persons altering their stratum statuses. In these respects African societies manifest wide variations. In most, mobility is both great and rapid, but there are also distinct exceptions, such as the Rwanda and the Marghi.

In most cases the differences between the strata are obvious and clear, but the societies described by Hoben (Amhara) and Lewis (Galla) have only minimal distinctions. Thus there appears to be a correspondence between the degree of mobility and the degree of distinctions between strata, such that where the differences between strata are vague, new members are likely to be recruited through diverse channels of mobility.

Where strata are vaguely defined, further ranked subdivisions within each stratum are either difficult to delineate or entirely absent. The converse situation is seen in South Africa, where the major groups of the society are most clearly separated. Van den Berghe suggests that further analysis would distinguish subdivisions within each. It is therefore likely that once a principle of stratum distinctiveness has been well established and institutionalized, that principle will create variants and further divisions within the major strata of the society.

One of the most critical comparative problems in the study of stratification concerns the primacy and interrelationship of the factors that produce and maintain hierarchial social groupings. The view is commonly shared that a society becomes stratified when some groups are excluded from access to strategic economic resources, and that it is around this economic discrepancy that stratification emerges (Fried, 1968). Economic power is postulated as having priority over political power in this process. Some authors, however, place primacy on honor, esteem, or prestige (Parsons, 1954; Fallers, 1964; Weber, 1958). The data from African societies do not inherently present a picture of the genesis of stratification.

African societies provide no clear correlation between economic power, control of the political system, and stratification. In a number of cases—Amhara, Galla, Marghi—the superior strata neither control economic power systematically nor consistently receive honor. Of all the societies included here only two—Ruanda and South Africa—manifest clear economic, political, and evaluative differences between strata; and perhaps significantly, the authors describe these in terms of caste systems. The examples presented in this volume generally support a view of a multicausal basis for stratification among traditional African societies.

Of course, it is impossible to neglect the fundamental importance of economic factors. The Tutsi of Rwanda and the South African whites clearly control economic resources in their societies, although in very different ways and to varying extent. Elsewhere, economic factors have less cogency. Cohen's essay on the Kanuri illustrates how various bases of support result in a flexibility of recruitment to the strata and a lack of consistency in the evaluation of stratum statuses. Among the Kanuri, royalty holds rights to the use of land, but other groups cannot be ranked solely according to their position in the economic structure. Furthermore, economic factors cannot be divorced from the networks of personal ties, and these, in turn, from political power. People in favorable political positions are able to influence the flow of valuables so as to attract followers and thereby further enhance their own political power.

The analyses offered here by Mitchell and Plotnicov also indicate a multiplicity of factors in the formation of social strata. The situations they describe show that, while economic considerations remain dominant, political power, ethnic and religious affiliations, and other factors are also significant for the emergence of stratified groups. Perhaps the significance of these noneconomic factors is ephemeral and only associated with rapidly changing societies.

When we try to draw conclusions some of the case studies may appear paradoxical. For instance, should we even consider the Marghi as an example of a stratified society? Among them there is a clear distinction between caste members and the rest of the population, but there is no clear (if any) ranking of these groups. The caste members not only mono-polize occupational activities that all members of the society consider vitally important, and which are held in high regard, but also carry out despised tasks. Elsewhere in Africa, the members or caste groups have been described as despised and feared. Not so with the Marghi, where caste persons are merely thought to be unusual, quite different, or perhaps strange. They appear to have no economic disadvantage, and their political position is ambiguous, although there is caste representation in the king's council.

Slavery in Africa shows a great deal of variation, and only for some comparatively few African societies can it be said that economic exploita-tion is the major factor in the appearance of slaves. In many places slaves have considerable economic freedom. They often emerge as political leaders in the community and, more rarely, as major political figures within the society. In some societies certain slave statuses were far more rewarding or powerful than those of the ordinary freeman.

An area in which we sorely lack sufficient data is that of ideology and the part it plays in relation to the structure of stratification. In this regard African societies again show great variation. Elaborate and well-defined ideological principles have been developed in Rwanda and South Africa, but the opposite is the case with the Amhara and Galla of Ethiopia, and the Nyoro of Uganda. The data suggest that where there are great dis-crepancies in the rewards offered by political control and economic power, the ideologies supporting the stratified groups and validating the inequities within the social structures will be strong and clear. All strata will be incorporated in the value structure, for it is impossible to maintain a hierarchical society by force alone. The case of the Marghi is an excep-tion to this rule, for here, while the ideology helps maintain a clear separation of the groups, these are neither clearly stratified nor in clear economic or political subordination to one another.

The explorations into the study of African social stratification collected in this volume confirm the necessity of much more extensive research. We are still far from the goal of definitive answers to such questions as the role of ideology or the relative importance of economic and political factors in the formation and shape of stratification. In the attempt to make some headway in this direction, let us proceed to discuss the types of stratification found in traditional and contemporary African societies.

TYPES OF STRATIFICATION

The task of identifying the principles of stratified systems would be easier if there was common agreement about the definitions of types of stratification, but writers have tended to advance their own definitions or to skirt this problem entirely. As a result, the critical issues of identification and definition have been obscured or ignored. The replacement of such terms as caste or class with the more general term *stratum,* as has been suggested (Lenski, 1966), simply begs the question.

Another obstacle in defining types of stratification has been the tendency to identify societies with particular types, and thereby to neglect making a clear distinction between a theoretical type and a concrete example. This confusion has obscured understanding in two ways: one, when the system of stratification has changed within a society and, two, where a society has had two or more types of stratification coexisting. Several African examples illustrate these conditions.

For instance, Perlman documents how the Nyoro changed from a kin-based society to one based on hierarchical status within a relatively short period. The problem of change—rapid change particularly—is compounded by the fact that the great majority of societies have not one but several coexisting principles of stratification. The Wolof of the Senegambia region and the Bachama of northern Nigeria are societies that possess both castes and slavery. Elsewhere, as among the Azande of northern Congo and southern Sudan, slavery coexisted with ethnic stratification. Perhaps the most salient example of such complexity is South Africa, where, as van den Berghe relates, there are, in addition to emerging classes, two types of caste systems, one traditional Indian, and the contemporary national one. Such complexity is not so anomalous when we consider that traditional African societies often incorporated different structural types contemporaneously.

These examples not only point to some of the difficulties in arriving at a useful definition but also point to an important theoretical problem—namely, that many complex societies possess a variety of principles of stratification. It is important to account for the variety of types of stratification within one overriding social system, and to discern whether these coexisting or incompatible principles of stratification force changes within the total society. They may indeed contain the potential for change insofar as in every society variant principles of stratification are in opposition to each other, or in potential conflict.

The range of accommodation in societies is obviously great, but if the structure of stratification in a society incorporates two divergent principles of organizing individuals there is the potentiality for change. For the Republic of South Africa, van den Berghe indicates that the variety of stratified groups, based on different organizing principles, are a source of structural discrepancies, and present a problem of articulation.

Definitions are necessarily in the order of ideal types that only approximate the empirical situations covered by the term. Compare, for instance, the castes of South Africa and of the Marghi, the Galla, and the Rwanda. In some societies the term *caste* applies to only a small percentage of the population; in others, it encompasses the entire society as the major system of organization. It might be possible in describing societies to suggest that in some cases we have a caste system structuring the society, while in others castes are merely present within the society. This approach would also be applicable to the examples described by Plotnicov and van den Berghe, where there are incipient classes but not class systems. In attempting to define the type of stratification within the society, we again must be aware of the scope or the importance of a principle of stratification for the total social system. Nowhere is this dilemma clearer than in discussing slavery. In societies possessing slavery there are by definition two different groups, organized on two different principles. It is wrong to characterize a society as a "slave society," for there are always free members. In any such example the problem we must consider is how important slavery is for the total social system.

SLAVERY

As in other parts of the world, slavery has an ancient history in Africa and does appear to have been more prevalent there than in other areas (Ethnology Appendices Vol. 1–Vol. 6). While widespread it was not found everywhere on the continent. Like other forms of stratification, African slavery is resistant to neat definition and classification. The forms of African slavery are varied, and sometimes they are indistinguishable from pawnship, serfdom, and other types of status subservience into which they may grade.

We propose defining slavery as *the legal institutionalization of persons as property*. As others have suggested, the crucial issue is how slaves are utilized and employed within a society and not how they are obtained (Siegel, 1945). African slaves were recruited by various means: raiding, purchase from dealers, or received in exchange for food from neighboring groups during periods of famine. Debtors, criminals, and convicted murderers, and sometimes their kinsmen, could be made slaves by the traditional governmental authorities. But the manner in which slaves were obtained did not determine the impact they made on the total society or its system of stratification.

All systems of stratification pose organizational problems, but slavery, more than any other type, presents a cognitive dilemma for the society. Objectively slaves are people like their masters and owners; yet they are socially defined as objects or things of property. Despite the great plasticity of behaviors and perceptions of which human beings are capable, there are inherent contradictions in the status of slaves that are irreconcilable. It has been recently suggested that permanent hereditary slavery may be an impossible condition that ultimately demands social change (Hopkins, 1967). All types of stratification are unstable and impermanent, but slavery systems are even more vulnerable to change. It is unlikely that a society can define and use humans as pieces of property and still maintain the conditions necessary for human organization. On the one hand, if slaves are recognized as potentially equal human beings, mobility will inevitably occur and slaves will be absorbed as freemen into the wider society. On the other hand, if slaves are treated as property and mobility is restricted, their physical and mental conditions are such as to inhibit the maintenance of their numbers through reproduction. Where mobility is restricted, slaves will also rebel against their condition with the inevitable result of forming independent new groups. In either case, slaves will not remain a distinct group without special recruitment from outside the society.

Where slaves are clearly defined as property and the social ties between them and the rest of the society are restricted or minimized, the slave group is distinct and the society most clearly presents a system of stratification. On the other hand, where the slave is viewed as only someone less than a full community member or kinsman, and where the slave is drawn into local networks of social relations, the social distinctions between slave and freeman are blurred and we can hardly speak of a well-defined stratum. In most African societies the social and cultural differences between slave and nonslave were minimal.

Nowhere in Africa (with some exceptions such as South Africa before the nineteenth century) were slaves defined as clear economic objects. Nowhere (again with some few exceptions, such as the early Portuguese sugar plantations and in Zanzibar) was there anything similar to the chattel slavery associated with the plantations of the Western Hemisphere. Doubtless, as others have noted, definitions of human beings as property emerges in a capitalistic context in which human resources are basic factors in the profit motive (Williams, 1944). Even where slaves were economically valuable, as in Dahomey and among the Hausa, Mossi, Wolof, and Ashanti, other factors mitigated the definition of a slave as an impersonal thing or object. It is true that some slaves were regarded as only and purely economic commodities, but these were marked for sale and export, and their sojourn in any one place was short. They cannot be taken into consideration in our discussion, for they were totally dehumanized and were no more a part of any social system than any item of trade or wealth.

From numerous African examples it becomes quite apparent that when slaves are not treated as chattel, the social category they form is amorphous. It is precisely under these conditions that we find slaves in a state of continuously merging with, and becoming indistinguishable from, the free members of the society. In his chapter on the Ila, Tuden describes the mechanisms by which mobility can occur by means of adoption, marriage, and fictive kinship affiliation. Generally speaking, slaves were introduced into Ila society as types of kinsmen. The bondage period itself was temporary and the inferior position transitory for the majority of slaves.

In these respects the Ila represent the general conditions of slavery in Africa.[2] Among the Ila, slaves were quickly absorbed into the community; in other societies it took a generation or two. The cultural distinctions and life changes between master and slave were not great. Slave and master usually worked and lived together under conditions that appeared virtually identical. Slaves participated in many of the same institutions as freemen. Among many West African peoples, for instance, slaves could gain considerable personal wealth through trading. In some societies slaves could themselves own slaves; some Hausa slaves did, and also employed free servants.

African slaves had many opportunities for mobility. In some African societies the owner's children by a slave woman both were free and had almost full rights of inheritance. It is likely that in the great majority of African societies strong personal ties were established between owners and slaves. Slaves were treated as slightly less fortunate kinsmen, and relationships were usually cast in a kinship idiom. No special distinctions

2. There is at least one exception to this generalization. Certain West African societies, among which the Ibo and Ibibio are the best known examples, had slaves devoted to the religious cults of their owners. The descendants of these slaves were despised and could not shed the stigma of their ancestry. They could never be redeemed, no free person would marry them, and they were feared and shunned.

in dress distinguished slaves from freemen in the great majority of cases. Where such differences did arise, and where there may have been special terms for slaves, we find other forms of stratification well established. For example, in the kingdom of Bornu, described by Cohen, male slaves were not permitted to wear the headgear associated with Islam. In some of the Interlacustrine Bantu states, all persons who were not nobility were called by a term meaning slave, although most persons covered by the word were free commoners, and merely owed service and tribute to their chiefs and lords.

By and large, however, slaves had minimal access to political power, although some African societies illustrate salient exceptions. Nupe slaves could hold posts at the royal court. M. G. Smith (1960) states that the royal slaves of some Hausa cities could appoint and dismiss chiefs entirely on their own. Indeed, among the Hausa, slaves could hold almost any office but the paramount chiefship. In many African societies slaves were the political support and military backing of an owner. Slaves formed the entire or the greater part of the armies of kings in the region of the Congo, and they could, if they felt they were mistreated, escape to their owner's enemies. The Fulani rulers of Hausa Zaria "appointed slave generals to command standing armies, as much through fear of internal revolt as for defense against invaders" (Smith, 1960: 242).

Therefore, the context and structure of African slavery is distinct from the forms of chattel slavery in the New World. In American chattel slavery, death rates were high; even under relatively mild conditions the birth rate of chattel slaves rarely approached the point where the slave population was self-sustaining. The high mortality rate and low birth rate appear to have been the result of the harsh physical conditions imposed on them. But psychological factors must also be considered relevant (Wade, 1964; Goveia, 1965).

There have been suggestions that slavery represents the earliest form of social stratification. Like Fried (1968), but for different reasons, we think this hypothetical reconstruction of the emergence of a system of stratification is untenable. The examples from Africa indicate that the social and cultural contexts determine the structure of slavery, and not vice versa. In the first place, the position of slaves in most societies is transitory, and slaves do not form a well-defined social group. Where slaves do form a distinct group, the society itself is already stratified. Even here the slave group requires constant replenishment from outside the society. In the latter case, associated with chattel slavery, there must be established economic and political preconditions for the perpetuation of slavery as a distinct social grouping. These include a complex cash economy of large-scale and widespread trade, occupational specialization, and international economic and political relations. These conditions, which are the hallmarks of civilization, could not occur without the co-existence of social stratification.

Although slavery in Africa was widespread, it was an ephemeral and transitory status. It has had no major influence on the systems of stratification that have since emerged and which exist today, with the possible exception of South Africa. This is true even where slaves were important as labor and commodities for trade.

The fact that most slave conditions in Africa lacked a strong ideology of status inferiority is in sharp contrast with postemancipation developments in the United States. There the stigma of slavery was maintained along with the belief in social and racial inferiority. In Africa, where slaves always had established ties with the total community, the abolition of slavery, which for most of the continent took place after 1900, was accompanied by only minor shifts in the structuring of society, usually in a recomposition of lineages or in the formation of new kinship groups. In America, on the other hand, the descendants of slaves still have not entered the mainstream of society after more than a century of emancipation.

CASTES

Like slavery, caste is polytypic and difficult to define. Four contributions in this volume deal with castes or societies with caste characteristics, and these illustrate some of the theoretical difficulties entailed in analyzing and defining this type of stratification. Vaughan (for the Marghi), Maquet (for the Rwanda) and van den Berghe (for the Republic of South Africa) use the same term *caste*, yet describe societies and stratification conditions that are very different. On the other hand, there are some structural resemblances between the Rwanda and the Amhara, described by Hoben. Yet Hoben chooses to designate his example as feudal, because of the importance of patron-client relationships, which also exist among the Rwanda. These examples not only illustrate the possible range of variation within a single type of stratification, but also show how these variations grade from one type to another.

There are two divergent scholarly views of caste. One group, represented by Cox (1959), Dumont (1956), and Leach (1962), insists that caste is a social phenomenon limited to Pan-Indian civilization. This group considers the application of the term *caste* to phenomena elsewhere as fallacious. Another group of scholars do not regard the examples from India as unique, and attempt to use the structural cultural, and functional similarities of caste for comparative analysis of stratification in Japan, Africa, the Near East, and the United States. Neither group agrees on the definition and precise nature of caste. Those who share the view that caste is coterminous with and limited to India stress the importance of cultural dimensions, as exemplified in the religious aspects of the Hindu heritage. However, they have generally remained sensitive to the variations within Indian caste systems and have recognized "normal" or "orthodox" types, by such designations as variant and marginal (Leach, 1962: 8). On the other hand, those scholars who attempt wide comparative analysis, by emphasizing the gross structural similarities, have at the same time tended to ignore the very wide range of variation covered by caste. Consequently, they have avoided coming to grips with the problem of what limitations should be placed on the application of the term to social phenomena outside India.

The concept of caste does have utility for comparative analysis but for it to achieve its full strength as an analytical category the conditions of groups called castes must be compared for their similarities and differences wherever they are found. For Japan, DeVos lists several requisites for its occurrence: (1) a centralized political structure, (2) social groups ranked on a permanent basis, (3) occupational specialization of groups, (4) group membership that is ascriptive, i.e., defined by birth, and (5) an ideological basis for group distinction that includes the concept of social pollution (1967: 332–33). Many of these features are characteristics of any stratified society, but three appear to differentiate caste from other types of social stratification.

These are the associations between *occupational specialization of endogamous groups,* in which *membership is based on ascription,* and between which *social distance is regulated by the concept of pollution.* While these three aspects occur in varying degrees in all stratified systems, they are indicative of castes when they appear in highly salient forms and in the special relationship just stated.

As with all systems of stratification, the complexity of the economic system remains fundamental to caste. In this regard, Leach (1962) stresses the symbiotic nature of caste relations. While recognizing the complementarity of caste economic relations we would call attention to the importance of the degree of occupational and economic specialization, and the complexity of the total economic system, as being critically important for the extent to which a society develops and elaborates caste principles. It is also clear that most authorities, basing their view on India, regard a caste system as consisting of a large number of caste groups woven into a fabric that covers almost every aspect of ranked group relations. But the African data indicate that the degree of casteness depends not only upon the factor of specialized economic activities, but also on whether these are allocated to one group or several. For example, the Marghi *aŋkyagu* are smiths. They also bury corpses, work leather, serve as drummers, and make pots. The Twa, among the Rwanda, make pots, hunt, and are court jesters. These are among the clearest examples of caste economic specialization in Africa, but it must be noted that these groups are approximately only two and one percent, respectively, of their populations. Obviously the Marghi are not a caste society, but the Rwanda, with the endogamous strata of Hutu and Tutsi, are.

It is likely that the ideological supports of group differentiation and the structural articulation of the society, such as ritual pollution, appear weakest in societies where the caste percentage is small, or the economic complexity is least elaborated. The Marghi are perhaps typical, for the concept of pollution is weak and ill-defined among them.

The Rwanda represent the clearest African example of a traditional caste system. The society displays many of the structural and cultural features attributed to Indian castes while lacking the Indian complexity of organization. This stimulates the question of whether the Rwanda illustrate an early stage of caste evolution. If so, would they have been able to achieve a greater proliferation of a subdivision, or caste groupings, with further economic specialization? This view, of incipient caste system development, is supported by the conditions of incomplete endogamy of Rwanda castes, the slight upward mobility from the lowest to the middle stratum, and the somewhat greater, but still slight, movement of Hutu to the top Tutsi level.

In other respects the African examples depart from Indian caste characteristics. Political power is monopolized by the top castes among the Rwanda, but this is not at all so clear among the Marghi, who also lack the emphasis on pollution. The Marghi, instead, show a concern with mutual avoidance which is maintained by caste endogamy. Political power also appears to be related to the relative ranking of castes. For instance, the Marghi have but one caste, which is not ranked relative to the rest of society; *aŋkyagu* persons are regarded as different, strange, and perhaps frightening, but they are not despised or rejected, nor lacking political power.

Some scholars have raised the question of whether the concept of a caste stratified society can be applied to relatively and absolutely large groups in a modern and industrial context, as van den Berghe does for South Africa. In his chapter he declares that the white, colored, Indian, and African groups satisfy the minimum definitions of caste—ascriptive membership, endogamy, clear ranking, and restricted mobility between groups—and that they tend to occupy different areas of the economy.

The application of the concept of caste to African societies clearly presents difficulties, even if we disregard the objections of those who are opposed to the employment of the term where there is no historical connection with the Indian cultural heritage and Hindu religion. The

Introduction

Marghi *əŋkyagu* appear most similar to the outcastes of Japan in size, but differ in being organized on principles of kinship and kin grouping. Therefore the Marghi lack a clear hierarchical structure (Leach). But the term *caste* appears to be more appropriate to describe relations between the groups in Marghi society than any other term.

We are aware that we have raised more questions on the nature of caste than we have been able to adequately answer. Still, we believe the term *caste* is best suited for the African examples presented here, and hope this discussion may clarify some of the theoretical issues that have been raised.

SOCIAL CLASSES

As Plotnicov indicates in his chapter, there are a number of pertinent reasons why scholars are debating whether social classes now exist in black Africa. That this should be a controversial issue, and that it has drawn considerable attention, is indicative of the associations we normally make with the concept of social class. The phenomenon is invariably related to industrial or modern economic development, factors that facilitate a large economic surplus. Social classes did not traditionally exist in Africa, but insofar as contemporary African governments have placed priorities on economic developments, one theoretically expects to find the concomitant rise of social class systems. Underlying this search is the assumption that social class systems are the inevitable consequence of industrialization as an iron rule of social change. What had originally been an observation of historical events for Western societies later became transformed, through imperceptibly minute alterations, into a universal generalization. We must recognize that the association of social class with industrialization is a concept that derives from limited empirical instances, and that its nature is that of a hypothesis which remains to be tested. The conditions in Africa provide only part of the test.

The lack of agreement over whether social classes are present in Africa is partly due to obfuscating empirical factors, but it is more the result of varying definitions of class and a lack of agreement of its components and associated features. Regarding the latter, we find that the populations of African countries embody groups that manifest many of the characteristics of a social class, but more often than not such groups—usually designated "modern elite"—remain different for each nation. Since we normally conceive of a social class within the context of a society possessing other social classes, it is difficult to accept a group possessing the characteristics of a class as a social class when other classes are absent, for one of the defining criteria of social class is the inherent conflict or competition of such groups within a society. This has not yet been empirically demonstrated for Africa, but on logical grounds alone the existence of a single class cannot be asserted if a defining attribute is its conflict with another.

However, the condition of competing classes is not relevant to a class, per se; rather, competition is a condition of a *system of classes*. This problem is analogous to the one raised regarding castes in Africa, where castes may be present in traditional societies lacking caste systems. In that connection we suggested that an elaboration of caste principles did not occur in traditional African societies because of the lack of economic complexity and differentiation of tasks that might be assumed under a diversity of castes. Might not the same solution apply to the question of the presence of classes? And just as there was nothing inevitable in the formation of castes and their elaboration into caste systems, may we not recognize the existence of one or two social classes without assuming that these must ultimately form part of a class system, however much we expect that to occur?

Turning to the empirical factors that obscure the presence of social classes, we may note that two contributors to this volume (Mitchell and van den Berghe) deal with areas of the continent where white domination over blacks so thoroughly overshadows other aspects of stratification, such as the formation of classes among the Africans themselves, that the issue of class formation is beclouded by a pernicious form of social pluralism. Other parts of Africa, particularly West Africa, provide clearer conditions for the observation and examination of emerging social classes. We do not mean by this that the areas under white domination are so anomalous that they cannot be dealt with by the application of social class theory, or that studies of stratification should exclude those case studies of historically alien domination. We merely mean that exploratory studies are best conducted where the research problems are not additionally complicated.

Before proceeding to the substantive problem of social classes in Africa we would do well to define our terms. It is our impression that most scholars, in defining social class, synthesize Marxian and Weberian views, and we would do likewise. Thus, following Weber, one of the conditions of a social class, which he calls a status group, is its sense of identity, style of life, and the degree of esteem conferred on it by the culture. This is similar to Marx's basic criterion of self-awareness or class consciousness. A characteristic derived from Marx, which Weber also employed, is the economic condition of the individuals in the stratum, and the implications of this for their material well-being. This, their "life chances," in Marxian analysis leads to political action, Weber's "party," once self-awareness has been achieved. This third characteristic tells us

Introduction

more about a class system than about the nature of one of its components. In fact, all of these characteristics can be applied to any system of social stratification, and in themselves do not distinguish classes from other forms of strata. A characteristic that does is the mode of recruitment.

In a class system there is an ideology which holds that a person's social position is that which he merits and earns by his achievements. This is the motivating force behind a class system. Not only does it provide justification for the reward or lack of reward of the deserving and the undeserving, it helps make a view of social mobility cognitively acceptable. There is a belief that although one may be born into a particular social class he need not remain in it. Regardless of the rate and extent of social mobility in a class system, the belief that it is occurring makes it difficult to set the precise boundaries between classes, and difficult for a person to determine his exact position.

Where there are fixed social groups ranked in unambiguous positions it is easy to recognize and identify them, but where social classes are present and stratum mobility is relatively fluid we may not only have difficulty in distinguishing between classes but have even greater difficulty ascertaining the existence of a social class where it is emerging. Researchers into social class are faced with the methodological dilemma raised by van den Berghe regarding the subjective and objective views of the subject—i.e., whether classes are analytical or concrete entities. In outlining social classes are we describing real social groups with self-awareness or are we imposing our own analytical categories?

This is not a new problem in social stratification for, as Dahrendorf has pointed out, Marx himself was not always consistent on this point (1959:20). Until a group within the society had developed a political consciousness it was, for Marx, a social class only potentially and not empirically. Subjective class identifications, by the actors involved, has been a defining characteristic stressed by social scientists, but such self-awareness is not to be expected in a situation where a developing class structure is associated with radical, wide, and rapid social change. Under these conditions people have only a dim awareness of the overall structure of the system. They are most knowledgeable of the ranking of others in social proximity to their own status, and they may have a vague idea of the thresholds that define major strata, but beyond this their cognitive map is murky. For scholars to attempt erecting more elaborate structures under these circumstances is to take unwarranted analytical liberties. For these reasons some scholars would go so far as to completely reject the empirical reality of social classes even for industrially advanced societies (cf. Brown, 1965:133–35), but we would insist that social classes are no fiction, and the concept of class remains heuristically useful. Applied to Africa today its use is limited because social classes are in the process of formation. In addition, they are associated with other types of stratification that are either retentions of traditional forms or those imposed by white colonists. All these conditions present great methodological difficulties and so, until further crystallization occurs, we regard social classes in Africa as more potential than actual, more analytical than concrete categories. One group of black Africans has emerged sufficiently, however, to possibly warrant its consideration as an almost fully developed social class—the modern elite.

The most Western in cultural orientation and occupational skills, the modern African elite are acknowledged as political, economic, and cultural leaders in national institutions. Since a majority of them hold high administrative positions in the governmental and commercial bureaucracies, they may, perhaps, more aptly be referred to as a managerial elite or managerial bourgeoisie.[3]

There is a warm debate regarding whether this group should be considered a social class. It is not, if one holds the view that "a social class can exist only in a system of social classes" (Lloyd, 1964:60), for one cannot observe a contrasting class or classes in the rest of the society. This group can, however, be considered a class, as we do, if one regards a class system as requiring time for its enfolding, and that it is analytically and empirically possible to distinguish between a class and a class system. For the time being, the Africans who are not modern elite lack clear manifestations of social class behavior and ideology, but there are some indications that this may be changing.

The recent African coups d'etat, for example, may be interpreted in terms of an emerging conflict of classes, but clearer indications than this appear in the growing resentment of persons of the potentially modern elite who are finding it increasingly difficult to attain the positions to which they regard themselves entitled because of the entrenched managerial bourgeoisie.

Additional reasons exist why scholars have been dissatisfied with their attempts to apply to the African scene the model of social class derived from Western experiences. One is the problem of inconsistency between the social statuses of family members. In the West the occupational and financial position of the nuclear family head—the breadwinner—is a determinant of not only his class position but that of the rest of the family members as well. As a unit, the family signifies its status in the type of

3. By no means would we dismiss the importance of inquiries into the problem of whether family lines tend to fall into the same relative positions when the forms of stratification change, and we applaud the efforts of those who have begun research in this area (cf. Fallers, 1964; Clignet and Foster 1964, and Goldthorpe 1961). We still know very little about the traditional family backgrounds of the modern African elite and African university students—the new recruits to the modern elite—although the picture appears to show ancestral backgrounds that are highly heterogeneous.

home and neighborhood in which it resides and in its consumption and recreational habits, esthetic tastes, and other behavior patterns regarded as indices of stratum position. To some extent, also, families are hereditary groups with internal status consistency among the close kinsmen.

This configuration is at variance with what we observe in Africa. Here family members frequently hold a wide range of hierarchical socio-economic positions, with a correspondingly wide spread between modern and traditional orientations. A modern elite man may frequently be found married to an illiterate wife, or wives, and his household may harbor an extended family of kinsmen who represent the entire gamut of social tradition and change. They are very likely to live in a house of modern design and construction in an urban neighborhood that is in no way residentially segregated by wealth, occupation, or Western cultural orientation. This picture is slowly changing, but it is the one with which observers are most familiar.

If status consistency has tended to be absent within the household, it has also appeared lacking in the behavior of individuals. In the West we are familiar with a syndrome of occupational elevation accompanied by residential mobility, loosening of kinship ties, and replacement of former neighbors and friends with others more appropriate for the higher social position accompanying the occupational promotion. We also tend to think of individual acculturation as an analogous process. The model we have apparently employed in viewing African social change is one in which Africans lose traditional social ties, behaviors, and cultural orientations to the degree that they become Western, modern, and achieve higher social standing. The evidence does not support this view. Africans have acquired new life-styles without entirely discarding their previous ones. Modern and traditional contrasting forms of behavior are turned on and off in accordance with the demands of modern and traditional institutional settings. Van den Berghe and Plotnicov, in their chapters here, recognize this complex transitional situation in which Africans become acculturated to Western institutions in the same process whereby they move stratigraphically upward; van den Berghe also regards situational selectivity or cultural commuting, as he terms it, as "invariably accompanied by value conflicts." Whether this is so—and we regard it as an empirical problem yet to be determined—it is clear that the persons who manifest class characteristics also resist categorization in a Western model of social class behavior because of their great degree of status inconsistency and their contrasting situationally selective orientations. It is still unclear whether these factors will change over a period of time, and what has been described is similar to any social group undergoing rapid change.

At present in Africa—and for some time to come—social classes only partially resemble those of the industrialized West, for the modern elite, who are in the most favorable position to break away from traditional institutions, have not done so. A number of other factors make it unlikely that the social context of the African societies will replicate Western social groupings. For example, traditional institutions, particularly those connected with kinship, have remained strong, and necessarily so, for they perform vitally needed welfare functions that modern African nations find difficult to assume. Because the national resources are so meager, economic development must take priority over the effective formation of those welfare institutions usually considered as crucial in industrial societies. Because Africans have thus been forced to draw from traditional institutional resources they have, correspondingly, had to support the very same institutions. It seems most likely this pattern will persist until economic developments render traditional sources of support comparatively unattractive.

Any attempt to evaluate the influence of traditional institutions upon social class formation must consider the following caveats. First, there were a variety of traditional forms of social stratification in Africa, and each of these will exert a different set of influences. Second, within these traditional forms were subvariations which would further complicate attempts at assessing the impact of traditional practices on contemporary developments. Third, contemporary conditions vary at least as widely as their traditional counterparts, and in the same ways. Finally, we cannot expect traditional forms to exert equal influences everywhere because they are not operating in precisely the same contexts.

MOBILITY

Compared with other forms of stratification, social class has been thought to be associated with a greater ease of vertical mobility. Previously we expressed our disagreement with this view, especially since it is contradicted by the rapid mobility within traditional African slavery. We also indicated that it was difficult, perhaps impossible, to compare rates of mobility between different forms of stratification. The structures, the shapes of the pyramid, the definitions of the strata, and the concomitant ideologies all differ widely. A question such as, "Will the future rate of mobility increase when social classes are forming?" cannot be answered definitively, but it will serve to raise for consideration some relevant theoretical issues.

The development of a modern elite and their associated social class in Africa has taken place under conditions that give the appearance of rapid

Introduction

upward mobility. During little more than two generations, the structures of the societies under colonial domination have undergone radical transformation. The colonial bourgeoisie established many new elite positions that they at first monopolized but which, over time, they increasingly shared with Africans until their departure, when the vacuum they created virtually sucked in those who have helped consolidate the modern elite stratum. But the formation of a social class is not the same as, and should not be confused with, social mobility. Social mobility involves the movement of persons between positions in the same structure, not between positions in different structures. What has occurred is best understood as social change.

It is theoretically untenable to attempt to compare positions between societies having different stratification structures, or even in the same society where the structures have altered radically through social change. Thus it is equally unsuitable to attempt to compare positions between different forms of stratification that are contemporary and coexistent within the same society. There are situations, as in South Africa, where an individual participates in two or more systems of stratification, yet his position in one has no necessary bearing on his status in another, for as van den Berghe points out, there is no single continuum between them. He asks, "Does a working class colored rank higher than a middle class African or a middle class colored than a working class white, or an African lawyer than a white bricklayer? There is simply no valid answer to that order of question."

From our point of view, the issue of social mobility and the related question of stratification in contemporary Africa cannot realistically be raised until social class systems have undergone more complete crystallization. Until then, we shall not be observing mobility so much as the formation of new strata, the opening of positions within them, and the recruitment to these positions from the population at large, and this is not social mobility but social change.

Most sociologists would agree that the occupational system lies at the heart of the contemporary Western social class system. The job and career not only determine one's income but also profoundly influence one's style of life, choice of friends, and other social and cultural characteristics that are indices of social class position. It is for these reasons that occupation has been the sociologist's primary index of class status in Western society, where its successful application has made it attractive to researchers in Africa and elsewhere. However, the indiscriminate application of this frame of reference can be hazardous for areas that are creating their own industrial revolutions as rapidly as possible. As stated earlier, it is fallacious to believe that all Western developments are necessary concomitants of industrial society and, hence, universal attributes of modernization. To do so courts the danger of turning an assumption into a conclusion. Let us recognize this ethnocentric bias along with the fact that it has yet to be demonstrated that occupation in Africa will bring the same results in stratification as in other industrialized countries. There may indeed be very strong parallels, but not necessarily as a natural outgrowth of modernization per se. The Western attributes of occupation could very well have diffused to Africans through the colonial experience. Those Africans who replaced the Europeans holding controlling positions, and who would maintain their advantages, now share an interest in legitimizing and buttressing a system of stratification that has been partially, if not largely, imposed from without.

The question of whether the job is a primary point of social identification in black Africa remains open to empirical investigation. In fact, sufficient evidence exists to believe that Africans have not internalized Western evaluations and perceptions of occupation and career. Only when we have considered the relative importance of other status characteristics will we be in a position to compare the essential criteria of social class position between European and African societies.

SOCIAL PLURALISM—ETHNIC STRATIFICATION

The difficulties encountered in attempting to define and isolate the principles of stratification generally arise to greater degree with pluralism —variously termed social pluralism, sociocultural pluralism, and ethnic stratification. The essential problem regarding this concept is not that it covers an extremely wide range of examples—all types of stratification are polytypic—but whether it is in fact a structurally distinct enough form of social stratification to warrant a special term. The concept has been applied so broadly and so loosely that it covers an enormous range of types.

We think that the criteria usually presented to demonstrate the existence of pluralism are those that are quite common for social stratification in general, and caste and class stratification in particular. Those societies that have been distinguished as plural appear to differ from other stratified societies by the presence of a group that not only is politically and economically dominant, monopolizes other valued positions, and has a distinct style of life, but also is racially distinct from the rest of the population. Therefore, pluralism seems to be racial stratification. If this is so then we must recognize that pluralism, as a *social* type, has been based on a *biological* characteristic, a feature that is theoretically and methodologically unacceptable. What we are observing in pluralism is the employment of

Introduction

phenotypic characteristics as marks of identification for status ascription—nothing more nor less—and this does not involve a difference in stratification structure. Otherwise it would be difficult to distinguish between stratification in plural societies and other forms of stratification. It is our conclusion, therefore, that social pluralism is best understood in terms of other forms of stratification; we are aware that, in taking this position, we disagree with scholars whom we highly respect, including one of our contributors.

Mitchell, for example, characterizes the societies described in his chapter as plural. He points out that in Rhodesia plural conditions began with British colonial rule in the late nineteenth century. From then on, white domination was reinforced by legal sanctions. Inequalities in economic opportunities, education, housing, and political power all stemmed from this condition. But the most salient characteristic that emerged was the strong correspondence between social class, status group, party, and race. However, each of these groups, while holding a distinct position in an overall hierarchy, is not itself a monolithic, undifferentiated entity. Within each, substratification also occurs. Furthermore, some forms of this substratification cut across all groups in such a manner as to create incongruities in the form of certain persons of low status groups holding higher positions than some persons of the dominating group. This description applies to South Africa as described here by van den Berghe; yet, he avoids the term *pluralism* in favor of *caste*. Such a difference of opinion—as between van den Berghe and Mitchell—is illustrative of the controversy surrounding the concept of pluralism.

M. G. Smith, perhaps the foremost contemporary scholar favoring the utility of the concept of pluralism, considers two criteria as singularly important for distinguishing pluralism as a distinct form. These are, first, that the system is maintained by the dominant group through its use of political force and, second, and related to the first, there is a lack of consensus among all the groups regarding the legitimacy of the system, just as there is a lack of cognitive agreement about what the system is. Again, this appears applicable to van den Berghe's description of South Africa just as it does to the areas of Mitchell's concern.

The latter agrees with Smith on these criteria. But whereas Smith regards the plural situation as inherently instable and requiring the continuous domination of the ruling group for its cohesiveness, Mitchell takes the opposite position. In his chapter he states that "as the subordinate race becomes more and more dependent for its subsistence and welfare on the economic and administrative system manned by the dominant race, it becomes less and less inclined to destroy that system by violent protests."

There seems to be a covert characteristic of social pluralism that is not normally brought into the open, and that is its degree of complexity. Conditions and situations that are usually described in terms of pluralism are invariably highly complex. It is our feeling that this complexity has influenced scholars to regard conditions, such as van den Berghe and Mitchell describe, as pluralistic. However, complexity, in and of itself, cannot be a criterion for distinguishing a *type* of stratification or any social form, for that matter.

Finally, we may note that the authors referred to point out that, under pluralism, legal sanctions are not applied equally to the members of the different groups. But is this very different from the situation in traditional Rwanda, traditional African societies in general, or, for that matter, all stratified societies? In traditional African societies these inequalities were manifestly expressed in the community's moral and political ideologies, whereas in the social class systems of industrial societies these are covert, but still recognized as objective reality. Invidious distinctions such as these may contradict a moral code associated with a class system that declares all persons equal before the law, but there is no necessary association between a democratic ideology and a class system. Otherwise one would have to declare Hitler's Nazi Germany a plural society.

What, then, makes a plural society plural? If we follow Smith's suggestion that a plural situation is inherently instable and requires application of political force by the dominating group for its maintenance, then we might ask whether the conflict and competition between black and white in Africa, before majority rule, indicates the condition of pluralism or whether, as Plotnicov has suggested here, there is a class conflict in the absence of a class system. Let us suppose that the preindependent African countries exemplified pluralism. We then find that when the whites are no longer politically dominant, no longer the colonial masters, the societies no longer appear to be good examples of pluralism. In fact, we see that the shift of power from one group to another has not resulted in a change in the form of stratification. If pluralism had existed previously, we would be forced to conclude that pluralism is not a form of stratification. The *system* has not changed.

As a matter of fact, it turns out that in the recently independent African countries the number of Europeans has increased, and they have retained the stratum positions they held during colonial days, without relinquishing their metropolitan citizenship. With this example we have another indication of the importance of factors external to a society for an adequate understanding of its internal systems. Certainly, a crucial area for further research lies in the evaluation of outside influences on the form and pattern of social stratification.

We previously indicated that Mitchell departs from Smith in stressing the importance of consensus as a force underpinning the stability of stratification in pluralism, in addition to the use of coercive measures. While consensus is not as easy to identify as the application of force, or coercion, it seems clear that Mitchell's point has universal applicability. All societies that are stratified rely, in good measure, upon consensus, but will apply coercion when other techniques of control have been exhausted. By and large, studies of social stratification have tended to ignore the application of political power, and not infrequently naked force, to maintain differential social positions. Contemporary conditions will surely alter this previous neglect.

In sum, we have taken the position that the criteria used to distinguish social pluralism from other forms of stratification are applicable to stratification generally. Sociocultural pluralism is no special condition that requires special descriptive methods and analytical tools. The term has been used to cover so broad a range of conditions that it has served more to obscure, rather than elucidate, our inquiries, and it is better to discard it in favor of the more precise and specific indicators of caste and class.

The initial purpose in collecting the following chapters was to provide comparative materials treating systems of stratification from an ethnographic area lacking these materials. During the process of editing and reading of the papers, theoretical problems concerning social stratification arose from the divergent analyses of social stratification and a wide variety of types of social stratification. Our discussion of these problems we hope will aid others to further clarify the structures and institutions of social inequality.

BIBLIOGRAPHY

Bendix, R. and S. M. Lipset   1966   Class, Status, and Power: Social Stratification in Comparative Perspective, 2nd ed. New York, The Free Press.

Brown, Roger   1965   Social Psychology. New York, The Free Press.

Clignet, R. and P. Foster   1964   Potential elites in Ghana and the Ivory Coast. American Journal of Sociology, 70:349-62

Cox, Oliver Cromwell   1959   Caste, Class and Race. New York, Monthly Review Press.

Dahrendorf, Ralf   1959   Class and Class Conflict in Industrial Society. Stanford, Stanford University Press.

DeVos, G., and H. Wagatsuma   1967   Japan's Invisible Race. Berkeley, University of California Press.

Dumont, L.   1956   For a sociology of India, in: Contributions to Indian Sociology, Dumont (ed.). Mouton.

Ethnology   Vol. 1–Vol. 6.

Fallers, L. (ed.) 1964 The King's Men. London, Oxford University Press.

Fried, M. 1968 The Political Evolution of Society. New York, Random House.

Goldthorpe, J. E. 1961 Educated Africans: Some conceptual and terminological problems, in: Social Change in Modern Africa, A. Southall (ed.). London, Oxford University Press.

Goveia, Elsa V. 1965 Slave Society in the British Leeward Islands at the End of the 18th Century. New Haven, Yale University Press.

Hopkins, Keith 1967 Slavery in classical antiquity, in: Caste and Race, pp. 166–76. Boston, Little, Brown & Co.

Leach, E. R. (ed.) 1962 Aspects of Caste in South India, Ceylon and North-West Pakistan. Cambridge, Cambridge University Press.

Lenski, G. 1966 Power and Privilege. New York, McGraw-Hill.

Lipset, S. and R. Bendix 1959 Social Mobility in Industrial Society. Berkeley, University of California Press.

Lloyd, Peter (ed.) 1964 The New Elites of Tropical Africa. London, Oxford University Press (for the International African Institute).

Parsons, T. 1953 Revised analytical approach to the theory of social stratification, in: Class, Status, and Power: A Reader in Social Stratification, R. Bendix and S. M. Lipset (eds.). New York, The Free Press.

—— 1954 Essays in Sociological Theory. New York, The Free Press.

Siegel, B. J. 1945 Some methodological considerations for a comparative study of slavery. American Anthropologist, 47(3):357–92.

Smith, M. G. 1960 Government in Zazzau. New York, Oxford University Press.

Tumin, M. 1967 Social Stratification. Englewoods Cliffs, N.J., Prentice-Hall.

Wade, Richard C. 1964 Slavery in the Cities: The South 1820–1860. New York, Oxford University Press.

Weber, M. 1958 Essays in Sociology. New York, Oxford University Press.

Williams, E. 1944 Capitalism and Slavery. Chapel Hill, North Carolina.

RANK AND STRATIFICATION AMONG THE ALUR AND OTHER NILOTIC PEOPLES

BY AIDAN W. SOUTHALL

SOCIAL STRUCTURE AND STRATIFICATION AMONG THE EASTERN NILOTES

In the Nilotic peoples we have a series of cultures that are somewhat scattered but largely in the same contiguous area of the southern Sudan, southwestern Ethiopia, northern and western Kenya, northern Uganda, and the northeastern Congo. By ethnographic standards they are closely related, whatever the precise source of this relationship. But at the same time they inevitably incorporate diverse elements which have links in different directions outside the Nilotic culture area. This area used to be conceptually split in two between the Nilotes and the Nilo-Hamites, who are now referred to respectively as the Western and Eastern Nilotes in the linguistic classification of Greenberg, which it is becoming conventional to adopt. Whichever appellation is used, the empirical similarities and dissimilarities of culture are obviously not affected. But we may note at the outset that the coincident dichotomy implied by both sets of terms is not the most relevant distinction from all cultural points of view. For example it is now clear that, in the basic structure of their religious ideas and moral values, the Nuer and Dinka have more in common with the Eastern Nilotic Masai, Samburu, Nandi, and Kipsigis than they do with most of the other Western Nilotes, mainly of the Lwo group, with whom they are customarily classified.

On the other hand, in social organization, despite its intimate connection with religion, there is a much sharper general distinction between

I wish to acknowledge the assistance I received from Mr. Kenneth Baer in the preparation and discussion of parts of this material.

Aidan W. Southall: Rank and Stratification Among the Alur

Eastern and Western Nilotes. This shows most strikingly in the age organization of the former, but perhaps this is just the easiest feature to pick upon. Both form and function differ markedly in the age organizations of these Eastern Nilotic peoples, while the institution itself extends far beyond them, most notably to the Cushitic Galla and also to the Bantu Kikuyu speaking peoples who, traditionally, were almost completely surrounded by the Eastern Nilotes. However, whatever form the institution takes, it has very important implications for the social structure, particularly in the strong sense of ethnic identity it imparts, the facility it gives to spatial mobility both of groups and individuals within the social framework, the emphasis it puts alike upon the status equality and solidarity of coevals, and the distinctions of either generational or individual seniority, all of which taken together are incompatible with the development of extensive segmentary lineages and of distinctions of rank and status between them, such as characterized the Western Nilotes.

Eastern Nilotic age organization is particularly compatible with elaborate complementary symbolic identifications, usually dichotomous, which do not appear with the same elaboration among most of the Western Nilotes. No interpretation of any profundity has ever been made of this distinction.

It would seem that there is a fundamental structural explanation. Where segmentary lineage organization is the major organizational principle, there is no need for an elaborate structure of cross-cutting symbolic oppositions and identifications. Not only is there no need, but there is nothing in the system likely to give rise to them. On the contrary, the self-regulating mechanisms of complementary opposition, discovered by Evans-Pritchard among the Nuer and subsequently much more widely, proceed inevitably from the principles of descent, residence, marriage, and inheritance in these societies. The composition of groups and the evolving pattern of segmentation may be quite irregular and in detail unpredictable, yet the overall balance of fission and fusion, superordination and subordination, in the continually unfolding situations of complementary opposition remains essentially the same. As long as such a mechanism is allowed, by the absence of other dominant principles, to proceed and work itself out unhindered, it is essentially incompatible with any fixed series of balanced symbolic oppositions, which would rapidly cease to match the empirical pattern of segmentation. While genealogies can be maneuvered and fabricated, there still remains a sense in which lineage structure must respond to varying forces of demography and ecology, the results of which must be allowed to find their own level in the constant readjustment of the pattern of complementary oppositions— the redrawing of the map of distribution of social forces—which is indeed the net outcome of all processes of solidarity and competition in these societies. Since the point of balance is not predetermined but is itself the outcome of empirical events, it is not useful or convenient that it should be tied to a fixed, unchanging framework of symbolic categories which would constantly come in conflict with the realities of the situation.

On the other hand, the principles of age organization, where it is the overriding structural mechanism, themselves guarantee conformity between the social strength (numerical, economic, political) of the groups formed by it and the balance and proportion of the symbolic categories into which they are fitted. All this is perhaps only to say very simply that the growth of lineages, over time and as compared with one another, can be almost infinitely varied and irregular, ranging from stagnation or total extinction to astronomically rapid growth, whereas the relative numbers in each successive generation or each successive cohort of the same age group can normally vary only within comparatively narrow limits. It may therefore properly be said that this stability in the proportions and balance of the crucial social entities over long periods of time is in conformity with fixed symbolic categories of balanced opposition, if indeed it cannot actually be said to encourage them. Some theories of the requisites of society would justify the latter statement. All that is necessary for the maintenance of this conformity between the balance of social groups and the balance of symbolic categories is that each pair of adjacent and successive generations or age groups should not be too disproportionate. Epidemics, famines, and other disasters may cause temporary dislocation, but the following generations inevitably return to a relative balance. The secular growth of the group is irrelevant; it is only the balance between adjacent generations and ages that matters, whereas it is precisely the secular divergence of lineage growth that has to be constantly adjusted to new points of balance in a segmentary lineage system.

Not only does age organization to this extent favor the expression of social structure and solidarity in fixed and balanced symbolic categories, but it determines that they should take a binary form with a potential trinary underlay. Opposition or complementarity is always necessarily between adjacent generations or age cohorts, usually tempered by the mediating force of the third generation or age cohort that has passed on ahead. Thus characteristically warriors, or youth, stand against elders, or middle age; junior warriors against senior warriors; but these binary oppositions are moderated by the alliance of junior warriors, or secondarily of senior elders with senior warriors over the heads of the junior elders.

This line of analysis cannot be pursued here with the empirical illustration it requires. Nor can it be denied that some societies (for example the Kakwa, Bari, and Lotuko, for whom our information is still too inadequate to permit effective analysis) show a considerable develop-

Aidan W. Southall: Rank and Stratification Among the Alur

ment of both age and lineage structure. But this in no way affects the fact that when the one or the other principle is fully developed as the major basis of social organization (as among Nuer or Kenya Luo on the one hand, or Masai, Kipsigis, Turkana, and Karamojong on the other) it has the characteristics and implications we have specified. The dichotomous or binary division and balance, imposed by the alteration of generations and the confrontation of adjacent age groups, tends to spread to other aspects of society. Thus Arusha territorial and descent groups all divide precisely into two at each level of organization, neither more nor less. The metaphysical characteristics of age organization are echoed and generalized in the social structure and symbolism of these societies.

We do not therefore argue that age organization and segmentary lineage structure are completely incompatible, but that the full and dominant development of the one is incompatible with the other. Thus, in a necessarily brief statement, it is fair to say that age organization, though present, is weak among the Nuer, and that segmentary lineage structure is hardly present among the Masai. Similarly, we cannot argue that symbolic dichotomies are entirely absent from the Western Nilotes, but they are certainly less prominent, less numerous and complex, often indeed lacking in symbolic content.

In giving a structural interpretation we have no intention of excluding the influence of diffusion and borrowing. This has occurred throughout between Nilotes and their foreign neighbors, but also among themselves. It is to be noted that the Kakwa, Bari, and Lotuko, technically classified as Eastern Nilotes, in fact form an enclave more than half surrounded by Western Nilotes. In language and many cultural features they are indeed linked with the Eastern Nilotes, but in respect of other elements they are closer to the Western Nilotes, who are also spatially nearer to them.

There are certain properties of age organizations that, if not ineluctable, are certainly logically simplest and therefore, *ceteris paribus,* most likely to occur. The major basis of social differentiation between men is based on the conventional evaluation of physiological or social age. The stronger this emphasis, the less likely is any stress on status differences between different descent lines within the system. Such distinctions could, of course, be made vis à vis groups in certain respects outside the system, such as the despised Dorobo and ironworking groups in conjunction with the Masai, or the serf stratum among the Bari. If conceived status differences between descent lines are unimportant, there is one less functional reason for solidarity (especially widespread territorial solidarity) based upon genealogical reckoning of unilineal descent and the generation of segmentary lineage structure. It is made relatively easy for a man to slot into an age organization structure, wherever he finds himself in the system, on the basis of criteria known and recognized throughout the

Social Structure and Stratification Among the Eastern Nilotes

system. It is therefore entirely in conformity with this that descent reckoning is either shallow or dispersed and in the form of nongenealogical clan identification. Such a system is appropriately articulated internally by alternative symbolic identifications (left and right, black and white, red and white, rocks and trees, elephants and buffaloes, etc.). These identifications fill out the substance of societal membership and give it body, while the automatic processes of recruitment (e.g., alternating attribution of father and son to different categories) cut across and overlap with other identifications, such as local settlement, descent group, and age group itself, so that society is closely knit, with little possibility of hostilities being channeled definitively along any one major cleavage.

These symbolic identifications, binary and complementary oppositions, afford a basis for horizontal differentiation, but provide little scope for vertical distinctions of rank and status. These latter are so focused upon differences of physiological and social age that, given the mechanisms of recruitment, they cannot easily become hereditarily entrenched. The position of laibons (Masai, Nandi, and Kipsigis *oiboni*; Lotuko *bwoni*; compare also Bari and Mandari *bunit*) may appear to constitute an exception, but it seems to prove the rule in not having given rise to any extensive noble stratum in society, such as is often found among the Western Nilotes. Furthermore, despite their apparent supremacy at times, the position of the laibons was ambiguous. They were by tradition of foreign origin in a number of cases and lacked the panoply and legitimacy of formal political rule. They invite comparison with other ritual and prophetic leaders among African peoples, whose power and influence is sometimes highly charismatic and also fluctuating, sometimes more or less routinized. They show a great capacity to react to opportunities, such as the general threat of external danger, demanding new and extended forms of solidarity within the society. This has been shown to have been in process among the Nuer in response to the growing menace of colonial rule. We do not know how far the dominant position of the Nandi and Masai laibons may have been due to a similar process.

The collective and egalitarian access to pastoral resources, as opposed to more specific individual and descent group rights to cultivated land, is greatly facilitated by the framework of age organization, and marks the contrast between the predominantly pastoral Eastern Nilotes and the more agricultural Western Nilotes. However, from this aspect, the Nuer and Dinka (Western Nilotes but predominantly pastoral) and the Arusha, Teso, or Lotuko (Eastern Nilotes but heavily dependent upon agriculture) represent intermediate points on the range of variation.

From this we conclude that, for most of the Eastern Nilotes, the scope within their system for important or lasting distinctions of rank is extremely limited, always excluding from this the depressed castelike groups in symbiotic relation but not fully within these societies.

The popular view of Nilotic peoples as a whole has certainly been one of egalitarian individualism. If such a slippery concept can be precisely defined, some truth may possibly be found in it, but the image may be most powerfully derived from the impact of the more superficially spectacular and exotic Nilotes, such as the Nuer and Dinka in the north, or the Masai in the south. But among the Western Nilotes in general there are more important distinctions which seem interesting from the point of view of a comparative theory of rank.

SOCIAL STRUCTURE AND STRATIFICATION AMONG THE WESTERN NILOTES

With the Western Nilotes it is the relation between genealogically based structures and territory that provides the main framework. Political offices are developed to a variable extent; and when they are present, differences of rank depend mainly on proximity by descent and access to them, for both the individual and the group. But it is by no means merely a question of proximity and access to political power, for all these offices are embellished with ritual and enshrouded in sanctity, and it is particularly this sanctity and ritual status, with certain accompanying privileges and immunities attaching to them, which spill over from chief office-holders, and their predecessors to those nearest to them by descent. Even when political offices are virtually absent, as among the Dinka, similar ritually defined sanctities are nontheless present. They confer a certain prestige, which is the embryonic form of rank and stratification present in such systems.

Thus it is important to note that among the Dinka, so acephalous and uncentralized politically, one finds many striking features attaching to the burial of certain venerable elders which, in an older ethnography, might well have been taken as cultural traits of divine kingship. Indeed, they demand comparison with death and succession rituals in other Nilotic societies, such as Alur or Acholi, in which such practices are much more distinctively crystallized around hereditary political offices. These in turn belong in considerable part to the same class of ritual practices that cluster around the much more elaborate kingship of their immediate Bantu neighbors the Nyoro. This is only to point out that there is a great similarity in form and meaning between ritual practices which in one society serve to confirm authoritarian political office, while in others they confirm the supernatural prestige of roles that lack political sanctions entirely.

Social Structure and Stratification Among the Western Nilotes

Dinka polities are focused upon the complementary validity of supernatural and political efficacy, symbolized by the division of Dinka lineages into two sorts, those of the fishing spear and those of the war spear. The distinction is symbolic in that it does not at all correspond to a division between those who fish and those who fight, although the war spear lineages are supposed to supply outstanding warrior leaders in each polity. Rather it seems a representation at the level of intellect of the parallel importance of religious and secular activities, for around the lineages and clans attached to "Masters of the Fishing Spear" (who seem to be simply those elders of such lineages who develop those qualities of seniority and excellence most valued in the society) focus the rituals and the myths that express most coherently the integration, articulation, and composition of Dinka society. Thus there seems to be a cultural integration of the Dinka fishing spear lineages, widely dispersed though they are, which embraces the war spear lineages only by virtue of their integration with the former in each Dinka polity. In this sense the fishing spear lineages seem to own a distinctive Dinka quality which the rest lack, and such a dichotomy runs through many other Nilotic societies, often in a largely secular form, but always related to the distinction between those granted the status of owners or aboriginals and those who are immigrants or settlers. There is no solid evidence to demonstrate whether this distinction holds true for the Dinka in a historical sense. But the myths and legends that distinguish and belong to Dinka society as an entity seem to belong to the fishing spear and not to the war spear lineages.

Among their Nuer neighbors the distinction appears in two forms: First between "nobles" and "commoners"—that is, between members of lineages which are held to be owners of the territory they occupy and those which are not. Nuer may be "commoners" in the sense that they are living outside the territory of their own lineage in that of another, or they may not be known to belong to a lineage which has territorial rights as "nobles" anywhere. But in the latter case it is likely that they are not of Nuer origin. Similarly, on reading Evans-Pritchard's account, it is difficult to resist the conclusion that all Nuer lineages with "totemic" identifications are of Dinka origin. This second distinction is one that might be empirically established by ethnography, but it is not one of general symbolic or practical significance to the Nuer, as is that between noble and commoner, or that between war spear and fishing spear lineages among the Dinka.

Among the Kenya Luo there is a similar distinction between members of lineages which own their territory, and are therefore politically and ritually dominant, and individuals, families and even lineage segments established as immigrants or settlers in the territory of other lineages. As would seem to be the case in Nuer, they may either be Luo displaced from

Aidan W. Southall: Rank and Stratification Among the Alur

their own territory or may be of non-Luo origin, usually Bantu.

Where political offices were more highly developed, the same distinction became clearly that between rulers and subjects, as in Alur and Acholi. Thus, in Alur all those belonging to lineages descended from chiefs are collectively called *rwodhi,* the term for the chiefs themselves, and incidentally the same etymologically as that applied to the Shilluk kings (*reth*), but which with this wide extension we must translate as "noble" or "aristocrat," as with the Nuer *dil.* Alur commoners are collectively called *lwak,* which etymologically suggests the masses of subjects. In Acholi the same distinction is made between *kal* lineages, or those derived from and focused upon the palace or homestead of the chief, and *lobong,* or subjects, a word that in other neighboring Nilotic languages refers rather to serfs.

It must not be thought that these "nobles" were a select minority, for they could often be even a majority in the local community. This was always in the nature of the system, although it is true that colonial rule weakened or broke the bonds between serf or commoner clients and their noble patrons, so that the proportions of the one and the other often appeared rather different, by the time the ethnographies were written, from what they had been in traditional times. Nonetheless, given the principles of unilineal descent, cattle bridewealth, exogamy and polygyny, noble lineages always on the average grew at a much larger rate than commoner lineages, thus constantly diluting their nobility to the point of virtual extinction at the margin, preventing the development of a very hard line of distinction between all nobles and all commoners as such. In Alur and doubtless also in Acholi, the more a noble lineage expanded, the farther its marginal members were pushed away from the source of their nobility in the reigning chief. The farther back in time and generations their link with a reigning chief, and the greater the expansion of the chiefly lineage during the intervening generations, the more the most distant segments and their members became indistinguishable from commoners for all practical purposes. Landmarks in this process were the breaking of the ban on intermarriage between them and the immediate agnates of the chief, and often their eventual invitation of a chief's son to come and rule over them directly, thus clearly signalizing their subject status.

Among the Shilluk the immediate royal family (*kwareth*), retaining in principle the right of royal succession, were distinguished from more distant members of the royal family (*ororo*), who were no longer eligible to succed. *Bang'reth* were the serfs clustering around the king and the shrines of past kings, while the mass of commoners were *collo,* the correct ethnic designation of the Shilluk. Such differentiations seem to be easily added to the simple collective distinction between rulers and subjects. Even within the same society the type and degree of distinction relevant depends upon the situation. Thus in Alur, while the general dichotomous distinction between *rwodhi* (chiefs and nobles) and *lwak* (subjects) is frequently made, it contains within it further refinements similar to those of the Shilluk. The general term *rwodhi* includes the *nyalwo,* or immediate lineage of a chief, which may equally well be designated *juparwoth* (people of the chief), and which implies a corporate agnatic group directly interested in succession to the office of chief and in privileged collective enjoyment of some of its perquisites; but *rwodhi* also includes the much larger number of more distant lineage members, who may also be called *lwo,* whose chiefly descent is hardly more than nominal, conveying little effective everyday privilege, however proud they may be of it. Closely attached to every reigning chief are special commoner lineages called *jukal* (those in the chief's village), whose leaders are guardians of the secrets and conductors of the rituals of chiefship. There were also slaves in small numbers in traditional Alur society and large numbers of non-Nilotes ruled by Alur chiefs, with the general status of subjects (*lwak*) but at a somewhat lower level than those of Nilotic origin. However, in the ultimate analysis the number of Alur commoner lineages of demonstrably Nilotic (*lwo*) origin is very few, most of them seeming to be of remote and therefore lapsed noble origin, or to have been immigrants or foreigners.

Thus it seems that alike for the Alur with their well-evolved chiefship and for the Nuer without it, "nobility" as we have used it, and as it is current in the literature, may mean little more than a claim to full membership of the ethnic group upon which the whole society is focused and identified. For the Alur this ethnic identity is *lwo,* and all who can claim to be *lwo* seem ultimately to be of chiefly descent, however shadowy and remote, while by the same token all other groups in the society seem ultimately to be of foreign extraction. However, the chiefly descent of some is so remote that their nobility is nominal, while the foreign extraction of others is also so remote that they are very fully integrated in the society and cannot in any present sense be considered foreigners. Not only does nobility depend on proximity of descent to ruling chiefs, but foreignness likewise depends on recency of incorporation.

Every phase of this process is illustrated among the Alur who, at least in their remembered history, have incorporated more numerous and more diverse foreign populations than any other Nilotic people. Some Alur chiefdoms incorporated Madi, some Okebo, some Lendu, some Abira, some Banyali, and many others besides. Some chiefdoms incorporated members of several or even all these foreign groups. Moreover, besides all these non-Lwo, there were groups of Lwo incorporated from other areas, who therefore counted as commoners in Alur, although they might have been able to claim some remote and scarcely verifiable descent

Aidan W. Southall: Rank and Stratification Among the Alur

and hence nobility from some Lwo rulers elsewhere. Their status was therefore of a similar order to that of Nuer or Kenya Luo living outside the territory which their lineage could claim as its own. Incorporated foreign groups retained their own distinct languages for several generations. In chiefdoms where the numerical proportion of Lwo was high, the foreigners became bilingual and eventually after many generations forgot their original tongue and spoke the Lwo language only. But in some chiefdoms rather remote from the main areas of Lwo settlement, where the proportion of Lwo was small and that of foreigners correspondingly high, it even happened that the Lwo rulers and nobles eventually dropped their Lwo speech and adopted that of their foreign subjects. Thus while political incorporation went in one direction, other aspects of cultural incorporation might proceed in another.

While the difference between a Lwo who could claim clear agnatic connection with a ruling chief, and a foreigner still speaking a non-Lwo language, was certainly a marked difference of rank, this cleavage was filled with many intermediate positions. A Lwo whose lineage diverged from a ruling line ten or twelve generations ago, and a foreigner whose lineage had been living in the same chiefdom equally long and who spoke no other language but Lwo, might differ very little in status. Many foreign groups of ancient incorporation could claim a special ritual or functional status which compensated them for their non-Lwo origin and gave them a parallel honor in the community. They might have special duties and privileges in the rituals of chiefship, of which they were very proud, while in the case of the Okebo they were the ironworkers who supplied tools and weapons to the Alur and justifiably claimed their indispensability. Lwo commoners affected to despise the other groups, and marriage with them was to some extent regarded as inferior; yet chiefs did not disdain marriage with non-Lwo women, nor was their status always inferior to that of their Lwo co-wives, and the sons of such unions could even succeed to chiefship. Thus the perspective and evaluation of rank and status varied somewhat according to a person's origin and position. Naturally each stressed those criteria most favorable to him, although others would in part discount his own evaluation. While individual bonds of kinship and affinity linked the various ethnic groups, and collective claims to special ritual functions, or the provision of indispensable services, satisfied personal esteem and supplied a minimum solidarity and common purpose to the diverse components of the society, there could be no doubt of the preeminent rank ascribed to chiefs and those near to them in agnatic descent.

The Padhola constitute an interesting variation for two reasons. On the eve of colonization they were in process of evolving two lines of chiefs, one in the west derived from a succession of prophets, the other in the East from a famous war leader. The western zone consisted primarily of *lwo* by descent and was known as *Jo·iye* (the inside people). The eastern zone consisted largely of Eastern Nilotic Itesyo, who had adopted the Padhola language instead of their own and had become integrated in Padhola society, with which they fought against the Itesyo from whom they were derived. They became known as *Jo·oko* (the outside people). Although their different origin was thus signaled, they were in no way of inferior status.

THE FACTORS RELEVANT TO RANK AND SOCIAL DIFFERENTIATION

From this brief appraisal it is possible to suggest the main factors relevant to systems of rank and differentiation in these Nilotic societies. First of all, the form of rank and differentiation depends closely upon the degree of political specialization in the society. The greater the political specialization, the more closely must the system of rank be integrated with the hierarchy of power, though rank and power remain overlapping but not identical, frequently with a time lag in the adjustment of rank to changes in power.

In uncentralized or stateless societies rank is defined, expressed, and even sanctioned much more in ritual terms, as indeed are most other aspects of social integration. Rank differentiation in such societies takes the form of complementarity much more than of hierarchy. One category or stratum may formally be said to be above another, but such hierarchy often seems of little social relevance. While all rank has ritual aspects, we may therefore speak of the varying politico-ritual balance and the varying balance between hierarchy and complementarity in the range of Nilotic societies from those which are most to those which are least centralized.

Rank differentiation naturally gives expression to the facts of history and ecology, especially in uncentralized societies, where power differences are not the main factor and differentiation is more complementary than hierarchical. It is impossible to give a comprehensive explanation of why some societies are more given to ritual than others, apart from the fact already stated, that society depends fundamentally upon ritual integration where centralized political authority is not developed. But there are obviously great differences in degree of ritualization between societies at the same level of political specialization, and this cannot be definitively explained. We are obliged to leave a place to the factor of cultural choice, which is a confession of ignorance. We may, however, suggest that the very age of a society is an important limiting factor. It would seem that a society which has had the opportunity to maintain its structure intact, with little radical change over a considerable period, and usually in much

Aidan W. Southall: Rank and Stratification Among the Alur

the same territory, has at least the possibility of considerable ritual elaboration, which a newer society has not. As ritual elaborates it may become ill-adapted to changed situations and eventually provoke a reaction. There is thus a cyclical tendency in many societies in which ritual elaboration builds up to a point at which it is more or less violently rejected and the process begins over again. This is a usual counterpart of political revolution frequently witnessed in our own day.

The American colonies, in winning independence and creating the United States, broke away from a system of rank and ritual that had been evolving for a thousand years. The Reformed Churches revolted (among other things) against what seemed to them the overritualization of the Roman Catholic Church, but the charisma of the reformers invariably became routinized and so the process has been repeated many times over. The Russian revolution was even more determined to eradicate rank and ritual, yet in the consolidation of the new state they have inevitably tended to creep in again. The twentieth-century convulsions in China are the overthrow of a system of rank and ritual which was in formation over an even longer period. The new nations of the *tiers monde* are all faced with the problem of developing an integrated system of rank and ritual which will provide dignity and solidarity. The attempt to throw out rank and ritual as such seems doomed to fail, but our age is witnessing the effective revolt against certain types of rank and ritual which are the counterpart of certain types of political system, and this revolt in a strange way constitutes a return to the complementary rather than hierarchical ranking systems of stateless societies.

We thus relate variations in ranking systems among the Nilotes to variations in the degree of political specialization and the consequent politico-ritual balance, to the opportunity for stable elaboration over long periods of time and to the expression of different sequences and processes of occupation and settlement in the context of local ecological variations. The ecological opportunities are, of course, a factor given outside the social system, but are quite differently exploited according to the direction of cultural interest and equipment. Thus, the Masai deliberately ignore the favorable opportunities for agriculture that exist within the territory they occupy. The historical sequences of occupation and settlement represent not only the successive choices made by the group but also its interactions with its neighbors, accompanied by reciprocal and selective borrowing. The political system, which we have so far taken as more or less given at any particular period, is obviously itself in large part a product of the same experiences. We are still confronted by the perennial functional dilemma, that if we can to some extent explain how a particular system works and continues, we cannot satisfactorily explain why it differs from those of its neighbors.

In Sahlins' ingenious theory, the Nuer segmentary lineage system is an instrument of predatory expansion. Now, we know that the Nuer had segmentary lineages, that they were predatory and that they expanded at the expense of the Dinka. But were the characteristics of Nuer segmentary structure the means or the result of their expansion? Both the Alur and the Kenya Luo expanded at the expense of their neighbors. Why then were the specific characteristics of the segmentary system different in each of these three cases? Nuer lineages were dispersed rather than localized, Luo lineages were localized rather than dispersed, while Alur lineages focused upon hereditary lines of political rulers which the other two people lacked. Furthermore, the Masai, with their structure based on age organization, quite different from the other three, were also successful predatory expansionists. It is unreasonable to suggest that these important variations on a common theme were caused simply by reaction to different local circumstances of expansion. We are left again with original variations of structure, which can to some extent be given a functional interpretation, but cannot further be explained without recourse to history. It is therefore with better informed and more rigorous diachronic functional analyses that interpretation can be improved.

The Shilluk and the Alur exhibit a higher degree of political specialization than most other Nilotes. The vital historical facts are lacking in both cases. The precise political powers of the Shilluk *reth* are still debatable, and the extent to which their development may have been due to borrowing from or reaction to the Turkish regime in the Sudan cannot be demonstrated. That Alur political specialization was influenced by Bunyoro cannot be absolutely excluded, but the evidence is quite inconclusive. On the other hand, if it could be demonstrated that Alur political specialization was a reaction to the opportunity for expansion and absorption, this would be important for political theory. For what is is worth, Nilotic tradition always suggests that it was prior possession of the idea of politico-ritual dominance that was important, rather than mere reaction to the opportunities of a situation.

COMMON THEMES AND VARIATIONS IN NILOTIC RANK AND STRATIFICATION

As examples of the more politically specialized Nilotic systems, we find a number of similar elements repeated among the Shilluk, the Alur, the Acholi, and the Eastern Anuak (see Table 1). In all three cases the population is ranked according to its proximity to the royal lineage. Both Shilluk and Alur distinguish the king himself (unique in the Shilluk case but repeated in numerous autonomous polities among the Alur), the

Table 1. Rank and Stratification Among the Alur and Other Nilotic Peoples

	King, Chief	Royal Lineage	Lapsed Royal Lineage	Commoner	Courtiers, Royal Serfs	Headman	Owner of Earth
Shilluk	Reth	Kwareth	Ororo	Collo	Bang'reth	Jyak	
Alur	Rwoth	Kwai Rwoth Juparwoth Nyalwo	Rwodhi Lwo	Lwak	Jukal Bong'	Jego	Won Ng'om Kwai Ng'om Monyekak
Acholi	Rwot	Kal		Bong'		Jago	
Anuak		Nyiye	Jowatong'		Bang'		
Bari		Lui			Dupi		
Nuer		(nobles/no totemic emblem) owners, natives Jo piny, Luo		(commoners/totemic emblem) settlers Jo dak			
Luo (Kenya)	Ruoth						
Mandari	Mar Lo Ban						(Lotuko) Lamonyefau Monyekak
Dinka	(warrior leader) Bany	Bany, koc bith (north/cattle)		Kic, koc tong' (south/crocodile)			
Shilluk		Ger, Gol Dhiang'		Lwak, Gol Nyikang'			
Lwo		Jo·iye (west)		Jo·oko (east)			
Padhola		Jo·iye (upper)		Jo·oko (lower)			
Lugbara/Madi		Lu		Madi			
Ahur		Ju malo		Ju piny			

royal lineage with residual rights of succession, the more distant segments of the royal lineage, whose rights of succession have lapsed, the commoners, and the serfs. The Acholi distinguish the king or chief (of whom there are many as among the Alur), the royal lineage, and the commoners. The Shilluk distinguish the ruler and all the nobles of his lineage, the lapsed nobles and the common people. The term *rwoth,* used in various forms for "ruler," appears again among the Kenya Luo in reference to the heads of maximal lineages, who were not strictly hereditary, but usually followed one another in the same agnatic line, acquiring recognition through wealth in cattle, wives, and children, and thus as heads of potential new lineage segments, and also through repute as war magicians. Their precise status varied from one part of the country to another, some lines showing a stronger tendency to become hereditary and gather special regalia to themselves. *Rwoth* could in fact be applied loosely to a leader in many contexts, having no unique reference to the ruler as in Shilluk; nor designating a particular descent category as in Alur.

Shilluk, Alur, and Acholi also use the same term (*jyak, jago, jego*) for the headmen of territorial sections under the chief or king. The reference of the term *bong'* or *bang'* varies from common people to serfs among these four groups. The Shilluk take their ethnic designation from that of the commoners (*collo*), while the Alur identify rather with the general designation of the nobles (*lwo*), as do most other southern Nilotes of the Western group (Acholi, Palwo, Padhola, Kenya Luo, and also the Luo of Bahr-el-Ghazal). The Alur use the term *lwak* for commoners, in the sense of "the masses," a term that appears also as designation for the southern moiety of Shilluk country, and which among the Nuer has the concrete significance of "cattle byre" where the men congregate.

The distinction between noble and commoner in those societies with a degree of political specialization would appear to correspond to that between owners of the country and settlers on sufferance. Such a distinction is made by all these peoples in the one form or the other. For the Shilluk, Alur, Acholi, and Anuak it has a definite connotation of rank; but for the less centralized Nuer, Dinka, and Kenya Luo it refers essentially to the different status enjoyed by those who live in the territory to which they properly belong by descent and those who for whatever reason do not. In the Dinka case it has the added significance of picking out in a symbolic distinction two of the primary activities of the society—warfare and fishing, the latter being intimately associated with the mythical origins of the Dinka and hence with their most important rituals. The word *piny* (earth), which in the Luo phrase *Jo piny* means owners of the earth or soil, seems to correspond to the word *ban* in the Mandari title of the earth chief and also to the Dinka *bany* designating the ritually dominant, more original, and hence in a sense higher-ranking clans of the fishing

Aidan W. Southall: Rank and Stratification Among the Alur

spear. For the Alur, the word *piny* (earth) has the further connotation downward, or below, hence *jupiny* refers to the lowland half of the Alur as opposed to *jumalo,* the highlanders. Such ecologically or topographically based dichotomies are made among a number of these peoples, sometimes incorporating other ritual or symbolic distinctions. Thus, Shillukland is divided into the northern and southern halves of Ger and Lwak, which have their counterparts in the religious moieties of Gol dhiang' and Gol Nyikiang', signifying respectively cattle and Nyikang', the founder hero who appeared in the form of a crocodile; so that in a sense the pastoral resources of the land and the fishing resources of the Nile are represented. As the fishing spear category of Dinka clans ranks higher than that of the war spear clans, so the southern Shilluk moiety especially associated with the culture hero and the Nile seems ritually preeminent. The ancient Nilotic root *lwo* finds a further echo beyond the Nilotes among their central Sudanic neighbors, the Madi and Lugbara, who divide themselves between the *lu,* or high people, and the *madi,* or low people, an apparently ecological and topographical dichotomy similar to that of the Alur who adjoin them to the south, but with additional mythical and symbolic overtones. Both the Kenya Luo and the Padhola use the terms *Jo·iye* and *Jo·oko* (inside and outside people) to distinguish the territory of early from that of later settlement, north and south in the Luo case, and west and east in that of the Padhola.

What we have endeavored to demonstrate by tracing these sometimes overlapping and sometimes superimposed social categories through this group of related peoples is that within such a group there appears to be from remote antiquity a certain common stock of concepts, with related sounds and social structures, which nonetheless vary somewhat independently of one another, so that with the variations of empirical social structure, the common stock of sounds and concepts has been drawn upon with independent shifts of sound and concept, the rules of which have not yet been defined. These closely related concepts cover a range of societies varying from those that are completely uncentralized to those with an appreciable degree of centralization and specialized political institutions. We have shown that among most of the Eastern Nilotes there is little opportunity for distinctions of rank to appear. However, the Bari cluster, as yet imperfectly known, displays quite a marked development of such distinctions, and seems intermediate between the Eastern and Western Nilotes in a number of structural features, as it is in geographical position. Among the Western Nilotes, such rank differences as appear among the uncentralized peoples are on a primarily ritual basis, with some economic implications, but of comparatively minor importance in secular daily life, while among the more centralized peoples ranking differences follow closely the form of the political system.

SLAVERY AND STRATIFICATION AMONG THE ILA OF CENTRAL AFRICA

BY ARTHUR TUDEN

Slavery, as a type of social stratification, has not received the same degree of attention that caste, plural societies, or class systems have. Slavery has been considered a type of class, and no detailed attempt has been made to analytically differentiate it from other forms of stratification. Further the analysis of slavery, as with many other earlier anthropological problems, has been viewed from a historical vantage-point. Attention has been focused on such questions as what the societal or economic forces leading to the adoption of slavery were, or whether or not slavery was the original and earliest form of stratification (Macleod, 1925; Nieboer, 1910; Siegel, 1945).

These questions, while critical for a picture of developmental sequences and historical change, have tended to obscure the forms of slavery and its importance for the structure of society. This chapter, therefore, will describe a system of stratification based upon slavery. It will emphasize the recruitment of slaves, their rate of mobility, and the relationships among the strata in society.

The Ila—or Mashukulumbwe, as they are also known—are a Bantu-speaking people of about 20,000 situated 200 miles north of Victoria Falls and 230 miles west of Lusaka in what now is called Zambia. They enjoy a plentiful supply of water and grass for their herds of cattle, and their territory is endowed with ample fertile land for agricultural pursuits.

I would like to express my thanks to the Ford Foundation for support of my field work among the Ila.

Arthur Tuden: Slavery Among the Ila

Before 1920, subsistence agriculture relied heavily on sorghum, maize, and millet, supplemented by ground nuts, pumpkins, sweet potatoes, various gather roots and wild fruit. Game and fish were easily caught in the nearby plains and rivers. The cattle provided fresh and sour milk, but were not, as with most cattle peoples, slaughtered for meat, but when killed at ceremonial occasions the meat was eaten.[1]

Resources such as land were not denied to any member of the group and were easily obtainable. Permission to farm land belonging to friends or relatives was not denied to a supplicant. The right to farm was so accepted that the Ila could not recall any instance when individual requests had been rejected if unused land was available, even though especially fertile plots of land were reserved for prominent kin heads and their closest relatives. The work unit was usually a man and his wife or wives. The elder members of the kin farmed rich land surrounding the villages, and brothers and immediate kin of the village headmen were allocated a share of kin communal holdings. Some men with more than one wife farmed multiple plots, one wife farming land near the village, while a second farmed more remote land.

The territorial framework was autonomous or semiautonomous divisions (*chisi*), which varied greatly in size and population. Within these divisions the dominant social relationships were based upon kin ties. In the more populous areas as many as fifteen to twenty kin groups resided in close proximity, while in the more sparsely populated areas only four or five groups resided. The basic structural unit and the primary political group was the *mukwashi,* or *chibuwe,* a small, exogamous-named group of agnatic relatives, three generations in depth and containing not more than twenty males. The agnatic members with their wives, children, followers, and slaves were the core of the village. Matrilineal relatives also resided in the villages, but rarely dominated numerically. Membership in the agnatic groups permitted rights to cattle held for the group, for payment of fines, contributions to bridewealth, mutual aid, and land. However, these functions were replicated in diminishing degrees by a group of dispersed matrilineal relatives called the *mukowa*. As no rigid descent system prevailed, there was a multiplicity of bonds of comparable and at times conflicting strength. The Ila social system allowed for a wide range of possible choices of affiliation for individuals and for the opportunity of changing an affiliation if the need arose. Within the smaller unit, the *mukwashi,* brothers from the same mother formed smaller discrete units and usually had strong ties of loyalty to each other.

In each of the territories usually one kin group was more powerful than the others, but a rotation of kin leaders and loss of their power

1. Earlier historical material is drawn from the study *The Ila-Speaking Peoples of Northern Rhodesia,* by Edwin W. Smith and Andrew M. Dale.

occurred over a period of time. Factors necessary for leadership, size of groups, or relative wealth underwent changes from generation to generation.[2]

Although, as we have suggested, no restrictions were placed upon land usage by individuals, and seemingly the kinship system ethic provided the major structural foundation for the social relationship, the Ila as perhaps many other non-Western societies resembled to a great degree an acquisitive society. They were and are scheming, grasping individuals constantly searching for methods to acquire property. Wealth distinctions are part of the value structure of the Ila—a poor man would be ignored. A wealthy individual was admired. The concepts of ownership and property among the Ila were complex and covered many items of property. However, property was divided into different categories, and no one item had clear convertibility for all other items. Cattle by far dominated most economic relationships and were at the apex of the economic system. Both land and foodstuffs were not usually considered items in the system of exchange.

While wide-scale trade was not a part of the economic system, tobacco, salt, and skins were traded internally and with other territories. These objects were exchanged for locally manufactured materials such as pottery, spears, and axe blades. Sea shells (*impande*) were also obtained by trade from neighboring groups. These items were owned individually and were inherited by close kinsmen, or later were buried with the owner.

Within the context of a kinship system and lack of economic complexity a slave group appears to be anomalous. But among the Ila, as with other societies where the development of a separate stratum such as slaves or classes had a political implication which strengthened an already hierarchical system, slaves were recognized as key elements in the society. Among the Ila, however, the slaves were incorporated into the social system so as to minimize and even offset the potential increase in stratification which might occur by weakening of kin ties.

RECRUITMENT OF SLAVES

Prior to a British edict of 1917 which released all slaves, the Ila augmented their numbers by adding slaves to their population. An estimated 40 percent of the present-day population are of slave ancestry, and this figure may be higher since slave ancestry may have been forgotten or concealed in genealogies. Information on slave ancestry was difficult

2. A more detailed discussion of the cyclical changes among a political system of this type appears in *Local-Level Politics*, Marc J. Swartz (ed.).

Arthur Tuden: Slavery Among the Ila

to obtain, because of the reluctance of the Ila to discuss the origin of a villager. Information as to the origin of slaves was always given in private, but no pride was evinced by informants in their own nonslave origin.

The recruitment of the slaves was not based upon any large-scale organization, but was rather a result of individual activities. Only one form of slave recruitment implied any societal organization or group activity, and this method accounted for only a minority of the slaves. In cases of warfare between different territories—and the Ila were an extremely warlike group—other villages were attacked, cattle seized, and younger children and women captured. But no organized distribution of slaves or cattle followed these raids; instead, each attacker seized and held his own spoils. In a few cases brothers did coordinate their action, but even this form of minimal organization was rare.

Slaves were also individuals accepted as payment of debts or fines. Among the Ila, a number of crimes were punishable by fines, and if cattle or other property was not forthcoming, children were sold or seized. In these cases it was likely that the children were later redeemed by relatives.

However, the majority of slaves were acquired by purchase from nearby culturally similar groups, primarily the Mbala, Tonga, Totela, or Twa. Cattle, salt, leopard skins, hoes, and grain were the standard media of exchange in the traffic. The amount of grain fluctuated with local crop conditions, but the average price for a male slave was sixteen bags (roughly sixteen pounds) of locally manufactured salt or a medium-sized heifer, and a female slave commanded twenty-one bags of salt or a slightly larger beast. Slave characteristics most eagerly sought by the purchasers were youth and an absence of physical deformities.

The information in Table 1, analyzing the recruitment of slaves in one

Table 1. Recruitment of Slaves

Sex	Age	Method of Recruitment	Origin
Male	20	Purchased by 15 bags salt	Mbala
Female	8–10	Purchased by 20 bags salt	?
Female	10–12	Purchased by maize	Mwila
Male	20's	Purchased by salt	?
Female	Old	Purchased by skins	?
Female	8–12	Purchased by one beast	?
Female	8–10	Purchased by salt	Totela
Male	10–12	Purchased by 15 bags salt	Tonga
Male	10–12	Purchased by one beast	Mbala
Female	10–12	Debt	Mwila
Female	10–12	Purchased by corn	Mbala
Male	10–12	Purchased by corn	Mbala
Female	10–12	Purchased by one beast	Mbala
Female	Old	Captured	Mwila
Female	Young (4–7)	Captured	Mwila
Female	Young (4–7)	Captured	Mwila
Female	Young (4–7)	Purchased by salt	Mbala
Female	Very young (2–4)	Purchased by salt	Mwila
Female	Young (4–7)	Purchased by one beast	?

village, is representative of other villages among the Ila, and indicates that female slaves outnumbered males four to one; slaves acquired under twelve years of age were almost ten times more common than older slaves. Fluctuation in price and the discrepancy of sexes should not be interpreted, according to the Ila, to indicate a stronger preference for females, since both sexes were eagerly purchased. Males were employed in economic tasks and in warfare, while females added cattle to the family herds when they married or, if they did not marry, produced children and labored in the fields.

SOCIAL DIFFERENTIATION

Although the majority of slaves were obtained by commercial trans-actions, it is impossible to talk about clear social stratification among the Ila based upon slave status or slave origin. Kinship ties absorbed the slaves, rather than slavery producing another distinct social grouping within the society. Essentially, no clear social differentiation existed between slaves and free Mwila. This ambiguous role and indeterminate status of slaves is reflected in the terminology and attitudes about status. The term *slave* is best defined in Ila terms as a person who was not reared in the village. It was impossible to elicit any stereotype concerning slaves, and consistently slaves were characterized as people who "didn't know where their ancestors came from," or "women who did not receive property in marriage," all references indicating minor social gradations based upon kinship criteria. One generic term applied to this category was *muzhike* (singular), *bazhike* (plural), translated in its broadest sense to include any individual of low status such as a slave, serf, or servant. A second term, *bantu bulyo*, was a polite and oblique reference to slaves meaning "people inside," and indicated individuals in a kinship group who were not true kinsmen.

The Ila stressed the unlikelihood of a slave being called either *bazhike* or *bantu bulyo*, since these terms could be construed as insulting. In one village a slave speared the son of his owner when he was called *muzhike* and the slave was not punished. A joking name, kinship term, or spirit name, the customary term of address for a free person, was the accepted procedure for addressing a slave.

Although we have asserted that the Ila society tended to absorb slaves into the kinship system, the absorption was not uniform. One social category emerged which did not even approximate social equality. The *nabutema*, translated "unmarried" or "heifer," denoted a special category of female slaves. As we shall discuss later, some women were not absorbed into Ila society, and their treatment and status were unenviable when we compare it to the majority of the slaves.

FREEMAN–SLAVE RELATIONSHIPS

The relationship between a slave and the free Mwila was not a clearly superior-subordinate one; it was clothed in a kinship idiom although not equated with other kinship ties. As soon as a slave was brought into the village, he was incorporated into his owner's kin group. A kin member shaved the slave's head and assigned him a spirit associated with a deceased member of the patrilineal group. During a communal ritual a kin member informed the ancestral spirits of the slave's entrance into the kin group and asked the family spirits to protect the new member. Thus, the initial relationship between slave and owner was structured within the framework of kinship bonds. The slave called his owner *achisha* (MoBR), and this genealogical fiction was adopted and extended to other relatives.

In outward appearance, the role and status of the younger slave was indistinguishable from that of the free Ila child, and no striking differences in behavior, costume, or duties separated the younger slaves from other children in the village. Both free and slave children lived within the village and aided in cattle herding, milking, running errands, and performing minor tasks. Subtle preferences may have been shown to actual kinsmen in choice of foods or presents; but impartiality was the rule, and the fact of slave status or ancestry was minimized. Some Ila stated that such pains were taken to avoid discrimination against young slaves that preference was actually shown them.

The lack of a special category for Ila slaves is perhaps best indicated in the attempts to incorporate the slaves into the kinship system rather than excluding them from key rituals within Ila society. The kinship emphasis of the relationship between slave and owner was expressed in the conscious enculturation of the slave children as Ila and kinsmen. Slave children underwent the same initiation rites as the free Ila with no curtailment of the ceremonies, and younger *bazhike* were members and at times leaders of a ill-defined age group (*musela*). During a slave's youth, economic ties symbolizing kinship affiliation were established by their owner's presenting them with cattle from the patrilineal herds. These animals became the slave's property and represented the nucleus of his private herd, and they were liable to kinship demands of the patrilineal unit with which the slave was affiliated. The owner assumed responsibility for his slave's debts and fines, and there were few if any differences in fines for slaves and for nonslaves. And in times of hunger both slaves as well as kinsmen could be sold or accepted as payment for debt.

Under normal social conditions a child slave's status was similar to that of a free child, although at times the position of slave status revealed the weakness of the fictitious kinship bond, and a property dimension emerged. On the death of an owner, for example, if debts were outstanding or if a slave had been purchased with property originally belonging to the *mukowa*, young slaves would be inherited by these groups.

Related kinship groups exerted the legal right to inherit young slave children, and slaves were removed to the village where the mother or grandmother of the deceased resided; however, older slaves were rarely inherited in this fashion. At these new homes, the slaves were fully part of the kinship group, and no discriminatory practices appeared to prevail. The Ila were vague about the age or social position a slave must attain before he was assured continuity of residence and stability of social relations, but they insisted that if a slave had lived in one village for a greater portion of his life he was a quasi-kinsman and therefore not property. This social dimension of the relationship was expressed in discussions of manumission by the Ila replying "How can a man buy himself from his relatives?"

ECONOMIC BASIS OF SLAVERY

Differences in the economic roles of slave and nonslaves were of quantity not kind. No clear-cut distinctions in the ability to utilize economic resources or in job allocation existed between these two social categories. Most slaves had their own fields and performed the same relatively undifferentiated tasks as the nonslave. But differences emerged with some of the older slaves, and they were exploited as a source of labor, thus relieving the owner and his kinsmen of some onerous tasks. For example, when the cattle were driven to the flood plains during the dry season, slaves performed most of the arduous work of building and repairing the temporary houses, rebuilding the cattle fences, and herding and milking the cattle, while the owner remained in the permanent villages as long as possible. Throughout the entire year, most of the herding was performed by these older slaves, and although such tasks as clearing the fields, hoeing, and assisting in the harvesting were also performed by the owner's sons and kinsmen, slaves seemed to provide the greater share of the labor. Further, a minority of the slaves did not possess fields of their own and worked exclusively in their owner's fields or herded his cattle. It was impossible to ascertain what the diagnostic factors were that separated

Arthur Tuden: Slavery Among the Ila

out these slaves, unless we accept the Ila statement that these slaves did not work well.

Troublesome slaves or those obtained in later life were restricted in movement and were separated from each other, and whenever possible, these slaves' houses were set between those of the owner and his true kinsmen. It appears that these were the slaves who were punished by having their ears branded or their tendons cut, or by being put to death, but physical punishment was not common and the sanctions controlling the behavior of slaves were similar to those applied to actual kinship members.

Slave status or ancestry did not hamper the partial participation of slaves in the Ila economic system, for they owned property, including other slaves. For example, a slave in one *mukwashi* owned thirty head of cattle and two slaves. *Bantu bulyo* obtained property in the same manner as free Ila did—through cattle raids, trading maize, inheritance and purchases. However, it was unwise for a *muzhike* to possess more property than his owner, for then it would have been possible to rival his owner in prestige and potential authority. Former slaves who had acquired property could establish their own patrilineal units by purchasing other slaves or by collecting the dissatisfied relatives of a deceased headman.

Crucial to understanding the economic differences between slaves and nonslaves is the fact that slaves contributed fewer cattle to the bridewealth than the adopted kinsmen did, and in return they obtained a smaller proportion of property from the potential wealth of the entire possible gamut of kin ties. In addition, upon the death of a headman, slaves or those of slave ancestry inherited a portion of the cattle held in the name of the patrilineal group. In all of these distributions and contributions, the fact remains that the economic activity of the slave was generally restricted to only one small area of the total social structure, the most closely related kin group, and the first generation slaves did not inherit from, nor participate in exchanges with, the broader kinship groupings.

At funerals, the cattle slaughtered by kinsmen of the dead man had a functional as well as a symbolic value, for this slaughter not only underscored bonds of kinship, but was also a means of distributing property. On the death of his owner or his owner's child, a slave killed a beast and shared in the inheritance of the *mukwashi* property. However, a slave did not slaughter cattle at the funeral of, nor did he share in the inheritance from, more distantly related kinsmen. Slaves, as pseudo-kinsmen, were outside the usual inheritance regulations, and the slave's owner and *mukwashi* were the major recipients of his property after death. The son or sister's son of a slave did not receive the same inheritance that a free son or sister's son would receive. After a slave's death, the owner "ate the name" (obtained his social position) and inherited most of his property, which in some cases was not incorporated into the *mukwashi* herd, but became the private property of the owner or kin head. For example, in one village, the kin head had inherited over sixty head of cattle from eight deceased slaves; as each slave died the owner and the *mukwashi* head collected the cattle. Therefore slave inheritance was in contradistinction to the usual patterns which dictated that only three names and associated property could be inherited by one individual. Since slaves were without the usual large number of kinsmen who would demand a portion of the property, their social position and cattle went to the head of the kin group, who usually was the owner. This is in contradistinction to the Ila freeman's cattle which circulated among a large number of affiliated relatives, but the distribution of property of newly obtained slaves was by definition restricted to those closely affiliated groups of his owner.

The role of older female slaves, as we indicated earlier, reflected more obvious discrepancies between the verbalized kinship affiliation and actual kinship roles, since female slaves were absorbed into the kinship system with more difficulty than the males. The *nabutema*, divorced or older unmarried slave women, lived in the center of the village in small huts of inferior quality, cleared the fields, planted crops, and gathered wood. If desired, they were assigned to visitors for their sexual pleasure. In isolated cases female slaves were sent along with the married daughter of a headman to work in her fields. They were later assigned to general labor in the village. Female slaves were also instrumental in free women's achieving a distinct social position. Wealthy women purchased female slaves, and their male kinsmen impregnated the slave women. By this means, women were able to form their own kin groups. The role of some women slaves appears to have been uniquely unfavorable, so as to form the only identifiable group within the society.

Slave ancestry presented no definite barrier to intermarriage with free Ila. Ila free women married male slaves, slave women married freemen, and interslave unions took place. However, there appears to be a definite pattern in the marriages which indicates slave marriages were not the preferred pattern. The most common status for a slave woman was that of a secondary wife. The head wife of a headman was usually the daughter of another headman, the marriage being arranged by the families; the second wife was affiliated usually with the mother's brother's patrilineal *mukwashi*; additional wives of the headman were usually slaves from within the village or from other villages. The genealogical fiction of kinship with slaves was ignored in these cases, and slave women were sometimes married to sons or kinsmen of their owner. When a free Ila woman married a male slave, the slave's owner and head of the *mukwashi* presented the *chiko* (bridewealth) to the bride's family, and the formal marriage ceremony took place. However, no cattle changed hands when an interslave marriage occurred within a village, but if both slaves were members of the same *mukwashi*, the girl was sent to another village for a period of time so that the male slave would not be marrying a kinswomen.

Any factor that allowed for further social relations eroded what few discrepancies existed between slave and nonslave groups among the Ila. The children of a marriage between a slave and a free Mwila further served to blur the distinction between slave and nonslave. Slavery, among the Ila, implied and was based upon a lack of kinship affiliation, but second-generation slaves established such affiliations through marriage and residence, since they had more opportunity to establish and extend kinship relations. The Ila summarized this fact by stating that anyone born within a village is a kinsman.

POLITICAL POWER

The Ila did not possess a centralized political system, and the access to political power was relatively open to all members of the society. These factors, plus an absence of a rigid unilineal descent system and the multiplicity of affiliations within the kinship units, appear to have operated in the political sphere to contribute to a lack of rigidity for the slave population.

The multiple bonds of loyalty which members of the community held were exemplified by the distribution of and the claims on property. Because slaves were considered responsible persons to supervise and maintain the patrilineal herds, and because of a slave's limited kinship affiliation, he could be and often was chosen to inherit the name of the kinship head in cases of bickering over inheritance between sons of different mothers. Thus, slaves represented compromise figures who served to lessen and diminish stress resulting from the fissioning of the family group, and they were critical in maintaining some degree of solidarity within the family group. Their elevation to kinship head obviously further minimized the differences between slave and nonslave.

The relationship of the slave to the social network, as indicated, was dependent upon a fictitious kinship affiliation and participation with only one kinship unit, while other members of the community maintained multiple ties with the various patrilineal units of their mother and grandmother. These genealogical relationships, although providing economic aid and support for participants, resulted in conflicting loyalties and responsibilities. As a result, the position of a leader was measurably strengthened by the presence in his village of a number of individuals who, as the Ila stated with relish, "had no place else to go." Since slaves fulfilled this criterion, and were oriented toward a single kinship unit, slaves were a type of floating vote, sought after by the local leaders. Slaves in many cases formed the core of support of the political leaders, and received special treatment in the villages.

A further factor contributing to the absorption of slaves within the kinship system was the lack of centralized leadership, which resulted in protracted and bitter struggles between kinship units for political power. Authority was diffused, so that power did not automatically devolve upon kinship heads or holders of specific roles. The most clearly defined role was that held by the kinship head, but he retained and strengthened his position principally by bonds of kinship, aided by distribution of property and gifts at strategic times. His authority, in essence, was built upon the number of dependents he could control, so a large number of slaves living in a village played a crucial role in the political framework. Since slaves, like kinsmen, were necessary for defense and for support in the constant maneuvering for property and regulation of village life, a slave who had been unfairly treated could run away from his village and a neighboring village would accept him gladly. The new owner, or new fictitious kinship member, would reimburse the previous owner, and the slave would be quickly incorporated into the village on a quasi-kinship basis. Another pattern, apparently widespread, was for the slave to incur a fine and ask to be sold to a new owner as payment for the fine. For example, a slave entering another village and insulted the *mukwashi* leader by throwing ashes on him. The fine for this act was two beasts, but the apparently injured party accepted the slave as payment for the crime. Therefore, the owner of a slave was careful never to unduly antagonize or punish his adopted kinsman, or make the status of a slave so onerous or so distasteful that he might leave.

CONCLUSIONS

The institution of slavery among the Ila did not produce fixed social classes with an unequal distribution of economic resources or political power. The unequal allocation of authority and economic resources were minor and were not permanent for the slave. Within a short period of time slaves were incorporated into the kinship system on a social basis similar to that of nonslaves. The authority regulations affecting slaves were, with minor variations, kinship authority patterns and did not indicate a reworking of the kinship structure.

The Ila, although only one case, are theoretically useful in analyzing the role of slavery in the formation of social stratification. It appears likely that slavery alone cannot be a factor that led to the formation of elaborate

Arthur Tuden: Slavery Among the Ila

social stratification, for in spite of the large number of slaves, and the long history of slavery among the Ila, they still remained a relatively egalitarian society.

As others have stressed, slavery is polytypic, and in some cases slavery is a critical factor in strengthening the preexisting social relationships within the society (Fried, 1968; Siegel, 1945). Among the Ila, as with other societies with weakly defined slavery, the slaves had a major function in adding numbers to the most critical structure of Ila society, the family. Their role was to enhance the strength of the family units, and because of particularly unique Ila kinship relations, slaves resolved internal conflicts.

No group among the Ila were able to employ the slaves as a means of consistently buttressing their positions. Even though the Ila were extremely concerned with amassing property, wealth was utilized within a kinship context, and slaves only facilitated the flow of property. Political positions were not so clearly drawn or potentially expandable that slaves further enhanced the allocation of power; rather they merely supported existing leaders as additional followers.

A key factor inhibiting the development of an exploited social group is the lack of a defined principle of stratification, and the slaves had the ability to move into different areas of Ila society in relatively the same manner, and on a similar basis to, the free Ila. Mobility was accelerated by the framework of the kinship system. Individuals were able to establish and extend their affiliations with other members of the community.

Further, among the Ila, occupational specificity or the assignment of special economic tasks did not exist. The economic system was not involved, as with other societies, for the production of goods in a cash economy, nor for large-scale economic trade. The slave's function was a social one devoted to internal needs, primarily within the framework of kinship relations.

BIBLIOGRAPHY

Fried, Morton   1968   The Political Evolution of Society. New York, Random House.
Macleod, W. C.   1925   Debtor and chattel slavery in aboriginal American slavery. American Anthropologist, 27(3):370–80.
Nieboer, H. J.   1910   Slavery as an Industrial System. Rotterdam, Nijhoff.
Siegel, Bernard J.   1945   Some methodological considerations for a comparative study of slavery. American Anthropologist, 47(3):357–92.

CASTE SYSTEMS IN THE WESTERN SUDAN

BY JAMES H. VAUGHAN, Jr.

The literature on caste in the Western Sudan is at once voluminous and vacuous—voluminous in that there are numerous references to craft-castes, particularly smiths, but vacuous in that the references are usually superficial and, in some instances, either incorrect, inconsistent, or seriously misleading. The great number of references to craft-castes may be seen in Walter Cline's classic study, *Mining and Metallurgy in Negro Africa* (1937); and C. K. Meek's widely used surveys of northern Nigeria illustrate the inconsistency in reporting on castes. Meek's generalization that "In Nigeria . . . there [is] no stigma attached, as in some parts of Africa, to the blacksmith's art—with the exception perhaps of the Kanembu, who despise all forms of industry" (1925:I, 149) is cited by Cline. Yet in his more detailed study we find the following statements: "This prejudice (against marrying a blacksmith's daughter) is widespread in Northern Nigeria" (1931:I, 228); "Blacksmiths are, as among many Nigerian tribes, regarded as social inferiors" (*Ibid.*: 284–85); and "Blacksmiths are commonly in Nigeria endogamous castes" (*Ibid.*: 423). It is also characteristic of Meek's study, as it is of many others, that his comments about smiths are hardly more than brief statements with little or no discussion. It is extremely difficult to get any kind of insight into the organization of the caste or into the operation of the caste within the society from published reports. It is not, therefore, possible to give a comprehensive analysis of the castes of the Western Sudan, if indeed a single analysis is possible. In this chapter, a summary of information

59

James H. Vaughan, Jr.: Caste Systems in the Western Sudan

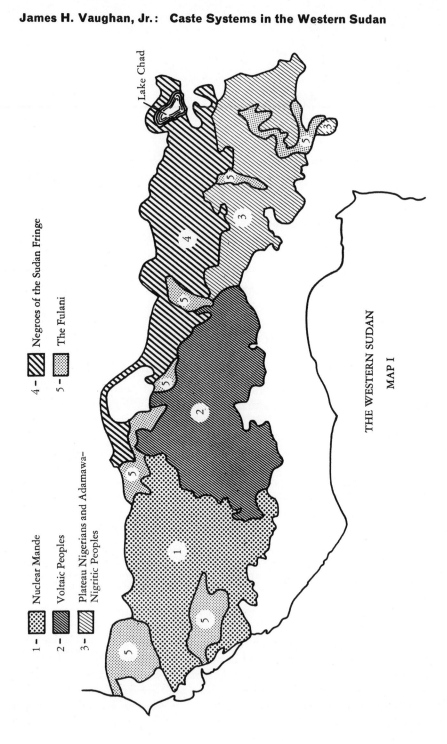

Lake Chad

1 – Nuclear Mande

2 – Voltaic Peoples

3 – Plateau Nigerians and Adamawa–
Nigritic Peoples

4 – Negroes of the Sudan Fringe

5 – The Fulani

THE WESTERN SUDAN

MAP I

about craft-castes is presented with a detailed description of one caste system, and some suggestions about Sudanese caste patterns.

Western Sudan, as used in this chapter, represents a compromise among the usage of Herskovits (1924, 1930, 1962), Baumann (1948), and Murdoch (1959). Our interest, of course, is primarily with the distribution of a single trait throughout an area and not necessarily with historical continuities. We have, therefore, kept generally to the traditional boundaries of the Western Sudan and excluded the Darfur, Wadai, and Bagirmi provinces of Murdock's Negroes of the Sudan Fringe area and excluded as well the southeastern groups of Baumann's Central Sudanese area. Furthermore, we have included with the Plateau Nigerians the Adamawa Cluster of Murdock's Eastern Nigritic peoples. The latter is done not only because it agreed with both Herskovits' and Baumann's discussions of the area but also, in the case of craft-castes, because the area was found to show specific relationships with the Plateau Nigerians. Map I shows the area we will consider in this chapter; the boundaries of the subdivisions are from Murdock.

Caste is not as clearly conceived as one might expect, or at least discussions of it often contain constructions which cause a great deal of difficulty when it is applied cross-culturally. With surprising frequency, one encounters usages which virtually limit the concept to India or the surrounding area, and almost all definitions are strongly slanted toward the Indian situation. This is unquestionably more characteristic of sociological than anthropological usage, though Kroeber's article on caste in the *Encyclopedia of the Social Sciences* (1931) discusses India at great length and only mentions that castes occur in Africa "presumably under direct influences from higher civilizations." A clear statement of the narrow sociological view is offered by Egon Bergel (1962:35–67). He begins, "The caste system represents a logical extreme approaching the ideal type of an absolutely inflexible order. Although it is to be found only in India and neighboring areas, it deserves our attention because of the great number of persons living under this system." Bergel then elaborately abstracts from the Indian system criteria which become *sine qua non* of any caste system, ultimately rejecting Dollard's thesis that Negro Americans form a caste on the grounds that they fail to satisfy two of his *Indian* criteria. This narrow view may be disappearing, for Rosser, in the *Dictionary of the Social Sciences* writes, "Of recent years there has been a notable tendency toward a wide-spread use of the term with the connotation of a rigid hierarchy combined with endogamous segregation" (1964:76). Nonetheless, Barber's assessment that "the archetype of a caste-type of social stratification system . . . is the one that has endured in Hindu India for nearly thirty centuries" (1957:341) is generally true, and the hierarchical ranking of castes in India with its implication of superior and inferior groups has had a very strong effect on caste typologies throughout the world. The hierarchical feature of castes has apparently so interested social scientists that they have often failed to consider the interrelationships between the caste groups.

Another point of contention concerning the definition of the term has to do with its occupational affiliation. Again sociologists, presumably under the influence of the Indian instance, generally include occupational uniformity as a characteristic of caste. This was not a part of either Kroeber's or Lowie's definitions; the latter used Jews as an illustration of a caste (1948:275). Since this chapter is only concerned with craft-castes, which are, of course, occupational in nature, the issue can be avoided, but it is not a point that can be dismissed generally. The question turns on the functions that a caste has in the society. If it is primarily, or if it was perhaps originally, a form of economic organization, then occupational uniformity may be central. However, under circumstances such as political or marital exclusiveness, occupation may be a minor consideration.

The materials from the "Ethnographic Atlas" taken from the journal *Ethnology* comprise a useful summary for a survey such as this. Furthermore Column 69, Caste Stratification, follows the broader anthropological definition of the category, though, of course, individual classifications are dependent upon given ethnographers' definitions, an admitted problem with surveys that rely upon the work of a great many anthropologists. The Codes used in Column 69 are as follows:

C Complex caste stratification in which occupational differentiation emphasizes hereditary ascription and endogamy to the near exclusion of achievable class statuses.

D One or more despised occupational groupings, e.g., smiths or leather-workers, distinguished from the general population, regarded as outcasts by the latter, and characterized by strict endogamy.

E Ethnic stratification in which a superordinate caste withholds privileges from and refuses to intermarry with a subordinate caste (or castes) which it stigmatizes as ethnically alien, e.g., as descended from a conquered and culturally inferior indigenous population, from former slaves, or from foreign immigrants of different race and/or culture.

O Caste distinctions absent or insignificant.

The use of two symbols, a capital followed by a lowercase letter, indicates a combination or a mixture of two of the types defined above (*Ethnology*, 2:114).

Our operational definition of caste, following anthropological usage, is *a hereditary endogamous group who are socially differentiated by prescribed behavior.*

DISTRIBUTION OF CASTES

Differences between the codes C, D, and E might have made it difficult to use the "Ethnographic Atlas" for we are only interested in craft-caste distinctions. However, of the societies within the Western Sudan and for which there is information in the atlas, only one, the Tazarawa, is classified other than D or O. Thus the only caste designation, D, refers specifically to occupational groupings. Tables 1 through 5 represent data from Column 69 of the "Ethnographic Atlas" except as otherwise indicated. In order to use Murdock's map, the divisions and subdivisions are his, and the tribal names and numerical designations from the "Ethnographic Atlas". In only two instances has this caused a problem; two of the societies Murdock subsumed under the Gude, the Fali of Mubi and the Cheke, seem to differ on castes, though the evidence for the Cheke is by no means clear. In the second instance, although the Hausa are reported as not having craft-castes, the Hausa of Zaria are listed as having them.

These tables present information on castes in 47 per cent, or 78 out of the 166 societies which Murdock has included within the area we have delineated as the Western Sudan. The distribution of the information in the tables is shown in Map II (p. 66), in which we divided the Gude into Fali and Cheke and show the Hausa with a Zaria subarea. Marked regional

Table 1. Nuclear Mande

Ag 1	Bambara	D	Ag 23	Kasonke	D
Ag 7	Bozo	D	Ag 25	Soninke	D
Ag 9	Malinke	D	Ag 26	Susu	D

Table 2. Voltaic Peoples

A	*Senufo Cluster*			E	*Mole Cluster*		
	Ag 31	Minianka	D		Ag 2 & Ag 47	Mossi	D
	Ag 32	Senufo	D		Ag 4	Tallensi[2]	O
B	*Habbe Cluster*				Ag 12	Nankanse[2]	O
	Ag 3	Dogon	D		Ag 41	Kusasi[2]	O
	Ag 30	Bobo	D	F	*Gurma Cluster*		
C	*Lobi Cluster*				Ag 10	Konkomba	O
	Ag 11	Lobi	O		Ag 48	Basari	O
	Ag 34	Dorosie	O		Ag 50	Moba	O
	Ag 35	Kulango	O	G	*Tem Cluster*		
D	*Grusi Cluster*				Ag 49	Kabre	O
	Ag 31	Kasena[1]	O	H	*Bargu Cluster*		
	Ag 37	Awuna[1]	O		Ag 51	Somba	O
	Ag 38	Builsa	O	I	*Intrusive Peoples*		
	Ag 39	Dagari	O		Ag 29	Samo	D[3]
	Ag 40	Isala[1]	O				

[1] Mapped as "Grunski."
[2] Mapped as "Gurensi."
[3] Classification taken from Cline, 1937: 130.

James H. Vaughan, Jr.: Caste Systems in the Western Sudan

Table 3. Plateau Nigerians

A	*Bantoid Peoples*			Ah 16	Angas	O
	Ah 1	Katab	O	Ah 34	Bata	D[4]
	Ah 2	Jukun	O	Ah 37	Gude	D[5]
	Ah 3	Tiv	O	Ah 38	Kapsiki	D[6]
	Ah 4	Mambila	O	Ah 39	Podokwo	O
	Ah 6	Gure	O	Cb 27	Bachama	D

	Ah 9	Anaguta[1]	O	C *Eastern Nigritic Peoples*		
	Ah 10	Chawai	O	Ah 28	Chamba	O
	Ah 13	Dakakari	O	Ah 29	Daka	O
	Ah 14	Kamuka	O	Ah 30	Longuda	O
	Ah 15	Reshe	O	Ah 31	Mumuye	O
	Ah 19	Kadara	O	Ah 32	Vere	D[7]
	Ah 20	Kagoro[2]	O	Ah 33	Yungur	O
	Ah 22	Yergum	O	Ai 9	Masa	O
	Ah 24	Kentu	O	Ai 12	Fali	D[8]
	Ah 25	Tigon	O	Ai 13	Laka	O
	Ah 26	Ndoro	O	Ai 15	Mundang	D
		Mbula[3]	D	Ai 16	Namshi	D

B	*Chadic Peoples*			D *Kwa Peoples*		
	Ah 5	Marghi	D	Af 31	Koro	O
	Ah 7	Matakam	D			

[1] Mapped as "Afusare."
[2] Mapped as "Katab."
[3] Classification from Meek, 1931: I, 8.
[4] Classification from Meek, 1931: I, 8, 284; and Murdock, 1959: 95.
[5] Classification from Meek, 1931: I, 304, for "Fali of Mubi."
[6] Classification from Meek, 1931: I, 257958.
[7] Classification from Meek, 1931: I, 415, 423.
[8] Classification from Lembegat, 1961: 163.

Table 4. Negroes of the Sudan Fringe

A	*Songhai Province*			C *Bornu Province*		
	Cb 3	Songhai	D	Cb 5	Buduma	D
	Cb 20	Zerma	D	Cb 6	Tera	O
B	*Hausa Province*			Cb 7	Bolewa	O
	Cb 1	Maguzawa	O	Cb 10	Karekare	O
	Cb 9	Hausa	O	Cb 18	Kanembu	D
	Cb 25	Tazarawa	E	Cb 19	Kanuri	D
	Cb 26	Zazzagawa[1]	D	D *Bagirmi Province*		
				A 18	Kotoko	O[2]

[1] Mapped as "Hausa of Zaria."
[2] Classification inferred from Column 42, "Absence of Metal Working."

Table 5. Fulani

Ag 6	Futajalonke	D		Cb 23	Tukolor	D
Cb 21	Djatun[1]	O		Cb 24	Wodaabe[2]	O
Cb 22	Libtako	D				

[1] Mapped as "Adamawa Fulani."
[2] Mapped as "Bauchi Fulani."

patterns are obvious; castes are most prevalent in the west and in the extreme east and possibly along the northern periphery.[1]

Murdock attributes castes to Arabic influences at least among the Nuclear Mande (1959:76) and presumably in some of the rest of the Sudan. He also notes that "endogamous depressed castes of smiths, leather-workers, hunters, and *griots* are commonly differentiated in the western-most provinces" of the Negroes of the Sudan Fringe area (*Ibid.*:144). Since he has already stated that "[The Negroes of the Sudan Fringe] must be regarded as constituting the African frontier of the Moslem world and of the great Middle Eastern culture area" (*Ibid.*:134), we may conclude that these castes are also the consequences of their Arabic influence. In the Voltaic region he regards endogamous castes as "clearly not indigenous to the area" (*Ibid.*:85). Among the Plateau Nigerians he notes the occurrences of castes but does not comment upon their origin. We shall defer discussion of this omission until after a discussion of the Marghi *aŋkyagu* caste.

Baumann's conclusions with regard to castes, though more restricted, are quite similar to Murdock's. Of the Upper Niger area, he writes, "La présence de *castes* est certainement une survivance du temps des grands états; ces castes sont échelonnées selon leur values et cela encore plus chez les Mandés que chez les Puels" (1948:397). Like Murdock, he does not believe that castes are indigenous in the Voltaic area and attributes them to Mande influence (*Ibid.*:406, 418). Although he notes the variety of craft specializations in the Central Sudan, particularly among the Hausa, he does not discuss the presence of castes there.

The picture of caste distribution is more complete if we refer to the "Ethnographic Atlas" for areas surrounding the Western Sudan. There is information on castes for 45 Guinea Coast tribes, and *all* of these are coded O, "castes distinctive, absent, or insignificant." If we include the Senegambians, only the two most northern societies, the Wolof and Serer, and the interior Tander, surrounded by Western Sudanese tribes, have castes. In the Saharan area *all* tribes for which we have information have castes. Apparently, then, castes are a northern phenomenon, possibly of Arabic derivation as Murdock suggests, while the custom seems to have been absent among the indigenous, sub-Saharan African cultures. The marginal character of the Western Sudan of which Herskovits wrote is illustrated in the spotty distribution of castes in the area, and those areas where castes are absent in the Western Sudan generally correspond to the Guinean zone first noted by Labouret and accepted as a subdivision of the Western Sudan by Herskovits (1962:104–5).

1. This map is comparable to Pierre Clément's mapping of attitudes toward blacksmiths in Africa (1948: 51). Unfortunately his references are so broad and the article so general that it is not possible to distinguish any pattern for the mixed attitudes exhibited in the Western Sudan.

James H. Vaughan, Jr.:   Caste Systems in the Western Sudan

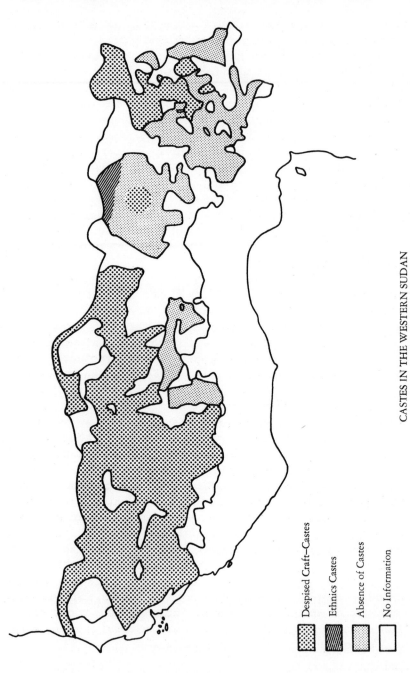

CASTES IN THE WESTERN SUDAN

MAP II

Despised Craft–Castes

Ethnics Castes

Absence of Castes

No Information

There is an important anomaly in this otherwise simple distribution. The southward extension of castes in the extreme eastern end of the area does not fit the pattern. First, these societies clustered in the Mandara Mountains and the northern portion of the Adamawa Massif are in the heart of the Guinean zone, and although one of the tribes, the Marghi, is in proximity to the Kanuri of the north, those Marghi areas in which castes are most in evidence are generally removed from Kanuric influences. However, the most interesting deviation from the pattern occurs in the nature of Mandara castes themselves—that is, the castes of the Mandaras, despite the "Ethnographic Atlas" classifications, are *not* despised castes. Admittedly this raises the question as to the meaning of despised and the validity of reporting; and rather than becoming involved in semantic distinctions about hypothetical issues, we will turn to a description of the caste system in a Mandara society.

CASTE IN MARGHI SOCIETY AND CULTURE

The Mandara Mountains form a part of the present boundary between Nigeria and Cameroun. The western slopes with which I am most familiar are today a part of Nigeria, though when I was there in 1959–60 it was Northern British Cameroons. They are a part of those mountains which Kirk-Greene called "the glory of Adamawa." (Adamawa was the Fulani emirate which spread across the present boundary of Nigeria and Cameroun and encompassed much of the Mandara area.) When viewed from Nigeria, the mountains rise abruptly from the plains; and in numerous instances, the mountain range proper is presaged by dramatic inselberge, isolated domes in the wooded plains. The mountains are extremely rugged, though rarely reaching heights of over 4500 feet. The sides of the mountains are frequently covered with boulders and large rock outcroppings, and along one portion of the summit of the range there are series of finger peaks which are probably volcanic plugs and which René Gardi has with good reason called a "Mondlandschaft" (1956:facing 45). These are mountains which, once seen, are never forgotten.

For all their ruggedness, the mountains are densely populated.[2] The administrative districts, which usually include 25 to 50 percent of their land in the sparsely populated plains adjacent to the mountains, have population densities from 150 to 200 per square mile. In the mountains, the densities must approach 300 per square mile. Usually villages are perched atop inselberge or at their bases. The topography is such that the

2. General surveys of the people of the Mandaras are by Lembezat, 1961: 7–61 and by Meek, 1931: *passim*. A comprehensive history of the region is to be found in Kirk-Greene, 1958.

population is clustered in the few habitable, defendable spots, each being relatively isolated from the other. The isolation is not complete, and intervillage travel occurs, but the orientation is such that the provincialism typical of mountain life is common. There is little significant social intercourse between groups and almost no political cohesion except among the Marghi, which will be discussed later. The villages are even more isolated from events outside the mountains than they are from each other. Although they have been subject to countless Fulani and Kanuri slave raids, they have been relatively little affected by the Islamization of northern Nigeria and northern Cameroun. To be sure the slave raids had important demographic consequences which resulted in cultural change, but it was not acculturative change, and the institutions of the Mandara Montagnards are to a striking extent indigenous institutions.

The Marghi are one of the tribal groupings inhabiting the western slopes and valleys of the Mandaras, but, unlike most of the other Mandara peoples, they extend westward into the plains of the southern portion of the Chad Basin. They divide themselves into four amorphous groups: (1) the Marghi *Putai* who reside in the west and have been strongly influenced by the Kanuri and Islam in general, (2) the Marghi *ti tǝm* in the south who show both linguistic and cultural affinities to the Kilba, (3) the Marghi *babal* who reside in the central plains, and (4) the Marghi *Dʒiryu*—literally "Marghi near the mountain"—the Mandara section of the tribe. The latter two exhibit the greatest number of similarities and for all practical purposes constitute the Marghi proper today. None of the groups constitutes structural entities with either political or geographic boundaries; they are rather references to varying traditions within a language group.

Marghi are basically mountain people although a great many today live in the plains. Many still live in the mountains, and most others have traditions of having migrated from them. In addition, the threat of slave raids even into the twentieth century has caused even the Marghi of the Chad Basin to cluster on or near the bases of inselberge from which they were better able to protect themselves. It is only since the establishment of peace that Marghi have been able to live imperiously in the plains. It might be noted that the tendency to move away from the mountains seems to have led to a wider identity among plains-dwelling Marghi. The Mandara Marghi, with whom we are mainly concerned, are noticeably more provincial than any of the other groups.

The official population of the Marghi is based upon tax receipts of adult males and their reporting of their family sizes. Two types of errors are prevalent: those resulting from a relatively high percentage of nontax-paying males, particularly younger men, and overestimates of family size by taxpayers. In part the latter is a consequence of varying definitions of marriage whereby a male counts as his wife a woman still living with her father who also counts her as a member of his family. There is also an obvious and unexplained variation in reports of children from year to year. With these reservations in mind, we may estimate the population of the Mandara Marghi at 30,000, most of it densely settled in the mountains.

It is very difficult to present a description of a typical Marghi village, since the patterns vary so greatly and are so dependent upon mountain topography. Compact villages seem to have been common, but when space became limited, smaller more scattered satellite hamlets or wards developed. Where plateaus or valleys were settled, a more disbursed pattern was followed. As population spreads into the plain, very wide disbursal is frequently the rule. There are actually two Marghi terms referring to residential groupings, and each refers more to organization than to spatial distribution. A *giwa* is a collection of compounds, ideally a single cluster but commonly several such clusters in a general area. For example, all the compounds in a valley which may be more than a mile in length might constitute a *giwa*, or a single large village with satellite clusters of compounds may similarly constitute one *giwa*. This is the basic residential unit and the one to which one hears most frequent references. The term *məlmu* refers to a collection of *giwa* and is usually translated "village." Actually it seems to refer both to the collection of *giwa* into an administrative unit, which might represent a wide dispersion, and to any very large compact settlement. Today the government refers to the smallest unit, presumably a *giwa*, as a "hamlet," and the administratively organized collection of hamlets as a "village," presumably a *məlmu*. Thus the "village" of Gulak in 1959 had a population of approximately 7000 living in 34 hamlets spread over approximately 45 square miles.

Perhaps a better notion of Marghi settlement and demography may be obtained if we leave the dubious statistics and nomenclature of the government and concentrate on a single *giwa*. The *giwa* of Kirŋu is the principal settlement of the *məlmu* called by Marghi Gulagu, but identified on maps and known to the government as Gulak. Kirŋu, which means mountain head, is a compact settlement located at the foot of Mount Gulak. Atop this mountain the original Kirŋu can be seen as obviously a larger and even more compact *giwa*. In 1953, the government "persuaded" the inhabitants to relocate and in fact built the new *giwa* for them. Since *Ptil* Gulagu, the king, resides in Kirŋu and since he is the most important king of the Mandara Marghi, the government was anxious that he be more accessible. It was perhaps also a deliberate attempt to make the people of this very conservative area more open to external change.

Early in 1960 the population of Kirŋu was approximately 355 living in 54 compounds. These figures are exclusive of my family and that of one Marghi immigrant in my employ. (For purposes of prestige and as a result of gerrymandering, Kirŋu's official population was 983!) There were 50 adult males residing in 48 homesteads (two adult men resided in the compounds of their fathers), 45 of whom were cohabiting with a wife or wives. In addition there were 16 young men, none of whom headed a residence and who constitute a transient population which fluctuates greatly in size; at times there were 25 or 30 such young men in the Kirŋu. There were 98 adult females in the *giwa*, 16 of whom are designated *malabjagu*, or women who have passed the menopause and are no longer marriageable. They are a part of every *giwa*; some are widows or ex-wives of men of the *giwa* who choose to continue to live in the vicinity; others are widows or ex-wives who have returned to their home *giwa*. Six of the *malabjagu* in Kirŋu had independent households, while the remainder lived with sons, brothers, or relatives of their deceased husbands. At the time of this census there were 6 young adult females, most of whom were recently divorced and had returned to their homes prior to remarrying. There were 185 dependent children in the *giwa*.

Polygyny is common among Marghi, and in Kirŋu there were 82 women married to the 45 men, excluding *malabjagu*. Of the 45 husband-wife households 22, or 49 percent, were polygynous. There were 23 men with but a single wife, 15 with 2 wives, 3 with 3 wives, 1 with 5, and 1 (the King) with 7. In addition many of these men had wives with whom they were not cohabiting either because the women were too young, because a traditional period of mourning for a deceased husband had not been completed, or because there were difficulties of one kind or another.

Although these figures for polygyny are relatively high, they fail to indicate the extent to which polygyny is a part of Marghi life. Traditionally we measure polygyny as an instantaneous occurrence—that is, the number of polygynous marriages at any moment. It is a truism, of course, that people live lives more than moments, so we might ask, in how many lives will there be a polygynous marriage? To this query, the answer for traditional Marghi approximates 100 percent, for all Marghi can reasonably expect that at some time during their life they will be involved in a polygynous marriage. The exceptions are the physically and mentally handicapped, the impotent, and the acculturated. The principal factor that permits a high expectation of polygyny is a very high divorce rate which has the effect of circulating women among men. This is revealed by data from fifteen *malabjagu*, who had of course completed the marriageable period of their lives. The median number of marriages among these women was three, and only one had never been divorced. In this sense divorce may be seen as maximizing marriageable females in the population.

Marghi are skillful subsistence farmers. For those who reside on mountains, farming is largely done on terraces which, while not very fertile, are easily worked. In the valleys the lands are much more productive, though weeding is a constant and arduous chore. The principal crop is guinea corn (*Sorghum vulgare*), of which at least eight types are recognized, though only four are usually mentioned. One type, *kuba*, is recognized as the traditional crop of Marghi and it has many ritual uses. Another type, *jiga*, is an early-ripening sorghum and quite prized both for its taste and because it is the earliest harvested grain. Beans are grown amid sorghum in fields near the *giwa*, while okra and a variety of other garden crops are grown in smaller plots within or near the compound. Marghi rotate crops and practice shifting cultivation along pragmatic rather than ritual lines. They do not abide by inflexible rules of procedure but change their crops when yield diminishes. Gardens are fertilized with goat manure. Formerly, religious ceremonies accompanied the first planting each year, but these are not often performed today. One interesting aspect of the ceremony, however, involved leaving some iron ore in the field. Iron ore, in the form of magnetite, is abundantly available in the soils of the Mandara region, and it may well be that it is conceived of as one of the "fruits of the earth."

All men and women are, by tradition, farmers. Even though a man may gather the greater share of his livelihood from some other economic activity, he will still list himself on census rolls as a farmer. When there was a registration of females for an election in 1960, all women listed themselves as farmers. It is not correct, however, to say that farming is an occupation, for to be a Marghi means to be a farmer. When I once suggested that in the future Marghi women might hold occupations, my listener was greatly shocked and said such would be the case only among harlots. Farming, he allowed, was different. That *is* Marghi. A person who does not farm cannot in the Marghi idiom be considered an altogether normal person.

A man's most important tangible asset is his farm. His most important intangible assets are the labor of his sons who will help him work the land and friends who will help him at appropriate times to weed his land. The sizes of farms vary greatly according to the fertility of the soil and family size, for each man has a keen sense of his needs and does not attempt to farm much beyond this. Farming for cash is not, even today, a significant part of the economic life of Mandara Marghi. Occasionally one finds a Marghi who will grow a small crop of ground nuts for sale but this is unusual. In the kingdom of Gulagu, where the soils are generally very fertile, farm sizes are small; about three to six acres would perhaps cover the range of most farms. These are usually divided up into several plots and include at least one small garden within or immediately surrounding the compound. There is no scarcity of land today, though when slave raids restricted farming to the mountains this was not the case.

James H. Vaughan, Jr.: Caste Systems in the Western Sudan

Ideally the family should work together as a unit farming the soil and sharing the harvest. In practice this occurs in only a very few instances. The household is the farming and landholding unit, but whenever there is more than one wife in the family there are potential internal divisions. In the majority of cases the competition between co-wives and their children necessitates dividing the farm into subfamilial responsibilities. In such instances, each wife and her children are responsible for the crops on the land allotted to her. This kind of division limits the responsibility of each wife, and frequently an industrious woman will have an additional farm which she works after having discharged her responsibilities to the farm of the compound. She may use the produce of this extra farm to make beer for sale or she may sell or barter it for household items, decorative jewelry, or the like. However, when a woman has such a farm she is solely responsible for it and must use tools of her own purchase. In this way, many women become relatively independent.

A family farms to live; no family, no matter how wealthy, allows itself to be dependent for food upon the market. The staple foods are ones they grow. To be sure, their diet consists of more than vegetables. It is supplemented by chicken, occasionally goat and mutton, and on rarer occasions by beef and game, but basically guinea corn and vegetables comprise the daily diet. In general there are few shortages, and everyone can grow an adequate amount on his farm. In fact, small surpluses are produced with relative ease, and each compound head is able each year to grow enough beyond his dietary needs to have something to sell or barter in the market for luxuries of one kind or another. As a consequence of their nearly rigid agricultural specialization, Marghi have other needs which they do not satisfy and for these they must rely upon weekly markets and direct trade with specialists. In the weekly markets they may buy cloth, supplementary foods they may wish, such as onions, fruits, sugarcane, or more important items such as beef. Then, of course, there are the myriad of new luxuries like beads, lamps, cloth, enamel ware, and the like, which they now find temptingly easy to buy in local markets. However, the most important needs are the implements of farming and the material culture of daily life, and almost all of them must be obtained from specialists called ŋkyagu, who by tradition are *not* farmers.

The descent system of the Marghi is embodied in the *fal*, a patrilineal clan which bears a masculine as well as a feminine name. There is no formal structure to Marghi clans, though in the past and in some kingdoms today each localized section has a nominal ritual head. However, ties between sections are tenuous and localized groupings frequently become new *fal*. It is probably incorrect to speak of these as "lineages," since the ties are so ephemeral. Authority within the *fal* is the authority of families and direct descent. It is undoubtedly relevant that the only ancestors ritually revered are the most recently deceased males. Thus in Figure 1 families A and B are essentially independent of each other, no longer even worshiping the same ancestor. Of course, they recognize that they are closely related members of the same *fal*, but there is no formal authority that binds them.

Clans are held together largely by custom and tradition. Each clan has unique characteristics which usually consist of variations in the performance of customary rites. The most widespread variation is in burial practices, but variations also appear in initiation and marriage rites, general religious beliefs and practices, diet, dress, *etc.* These variations are of importance to Marghi as identifying criteria, but failures to observe them are not punishable so much as incomprehensible. Although clans are of little material consequence in the life of an individual, they are of great psychological importance. To be a Marghi means first to be a member of a *fal*, and rejection of this is rejection of normality. There are as yet no alternatives to clans, although there is some evidence that political loyalties may be superseding those of the clan.

The regulation of marriage is not an exclusive prerogative of the clan. There are several stated rules concerning marriage: no one may marry an individual more closely related than third cousin on *either* side of his family; no one may marry the former wife of a patrilineal kinsman; and no one may marry the former wife of any man who lives within one's own neighborhood. The first of these rules is regarded as the most basic, yet I discovered that in practice it is consistently altered. Once, after two men asserted that it was permissible for what we would call third cousins to marry, they were shocked when I pointed out that under this rule their

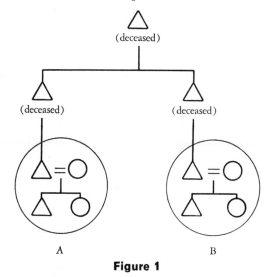

Figure 1

James H. Vaughan, Jr.: Caste Systems in the Western Sudan

children would be able to marry. Actually patrilineally related men living in the same village think of themselves as brothers, a custom facilitated by their Hawaiian cousin terminology, and I believe that the "third cousin rule" in practice means two generations removed from coresidence. This means that certain small clans are virtually exogamous, though there is no formal requirement of clan exogamy. In contrast to the careful reckoning of descent on the patrilineal side, on the matrilineal side second cousins with a sufficient number of female links may never be reckoned as kin and, in fact, might marry. In general one finds a certain looseness about reckoning matrilineal kin in both males and females. In this regard it should be mentioned that though clans usually have masculine and feminine names, in several instances I have known men to be unfamiliar with the masculine names of their wives' clans although they recognized the name when they heard it. In almost all instances of general usage, clans go by their masculine names.

When it comes actually to choosing a mate, virgin brides (in the social if not physiological sense) are likely to marry men who live relatively near. The betrothal of such couples (Vaughan, 1960) is protracted and involves considerable bride service in addition to bridewealth. A wise father sees that his daughter's betrothed lives near enough to be called upon frequently. This practice is not quite so noticeable in those instances where older men take an additional virgin bride, and not a custom at all when the wife has been married before. (All men take as their first wife a virgin, though the terms "marriage" and "wife" are used within the context of Marghi custom.)

Members of a clan know only its history, and this is only incidently collated with the history of other clans and events as, for example, when one says, "That was when Kamavudu was king," or "When we came to this place, Ishidi was the only *fal* here." The histories of kingdoms become largely the history of the royal clan, with incidental facts from the histories of commoner clans. Furthermore, the span of any history is limited to the events relevant to that group. The Gidəm clan at Gulagu, for example, recounts only its history since migrating from Sukur. Members know little or nothing about the legends of the original migration to Sukur. Of course at Sukur this is known, though nothing is known of the events of the clan at Gulagu. Similarly, there are Gidəm at Dluku who recount a migration from Gulagu but know little or nothing about either of the two preceding migrations.

It may be seen that Marghi do not have a strong sense of clan continuity. Migrations, which have been frequent, usually result in complete breaks and the formation of virtually new clans, sometimes with significantly modified or totally new names. Indeed the most unusual thing about the Gidəm clan migrations is that the name has not changed. Marghi clans are given to fission without fusion; they have only a mechanical solidarity—in the Durkheimian sense. However, this is true only of mass movements and not of individual emigration. An individual or family which has moved to another area is still likely to perceive of itself in relationship to the history of its homeland.

None of the clans whose histories I have been able to collect fail to have a migration legend. Migrations are usually from one of three directions. Perhaps the oldest tradition is from the east, the Mandara Mountains and the Cameroun Highlands beyond. Many say they have come from Gudur, which is called Mcakali by Marghi. A second group of Marghi clans has come from the west, particularly from the Pabir area, but most of these people claim a prior Camerounian origin as well. The third stream is from the north and shows a marked Kanuric and Moslem influence. These migrations have undoubtedly been in successive and sometimes simultaneous waves, and it is probably pointless to ascribe any temporal priority to them, although the Kanuric influence which has virtually inundated the northern and western areas is only slightly felt in the central areas and not at all in the east. Among Marghi living in the Mandaras, the majority of clans have Mandara and Camerounian origins, though several have Pabir-Camerounian traditions.

Political organization among Mandara Marghi is in sharp contrast to that which is reported as typical of Mandara societies (Lembezat 1961: 37–39). Among the Marghi there are several hierarchical kingdoms, one of which we have already mentioned, the kingdom of Gulagu. This dynastic tradition among Mandara Marghi probably dates from about the middle of the seventeenth century when two kingdoms were founded. One was started among the Marghi at Sukur and claims an origin at Mcakali; the other, of Pabir tradition, was established at about the same time at Madikaŋkaŋ (Madu-Kaŋkaŋ) though it later moved to Mazhini. Most of the Mandara dynasties are derived from Sukur, as most of the clans come directly from Cameroun. Gulagu was the second Mcakali-Sukur kingdom and is today the largest and most powerful Mandara kingdom.

Predynastic Marghi, like other Mandara societies today, were undoubtedly little more than an acephalous collection of autonomous clans each with little more than a head priest over it. They shared certain basic cultural features, but were probably bound largely through language and by intermarriage. Although they were localized groupings of patrikin, as we have seen, Marghi lack the cohesiveness to keep them from frequent segmenting into new clans. There was, for the area in general, considerable mobility and heterogeneity among clans.

Each kingdom associates its founding with the advent of a single royal clan who provided a centralized government, which gave a new order to

Marghi life. So far as legends tell us, the establishment of these dynasties was in every instance peaceful and welcomed by the commoner clans.

The organization of Marghi kingdoms consists primarily of a divine king with hypothetically unlimited power and two subsystems to assist him in his duties. The first system is the council of advisors, about which we shall also speak later. It is sufficient here to note that it is comprised of the ceremonial heads of the indigenous clans along with certain other representatives of the populace of the kingdom and that membership is based upon descent. Theoretically this is a powerful body, advisors to the king, electors and installers of new kings, but actually it is very weak and always has been because members simply have no effective power. They have never had power over their clans—that is the ancient problem of Marghi political organization—and lacking any effective clan structure they are not true representatives of their clans. But the greatest weakness of the council is that the king—whether by design or not, we cannot say—does not use them as agents of his power.

His agents are appointed heads of *giwa*—the *bulama*. The *bulama* is the king's representative in the *giwa* and as such is a relatively powerful person. But it is important to grasp that his power is entirely dependent upon the king. Although he is likely a member of the dominant clan in the *giwa*, he is not a clan head and he is never a member of the council of advisors. Although today the office of *bulama* is one of the most powerful commoner statuses in a kingdom, it would seem that it was not so regarded when the dynasties were established. If there are two clans of approximate size in a *giwa*, the senior one provides the local priest or *zuli* while the junior provides the *bulama*.

The Marghi kingdom is, then, a hierarchical organization of power, all authority being concentrated in the office of the king and his appointees. The older descent system does not offer a realistic alternative, partly because of the absence of a traditional power structure, but also because the king does not use the *fal* in administering power. Citizens of a kingdom are divided in their loyalties between the traditional ties to *fal*, which are so important culturally, and ties to their *giwa*, which in a materialistic sense are of such importance.

Hierarchical power systems frequently lack checks upon excesses of power, doubly a problem when the head is a divine king. However, the divine king concept frequently embodies its own check, one that Mandara Marghi have often used—institutional regicide. This custom has persisted into the twentieth century at Gulagu, the last attempt upon the life of a king having been made in 1939. Contemporary developments have, of course, modified the system, as I have discussed elsewhere (Vaughan 1964a). In general, the preceding description of Mandara

Marghi political organization can be considered typical as of two generations ago.

Marghi conceive of a world ordered by a supreme supernatural, *Iju*, who is the cause of everything—both good and bad. *Iju* is remote, largely nonanthropomorphic, and not truly amenable to persuasion. *Iju* is perhaps best translated as *fate*—something that exists for which one can be thankful or sorry but not something over which one has a great deal of control. But Marghi are not passive, for their view of the world also includes two categories of anthropomorphic supernaturals who are intimately concerned with human behavior and who are susceptible to human manipulation. These are the *shatar*, who are mischievous, and the *yal*, who are malevolent and dangerous, the cause of most serious illness, death, and calamity.

Ancestors, to which we have already alluded, are of little importance in Marghi religion. They are the subject of only one annual ceremony, and even this is the responsibility of only the eldest surviving son of the deceased. Like *shatar* and *yal*, ancestors seem to do good by not doing bad and the annual remembrance is to keep them happy. However, it should be said that ancestors are likely to cause harm only if they have been deliberately offended; they are otherwise a neutral and minor force in the Marghi pantheon.

Except for the annual ceremonies associated with the growing season, which are vaguely associated with *Iju*, the bulk of Marghi ritual is directed toward the propitiation of *yal* and *shatar*. The solution to specific problems and ills is sought through *yal* and *shatar*, who are the usual causes of such. However, if these propitiations are unsuccessful, this is not an indication that the rituals are worthless but that the difficulty was, after all, fate or *Iju*. In this we are able to see the closed quality characteristic of religious systems.

From this general description of Marghi society and culture it may be surmised that cultural heterogeneity within the society is primarily based upon minor variations in behavior between clans. There is, however, an additional variation superimposed upon the clan differences. There are a group of Marghi clans, each with its own clan customs, which are differentiated as a group from other Marghi. Collectively they are called *əŋkyagu* (feminine, *kwiŋkyagu*). There are no physical criteria that set *əŋkyagu* apart from other Marghi. Although they may be frequently recognized by their rustic, conservative behavior and dress, they might pass unnoticed through a strange village. In the generic sense they are Marghi, and this is generally recognized, but at the local level they are not referred to as Marghi but as *əŋkyagu*. No *əŋkyagu* will marry a Marghi woman, and with one exception to be explained, no Marghi will marry a *kwiŋkyagu*. They form an endogamous caste within Marghi society.

James H. Vaughan, Jr.: Caste Systems in the Western Sudan

It is difficult to estimate the number of *aŋkyagu* in Marghi society, although census figures list "blacksmiths," and *aŋkyagu* are so considered. The numbers are significantly in error; in the kingdom of Gulagu, for example, the 1959 census listed ten blacksmiths, though I must have known fifty. For the village of Humbili, in which the largest collection of *aŋkyagu* are known to live, *no* blacksmiths were listed on the census. I would estimate that they comprise between one and two percent of the society.

The quality of the differentiation of *aŋkyagu* is difficult to explain, largely, I believe, because too much is assumed from the use of the term *caste*. There are important differences, to be sure, and this chapter dwells upon them at length, but we might well begin by stressing the similarity— even the sameness—of these Marghi to others of the society. They share the same world view, and the differentiae which characterize their clans, viewed in isolation, are of the same type as those that distinguish other clans. Apart from unique clan rituals, they observe the same rituals as their neighbors. When an *aŋkyagu* dies, his funeral is attended by Marghi in accordance with his age, status, and the canons of neighborliness. Like all other descent groups, *aŋkyagu* have a tendency to live in clusters as a consequence of patrilocality, but there are no *giwa* composed even predominantly of *aŋkyagu*. Daily intercourse between *aŋkyagu* and other Marghi follows the usual pattern of relations between nonkinsmen, tinged only with constraint in areas to be mentioned. In the *giwa* of Kirŋu there was a single *aŋkyagu* compound when I first established my residence there. (The family subsequently moved because of a death.) The compound, like all those added since the initial relocation, was on the periphery of the royal *giwa*. Most of the villagers were related to one another and, as royalty, were intimately concerned and interested in the kingship, but at the routine level there were conversation, visiting, and cooperation with the *aŋkyagu* family. Because of most of the villagers' connection to the king, the general economic level of the *giwa* was higher than that of the *aŋkyagu*, but in general the wealth of *aŋkyagu* is little different from that of other Marghi. There is today perhaps less of a tendency among *aŋkyagu*, who are usually quite conservative, to take advantage of the changes brought about by acculturation, but at the time of my field experience only a few of the Mandara Marghi seemed to see the possibilities of expanded markets, cash crops, education, etc.

In the preceding paragraph I have stressed the predominant normality of social relations between Marghi and *aŋkyagu*. However, there are areas in which normal behavior ceases. In addition to the marital prohibitions, Marghi and *aŋkyagu* will not eat together, nor will they share the same food or eating vessel. A Marghi will not drink the beer brewed by a *kwiŋkyagu*, although *aŋkyagu* will drink Marghi beer. In the latter instance, however, they must provide their own drinking vessel. This means *aŋkyagu* are sometimes recognized by the distinctive drinking basket which they carry to beer markets and when they travel.

When one asks a Marghi what is the nature of the difference between the two groups, the answers tend to be typical "social distance" responses A Marghi when asked to say why *aŋkyagu* are not like other Marghi, responded, "Because an *aŋkyagu* is the most '*talaka*' [commoner] in our area, and moreover they eat things like donkey, monkey, snakes, and others which we will not eat." This statement was not made by a member of the royal clan and is the only time I ever encountered degrees of "*talaka*-ness." Actually, the statement is misleading, for other Marghi groups, particularly some of Kanuric origin, are said to eat snakes, but these people are not considered to be different or strange, and for that matter *aŋkyagu* deny that they eat donkey. It is difficult to assess the quality of the social distance between Marghi and *aŋkyagu*, but the most important element of it emphasizes the *difference* between the two or the strangeness of the *aŋkyagu*. It would be an unwarranted conclusion to say that Marghi detest *aŋkyagu*, for there is no enmity between them whatsoever. It would not be amiss, however, to say that Marghi hold *aŋkyagu* in awe or, in the case of Marghi children, it would be fair to say that they fear *aŋkyagu*.

For a Marghi to indicate that an *aŋkyagu* is "different" is to say a great deal more than we may mean by the term. The essence of the ideal Marghi life is predictability. As I have previously discussed, they have a very low tolerance for ambiguity (1965:17–19). To imply that someone is different from the rest may in fact be taken as a reproof (*nagə ŋadzugwa jamna kər!*). Even when the kindest motives are apparent, offense may be taken. Self-depreciation, modesty, reliability—these are expected virtues. A Marghi who deviates, who, for example, acts proud, is censured, but in the case of group deviation the reaction is more one of bewilderment. This type of reaction is very clearly noticed in the attitudes of unacculturated Marghi toward Europeans. They believe and are willing to believe the most outrageous things about them. Once as I walked with a companion on a remote path, we suddenly came upon a woman who immediately ran into the bush. Under no encouragement would she come out, and she asked my friend if he was not afraid that I might eat him. It is inconceivable to me that this woman had not seen other Europeans and I do not believe that she could have been as naive as her question seemed. Rather I believe it revealed the magnitude of the social difference she perceived between us. This is the connotation which I think appropriate to the Marghi statement, "*aŋkyagu* are truly different people."

In contrast to the affectual responses of Marghi to characterize the contrast between themselves and *aŋkyagu*, the latter see the difference as one based in the division of labor. The *aŋkyagu* point out that there are mutually exclusive activities characteristic of each group. Furthermore, one *əŋkyagu* emphasized the mutual dependence that characterizes the two groups, something I never heard the Marghi suggest.

When we examine these two views of the difference between Marghi and *əŋkyagu*, we might conclude that *əŋkyagu* have a more realistic view of the situation. This might be a consequence of the differential contact between the two. On the average, Marghi encounter *əŋkyagu* infrequently and under rather special circumstances, as when the services of an *əŋkyagu* are needed. On the whole, Marghi are not very well informed about *əŋkyagu* customs. In contrast, *əŋkyagu* live surrounded by Marghi, and may know a great deal about their particulars. Despite the realism in the *əŋkyagu* assessment of the situation, it is completely deficient in explaining the social and ideational aspects of the relationship. Ask why Marghi and *əŋkyagu* do not intermarry and an *əŋkyagu* replies simply, "It is not our custom." For all its truth, the statement lacks any rationale. To a Marghi the answer is "Because they are different" or "Because they do strange things," and for all its brevity, this is understandable and consistent with their view of proper human relationships as previously discussed.

In neither case is the one ignorant of the conditions cited by the other. Marghi are well aware of the occupational specialization of the *əŋkyagu*, indeed unrealistically aware, for they often attributed specialities to *əŋkyagu* which in fact they did not have. After this occurred on numerous occasions, I finally concluded that if the term *əŋkyagu* must be translated, it should be translated as "traditional craft specialist" rather than "blacksmith," as is customarily done, though admittedly the smithing of iron is the principal speciality of *əŋkyagu*.

The attitudes and feelings of Marghi toward *əŋkyagu* are known by the latter, and in many instances they encourage them. The widely held belief that *əŋkyagu* eat snakes resulted in several instances to my knowledge of Marghi giving dead snakes to a nearby *əŋkyagu*. Later I discovered that neither this man or any of his *əŋkyagu* neighbors—approximately twenty persons—ate snakes, although they gladly accepted them as though they did. I surmised that to an extent *əŋkyagu* enjoy their status, particularly when they are among Marghi.

The most accurate description of the caste system combines the contrasting views of Marghi and *əŋkyagu*, and when we accept that these two facets of the system are both present, we come to the heart of a caste system. Not only are its members set apart in terms of behavior or occupation—this is characteristic of many forms of social differentiation and stratification—they are set apart on ideological grounds. Bergel describes the religious foundation of caste (1962:49), and though I find the term *religious* somewhat narrow, I would agree with its use in a broader context. If by religion we can include the "ordering of the world," then I would agree that the caste system of the Marghi is a part of their religion. The separation of Marghi from əŋkyagu is for them *de rerum natura*.

The differences that Marghi and əŋkyagu perceive as so important do not constitute an adequate explanation of the caste system. The differentiation, for all its rigidity, is not simply a mechanical division. The əŋkyagu was correct in pointing out that the two groups need each other. The interdependence of Marghi and əŋkyagu is undoubtedly the most critical part of the system. The facts of social differentiation are vacuous until their functional relationships are revealed. In this instance we turn first to Marghi economics, in which the foundation of the caste system lies, and finally to political organization to demonstrate how the ordering of the economic system, which is justified in the rationale of a caste system, is translated into the political ordering of the society.

We have already noted that əŋkyagu are the specialists of the society. There is, however, one important specialization—not an occupation to be sure—which is the province of Marghi, yet intimately related with əŋkyagu. The smelting of ore is done by Marghi. Smelting was the province of each Marghi compound head, and apparently very many of them smelted ore. It might seem logical that perhaps in a hamlet or village only one or two men would smelt, but one can find dozens of abandoned smelting furnaces in the areas surrounding old villages. Today the process is not necessary, since scrap iron and steel of European manufacture are readily obtained, although in the more remote areas of the Mandara Mountains one finds that smelting continues. At Sukur, locally smelted iron is used for farming implements specifically, for the people believe that iron of European manufacture is not suitable for Marghi soils.

The technical aspects of the process of smelting by Marghi has been described (Sassoon, 1964; Vaughan, in press), and since it is not in the domain of əŋkyagu, I will not go into it here beyond relating it to the activities of əŋkyagu. Primitive smelting does not produce a molten metal which might be poured into bars or other more useful shapes. Instead, only a spongy bloom is extracted from the furnace, which must then be fabricated either into a bar, as a repository of value, or directly into a utilitarian implement. Consequently, the Marghi smelters are still dependent upon the əŋkyagu smiths, but conversely the əŋkyagu are dependent upon Marghi for the raw materials of their trade. This mutual dependence is characteristic of the Marghi who live in the Mandara Mountains where ore is very readily available, but apparently this was not the case for Marghi who lived in the Chad Basin.

One has difficulty collecting information about smelting from Marghi who come from the plains. Admittedly this may be a consequence of differential acculturation in which European-fabricated scrap iron and steel have supplanted indigenously smelted ores. However, Heinrich

James H. Vaughan, Jr.: Caste Systems in the Western Sudan

Barth, the German explorer, encountered a smith on the northern borders of Marghi land in 1851 who told him that his iron was brought from Madégelé in Búbanjídda (1857:376). I believe Barth has the wrong Madégelé, largely on the basis of distance. Búbanjídda was an unlikely journey of 275 miles, while Madágelé of Ardon Jídda (*Ibid.*:398) was a very easy journey of 50 miles. Furthermore, the latter is at the western edge of the mountains where even today iron can be obtained in bar form. It is probably significant that in the Marghi areas in which iron is not smelted, such as the plains, the *əŋkyagu* caste either is poorly delineated or follows patterns other than those described here. I have even been told by Marghi from the plains that there are no Marghi *əŋkyagu*, only descendants of Higi who live amid Marghi. Although my experience with plains Marghi was limited, I felt that they had a very different attitude toward *əŋkyagu*, an attitude that might well reflect Kanuric influence.

For Mandara Marghi the interlocking specialities of smelting and smithing are of crucial importance to the traditional operation of the caste system. Although Meek, Lembezat, and others carefully mention the blacksmith caste in Nigerian and Mandaran tribes, unfortunately smelting has been neglected. Today, with the easy accumulation of scrap iron, smelting is rapidly disappearing, and we may never know if the Marghi dichotomy between smith and smelter was typical.

Unquestionably smithing is the basic component of the *əŋkyagu* caste. The symbols of the caste are the forge and the tools of the smithy. The tuyère has special symbolic importance to all Marghi. Unlike the bellows, which are also made of clay, the long cylindrical tuyère is made by males of the *əŋkyagu* caste. It is believed to have mystical powers and when placed in a field protects it from thefts, particularly from the thefts of women. Not only is the tuyère symbolic of the power of the *əŋkyagu* caste, but the sexual symbolism in its shape, manufacture, and use is obvious. Without going into the technology of smithing, let us note that it is a complex technology requiring skill and a great deal of training.

The *əŋkyagu* are far more than smiths, however. The ram-skin loin garment called *pəzhi* worn by men and the goat-skin fringe apron, *dzar*, worn by women are made by *əŋkyagu*. They make other items of leather as well, such as the sling in which infants are carried, belts, and leather-covered charms. Marghi wear a great many different kinds of iron ornaments: bracelets, iron beads which are now rare, chains, and their well-known hooks (*mpiəmə*), and all of these, of course, are made by the *əŋkyagu* smiths. Marghi are very interested in and proud of their weapons, all of which are made by *əŋkyagu*. There are three types of throwing knives, several styles of knives, two types of arrowheads—one of which is used exclusively by *əŋkyagu* hunters—and spears, the most commonly seen weapons. There are as well a host of less frequently seen items such as pipes, pipe scrapers, needles, tweezers, and picks, which are made from time to time.

The main household items of Marghi are pots, calabashes, knives, stools, and beds; and except for calabashes, which are grown and decorated by Marghi women, the rest are considered specialties of the *ŋkyagu* caste. *Kwiŋkyagu* are the potters of the society, and pots are ubiquitous in Marghi compounds. The exact status of wood carving in Marghi society is ambiguous; beds are no longer carved, having been supplanted by a corn-stalk or stick composite bed sold in the local markets. These are called "Fulani beds" and may be made by anyone. The carved stools are always said to be *ŋkyagu* products. However, the most successful carver I knew was a deaf mute who was not an *ŋkyagu*, though he may have been an exception to the rule. It is surely significant that the Marghi word for stool, *aghwa*, is the name of the shallow mortarlike mold used in forming pottery and which also serves in *ŋkyagu* compounds as a very comfortable seat.

Unquestionably the most important items made by *ŋkyagu* are agricultural implements, specifically hoes, axes, and sickles. Hoes are the most common and probably the most important products manufactured by smiths. They are the most frequently used farming implement and are used over a longer period of time than axes, which are used only in clearing land, or sickles, which are used only during harvests. In addition, hoes have to be replaced more often since the relatively soft iron is frequently worn down in the heavy soils of the area. Hoes and pottery are the only products that *ŋkyagu* consistently make in anticipation of their sale, and they are sold in markets regularly. Other products are generally made on commission, but occasionally they may be manufactured because the materials happen to be at hand or because a likely customer is known.

The cicatrization of females is another activity monopolized by *ŋkyagu*. The process takes place over a number of years. Young girls have their faces scarred in a traditional pattern starting when they are six or seven and culminating before they reach puberty. After they marry, their bodies and arms will be scarred. This is almost a trivial occupation of *ŋkyagu* though it requires a certain amount of skill to obtain the desired design without unduly hurting the customer.

The *ŋkyagu* are the morticians in Mandara Marghi society, and this must be rated as one of their most distinctive and important activities. They are responsible for digging the grave and carrying the corpse from its compound to the grave. In addition, they will assist the family of the deceased in preparing the body for burial. The bodies of adult men are carried on the shoulders of *ŋkyagu*, who usually dance amidst the mourners before carrying the corpse on to the grave. It is not clear in just what way this profession affects Marghi attitudes about *əŋkyagu*. It is difficult not to see some relationship between corpse-care and caste, yet Marghi are not unduly disturbed by corpses or the presence of death.

There is a Marghi tradition that drumming is an *əŋkyagu* speciality. There is some tendency for this to be true, but today, at least, there are deviations from the rule. The present practice is not without patterning, however. A large kettle drum called *dlumbwadu* is played on very special occasions such as the funerals of important or esteemed persons and at religious festivals. I never saw an *əŋkyagu* play a *dlumbwadu* except at the funeral of an *əŋkyagu*, and I cannot believe that this drumming was ever reserved for *əŋkyagu*. A smaller drum, *nʒir*, held under the arm and struck with the hands, is exclusively an *əŋkyagu* instrument. It is traditionally played at funerals by *əŋkyagu*, and it is said that formerly it was played at social dances. At present a large drum called *kaŋga*, of general Sudanese style, which is struck with a carved stick, is the most common dance drum. It is usually played by anyone who has the talent, though professional musicians are not uncommon. Only one of the professional musicians I knew was an *əŋkyagu*, and he was blind. The *kiriharahara*, a single-stringed bowed lute, is played by *əŋkyagu* exclusively. In general, it may be said that certain types of instruments are the exclusive province of *əŋkyagu*, and they are probably the traditional social musicians of Marghi society. However, the playing of other instruments, not associated with the caste, which have come into use in recent years, is not limited to *əŋkyagu*.

It is also said that *əŋkyagu* are diviners, *malaga*, and "doctors," *pitititima*, and it is often so. But in neither profession do *əŋkyagu* form a majority. Both *malaga* and *pitititima* are regarded with awe among the general populace, and both clothe themselves in a certain amount of secrecy. The mystery that surrounds these professions is similar to that which Marghi see as surrounding *əŋkyagu*; and to the extent that they deviate from the norm, these professions are like *əŋkyagu*. It is to this that we may generally attribute ascription of these roles to the caste. When one asks a Marghi, who is a doctor? who is a carver? who is a hunter? there is a sense in which he has been asked, who is different? who does things that other people do not do? It is not surprising in this context, then, that the answer so frequently is *əŋkyagu*, even though in practice the facts may indicate otherwise.

There are, of course, minor specializations which are not traditional ones but are now fully sanctioned within Marghi society. These are not reserved for *əŋkyagu*. Occupations connected with the government, such as teachers, scribes, and agricultural assistants, and other occupations, such as petty merchants and laborers, fall into this category.

The Marghi system of economics provides a relatively stable base for their society. Production of food is generally adequate; their diets may not be well balanced, but except for infrequent famines there is generally no shortage of food. They have achieved this mastery over food production by virtue of a value system, which emphasizes that farming is the only proper activity, and a technology, which provides them with the tools necessary for the exploitation of their environment. There is, however, an incongruity in the system; although Marghi values dictate that all men must farm, they require the services of skilled technicians to produce their farming implements. The dilemma is resolved by having a group within the society who are permissible deviants—technologists who do not farm or, for that matter, who probably have little time for it. Marghi are dependent upon *əŋkyagu* for tools, but the technologists are dependent upon Marghi for food and the raw materials of their most important craft. I have previously commented about the reluctance of Marghi to be dependent upon others (1964b:396). In this instance, I believe the situation is mitigated by the mutual dependence implicit in the situation and perhaps by the caste status of the *əŋkyagu*, which makes the situation one of institutional dependence. In the latter instance, it may be said that the dependence is at least customary. I also believe that this general abhorrence of dependency might partially account for Marghi characterizations of the caste systems which seem to ignore the interdependence involved.

The economic interdependence of Marghi and *əŋkyagu*, although formalized in the caste system, has few exchange formalities. The *əŋkyagu* are not slaves nor are they clients of Marghi. They practice their specialties with the unconscious understanding that they are needed. At the same time they are acutely aware of the requirements of skill, the necessity to reflect change, the seasonal fluctuations of demand, and even the vagaries of fads. With respect to any individual, we might characterize the exchange pattern as one of economic contract either directly between persons or implicitly in the market situation. However, at the sociological level of abstraction, the relationship between Marghi and *əŋkyagu* is best characterized as symbiotic in that they are bound together to their mutual benefit through group specialization within the division of labor. A caution should be entered, however, lest the term *symbiosis* be taken as an emphasis upon the dissimilarity of the groups involved and thus overstate the difference between Marghi and *əŋkyagu*.

There is another aspect of society in which the two come into conspicuous contact. In Marghi political organization, the *əŋkyagu* caste occupies a curiously distinctive status. If we examine the organization of a kingdom, such as Gulagu, we find that the members of the council who advise the king reflect the history of the founding kingdoms and a great deal more about the organization of the society. Today the national government has emasculated the council, and in some kingdoms it is beginning to diappear. This description of the council is as it functioned a generation ago at Gulagu. The council members are as follows:

Ptil Gulagu. The king. He must be the eldest living son of a deceased king and at Gulagu is of the clan *Gidəm*.

Makarama. The king's administrative assistant. He is of the *Gidəm* clan and a legitimate heir to the throne. Appointed by the king, he is likely to be the king's next youngest brother or possibly a very close kinsman.

Thlifu. The highest-ranking commoner in the kingdom. This position is hereditary in the clan *Kwazhi*. In ritual matters he ranks just after the king and carries a staff identical with the royal staff of the king. He often represents the commoners on ritual occasions.

Zuli Tra. Hereditary in the *Ishidi* clan. *Zuli* means priest, and this *zuli* is in charge of a number of shrines in the vicinity of the ancient royal village.

Zuli Dagu. Priest in charge of the remaining shrines at the old royal village. It is hereditary in the *Ghwa* clan.

Ŋgwoma. A master of ceremonies. This role is also hereditary in the *Ghwa* clan, and its occupant is in charge of many of the religious ceremonies of the kingdom.

Midela. The leader in war, hereditary in the clan *Ghumdia*.

Adaŋyaptil. Literally "father of the king." Its occupant cautiously plays this role. *Adaŋyaptil* may censure the king and grant sanctuary to refugees. He is of the royal clan *Gidəm*, but *not* a possible heir to the throne. In Gulagu, where kings have always been strong, it is an appointed position.

Birma. The king's ceremonial assistant. He also acts for the king in the king's private customs. The position is quasi-hereditary in the slave or *mafa* class.

Ptil ∂kyagu. The hereditary king of the *əŋkyagu*. He judges their disputes and collects their taxes. He wears a royal hairlock as does the Marghi king and, in addition, wears an iron bracelet distinctive of his office.

The council reflects the composition of the society at the time of the founding of the dynasty and shortly thereafter. By tradition the clans *Kwazhi*, *Ishidi*, and *Ghwa* were the inhabitants of the mountain on which the kingdom was founded prior to the immigration of the royal clan of *Gidəm*, and *Ghumdia* arrived shortly thereafter. The *mafa*, while not constituting a migratory group, is a traditional status in the society. *Mafa* were war captives, enslaved criminals, and persons bartered into slavery. The status continues to the present. One very old *mafa* I knew had been traded with his father to the king of Gulagu in exchange for guinea corn for his famine-stricken Higi village. This probably occurred in 1904, but the custom was still practiced in the great Mandara famine of 1921 (Kirk-Greene, 1959:65–66). Kirk-Greene also reports that in 1926 "the hill tribes of the northern mandated areas were still trading in slaves" (*Ibid.*:180).

The *əŋkyagu* were not only residents of Gulagu when the *Gidəm* dynasty came, they were instrumental in the founding of the dynasty. A similar role is attributed to *əŋkyagu* in the legends of other royal clans among the Mandara Marghi. In the case of Gulagu the founding ancestor used the arrows of *əŋkyagu* to kill hyraxes, which he shared with the autochthonous inhabitants. A legend in another kingdom recounts how the founding ancestor caused a *kwiŋkyagu malabjagu* to conceive. Such legends are used to explain the peculiar affinities between Marghi kings and *əŋkyagu*. The most startling feature of this affinity is the custom of the king taking a *kwiŋkyagu* bride in conspicuous violation of the rule of endogamy. She becomes one of his wives, living in the royal compound, and bearing him children who, by virtue of patrilineal descent, are not considered to be *əŋkyagu*.

A second linkage between king and *əŋkyagu* at Gulagu, and at some other Mandara kingdoms, occurs at the investiture of the king. It is popularly said that the *əŋkyagu* "make" the king because one of their number from the ancient home of the *Gidəm* clan, Sukur, shaves the king-designate's head, leaving the royal hairlock, after which he is acknowledged as *ptil*. An even more common relationship is the widespread Marghi custom of burying deceased kings as though they were *əŋkyagu*— that is, seated on an iron stool and surrounded by charcoal.

The explanations for these ties between political structure and *əŋkyagu* may in part be historical, but there are much more suggestive and convincing explanations to be found in the traditional organization of the kingdom. The council is clearly a representative one, although it is not representative for later-day immigrating clans. This is even more apparent if we collate the three major duties of the council with the clans of the council members.

In Table 6 the balanced distribution of power can be seen. Only

Table 6. Functions of Council Members by Clan

Clan or Social Category	Electors	Legal Advisors	Major Ritual Duties
Gidəm		Makarama	
Gidəm		Adaṇyaptil	
Kwazhi	Thlifu	Thlifu	Thlifu
Ishidi	Zuli Tra		
Ghwa	Zuli Dagu		Ɗgwoma
Ghumdia	Midela		
Mafa		Birma	Birma (as acolyte of Ptil)
Əŋkyagu			

James H. Vaughan, Jr. : Caste Systems in the Western Sudan

commoner clans are electors, and no clan has more than one elector. Royalty, commoners, and slaves are all legal advisors. Furthermore, the second member of the royal clan does not overbalance this group but, on the contrary, acts as a ritual check on the excesses of the king. In a sense all the council members have ritual functions, and none of these constitutes viable power, but it is interesting that the only commoner clan with two members has one of them, in effect, shunted off into ceremonial duties only. The *Thlifu* is the only member of the council with broad responsibilities, and he is the representative of all commoners. Even though the *Ptil ƏŋΚyagu* has a role at all the major religious festivals and, for example, receives a stated portion of the sacrificed cow at the important religious festival of *Yawal*, the position as outlined seems relatively powerless.

This is not the case, however, for *əŋkyagu* are to a greater extent than any other group in the society autonomous. They have their own *ptil*, which makes it unnecessary for them to be electors of the Marghi *ptil*, and since *Ptil ƏŋΚyagu* adjudicates *əŋkyagu* disputes, there is no need for *əŋkyagu* to be associated with the legal advisors. The power of *Ptil ƏŋΚyagu* over his people is unique among members of the council, none of whom have any control over their clans. Today the powers of *Ptil ƏŋΚyagu* are undermined by a regional and provincial administration which only recognizes the authority of *Ptil* Gulagu, and I once witnessed *Ptil* Yarkur, the present king, trying to settle a dispute between two *əŋkyagu*. He obviously found himself in a difficult position and remarked with exasperation, "Why can't you *əŋkyagu* behave as you used to!"

The council of the Marghi *ptil* is organized in such a way as to give representation, distribute power, and limit power among sections of the kingdom. That the *əŋkyagu* fit into this scheme is no less surprising than that any other member should. Nor is the peculiar status of the *əŋkyagu* representative unusual, given the status that the group occupies in the society. It is interesting that the balance of power and representative quality implicit in the council are apparently unrecognized by Marghi themselves.

The special relationship between the office of *ptil* is to be understood in terms of the Marghi concept of kingship. If it were simply the legendary tie between a royal clan and a caste, it would hardly be limited to one person in the caste nor be so common among other ruling clans. It will be remembered that the Mandara Marghi king is a divine king; he is identified with his kingdom, and his health and his person are mystically related to the land and population he rules. An important part of that population, of course, are *əŋkyagu*. The king's ties with them emphasize the completeness of his realm. They also signal his elevation above kith and kin, for it should be noted that the royal clan has a representative in the council *other than* the king. Meek suggests that the ties between king and smith are a consequence of the dynastic principle having been introduced by immigrant blacksmiths (1931:I,228), but a historical explanation lacks evidence and is unnecessary. It does not take into account the social dichotomy between smelting and smithing, and more importantly it ignores the congruence between the king-*əŋkyagu* relationship and the African concept of the divine king.

To summarize the Marghi caste system, we may say that its basis is clearly technological. Most of the important distinctions that characterize *əŋkyagu* lie in this area. We have seen that the caste system provides necessary technologists for the society but, more than this, as an ascriptive role system, the caste *qua* caste ensures that the necessary technological roles will be filled. The general insecurity characteristic of nonliterate society unquestionably accounts for the greater importance of ascriptive role systems such as kinship and hereditary occupations. An achievement-oriented role system might under conditions of population instability result in a loss of a technological speciality. However, hereditary occupations, especially as characterized in a caste system, solve the problem of role recruitment. In this way a society is assured of role occupants; there is an occupational continuity implicit in craft-castes which avoids the vagaries of individual motivation and life expectancy. (This, of course, cannot be given as an explanation of the origin of caste systems. Although we may conclude that the caste system solves certain problems of Marghi economics, it would be meaningless to say that they developed the system to solve the problems.) The caste system works, in effect, because the group provides needed specialists; but it persists because the specialists are socially distinctive or, as Marghi say, "*əŋkyagu* are different." This difference is manifest not only in economic specialization but in perceptions of one another. Lacking criteria of physical appearance, the differentiae tend to be statements about behavior in which one or the other of the caste groups is seen as being incomprehensibly different. For the Marghi, caste characteristics are the inevitable consequences of economic deviation. As the formal structure uniting the kingdom, Marghi government integrates *əŋkyagu* into the political structure and thereby illustrates the organic solidarity of the community. Furthermore, given the peculiar nature of Marghi kingship, the peculiar affinity of king and *əŋkyagu* is almost necessary. However, it should be remembered that other of the Mandara societies that have castes do not, so far as we know now, have the concept of kingship (Lembezat, 1961:37–39).

Why technological specialization should be reified in a caste system is not knowable in this instance, and I confess to being less interested in how it came to be than how it operates. Actually, our conclusions today on this matter are little different from those offered by Cline over thirty years ago when he wrote, "I cannot believe that the mysterious quality of metals accounts for the rituals described above or that the latter expresses an original division of the population between immigrant and indigenous peoples" (1937:140).

CONCLUSIONS

At the beginning of this chapter we saw that the castes in the Western Sudan have uniformly been characterized as "despised" castes. That characterization is incorrect for the Marghi. To be sure no Marghi wants to be an *əŋkyagu*, and there are avoidances that must be observed, but *əŋkyagu* do not resent their status and generally recognize that they are important parts of the community. There is a sense in which one might say that Marghi have more political power than *əŋkyagu* since the king of all is Marghi, but we have seen that this is not a simple matter by any means, and furthermore at an individual level there is little difference between the prerogatives or wealth of Marghi and *əŋkyagu*.

The Marghi are not alone in having nondespised castes; other Mandara and Adamawa Massif tribes also follow this deviant pattern. This has been recognized by Murdock, who wrote, "In a few groups, i.e., the Bachama, Bata, Gude, Marghi, and Matakam, smiths form an endogamous *but not a despised caste*" (1959:95, italics added). To this one should probably add the Kapsiki or Higi, knowledge of whom I have from personal experience.

Having established that there is a deviant caste pattern in one part of the Western Sudan, I wish to conclude by suggesting reasons for the difference. It might be assumed that we merely have a variation in a single caste pattern, but this seems unsatisfactory when most scholars accept that the despised castes of the Western Sudan are Arab-derived while the tribes of the Mandara and Adamawa Massif are relatively independent of Moslem influences. Baumann, who it will be remembered characterized these mountains as belongings to the Paleonigritic tradition, describes siderology in that tradition as follows:

> La profession du forgeron est très estimée et le forgeron, ainsi que des ustensiles en fer jouent un rôle assez important dans les cérémonies cultuelles. . . . C'est précisément dans leur domaine [les Paléonigrites] que l'on rencontre en nombre considérable les meilleurs hauts-fourneaux de l'Afrique. On fait appel aux forgerons pour le stérilité, la secheresse, les fêtes en champêtres, la circoncision et les associations secrètes. (1948:67–69)

Although Baumann does not consider castes as belonging to this tradition, the description otherwise sounds generally quite appropriate to the Marghi.

It will be remembered that Murdock, who attributed the despised castes among the Nuclear Mande, Negroes of the Sudan Fringe, and the

Voltaic regions to Arab influences, made no comments about the origins of caste among the plateau Nigerians. I suggest that he had good reason not to attribute that to Arabic influences, too, for the difference between despised castes of the Moslem Sudan and the nondespised more organic caste system in the areas we have discussed is truly fundamental. Furthermore the necessary criteria of caste differentiation, craft specialization, and differential status ascribed to craft specialists, as indicated by Baumann, clearly antedates significant Arabic influences in Sub-Saharan Africa. The more probable explanation for the variant caste system is that it is a parallel, but essentially indigenous, development based upon indigenous patterns of specialization. This hypothesis has the advantage of accounting for the differences in caste patterns and also accounting for the noticeably syntonic symbiosis achieved among the Marghi.

SUMMARY

We have concerned ourselves with the distribution of but one cultural trait, craft-castes, in the Western Sudan, and we have found that their distribution tends to confirm the existence of a distinctive southern zone— a Guinean zone. We concluded that there are three patterns concerning castes in the Western Sudan: depressed craft castes in the northern and western areas presumably of Arabic derivation; a general absence of castes in most of the Guinean zone, though there are distinctive customs surrounding the smithing profession; and finally a Guinean caste system, limited apparently to parts of the Mandara and Adamawa Mountains and exemplified by the Marghi, derived from indigenous siderological traditions.

BIBLIOGRAPHY

Barber, Bernard 1957 Social Stratification: A Comparative Analysis of Structure and Process. New York, Harcourt, Brace & World.

Barth, Heinrich 1857 Travels and Discoveries in North and Central Africa, 1849–1855. London, Longman, Brown, Green, Longmans, & Roberts.

Baumann, H., and D. Westerman 1948 Les peuples et les civilisations de l'Afrique suivi de les langues et l'éducation. Paris, Payot. (Translation of Völkerkunde von Africa [1939].)

Bergel, Egon Ernest 1962 Social Stratification. New York, McGraw-Hill.

Clément, Pierre 1948 Le forgeron en Afrique Noire. La Revue de Géographie Humaine et d'Ethnologie, pp. 35–58.

Cline, Walter 1937 Mining and Metallurgy in Negro Africa. General Series in Anthropology, No. 5. Menasha, Wisconsin, George Banta.

Gardi, René 1956 Mandara. Unbekanntes Bergland in Kamerun. Zurich, Orell Fussli Verlag.

Herskovits, Melville J. 1924 A preliminary consideration of the culture areas of Africa. American Anthropologist, 26:50–64.

——— 1930 The culture areas of Africa. Africa, 3:59–77.

——— 1962 The Human Factor in Changing Africa. New York, Alfred A. Knopf.

Kirk-Greene, A. H. M. 1958 Adamawa, Past and Present. London, Oxford University Press.

Kroeber, A. L. 1931 Caste, in: Encyclopaedia of the Social Sciences. New York, Macmillan.

Lembezat, Bertrand 1961 Les populations païennes de Nord-Cameroun et de l'Adamoua. Paris, Presses Universitaires de France.

Lowie, Robert H. 1948 Social organization. New York, Holt, Rinehart & Winston.

Meek, C. K. 1925 The Northern Tribes of Nigeria. London, Oxford University Press.

——— 1931 Tribal Studies in Northern Nigeria. London, Kegan Paul, Trench, Trubner.

Murdock, George Peter 1959 Africa: Its Peoples and Their Cultural History. New York, McGraw-Hill.

Rosser, K. C. 1964 Caste, in: A Dictionary of the Social Sciences. New York, The Free Press.

Sasscon, Hamo 1964 Iron-smelting in the hill village of Sukur, north-eastern Nigeria. Man, 64:Art. 215.

Vaughan, James H., Jr. 1960 Rock paintings and rock gongs among the Marghi of Nigeria. Man, 62:Art. 83.

——— 1964a Culture, history, and grass-roots politics in a Northern Cameroons kingdom. American Anthropologist, 66:1078–95.

——— 1964b The religion and world view of the Marghi. Ethnology, 4:389–97.

——— 1965 Folklore and values in Marghi culture. Journal of the Folklore Institute, 2:5–24.

——— (in press) ∂ŋkyagu as Artists in Marghi Society. The Traditional Artist in African Society. Warren d'Azavado (ed.).

RWANDA CASTES

BY JACQUES MAQUET

Caste is a concept which has not yet been completely accepted as a common term in the sociological language. It is one of the words that some scholars, mainly historians, think to be suitable only to denote singular institutions which appeared once in the course of history —in a certain region at a certain time. In that view caste should be exclusively applied to one of the hereditary divisions of society in classical India. Feudality is another of these words which, according to some historians, should be restricted to designating certain institutions of western Europe during the Middle Ages and should not be used in any other connection.

Since we are going to use the caste concept in the following analysis of the Rwanda social organization, we feel obliged to justify our position. To abstract from a particular phenomenon some aspect, designate it by a name, and then apply the latter to other phenomena in which the same aspect may be found, is a process so basic to our thinking that it seems preposterous to appeal to it. Social science could not go beyond pure description without the constant use of concepts obtained by abstraction from a concrete situation. When we speak of kings and priests among the Maya and Aztec, we apply to New World peoples words that have been evolved from very different civilizations—the former from old German institutions and languages, the latter from ancient Greece. On theoretical grounds, then, one cannot object to the attempt to extend, in similar fashion, the application of caste to institutions other than Indian social divisions.

Jacques Maquet: Rwanda Castes

In addition to theoretical possibility, justification also requires that the concept appear to fulfill a useful function in its new applications. The proof of this will result, we hope, from this chapter and cannot be given at the very outset, but it may be relevant to indicate here that when the Rwanda material was collected, caste was to us just another word of the current language. Later on, when we tried to analyze and interpret our field records, we felt the need for an analytical concept whose content was very close to that of caste. Consequently we thought it convenient and advisable to assign a precise meaning to the term *caste* and to make it a part of the sociological vocabulary. It may be useful in two connections; first, as an analytical category under which we may gather social phenomena that have appeared in different societies at different times but that are significantly similar; second, as a minimal definition which certainly does not take into account the complete richness of the phenomenon, but which, acting as a guide mark, permits us to locate it in the continuous fabric of collective life.

TRADITIONAL RWANDA, END OF THE NINETEENTH CENTURY

For Rwanda, the traditional period was brought to a close at the extreme end of the nineteenth century: in 1899, the king was led to accept the German Imperial Government's protection. Of course, many important sections of the traditional culture continued to dominate the life of Rwanda people—and still do—but 1899 marks the end of the king's political sovereignty and the beginning of the opening of Rwanda to the influence of external forces.

To the first European explorers, colonial officers, missionaries, and merchants, Rwanda appeared as a densely populated kingdom situated in a pleasant environment with a temperate climate, isolated by its highland relief.

Rwanda is a part of the interlacustrine area of central eastern Africa, a region particularly well suited for human occupation. Because of its elevation (above 3000 feet), its latitude (between about 3° north and 5° south), and its vegetation (mainly savanna and occasional forest), the land delimited by the Great Lakes (in the west, Lakes Albert, Edward, Kivu, Tanganyika; in the south, a line running eastward from Malagarasi River to Muanza Bay on Lake Victoria; in the east and north, Lakes Victoria and Kyoga) had attracted invaders from the north who came and settled. Cattle-rearing and cultivation were productive activities easily carried on in the interlacustrine area.

Though somewhat peripheral in the area and not easily accessible (it is situated in the southwestern part of the highland region and divided by the chain of mountains which separates the Congo and Nile drainage basins), Rwanda had a population estimated by the German administration at approximately 2,000,000 in 1900. In spite of this large number and of the difficult communications across the high-altitude forests of the Congo-Nile divide (its peaks reach 9000 feet and its passes are not under 6750 feet), the Rwanda king had under his political control practically all the people speaking the Rwanda language; they were all situated on the kingdom's territory, which had a north-south extent of about 100 miles and a west-east extent of about 140 miles.

The Rwanda global society thus consisted of a numerous population living in a centralized political unit, under the authority of a monarch who was assisted by a well-organized administration. The population was not homogeneous. Three groups could easily be distinguished among the Rwanda people: Tutsi, Hutu, and Twa. The immediately noticeable differences among these groups occur in their activities, their social statuses, and their physical types.

Tutsi were cattlemen. They were proud of their herds; they attached an immense value to them, and not exclusively an economic one. They were also warriors; their young men received a specialized training, and only Tutsi were allowed to enter into military organizations. Government, at almost all levels except the lowest ones, was for the Tutsi exclusively. Tutsi constituted a minority—between 15 and 20 percent of the Rwanda population—which had social preeminence over the other groups. A distinct physical appearance was considered typical of them and "nicer" than the characteristics of the other groups: Tutsi were supposed to be slender and tall, to have a straight nose and a light-brown skin color. Many had these characteristics but not all; however, they represented a culturally important stereotype.

Hutu were hoe-cultivators. They could take care of the cattle of Tutsi; they were allowed to dispose of a few head under certain conditions, but it was exceptional for them to own cattle. On the other hand, Tutsi considered tilling the soil completely undignified for themselves. Representing between 80 and 85 percent of the population, the Hutu constituted the peasant mass and had a definitely lower position in society than the Tutsi. Their physical stereotype included short or middle stature, thick lips, often everted, and a flat, broad nose.

Twa were traditionally hunters; but game being rare in most parts of Rwanda, owing to the scarcity of forest, many Twa were craftsmen (potters) or servants of important Tutsi. As servants, they were often singers, dancers—in the buffoon tradition—or killers on behalf of their masters when the latter wanted to quietly suppress somebody. They were not numerous—1 or 2 percent—but socially highly visible; they were looked upon with amused interest by Tutsi and Hutu, who did not see them as completely human and responsible beings. Physically, Twa were short, pygmoid rather than pygmy, with a head low in the crown, flat face and nose, prominent cheekbones, bulging forehead, and narrow and slightly oblique eyes.

At the end of the nineteenth century, any observer of the Rwanda society could easily perceive the main features we have just mentioned. And they did, as appears for instance in the reports of Kandt, Arnoux, and Czekanowski.[1] Another aspect of the social organization which appeared very striking to the early observers was the personal tie between a Tutsi and a Hutu which established for both of them reciprocal but different obligations and which made it possible for the Hutu to enjoy the usufruct of a cow.

The different institutions of traditional Rwanda have been described more than once;[2] therefore, these brief indications of them should suffice here. They convey, we hope, the impression of a rich array of social relations among Tutsi, Hutu, and Twa, kings and chiefs, warriors and peasants, lords and subjects, etc. Different terms have been used in connection with the Rwanda setup: nobles and commoners, aristocrats and vassals, clients and superiors, etc. In order to attempt an analysis of this complex situation, we have first to consider a few sociological categories.

ROLES AND SANCTIONS

For a brief time, let us go to fundamentals and make clear the perspective in which our categories are set. In any human group which presents some permanency (that is to say, in any society), the activities of the interacting members are not left to chance or pleasure but are organized. Organization is particularly important in that kind of society called *global*, because it provides for the needs of the individual from birth to death and for the necessities of the survival of the group as such. To obtain these results, the activities of the members must be complementary and harmonized.

Traditional Rwanda was obviously a global society. It was possible to live one's life in it without entering into any relation with people from outside; and when they occurred, these outside relations were not essen-

1. Czekanowski, 1911, 1917; Kandt, 1919; Arnoux, 1948.
2. See, among others, Kagame, 1952; Maquet, 1961; d'Hertefelt, 1962. It is useless to give here an extensive bibliography on Rwanda; there are several easily available, for instance, in Maquet, 1961:186–94, and in d'Hertefelt, 1962:99–112.

tial to the lives of individuals—some encounters with foreigners, cattle-raiding on the borders, military expeditions. For many men and women of Rwanda, the social horizon was even more restricted; it encompassed only a region of Rwanda for most of their activities. Yet for all of them, Rwanda was a perceived reality; they were identified by the name that set them apart from outsiders belonging to neighboring global societies; they were subjects of the same king, and we know that his power was effective over the whole territory of Rwanda at the end of the nineteenth century.

In Rwanda, as in any global society, each individual member is linked to many others by a great number of relations, each representing a specific interaction between two actors. If each actor were represented by a dot on a chart, and each interaction by a line between two dots, the chart would look like a confused web of intersecting lines going in all directions.

To describe and analyze the continuous web of social relations, the latter have to be gathered under a few categories. This is usually—we may even say always—done in sociological literature as well as in common parlance: we speak as a matter of course of political, economic, or kinship relations. Criteria used to attribute such qualifications to concrete relations differ more or less and are not always very clear, particularly in everyday language. We will, therefore, attempt here to make our criteria as explicit as possible.

It seems to us that from a certain number of observable concrete interactions between members of a global society, it is possible to abstract a few relational models which express the specificity of different fields. These models allow us to locate what is common to a great number of interactions and, consequently, to consider them together. Of course, we suppose that common element to be important, even fundamental. Models are elementary in the sense that they attempt to delineate the core of the relation.

Structure in the different models is identical and simple. It consists of two elements: the roles of the two interacting actors and the sanctions of these roles. From Ralph Linton to Ward Goodenough, the term *role* has been subjected to different reappraisals and refinements.[3] Here, we understand role as a collection of rights and duties of an actor toward other actors; role encompasses the static aspect (the description of the collection) as well as the dynamic one (the practice of the rights and duties). For Linton, the static aspect was called status, and the dynamic one, role. We shall reserve the term *status* and use it only in the model of social stratification. *Actor* refers to the individual member of the global society as he is apt to enter into different social relationships and thus carry on different roles and fulfill different social identities. To describe the roles

3. Linton, 1936; Goodenough, 1965.

Jacques Maquet: Rwanda Castes

of both actors in a relationship is to describe the content of it. There is nothing else in the relationship from the anthropological point of view; the manner in which A plays his role of husband, with tenderness or coolness, with intelligence or stupidity, is not to be taken into account in role analysis as long as he remains within the boundaries of his rights and their duty counterparts as defined in his culture.

Sanction is a term pertaining to the legal field, where it is "the specific penalty enacted in order to enforce obedience to a law," as the *Oxford Dictionary* puts it. But it may be extended to rules of action other than the legal ones; sanction is applicable then to any kind of reward or punishment following observance or nonobservance of rules. Now, we may consider a role as a set of rules that an actor is obliged to observe as regards the other actors; the latter have another set of rules to observe as regards the former. If one does, or does not, comply with the rules, there are agreeable consequences in the first case, unpleasant in the second; such consequences are what we call here sanctions.

Sanctions are not necessarily punishments; they may be positive rewards. Sanctions do not necessarily require the intervention of an agency whose explicit function is to punish or reward; diffused, moral, magical sanctions have been known for a long time in anthropological literature.

By defining the reciprocal roles of two actors and the sanctions of their observance, we shall attempt to build elementary models of government and stratification relations with reference to the Rwanda.

RWANDA POLITICAL RELATIONS

Political relations are not easily distinguished from the stratification relations. Yet it seems important, from the point of view of social analysis, to set them clearly apart at the beginning even if, later on, it will be as important to point to the partial overlapping of the two networks.

Members of a global society, as actors in a political relation, may be called ruler and subject. The subject's role is to obey the ruler and to provide him with goods and/or services; the ruler's role is to command and to maintain the subject's survival. The ultimate sanction of the observance of both sets of duties rests on force: physical coercion on the part of the ruler to oblige his subject to fulfill his duties; resistance or rebellion of the subject whose survival is threatened by the excessive demands of the ruler.

The Rwanda traditional society was divided into two groups: rulers and subjects. Rwanda was a monarchy but, as in any monarchic state, the ruler's role was not restricted to a single actor, the king. The *mwami* (king) was not the only actor who could make use of the coercive power and who could obtain labor and tributes from other actors; chiefs residing at the court, chiefs representing the king in the provinces, military and administrative officers shared with the king the control of physical force and the benefits of tax collection. There was not a ruler, but a ruling group.

Of course, in that group, the *mwami* had a prominent place. He was a sacred king. The official genealogists could trace his descent through patrilineal direct links to the first kings who came from the heavens, the invisible and powerful world of the gods and of the high god creator, *Imana*.[4] In addition to his divine origin, the *mwami* was Rwanda; there was a deep identification of king and country. What happened to him would reverberate, as it were, over the country: as the king was growing old and weak, his physical decrease would endanger the health and prosperity of Rwanda; when a battle was waged against an enemy, on the borders of Rwanda, the king, in his capital, had to avoid any backward move lest the Rwanda army retreat; the *mwami* had also to refrain from bending his knees for fear Rwanda's territory would shrink.

The king's power was absolute in theory. Ideologically, there was no limit to his powers over the inhabitants, cattle, land, and even commodities of Rwanda. There was no human authority above him to which he had to render an account of his management, and *Imana* was far away and rather indifferent; there was no man-made abstract institution (such as a constitution or tradition) which could be opposed to his will. And in addition, nobody else could claim to have a similar power over a part, even very small, of the Rwanda territory. Some high dignitaries who were also heads of ancient and important lineages enjoyed a certain fiscal immunity and other privileges exempting them from some obligations toward the *mwami*, but none of them was completely independent of the *mwami*.

This does not contradict our assertion that Rwanda was ruled by a group and not by a single actor. Absolute power was the theory, and it was true in the sense that the right to rule had a single origin, the *mwami*, and was delegated by him, explicitly or implicitly, to any other actor who could control physical coercion. But the ruler's role does not exclude delegation or limit of power. The *mwami* was the symbol of the perfect political power of the ruling group which was organized around him.

Theoretical absolutism and a well-organized structure of the ruling group are not sufficient to suppress the sanction of resistance of the subjects by escape or revolt. Revolts of subjects of the inferior caste are not known to have happened in Rwanda traditional history, and if they did, it is most unlikely that they succeeded; but struggle for power among factions of the superior caste (that is to say, opposition of subjects of the

4. Kagame, 1959:81; Vansina, 1962:43; Maquet, 1954b:166; d'Hertefelt and Coupez, 1964:457.

superior caste to a part of the ruling group, and particularly to the *mwami*) was not infrequent.

Rules of monarchic succession entailed struggles. They designated, not a single heir (e.g., the eldest son of the first wife), but a category of possible heirs (any son of the king). The choice belonged to the *mwami*, but it was kept secret till after his death; then it was made public by three high dignitaries. As each candidate was supported by a faction of influential people, there were many intrigues and pressures before and particularly after the king's death; sometimes the losers did not easily acknowledge their defeat and attempted a coup d'état. Consequently the *mwami* had to take into account these possibilities: he had to secure the support of some factions among the ruling group. His power was not limitless.

To rule two million people, the king needed assistance. He delegated his rights and duties; that is to say that in fact he shared his ruler's role with many other actors. They were organized: court, administration and army were the main political institutions of Rwanda. Any ruler (in the sense of member of the ruling group) belonged to one of these institutions.

The court has sometimes been called the central government; certainly it performed the functions of a central government, but we prefer the term *court*, which calls to mind different ideas—loyal followers of the king chosen by him because he felt he could rely upon them, counselors who advised but had no legal power of decision, courtiers who resided permanently where the king lived, relatives of the monarch who took advantage of their kinship ties and hoped to influence the king, sycophants who flattered and enemies who intrigued.

The *mwami* and his court were the capital of Rwanda. It was not permanently located; it moved from one province to another. Wherever it was, it was the center of political decision and power. All the important chiefs in the administrative or military hierarchies regularly and frequently had to spend some time at the court. They reported to the *mwami*, advised him, and took his orders.

The court was also the center where consumption goods were concentrated. A part of the surplus produced all over the country was canalized to the court. To collect goods without economic counterpart is a function of any political system, and its necessary condition. To be obeyed, the *mwami* needed his court, his administration, his army; thus an important number of men and their dependents were exempted from productive activities; they had to be fed by peasants and cattle-herders. Through the tribute imposed by the king and collected by his administration, peas and beans, banana-beer and milk were gathered at the court and distributed to all the court officials.

The main function of the second political institution of Rwanda, the administration, has just been mentioned: to collect dues and taxes. The extent of the country and the number of subjects of the *mwami* made obligatory the division of the country into districts and the delegation of the royal power to "civil servants" who would act as representatives of the king in each district.

It was a complex organization. Each district was ruled by two chiefs, neither of them dependent on the other. Their authority extended over the same territory but from different points of view. The land-chief took care of the dues from agriculture and the cattle-chief of the dues from stock. The district was divided into hills; there was no duplication at that level: the hill-chief was the subordinate of both the cattle- and land-chiefs. On each hill, there were usually several neighborhoods: they constituted the smallest administrative units; one of the family heads living there was chosen as the answerable representative of the few neighboring families.[5] Between the district authorities (cattle- and land-chiefs) and the king, there were high chiefs. The administrative structure was thus a multilevel hierarchy.

Again, we consider the officers of the administration here as "rulers" because they could enforce the decisions they made, within the limits of their capacity, by coercion, and because they received benefit from the collecting system they operated. According to my informants, about two-thirds of the impositions on agricultural produce was retained by them before it reached the court.

It should be added that, like any authority in Rwanda, the "chiefs" of the administrative hierarchy had to maintain peace among the subjects of their territories, and act as judges or arbitrators when a dispute occurred.

Army—or rather armies—constituted that force upon which finally the political sanction rested. At the beginning of his reign, every *mwami* recruited a new army; he asked Tutsi chiefs to bring to the court their sons who had not yet had any military training. About 150 to 200 young men constituted a company; they were trained for several years in military skills and warlike dances, and they were taught to memorize poems in which military high deeds were recalled and to compose new songs on the same topics. After a few years, other companies were formed according to the same procedure. These new companies constituted the army of a particular reign. But the armies founded previously, during other reigns, continued to function up to the death of their members. In spite of this plurality, armies may be said to have constituted an efficient force put at the disposal of the king.

The ruling group was thus made of all those who participated in the king's power and privileges, whether at the court, in the administration,

5. For a discussion of the Rwanda names given to districts and administrative authorities, see Maquet, 1961:101.

Jacques Maquet: Rwanda Castes

or in the army. In theory, the *mwami* was the single source of authority, and consequently all other rulers were such on behalf of the king; this is why we have spoken of civil servants in connection with the administration. In fact, there were other sources of legitimacy (kinship in the case of old lineages settled in a part of the country before the royal dynasty was able to extend its predominance there) and of actual power (as in the European Middle Ages appointed deputies tended to become hereditary, i.e., to transmit their charges to their heirs). When the king was strong, he could in fact appoint and dismiss; when weak, he had to confirm choices which were not his.

In this brief discussion of the Rwanda system of political relations, we have emphasized the profits in consumption goods made by the members of the ruling group. These profits do not belong to the field of economics, as there is no counterpart in goods for the subjects. What about the duties included in the role of rulers? They are very general: to maintain the conditions making the collective survival possible. In Rwanda and societies living in similar conditions of productive techniques and economic organization, to ensure the continuity of the cultural heritage—in fact, it amounts to that—is not a heavy charge for the rulers, as kinship units (such as the lineage) and local units (such as the neighborhood) take care of production, education and transmission of cultural patterns. Defense against aggression from outsiders was the only protective function of the army. But such aggressions were not so detrimental to the subjects as to the rulers. The latter were threatened with deprivation of their privileges, the former with a change of rulers; was it so important?

THE RWANDA STRATIFICATION SYSTEM

The phenomenon of social stratification corresponds to a very common experience in many global societies—in most of them in fact: they are visualized by their members, as well as by outsiders familiar with them, as divided into a few horizontal strata which are ranked, that is to say, situated one above the other in a hierarchy. It is usually easy to locate an individual in his stratum, and when this is done, one knows how to deal with him even without knowing him personally. If A belongs to the first stratum and B to the second one, A will be considered socially superior to B, irrespective of their personal qualities, and be treated accordingly.

This very common phenomenon is easily grasped but difficult to formulate in an elementary relational model because the criteria permitting attribution of rank in a hierarchy of groups vary in different cultures, and because a pure ranking relation rarely occurs in isolation between two actors; usually the ranking relation accompanies, as it were, another one. Yet, let us try.

Members of a global society, as actors in a relation of stratification, may be called superior, inferior, and equal. These terms refer to their affiliation to a division of their society which is considered superior or inferior to the division to which the other actor belongs. The actors are equal when they belong to the same division. Thus inferiority, superiority, and equality of actors are determined by the mediation of a horizontal division of the global society. Such a division is called a stratum. The image of the horizontal layers is useful, since it indicates two characteristics of stratification: these layers constitute a system that encompasses the whole global society (every member of the society belongs to a stratum; it is impossible to be in the society and out of the strata), and they are ranked (strata are always hierarchical; they are not segments which, like kinship groups, are situated side by side).

Each actor must behave toward the other according to the place of their respective strata in the hierarchy existing in their particular society. If there are two strata, the actor belonging to the upper one must act as superior in relation to an actor belonging to the lower one. The content of each role varies in each global society, but everywhere the superior expresses by his behavior that the prestige of his rank is higher than the one of the inferior, and the latter must manifest recognition of the superior's priority. The sanction for the observance of both roles is collective pressure. Collective pressure is not easily analyzed; it covers all the means through which a community may oblige an individual to conform to its norms short of legal or coercive sanctions; it begins with an ironic smile and goes up to ostracism (which may, in fact, force the sanctioned person to leave the community), with the intermediate stages of mockery and insult. Such sanctions are often termed diffused or indirect because they are not institutionalized or precisely measured; all the means indicating reprobation may be used. Their efficiency depends on two conditions: small size of the group and unanimity in the reprobation. If all the members of the society do not personally know each other, the deviant can escape public censure through anonymity (as happens in large urban societies); if a minority do not share the common feeling of indignation, the collective pressure will be jeopardized. If, when dealing with a superior, an inferior does not keep his proper place, disapproval by the superior, the superior's stratum, or even the whole group will entail reactions very unpleasant for the inferior, and if he does not "understand" and does not comply with the duties of his role, the pressure will increase, and eventually he will be in serious trouble.

The elementary relational model of social stratification we have just attempted to delineate is focused on rank—that is to say, on the relative position of a unit in a series of units of the same kind. It does not indicate the basis of the ranking order, which may be landed property, kinship, wealth in cattle, gold, learning, type of activity, etc. Where there is stratification one or several of these values are taken as the basis, and the justification, of the hierarchy of horizontal divisions of society. For instance, the classical Indian system of castes was originally based on type of activities: at the top, the priests, then going down, the warriors, the merchants, and finally the artisans and laborers; in medieval Europe, the landed and military nobility, the men of religion and learning of the Church, the wealthy bourgeoisie of city merchants, the peasants and other manual workers of the countryside. Obviously, a ranking system always has a content of values, but as it varies in different societies, it seems to us that the elementary model should not take it into account, but be restricted to what is common to all stratified organizations—that is to say, the hierarchical order of horizontal divisions.

We have already indicated that the traditional Rwanda population was heterogeneous—three groups clearly differentiated by their physical types, their activities, and their relative numbers. They constituted also a system of social stratification. The Rwanda global society may be analyzed as having been divided into three hierarchical strata: every Rwanda man or woman was either a Tutsi, a Hutu, or a Twa. And to be a Tutsi, a Hutu, or a Twa gave an individual a different status in the society.

It may be useful to introduce here the term *status*. In this chapter it has already been written without any explanation, as it is a word of common language; but as some anthropologists and sociologists have given it a particular meaning when associated with *role*, some clarification seems required here. For us, status is not a general concept having an extent as wide as role; it is used here to designate the position of an actor as determined by his membership in a stratum. To say "Misigaro's status prevents him from being a warrior" means that his unfitness to become a warrior is not due to physical incapacity, lack of training, poverty of his family, etc., but is only due to the fact that he belongs to a stratum for which military activities are considered inappropriate.

A distinction is thus made here between the status and the role of, say, a Hutu. Status refers to his position in the Rwanda global society as member of the Hutu layer; role refers to his rights and duties toward another actor in a social interaction. Of course the role of superior, inferior, or equal of A toward B is based on the statuses of A and B. If they belong to the same stratum, they have the same status and thus assume toward each other a role of equality; if they do not have the same status, one of them will necessarily play a role of superiority toward the other. Again, it is the statuses of A and B that will determine the orientation of their relation.

Because of his status, each inhabitant of Rwanda has a certain power different from the one commanded in another status. A has more power than B because he is Tutsi whereas B is Hutu. Power is understood here in its broadest sense—the ability of an actor to oblige others to supply him with goods or services. Obligation does not imply the threat of physical coercion; such threat is only one of the different ways to oblige somebody to do something. As we have seen, that kind of sanction indicates the political field. There are other ways to obtain something from somebody. To cover all cases, Lasswell defines power as an inter-personal situation in which a severe deprivation may be inflicted by one person on another.[6] Deprivation may be economic, psychological, physical, etc. Whatever it may be, the person in position to inflict it may oblige the other one to do something; he has thus power over the other one. It should be emphasized here that the fact that it is possible to avoid the deprivation by complying or by escaping does not suppress the power relationship: if one complies or if one flees, it is because one fears the deprivation so much that one is ready to suffer disadvantages to preserve what one has been threatened with losing.

In order to distinguish power pertaining to a status from other kinds of power (political, parental, religious, magical, etc.), let us call it *status power*. It is entirely independent from the personal characteristics of the actors. An intelligent, active, and wealthy Hutu had less status power than a Tutsi devoid of these qualities. Of course, in concrete relations, personal qualities had their importance, but the difference of power entailed by the difference of status was never overcome. And, as we have pointed out elsewhere, "when two persons are involved in any kind of social relation, it is their mutual hierarchical situation which is regarded as the most relevant element of the relation."[7] Status was never forgotten; on the contrary, it permeated any social intercourse, and both actors were conscious of their respective status power.

RWANDA BASES OF STATUS POWER

The basis of political power is easy to understand: it is the final recourse to physical force which maintains the rulers in their privileged position. They are able to oblige others to supply them with goods or services because they control coercion. But what about the superiors, i.e., the members of the first stratum?

Status power was based in Rwanda on an image of the past, on a

6. Lasswell, 1948:10–14. See also Russell, 1938:35.
7. Maquet, 1961:165.

Jacques Maquet: Rwanda Castes

special kind of particularly valuable wealth, on a certain immunity from legal sanctions.

The past of the three Rwanda strata was not forgotten. By their songs, poems, oral traditions, Tutsi impressed the memory of the past on the whole Rwanda society. On the basis of such traditions, those of neighboring kingdoms, and archeological evidence, a historical reconstruction has been made. For the essentials, it corresponds to the popular image shared by the Rwanda people at the end of the nineteenth century.

The interlacustrine region had been reached by agriculturalists before the thirteenth century. They spoke Bantu languages and they had perhaps assimilated early Ethiopid waves. Invasion—or infiltration—of groups of Ethiopid nomads continued, and from the thirteenth up to the fifteenth century they entered the Rwanda Plateau where they remained under the names of Hima or Tutsi. It is very likely that the late Ethiopid invaders were organized from small groups of warriors moving slowly with their cattle (up to now, Hima nomads have kept, in the northeastern region of Rwanda, nomadic patterns).[8]

Ancestors of the Tutsi stratum were thus invaders. They were not conquerors: the term *conquest* suggests a sudden, complete defeat after a military encounter, and nothing of that sort happened. Forebears of the Hutu were peasants living by agriculture. It is very likely they had maintained the same kind of life up to the twentieth century in the small peasant communities of northern Rwanda. These communities were not gathered in larger political units: all their inhabitants belonged to a few patrilineages; social order was kept and conflicts were solved by the kinship heads whose authority was based on their position in the lineage.

In fact, two types of global societies came into contact, and if there was no conquest, there was a progressive domination of the sedentary peasants by the nomadic warriors. Precisely how that domination was achieved does not matter at this point of our argument: the military superiority was, of course, the most significant factor. But what is important to point out here is that the Tutsi has continuously kept for himself and for the other strata the image of his successful invasion and of his domination over the peasants. He has even distorted the past by emphasis on the superior force and on the rapid submission of the peasant communities. Of course, every group manipulates history, but it is interesting to see in what sense it manipulates it: in Rwanda it was to assert the rights of the present-day Tutsi to their high status power. As late as 1958, when the Tutsi superiority began to be questioned by Hutu, a group of high chiefs living at the court of the king, Mutara, wrote a declaration to justify the Tutsi status in the stratification of Rwanda. Their argumentation is historical: When the ancestor of the Nyiginya (the Tutsi dynasty),

8. Fage, 1958:21–22; Oliver, 1963:180–91.

Kigwa, arrived in the country, it was occupied by the Zigaba, whose king was Kabeja. Kabeja's subjects became the servants of Kigwa; "now Hutu claim a share in the common heritage . . . as our relations with them have always been of serfdom, not of fraternity," they have no patrimonial rights. Tutsi chiefs pointed out further that Ruganzu and other Rwanda kings had killed many Hutu petty monarchs and thus had conquered the country of the Hutu. And they concluded by these words: "As our kings have conquered the land of the Hutu by killing their king-lets and have consequently subjugated the Hutu, how can the latter pre-tend to be our brothers?"[9] After sixty years of exposure to Western ideas, of life under a colonial administration, of deep social and economic changes, such were the views of important Tutsi chiefs. At the end of the nineteenth century, when the whole traditional Rwanda society was still a going concern, it is easy to imagine the bearing of the image of the past conquest on the status of descendants of the victorious invaders and of the vanquished peasants. To be a Tutsi was to be identified with the group who had gained control of Rwanda through the right of conquest.

Cattle were another basis of the Tutsi status power, and, it seems to us, the main one. Cattle have been a privileged kind of wealth all through the history of Rwanda—at the time of the nomadic pastoralists settling in the hilly highlands of the interlacustrine area, and at the time of the centralized kingdom of the precolonial decades.

The Ethiopid pastoralists had the superiority of the trained warrior over quiet peasants accustomed to tilling the soil. But they had another, more fundamental advantage—in the sense that it made possible the specialization in warlike activities—cattle as a system of production of goods.

Indeed, from that point of view, cattle have some characteristics mak-ing of them an instrument of subsistence very different from land.

Land in Rwanda, as practically everywhere in precolonial Africa, had no scarcity value. Like water, or air, it was not privately owned. When somebody—for instance, a newly married young man who had to care for the needs of a new nuclear family—needed a plot of land to cultivate, he was granted one by his lineage head or by the community chief. This means that the value of land was measured only by the labor that could make a field producing crops out of a piece of uncultivated soil. In itself, land was without any value because it did not produce any commodity. By contrast, a herd of cattle is a remarkable instrument of production. It does not require much work: a few experts in cattle breeding and a few herdsmen who know where to find grazing grounds are sufficient to ensure good returns in milk, meat, blood, leather.

Although animals die, a properly kept herd never disappears: young

9. Nkundabagenzi(ed.), 1961:35–36.

Jacques Maquet: Rwanda Castes

beasts replace the old ones. Even if an important part of its products is consumed, a herd will last forever and increase. If one ceases to work on a field, it does not produce anything and very soon it returns to its natural state.

Finally cattle are an instrument of production which has mobility. If a peasant has to leave the place he has cleared, he can take with him only the year's crop, whereas pastoralists can move and migrate without losing their means of subsistence. This mobility seems to account for the warlike character of the pastoral groups of the interlacustrine region: because they were very valuable, cattle were coveted goods, and because they were easily moved they could be raided. Consequently the group owning cattle had to be able to defend its precious possession.

Because of these favorable characteristics, cattle were an important asset for the invaders, who were able to subsist entirely on them when the circumstances made it necessary (up to recent times, the Hima nomads of Rwanda lived almost entirely on pastoral products). And cattle-raising was envied by the hoe cultivators. It should be added here that herding was an efficient technique of production in the conditions prevailing in that region of Africa during the traditional period. Pastoralism without stalling and feeding the cattle requires very large superficies and thus constitutes a waste of land. But when there is no shortage of land, when the soil is poor, when advanced agricultural techniques such as irrigation and fertilization are not available, herding is more rewarding than agriculture can be for a small group of people. It is in that perspective that possession and use of cattle carried more prestige than tillage.

After they settled in the country, Tutsi had the ability to keep ownership of cattle for themselves. As we have pointed out elsewhere, cattle had some characteristics analogous to those of capital in the Western economic systems.[10] The cattle-owner gets returns without working; if he does not spend them, they are capitalized and produce, in due course, new returns. It is a "natural" capital in the sense that the returns are not founded on a complex economic system but are inherent in the biological nature of cattle. It would be preposterous to press this comparison, but it helps to understand how the exclusive ownership of cattle gave the Tutsi stratum a high status power: the control of this self-increasing wealth remained in the hands of the top layer. This, obviously, offered opportunities for the Tutsi "to oblige others to supply them with goods or services." We shall see later on how they made use of this possibility.

A certain immunity from legal sanctions was the third basis of the high status power in ancient Rwanda. This was not a *de jure* exemption from common sanctions when an offense had been committed by a

10. Maquet, 1962:151–52.

Tutsi. If he had injured somebody, he had to compensate for it; if he was guilty of a breach of peace, he had to be punished. But such legal sanctions were decided by a chief or even the king. As mentioned in our discussion of the political organization of Rwanda, any ruler had, among the duties of his charge, to sentence the delinquents and to settle the conflicts. Now, all the persons belonging to the political hierarchy were Tutsi. Thus when a Hutu and a Tutsi were opposed, when a Hutu complained that he had suffered tort from a Tutsi, the judicial authority was always a Tutsi. It is certain that the chief was biased in favor of the Tutsi. There is no need to insist on that; one has just to be reminded of similar situations in the Western societies (for instance, in a colonial regime) to know that it is a distinct advantage for the plaintiff or the defendant to belong to the judge's social stratum. Yet, there is for us an abstract ideal of impartiality, a possible control of public opinion, the legally protected independence of professional judges. Such obstacles to a stratum bias did not exist in Rwanda.

To sum up, it may be said that the Tutsi status power was based on several factors. We have indicated here three which appear to us to have been most significant. Alone, each of them could not account for the power each Tutsi was endowed with, but their sum resulted in a somewhat diffused influence. Influence is understood here as the ascendancy of the Tutsi stratum which, when exercized, gives the power to attain specific goals.[11] Elusiveness of these phenomena makes their analysis difficult.

CASTES AND CLASSES

A system of social stratification manifests permanence; it has a continued existence through several generations, usually many; it changes slowly or it meets an abrupt end by revolution. From the point of view of the individual member of the global society, stratification appears as fundamental and solid as society itself: it has existed "forever" before his birth and it will last "forever" after his death. Of course, this sense of perenniality is jeopardized in times of deep social upheavals, but such crises are not frequent, less frequent anyway than wars, invasions, and dynastic changes. For instance, in Rwanda, the social stratification we are analyzing here has practically lasted up to the Hutu revolt of 1959; that is to say, it survived the loss of political sovereignty of the kingdom for sixty years.

Within the limits of one individual life, what matters is not the existence of the stratification, but the openness of the strata—that is, access

11. Lhomme, 1966:10.

Jacques Maquet: Rwanda Castes

to the higher strata and intercourse across the strata lines. A stratum is open when it is possible for an individual to climb into it during his lifetime, and when a large number of social relations admit actors belonging to different strata. It is closed when the only way of access is to be born of parents belonging to the stratum and when social segregation between classes reaches most fields of social interaction.

We suggest calling *caste* a closed stratum, and *class* an open one. We are aware that it is rash to give such apparently simple contents to concepts which have been discussed at length and in depth and which sometimes have been given specific meanings within the framework of vast theories. We will not, however, discuss them here; this problem, despite its considerable interest, falls outside the scope of this chapter, whose purpose is to analyze the social stratification of traditional Rwanda. Of course, to carry on that task, concepts have to be utilized. Caste and class seem to be useful; we take them thus and indicate what we mean by them. It should be added that the meanings we propose follow closely such classical anthropological works as Lowie's.[12]

The criterion just mentioned—openness of the stratum—indicates that caste and class are not seen here as clear-cut categories: culturally accepted relations across the stratum lines may be more or less numerous; the stratum is thus more or less open. Consequently the caste and class duality is conceived here as a polarized opposition; they constitute two extreme positions separated by a continuum on which there are many possible intermediate positions. Some of them may be spotted on the continuum and given numerical values, and a concrete stratum can then be marked on the scale according to its degree of openness. When there is only one case to study—as in this chapter—it is obviously pointless to attempt to set it on a numerical scale, but when several stratification systems are taken into account, situating them on a scale may help comparison.

Rwanda society was divided into three strata, it is often repeated by Rwanda people and by outside observers. In fact, one of them, the Twa group, had a very restricted demographic importance—probably less than 2 percent of the total population, perhaps less than 1 percent—and was at the bottom.

The Twa layer deserves to be studied with special attention, as the Rwanda, visualizing their own society in terms of three groups collectively, tended to apply the same patterns to the different interstrata separations. Now, the social borders of the Twa group were certainly those of a caste.

As the Twa layer was at the bottom of the hierarchy, it may seem

12. Lowie, 1948:273. For a more recent bibliography on social classes in Africa, see Verhaegen, 1965.

ironic to state that the only access to it was by birth. Yet it is true: a socially deviant Hutu or Tutsi, living very poorly and irregularly, did not become a Twa. If, except by birth, it was impossible to get in, it was impossible also to get out. The absence of any access in both directions was due to the fact that Twa appeared to other Rwanda to belong to another race, almost to another species: they were said half-jokingly to be more akin to monkeys than to human beings. Of course, this was not really believed, but it was a way to insist on the racial basis of the Twa caste.

This idea is fundamental in the Rwanda conception of strata differences. We have indicated at the beginning the physical stereotypes of Tutsi, Hutu, and Twa. To them, moral qualities were added. I have described them elsewhere in this way: "Tutsi were said to be intelligent (in the sense of astute in political intrigues), capable of command, refined, courageous, and cruel; Hutu, hardworking, not very clever, extrovert, irascible, unmannerly, obedient, physically strong; Twa, gluttonous, loyal to their Tutsi masters, lazy, courageous when hunting, without any restraint."[13] Of course, national and regional stereotpyes of that sort are very common everywhere, but when in the field I insisted on knowing to what cause such characteristics were attributed (innate vs. acquired, to simplify). For instance, I asked if a Hutu brought up with Tutsi, and as a Tutsi boy, could not develop the Tutsi qualities. To that question, Hutu and Tutsi informants answered that such a training could change the boy to some extent, but not completely. For them, differences pertained to nature.

In the case of the Twa, who were pygmoids, the racial basis of the caste was particularly stressed. But in the Rwanda ideology, the same principle was applied to the Hutu and the Tutsi groups. And the same consequence was drawn: membership in a stratum results from birth. This is why we think that Rwanda strata are more on the side of caste than class. It is not the only argument, but the criterion of access is in favor of caste.

One is born Twa, Hutu, or Tutsi. Physical and moral conformity to the caste stereotype does not obtain membership in the caste, and it is not required either. Tutsi shared the usual lack of logical consistency of racists who give the greatest importance to physical type but consider it neither sufficient nor necessary to belong to a certain race.

To be born in a certain caste, is it required that both parents belong to that caste? Castes were endogamous. Consequently the most common case was that both parents were members of the same caste. Marriages across the caste line were exceptional, in the sense that they were rare and in the sense that they were due to special circumstances which indicated

13. Maquet, 1961:164.

who was assimilated to the spouse's caste. If a rich Hutu dear to his Tutsi lord was granted by the latter a Tutsi girl (perhaps one of the lord's daughters) as a wife, their children were likely to be considered as Tutsi, and their grandchildren almost certainly (if the "children" marry Tutsi, of course). If a Hutu marries a Tutsi girl who for some reason has not been able to find a Tutsi husband (because of some physical disability, or because she has already had a child—which was very objectionable in Rwanda where girls were supposed to remain virgins up to marriage— or because her father has lost the trust of the king) and who lives with her husband cultivating a plot as a Hutu wife would do, their children will be considered as Hutu. If an important Tutsi takes a Hutu girl as one of his wives—because she meets his fancy—he will oblige others to consider her children as Tutsi. If a Tutsi who has lost his cattle, and for some reason pertaining to a serious offense he has committed cannot obtain the protection of a lord, marries a Hutu girl and lives near his wife's father, their children will be Hutu. As these four examples indicate, there is no general rule for intercaste marriages, except perhaps this one: children will be considered Tutsi if the marriage constitutes a social promotion for the Hutu spouse, and Hutu if it marks the downfall of the Tutsi spouse.

And what about children born to unmarried mothers? For a girl, it was a serious fault and, in theory, she could be put to death. But in fact, there were concubines, of course. Concubines were women for whom the bridewealth had not been paid: their children were supposed thus to belong to their mother's lineage, and consequently they belonged to their mother's caste. If it was adultery, the child was supposed to have been begotten by the husband of the mother.

Intercaste marriage was exceptional; it was a very slow mechanism of social mobility: by marrying a Tutsi (man or girl), a Hutu (girl or man) did not become a Tutsi but could hope to see his or her children become Tutsi. There was a shorter way but still more exceptional. It has been called, in anthropological literature on Rwanda, *ennoblement*. In spite of the unavoidable associations with the medieval chivalry, that word expresses very well the phenomenon: the king decided to raise a Hutu (or even a Twa) to the higher rank of a Tutsi. The existence of such practice gives a strong confirmation of the closed character of the Tutsi caste.

SEGREGATED CASTES

Born in a caste, the Rwanda individual lived a great part of his life in it. Hutu, Tutsi, and even Twa had many relations: servants attending rich

Tutsi in their residences were Hutu; singers, dancers, performers of farcical plays amusing Tutsi chiefs were Twa; laborers working in the fields for Tutsi were Hutu; hunters providing Tutsi with hides and furs were Twa; herders taking care of the precious cattle owned by Tutsi were Hutu; potters making household utensils used by Tutsi and Hutu were Twa. Yet castes were segregated for practically all the other domains of collective life; intercaste relations were restricted to the field of services and commodities. Outside that field, they were kept to a minimum.

We have already mentioned the rule of endogamy prohibiting marriage between people belonging to different castes. There were obviously no kinship or affinity relations between Hutu and Tutsi; clan names (*ubwoko*) were the same, but it does not mean that Tutsi and Hutu belonged to the same clans. Then why the identity of names? Probably because, a long time ago, Hutu servants and dependents took the clan name of their masters. This is a hypothesis proposed by Tutsi; some Hutu informants prefer to think that the similarity of names indicates a common origin.

There was a similar ambiguity in the Ryangombe ritual. Ryangombe was believed to have been, during his life, the leader of a small group of friends. There are many stories about events of his life. Eventually he was killed by a buffalo during a hunting party. Unwilling to leave Ryangombe, his friends threw themselves on the buffalo's horns. The high god of Rwanda, Imana, gave them a special place in the world of the dead where they enjoy a more agreeable life than the other spirits. To join them and be protected by them while living, many Rwanda people were initiated into Ryangombe's sect, Tutsi as well as Hutu. But it did not imply a common participation in a ritual or a common membership in an association. There was no religious association of Ryangombe's initiates, and initiation was a lineage ceremony. Ryangombe and his friends were impersonated by kinsmen (who had previously been initiated). In spite of the fact that there was a single Ryangombe cult, and that there were Hutu and Tutsi initiates, Hutu and Tutsi held separate ceremonies.

Hutu were also said to belong to armies. To our question: "Was any Rwanda man a member of an army?" 298 informants out of a sample of 300 answered "yes."[14] But Hutu were not warriors; their participation in the army consisted in providing it with agricultural produce and with services (such as carrying water and other charges when there was an expedition).

Hutu and Tutsi did not eat together. It should be pointed out here that Tutsi were extremely reserved about solid food. They behaved as if the need for nourishment were somewhat shameful. Even friends did not share a whole meal; they drank beer or milk together. On the other hand,

14. Maquet, 1961:177.

Jacques Maquet: Rwanda Castes

Hutu were supposed not to be restrained about food. It is thus understandable that there was no intercaste conviviality, as it was practically absent among Tutsi. But Tutsi and Hutu did not drink either as friends. They did not enjoy themselves together. Segregation was maintained during social occasions.

The result of that segregation was the existence of three subcultures within the Rwanda culture. These subcultures were in fact in continuity with the cultures of the three types of societies—forest hunters, hoe cultivators, nomad pastoralists—which made up the Rwanda global society by incorporation. Obviously this was not a consequence of the initial situation but the result of the Tutsi will to maintain segregation, against the Hutu desire to abolish it. In their answers to questions about caste differences, Hutu informants tend to minimize them, Tutsi to stress them. This is not peculiar to Rwanda: superiors (in the sense we give here to that word, members of the first-rank stratum) like to distinguish themselves by speech, dress, alimentary habits, leisure pursuits, from the inferiors; and inferiors tend to imitate the symbols of higher status. In both cases this is not just snobbery as it is often said but, for the superiors, means to defend the caste system, and for the inferiors, means to contest it. (The derogatory term *snob* expresses the view of the superiors who judge ridiculous and vulgar the inferiors who question differences and distinctions.)

Segregation of the three Rwanda strata is another argument in favor of calling them castes. On our scale extending from the open stratum to the closed one, Rwanda social layers are very near the extreme seclusion of the abstract model of a caste.

RULERS AND SUPERIORS

Because all Rwanda rulers were Tutsi, because all Rwanda superiors were Tutsi, and because both roles (of ruler and of superior) had in common dominant features, respectively, to the corresponding roles of subject and inferior, political organization and social stratification have not always been sufficiently distinguished. Referring to an analysis of the Rwanda society published in 1954, Lucy Mair writes:

> Maquet argues that in the days when the kingdom was independent not only chiefs but *all* Tutsi were able to exercise power over *all* Hutu and Twa, and that Hutu and Twa had to behave towards *all* Tutsi as their superiors. But he does not show that a similar relationship of superiority and inferiority exists between Hutu and Twa, as it would if this system conformed to the Indian model of a caste structure.[15]

15. Mair, 1962:136. She refers to Maquet, 1954a.

The difficulty raised by Lucy Mair disappears, I think, if one distinguishes clearly—more clearly than I had done in the 1954 text that she mentions—political power exercised by Tutsi chiefs as rulers over the Hutu subjects under their jurisdiction, and status power exercised by Tutsi as superiors over all the Hutu as members of an inferior stratum. We grant that the status power of Hutu over Twa was not similar to the one of Tutsi over Hutu; yet, for the reasons already put forth, Hutu and Twa groups exhibited caste characteristics: access by birth, segregation, and rank. The Twa group was indeed seen as inferior to the Hutu one: Twa ate any kind of meat, even the meat considered disgusting such as mutton, whereas Hutu, like decent beings, had many food interdictions; moral and physical stereotypes of Hutu were more flattering than those of Twa; for a Tutsi, to marry a Hutu girl was "not done," but to marry a Twa girl was unbelievable (a naïve anthropological query on that gave rise to laughter). As for status power, a Hutu could certainly not obtain from a Twa what a Tutsi could obtain from a Hutu; however, a Hutu was not as socially weak as a Twa (a Hutu would not be as ill-treated by a Tutsi as a Twa could be), and a Hutu could (and would) push away very rudely a Twa for forgetting to keep the distance becoming to his low rank.

We have stressed the economic advantages of the rulers: consumption goods were collected by the tax system sanctioned by coercion. Now, what were the advantages of the superiors who were not rulers, the ordinary Tutsi who were not endowed with any fragment of political authority?

We have indicated that their high status gave them a diffused influence which could be translated into power, permitting them to obtain services and goods. But this could not be done directly. The passage from status to profit can be obtained in three different ways.

The first one is sheer prestige. It is certainly not the most important but it should be noted, as ascendancy has an efficacy often ignored. Simply because he has ancestors who conquered the country, because he has friends at the court of the king, because he has cattle, that precious wealth, because he is a warrior, a Tutsi inspires respect in his Hutu neighbors, and they do not dare to refuse an occasional service he asks, some agricultural produce he wants, the right to graze his cattle where the soil is good and fertile even during the dry season, etc. Colonial situation has shown that a white man, any white man, just because he shared the prestige of the dominant group, could obtain easily what Africans could not get without many difficulties. (Colonial society—I mean all the people living and interacting in a colony—was also stratified; therefore it is permissible to draw some analogies which help us understand the Rwanda system. Some Tutsi were aware of the similarity of the two types of social organization; one of them told me that colonization had just added one more caste on the top.) It was not a question of coercion, not even of pressure, but the utilization of the prestige linked to membership in a superior group.

A second way to translate status into profit, much more efficient than the first, was to use the Tutsi status as a stepping-stone toward political power. To become a ruler, the first condition was to be a Tutsi. According to a large majority of our Tutsi informants (275 out of 300), Hutu could be land-chiefs (in charge of collecting dues from the peasants). In order to check that general opinion, the informants were asked to give the names of the Hutu land-chiefs they knew: 258 informants were able to give the names of Hutu land-chiefs but they mentioned only 34 different names (one of the Hutu names came up 180 times, another 109 times, another 97 times). It is thus very likely that the cases of these three men were exceptional and that, in fact, Hutu were not very numerous among land-chiefs.[16]

Tutsi caste was the minority within which rulers were recruited. How? By heredity, by connections, and to some extent by personal qualities. Chiefs of all levels, in spite of the fact that they were representatives of the *mwami*, appointed by him and dismissed by him, attempted to make their charges hereditary. In the course of the three centuries of the Tutsi regime in Rwanda, there have been many variations in the success of these attempts, depending on the regions (in the peripheral districts where recently conquered Hutu were still turbulent, efficient local Tutsi authorities have sometimes been able to make themselves indispensable and to take roots), depending on the influence of the lineage (a chief belonging to an important kinship group was not easily dismissed by the *mwami*), and depending on the relative power of the *mwami* (there have been in Rwanda, as in most dynasties, strong reigns and weak reigns; during the latter the situation of the chiefs was more favorable to hereditary implantation).

Where there is a large power of decision maintained by a monarch, to have influential friends in the court is most important; the right connections constitute an invaluable asset. And obviously the personal talents of a young Tutsi made easier the task of his protectors at the court.

This inequality of opportunities, regarding access to the group which commands political power and consequently has the largest share of economic advantages and the highest prestige, is not a phenomenon peculiar to Rwanda, of course. It is, it seems to me, what constitutes essentially a "ruling class"; it is not made only of the group of rulers, but it is the social stratum which is associated with the group of rulers— that is to say, which monopolizes in fact access to the different rulers'

16. Maquet, 1961:105–6.

roles available in that society. In Rwanda, Tutsi constituted a "ruling caste" in that sense.

A Tutsi was a potential ruler whereas a Hutu was not. To become an actual ruler was certainly, for a Tutsi, the best use he could make of his status if he wanted to reap all the economic advantages he could hope for. The shortest way from status to profit was to become a chief. But, obviously, not every Tutsi could achieve that; they were about 20 percent of the Rwanda population! For the Tutsi nonrulers, the third way to exercise their status power was the most efficient: it was the institution of the *buhake*, the feudal relation.

THE RWANDA FEUDAL INSTITUTION

There have been many discussions on the applicability of the term *feudal* to Africa, and in fact to any situation other than medieval Europe. At the beginning of this chapter we justified the principle of extension of a concept abstracted from a particular historic phenomenon to other phenomena which are fundamentally similar to the original one. We now have to construct the model of the elementary feudal relation.

As actors in a feudal relation, members of a global society may be called lord and dependent. The lord's role is to protect his dependent, the dependent's is to perform the services required by the lord. The respective duties are sanctioned by a voluntary agreement.

Feudal relations are institutionalized, not only in the sense that they are culturally patterned but in the sense that they constitute a complex institution, identified by a name, and known by the members of the society. This is not one of those covert features of a culture discovered through anthropological analysis and of which the members of a society are not aware; it is an important part of the overt culture. Anthropologists may argue about the feudal character of a particular institution, *buhake* for instance, but not about the existence of *buhake*, which is known by any Rwanda person.

Institutionalization permits distinguishing the feudal relation from simple ties of dependence. In any society, there are many kinds of dependence relationships: in a family, between the children and their father; in a workshop, between the master and his apprentices; in a political party, between the boss and his followers. These relations are culturally patterned but they do not constitute institutions; besides, dependence is not the only content of the relation; it may even appear incidental to generation (in the family), to learning of skills (in the workshop), to promotion of a candidate (in politics). In the feudal relation, dependence is at the core of the relation. I now consider that the clientage relation, between a patron and a client is one of these noninstitutional forms of dependence; I would no longer use the clientage vocabulary in the analysis of the *buhake* institution, as I did previously.[17]

The *buhake* institution has been frequently described in anthropological literature. It will be sufficient here to give an outline. The word *buhake* comes from *guhakwa*, a verb meaning "to pay one's respects to somebody." This verb summarizes the *garagu*'s duties toward his *shebuja*. This relation was created when an individual who had less power than another offered his services to him and asked protection from him.

> The following sentences were usually, but not ritually, said by the man offering his services, after he had given a jug of beer or hydromel to the other: "I ask you milk, make me rich, always think of me, be my father, I shall be your child." If the offer was accepted, the man in higher position bestowed on the other one or several cows. From that time on, they were in the institutionalized relation of *shebuja* (that we may translate by "lord") and *garagu* ("dependent").[18]

The rights the dependent enjoyed over the cattle granted to him were those of usufruct: he had full rights of ownership over milk, the male increase of the cattle, and the meat and skin of a cow that had died or had to be slaughtered. The female increase of the cattle remained at his disposal under the same conditions as the original cows given to him by the *shebuja*.

The protection granted by the lord included support in lawsuits (it was usual and very useful to be accompanied by one's *shebuja* if one wanted to be judged by the *mwami*). Moreover the lord extended help to his dependent if the latter was in a state of poverty (he gave milk for the *garagu*'s children if the father's cows did not yield enough; he contributed to the payment of the bridewealth if the dependent and his lineage could not meet the expenses; he provided his Hutu *garagu* with a hoe when it was needed; he granted meat and hides to his dependent if, on certain occasions, they were badly needed). When the *garagu* committed an offense, his lord had to help him out of his predicament by paying the fine or the compensation to the victim. If the dependent was murdered and his lineage was too weak to do anything about it, the *shebuja* had to demand justice from the *mwami* or even avenge his death by blood feud. Finally, if, after the *garagu*'s death, his widow and children could not be taken care of by his brothers or parallel cousins, the lord had to help them.

On the other hand, the dependent had to go and pay his respects to

---

17. Maquet, 1954a: 151–65; 1961: 129–42.
18. I closely follow here and in the subsequent paragraphs, the description of *buhake* given in Maquet, 1961: 129–33.

his lord. This included personal service which required the presence of the dependent at the lord's residence for a certain time. Some obligations were common to Hutu and Tutsi *garagu*. They were: to accompany the *shebuja* when he was traveling, for instance, when he went to the king's court or participated in a military expedition; to carry the lord's messages; to build or repair a part of the *shebuja*'s dwelling. It was advisable also for dependents, Hutu as well as Tutsi, to offer from time to time to their lord some presents such as jugs of beer. If the lord happened to lose his herds, the *garagu* had to provide him with cattle and jars of milk. Some services were imposed only on Hutu dependents, such as working in the *shebuja*'s fields, or joining the night watch in the lord's enclosure.

The measure of the different obligatory gifts and services (number of days, etc.) was not fixed. It depended on the *shebuja*'s temper, his requirements, the number of cows granted to the *garagu*, and the dependent's expectations. Moreover, each dependent was usually not requested to fulfill all the obligations we have just mentioned. The lord, particularly if he had many *garagu*, frequently gave to each of them a precise task in which he was particularly competent (to brew beer, to cook, to mind the cattle, etc.).

In spite of the fact that we are interested here in the *buhake* institution only as an instrument permitting ordinary Tutsi to actualize the potential power of their status, we have given a general, if summary, description of it, in order not to distort it. Let us now stress the features which are relevant to our purpose.

Before they conclude the agreement initiating the *buhake* relationship, the two parties are unequal in power, either because they belong to different castes (then it is inequality in status power), or because, within the same caste, individual differences due to circumstances, personal talent, etc., result in more power for one and less for the other.

The second case is not of direct interest to us here. For the Rwanda people, *buhake* was first an intercaste relation between a Tutsi and a Hutu; however, there were *buhake* relations among Tutsi. But the services asked from a Tutsi dependent were partly different from the ones required from a Hutu, as has just been mentioned. *Buhake* among Hutu could exist but was exceptional: Hutu had no cattle of their own; to be a lord, a Hutu had to be himself a *garagu* provided by his Tutsi lord with enough cattle to be able to grant some of it to another Hutu. Incidentally, to indicate rank within a stratum, the term *situs* seems very useful; it denotes the ranked position of an individual among others sharing the same status. It may thus be said that the prospective *garagu* is ranked behind the prospective lord either in status or in situs.

In the Tutsi-Hutu *buhake*, it may be said—and it has been said by Tutsi when the privileges of their status were challenged by the Hutu, at the end of the fifties—that there is an exchange of commodities and services: pastoral consumption goods for agricultural produce and labor. It could have been so, but it was not. The usufruct of one head of cattle— an ordinary peasant usually did not get more—was very poor, whereas the Hutu had to provide his lord with what the latter asked. The granting of cattle was no economic counterpart; it was the symbol and the proof of the *buhake* relation. Because I had received a cow from a Tutsi, I knew —and everybody else knew—that he was my lord.

The *buhake* agreement was voluntary. Nobody was obliged to offer services to a Tutsi; when the dependent died, his son had to renew the agreement, and when the lord died, his son had to confirm his acceptance of his father's dependents. The *buhake* relation could also be ended when both lord and dependent or only one of them wanted this.

As being the dependent of a lord was neither economically profitable nor obligatory, then what prompted a Hutu to offer a Tutsi services and goods? His need for protection. Segregated but living scattered in the same regions, Tutsi and Hutu were neighbors. For a Hutu, to have one or several neighbors to whom status conferred prestige, influence at the court, ownership of cattle, and some measure of immunity was a situation bound to result in many inconveniences, troubles, and finally loss of various rights or things. Pressure might be exerted on him, and he was practically defenseless. He needed to be protected by somebody who was equal to those who pushed him around, who had the same status. He had to pay for that protection with what he had—his crops, his labor.

One sees how an ordinary Tutsi (who did not belong to the political hierarchy) could translate his status into material advantages, not directly but through the *buhake* institution.

CONCLUSIONS

Stratification—not political organization, not feudality—was the focus of this chapter. *Buhake* has been considered in that perspective only. Its function was to provide the upper stratum with agricultural goods without significant reciprocity in goods, and without the obligation to participate directly in the productive processes—that is to say, to work. Another function of *buhake* was to limit the exploitation of peasants by giving them the opportunity to have recourse to the protection of a member of the exploiting caste against overexploitation by the others. In that sense the feudal relation may be understood as a regulating device of the caste system, which in itself would have led in Rwanda to its own destruction much earlier than it happened, and probably in a very different way, not revolutionary.

Helen Codere is opposed to the "functional interpretation" of Rwanda which, she writes, is "best exemplified by the work of Jacques Maquet [1954], and [by] the views of Fortes, Evans-Pritchard and Radcliffe-Brown on the nature of the general type of African political system to which Rwanda would be assigned."[19] She presents what she calls a "power interpretation" of Rwanda social structure. According to that interpretation "power can be held and exercised by a minority against the interests and without the consent of the governed; . . . this state of affairs can last for long periods of time."[20] Another quotation concerning the Tutsi protection we have just discussed indicates very clearly what kind of power she has in mind: "[Maquet's] presentation of the compensatory advantage to a Hutu of having a Tutsi overlord in order to give him protection from the exactions and oppressions of other Tutsi is such as to deserve a description in more forthright terms. 'Protection' in such a sense deserves the quote marks it is usually given in describing U.S. gangsterism in the 1920's."[21]

Commenting on Helen Codere's views and mine, René Lemarchand points out the differences of circumstances under which the fieldwork was carried out: Codere was in Rwanda in 1959–60, "a period of great tension and turbulence," as she herself admits, "heavily colored by the emotions and racial antagonisms triggered off by the upheaval of November, 1959," as Lemarchand adds;[22] my 1954 book criticized by Codere is based on fieldwork done in 1950–51, which was a very quiet period. As a determined advocate of the importance to be granted to socially conditioned perspective in anthropological studies, I cannot fail to approve that approach.[23] But it does not exclude a discussion, and I think that the divergence is more on the conceptual level than on the interpretative one.

If I understand her rightly, Codere establishes a dichotomy between a society based on power, by which she means violence and the constant use of oppression and terror, and another one based on consent and control by the majority of the power exercised by a minority. Now, as the previous analyses have made clear, it seems to me that there are different kinds of power according to the sanctions, that many kinds are in operation in any society, and that political power is defined by coercion everywhere. Actual terror, the direct use of physical coercion, is occasionally used in times of crisis, as in the 1959 Tutsi counterrevolution, but usually the threat of it is sufficient. But that threat is present wherever there are rulers, even if the subjects consent. Control and consent are important in the choice of rulers, but the political relation is fundamentally everywhere a relation of coercion. And everywhere, except in times of crises, there is consent, even if reluctantly given. Protection, as understood in the

19. Codere, 1962:46. 20. Codere, 1962:51. 21. Codere, 1962:83.
22. Lemarchand, 1966:597. 23. Maquet, 1964a.

Chicago of the twenties, does not deserve the quote marks: when protection is needed, it always means that pressure is exerted, even if it is done more elegantly than by the gangsters.

Lemarchand, in his attempt to reconcile the contrasting views of Codere and myself, distinguishes the central region of Rwanda and the northern region: in the former, my interpretation could be applied, whereas in the latter, it would not be suitable. In the first case, there is "a situation of optimum functional integration, characterized by a caste structure"; in the second, a situation of "ethnic coexistence,"[24] which implies the absence of functional integration and the persistence of vertical cleavages among groups. I agree with Lemarchand's contention that the situation in northern Rwanda was, at the end of the traditional period, different from the one in the center: in the north, the Tutsi expansion was still in process, whereas in the central provinces, the Tutsi domination had been stabilized for many generations; but what was going on in the north was following the same pattern (incidentally, in my sample of 300 Tutsi informants, there was no overrepresentation of the central region, as Lemarchand thinks: in order to interview the informants, I had to move between 74 different places which were about evenly distributed through the whole area of Rwanda). What was happening in the north, at the end of the nineteenth century, was similar to what had happened in the "nuclear" kingdom, a couple of centuries before. This is why it seems that my analysis is valid for the north also.

If the Rwanda traditional society had to be described in a single word, I would choose "stratified." Inequality of statuses went deeper in the life of Rwanda people and in their culture than other characteristics of their social organization—monarchy, feudal institution, patrilineal kinship, etc. The importance of the caste system has been confirmed by the 1959 Hutu revolution, whose target was its destruction.[25]

BIBLIOGRAPHY

Arnoux, Alexandre   1948   Les Pères blancs aux sources du Nil. Paris, Editions Saint-Paul.

Codere, Helen   1962   Power in Ruanda. Anthropologica, 4(1):45–85.

Czekanowski, J.   1911   Forschungen im Nil-Kongo-Zwischengebiet. Vol. 3: Ethnographische-anthropologischer Atlas. Leipzig.

——   1917   Forschungen im Nil-Kongo Zwischengebiet. Vol. 1: Ethnographie (Mpororo-Ruanda). Leipzig.

d'Hertefelt, Marcel   1962   Le Rwanda. Les anciens royaumes de la zone interlacustre méridionale: Rwanda, Burundi, Buha, par M. d'Hertefelt,

24. Lemarchand, 1966: 608.   25. Maquet, 1964b.

A. A. Trouwborst, J. H. Scherer. Tervuren, Musée royal d'Afrique centrale. 9–112.

———— and André Coupez 1964 La royauté sacrée de l'ancien Rwanda. Tervuren, Musée royal d'Afrique centrale.

Fage, J. D. 1958 An Atlas of African History. London, Edward Arnold.

Goodenough, Ward H. 1965 Rethinking "status" and "role": toward a general model of the cultural organization of social relationships, in: The Relevance of Models for Social Anthropology, Max Gluckman and Fred Eggan (eds.). London, Tavistock Publications (A.S.A. Monograph No. 1), pp. 1–24.

Kagame, Alexis 1952 Le code des institutions politiques du Ruanda précolonial. Bruxelles, Institut royal colonial belge.

———— 1959 La notion de génération appliquée à la généalogie dynastique et à l'histoire du Rwanda des Xᵉ-XIᵉ siècles à nos jours. Bruxelles, Académie royale des sciences coloniales.

Kandt, Richard 1919 Caput Nili. Eine empfindsame Reise zu den Quellen des Nils. 2 vols. Berlin, Dietrich Reimer (4. Auflage).

Lasswell, Harold D. 1948 Power and Personality. New York, W. W. Norton.

Lemarchand, René 1966 Power and stratification in Rwanda: a reconsideration. Cahiers d'études africaines (Paris), 6,4(24):592–610.

Lhomme, J. 1966 Pouvoir et société économique. Paris, Editions Cujas.

Linton, Ralph 1936 The Study of Man. New York, Appleton-Century-Crofts.

Lowie, Robert H. 1948 Social Organization. New York, Holt, Rinehart & Winston.

Mair, Lucy 1962 Primitive Government. Harmondsworth, Middlesex, Penguin Books.

Maquet, Jacques 1954a Le système des relations sociales dans le Ruanda ancien. Tervuren, Musée royal du Congo belge.

———— 1954b The kingdom of Ruanda, in: African Worlds: Studies in the Cosmological Ideas and Social Values of African Peoples, Daryll Forde (ed.). London, Oxford University Press, pp. 164–89.

———— 1961 The Premise of Inequality in Ruanda. London, Oxford University Press.

———— 1962 Afrique, les civilisations noires. Paris, Horizons de France.

———— 1964 Objectivity in anthropology. Current Anthropology, 5(1):47–55.

———— 1964b La participation de la classe paysanne au mouvement de l'indépendance du Rwanda. Cahiers d'études africaines (Paris), 4,4(16):552–568.

Nkundabagenzi, F. (ed.) 1961 Rwanda politique 1958–1960. Bruxelles, Centre de recherche et d'information sociopolitiques.

Oliver, Roland 1963 Discernible developments in the interior, c. 1500–1840, in: History of East Africa, Roland Oliver and Gervase Mathew (eds.). London, Oxford University Press, pp. 169–211.

Russell, Bertrand 1938 Power. London, George Allen & Unwin.

Jacques Maquet: Rwanda Castes

Vansina, Jan   1962   L'évolution du royaume rwanda des origines à 1900. Bruxelles, Académie royale des Sciences d'outremer.

Verhaegen, Benoit   1965   Bibilographie sur les classes sociales en Afrique. Bruxelles, Centre de recherche et d'information socio-politiques (roneotyped).

THE TRADITIONAL SYSTEMS OF STRATIFICATION AMONG THE GANDA AND THE NYORO OF UGANDA

BY MELVIN L. PERLMAN

The general characteristics of the Interlacustrine Bantu societies clustered around the great lakes of East Africa have been described in the first chapter of *East African Chiefs* (Richards, 1960). Although the conclusion to this same book briefly compares these societies and indicates some of the differences between them, the topic of social stratification has not, to my knowledge, received any systematic treatment on a comparative basis.

It was not possible to include all these societies, and I decided on the Ganda[1] and the Nyoro for a number of specific reasons. First, for centuries before the arrival of the Europeans in East Africa, the Ganda and Nyoro dominated the region. Second, the data for these two societies are by and large better than for the others. Third, they offer the possibility of a strongly controlled comparison because, although similar in certain important respects, they are different in others.

The Ganda and the Nyoro are sometimes classified together as "Interlacustrine Bantu Kingdoms," a classification that stresses the many similarities between them, and emphasizes their differences from other types of kingdoms. In this chapter, I propose to capitalize on the similari-

1. Following current practice, I have dropped the use of the prefix *Ba* for these Bantu peoples.

A Comparative/International grant from the Institute of International Studies, University of California, Berkeley, has provided financial support for a project on Uganda, of which this chapter is a part, and this support is gratefully acknowledged. For valuable criticisms I would like to thank John Beattie, Elizabeth Colson, and Erica McClure. Anne Brower kindly provided editorial assistance.

Melvin L. Perlman: Stratification Among Ganda and Nyoro

ties between Ganda and Nyoro in order to illuminate the importance of their less obvious and less often stressed differences. This chapter is thus an example of what Eggan called the method of controlled comparison (1954).

The Ganda and the Nyoro are located in southern and western Uganda respectively. These two states have been traditional enemies for a very long time. Until approximately the middle of the eighteenth century, Bunyoro maintained much of its great empire, which is said to have encompassed not only much of present-day Uganda but other territories to the west and south as well. Thereafter much territory was lost, especially to the Ganda. During the nineteenth century, Buganda increased its power at the expense of Bunyoro until it became one of the most powerful states in traditional Africa.

What were some of the important similarities between these two kingdoms? Buganda and Bunyoro had about the same level of technology. The hoe was the basic tool in cultivation. In both societies metallurgy was practiced for the manufacture of tools of cultivation as well as of spears, which were the main weapons.

Both societies were monarchical states, each being headed by a king who was the source of all political authority and "owner" of all the land. There was a close connection between political authority and the possession of rights over land, so that when a king granted authority over a territory, this also meant authority over the people living on it. Chiefs fell into two broad categories, with each society having only ten or a dozen great territorial chiefs. Lesser chiefs as well as members of the royal clan and other favorites of the king were granted estates within the boundaries of the great territorial divisions. Every adult male in both societies was expected to participate in military campaigns.

Within the framework of these broad similarities, there were also some important differences between these two states. Originally the Ganda king was little more than *primus inter pares* among clan heads. By the nineteenth century, however, the clan heads had lost most of their powers to the king (or Kabaka, as he is called in Buganda), who had established a supreme position largely through the acquisition of new territory by force. The Kabaka was a despotic, almost absolute ruler against whose abuse of power there were few checks. Only a few positions remained hereditary, and the Kabaka considered himself to be in control of the gods.

Bunyoro had a more complex history, in which there was an overlaying of three ethnic groups: first, the agriculturalists (Iru), then the cattle-keepers (Huma), and finally the present rulers, the Bito, from whom the present Nyoro king, the Mukama, is descended. It seems likely, however, that the "conquest" by the Bito was not through overpowering numbers and large armies, but a kind of infiltration and eventual usurping of the throne of the earlier Chwezi rulers.[2] Although at a later date Bunyoro also expanded her territory through conquest by force (and still later lost much of it again to Buganda), the Mukama of Bunyoro never gained as extensive control over appointments as did the Kabaka. One of the important reasons for this was that the Huma were also to maintain considerable power in entrenched hereditary positions, this being related probably to the nature and extent of the original Bito "conquest." The Mukama of Bunyoro was thus a less powerful king than the Kabaka, and there were more checks on his power. Hereditary positions were more numerous in Bunyoro, and the system of ritual belief was an important buttress to the Mukama's power, whereas the Kabaka's position was largely based on force.

In addition to the differences already mentioned, Buganda and Bunyoro differed also in demographic patterns, environmental conditions, type of economy, and the extent of economic surplus. Buganda had a smaller territory but larger population (and therefore higher density of population) than Bunyoro. The Ganda were more permanently settled than the Nyoro, and they also had a much better system of roads.

The most significant environmental difference between the two societies was that Buganda, on the one hand, had an environment that was far more favorable to the growing of bananas than to pastoralism; most of Bunyoro, on the other hand, was particularly well suited to pastoralism, and although they formed a subsidiary part of the diet, bananas apparently grew less well there than in Buganda.

The Ganda cultivated bananas, a permanent crop which left men almost entirely free for other activities, including especially warfare. The Nyoro practiced shifting cultivation, with millet as their staple, and there was a strong emphasis on pastoralism. Because they herded and helped their wives in cultivation, Nyoro peasants had less time for other activities, including warfare, than had Ganda peasants.

The Ganda had much more than a subsistence economy; they had an abundant and secure food supply, and famine was rare. Moreover, the level of their productivity was increasing during the nineteenth century as they won victories in war against the Nyoro; this success was an important source not only of consumer goods but also of capital goods (wives, slaves, and cattle). By contrast the Nyoro had a subsistence economy, which provided a less abundant and less secure food supply than that of the Ganda.

2. It is probable that the Chwezi and the Huma were not one and the same people, a view that is supported by Nyoro tradition. Both Oliver (1959) and Posnansky (1966) see the Chwezi as the builders of the Bigo site which is the principal archaeological evidence of the establishment in about the fourteenth century of a loosely knit centralized state.

Melvin L. Perlman: Stratification Among Ganda and Nyoro

These similarities and differences, then, provide the opportunity for a controlled comparison of social stratification between these two kingdoms. Following the work of Gerhard Lenski (1966), I view the field of social stratification in terms of the distributive process in human societies. Similarly, I accept his definition of a class as "an aggregation of persons in a society who stand in a similar position with respect to some form of power, privilege, or prestige" (pp. 74–75). I also accept his emphasis on the importance of power, and his definition of a power class: "an aggregation of persons in a society who stand in a similar position with respect to force or some specific form of institutionalized power" (p. 75). Also following Lenski, "class," unless otherwise indicated, will hereafter refer to aggregations defined in terms of power, though of course this does not mean that they all *have* power. The major exception to using "class" to refer to a "power class" in this chapter will occur in reference to *ethnic* classes among the Nyoro. As we shall see, power and ethnic classes tended largely to overlap; at least this is true of two of the three Nyoro ethnic classes, for the rulers were of one ethnic class and the agricultural peasants of another. The third ethnic class, the pastoralists, were somewhat more diversified; many of the Nyoro chiefs belonged to this class, but there were also many ordinary herdsmen who were not chiefs.

The systems of social stratification in traditional Ganda and Nyoro societies were similar in a number of ways, which will be noted and summarized later. They were also different in three important ways, which will constitute the three stratification variables of this chapter: X—degree of social inequality; Y—rate of vertical mobility; and Z—degree of class institutionalization (including "class consciousness").

The degree of social inequality (X) simply refers to the range and magnitude of differences in the share of the rewards of society that each class has. The rate of vertical mobility (Y) refers to the ease and rapidity with which individuals move into and out of the most favored positions in society (i.e., both upward and downward). I am particularly concerned with intragenerational mobility—that is, with the ease and rapidity with which persons cross class lines within a single generation. The degree of class institutionalization (Z) refers to the degree to which "the rights and duties of the several classes are firmly embedded in custom and undergirded by a universally accepted ideology which serves to legitimize inequalities" (Lenski, 1966:82). This includes the degree of "class consciousness," which refers to the degree to which those people who occupy a common status in society also share a "consciousness of solidarity, a consciousness that the values and beliefs embodied in the group culture define common rights and duties" (L. A. Fallers, 1959:12).

The following part of this chapter contains a basic descriptive account of the Ganda and Nyoro systems of social stratification, with particular attention to the three stratification variables just mentioned. The description of each society will be separate and will include a discussion of each major class. As I have not done fieldwork in these districts, I have attempted to stay as close as possible to the authorities. I emphasize the traditional period, which means the middle to the latter part of the nineteenth century. Although more detailed data are available on the more recent past, a proper understanding of this recent past (i.e., the modern period) really depends on a better understanding of the more distant past. It is hoped that future studies will analyze the modern period in systematic fashion.

The final part of the chapter compares the Ganda and Nyoro systems of social stratification.

THE GANDA

The King and Other Royalty

With a few exceptions, a Kabaka could marry a woman of any clan. Such alliances were eagerly sought after, for royal fathers-in-law were often rewarded with gifts and office. Moreover, in the next generation, the lineage of the queen mother (Nnamasole) would be even more richly rewarded (L. A. Fallers, 1964: 106–7).

Children of the Kabaka belonged to the clans of their mothers. Thus, there was no royal clan, but only a royal dynasty composed of the sons and grandsons of a ruling king who were called "Princes of the Drum." Ganda princes, however, never formed a privileged class as did the members of the royal clan in Bunyoro (Richards, 1960:47).

More distant descendants of kings were known as "peasant princes" and were ineligible to succeed to the kingship. Their style of life was the same as that of peasants, and they had no special privileges. Nevertheless kings were very reluctant to appoint princes to important chieftainships, which could have been a threat to the ruling king; such reluctance indicates that these "peasant princes" retained a residue of royal eligibility (L. A. Fallers, 1964:69).

Only "Princes of the Drum" were eligible to succeed to the throne. The choice between them was a decision for the Katikiro (prime minister) and two important chiefs (Kasuju and Kimbugwe). Roscoe (1911:189) describes the matter as follows:

> The reigning king generally made his wishes known to the Katikiro and the Kasuju, and his wishes were adhered to, if possible; but if these chiefs thought that there was another prince who would make a better sovereign, they did not hesitate to appoint the latter.

> The question was usually amicably settled by these chiefs; they would call a meeting of the other principal chiefs and tell them of their choice; then, if all the chiefs (amasaza) concurred, no danger arose; but if they differed, there would in all probability be civil war.

Such civil wars seem to have been more frequent in the reigns of the early Kabakas when brothers fought for the throne. Later, princes not chosen were generously compensated with private estates, though not with political authority; but by the early part of the nineteenth century, princes in direct succession to the throne were killed on the accession of a new Kabaka (Richards, 1960:47).

Like the king, the new "queen" (Lubuga),[3] who was a sister of the Kabaka, was also chosen by the Katikiro and two important chiefs (Mugema and Kimbugwe), in this case assisted by the ex-"queen." Roscoe states that although the Ganda accepted the rights of the "queen" and the queen mother (Nnamasole) in their own districts, they had a deeply rooted objection to women rulers. A "queen" has never sat on the throne, and when a prince was too young to govern, it was the Katikiro who was appointed regent. But officially these ladies ranked second only to the king; each also had the title of "Kabaka," held her own courts, and had a certain measure of administrative power (Roscoe, 1911:187, 191, 232, 236–37).

We have already noted the progressive extension of the authority of the Kabaka in the appointment of officials and the concomitant decline in the political importance of descent groups, as well as of royal princes. All the land belonged to the king and he alone could dispose of it. This was the basis of his power to allocate land and authority over the people on it, and in this way, and through gifts of slaves, women, and cattle, he rewarded loyal followers and military heroes, and bound them to himself in a strong central government (L. A. Fallers, 1964:97, 101; Roscoe, 1911:238; Richards, 1960:352).

By the end of the nineteenth century, the Kabaka had acquired complete administrative control over Buganda. He was the source of all legitimate authority; he was the head of a standing army and a regular "navy"; he was the supreme judge in court cases, the head of all the clan authorities, and the recipient of taxes from the whole country, as well as of the largest single share of the spoils of war. The Kabaka was unapproachable; it was impossible, even for a noble, to come into his presence unannounced. Labor was exacted as a demonstration of the king's power over his subjects, and there were ceremonial killings in order to make the king strong. The prosperity and general well-being of the country

---

3. The Ganda term *Lubuga* has usually been translated as "queen," although she was not really a queen in the ordinary sense of this term, for she was not married to the king.

were thought to depend upon him, and the nation looked to its king to maintain the balance between the different pyramids of authority within the kingdom, such as the clan heads, administrative chiefs, military leaders and others (Richards, 1960:45; L. A. Fallers, 1964:112; Richards, 1964:275, 276, 279, 281, 283).

Ganda kings were surrounded by ritual acts of a most complex nature, generally carried out by representatives of one or more of the clans. The ceremonies emphasized the king's despotic powers; they reinvigorated him and secured for him the support of his ancestors. But the Kabaka was not the center of a hierarchical system of ancestor worship. It is clear that the Kabaka thought of himself as controlling the gods. Roscoe makes this explicit (1911:273):

> The worship of the national gods was under the immediate control of the King; their first and principal duty was the protection of the King and the State. Although the King consulted them, sent presents to propitiate them, and followed their instructions, he would, if one of them vexed him, send and loot his temple and estate. He alone in the country dared commit such an act of sacrilege.

Kabaka Mutesa was quite cynical about the cult of the royal spirits, and once had an important shrine destroyed; he is also recorded as having treated the priests very roughly. Kabakas also controlled appointments of men and women to serve in all the national shrines in the country. Mair states that the king consults the gods out of recognition of his responsibility for the general welfare of his people, and that such consultation is on a par with his duty to administer justice (Richards, 1960:43–44; L. A. Fallers, 1964:100–101; Richards, 1964:280; Mair, 1934:242). Mair (1934:242) sums up the position as follows:

> Religious beliefs do not here serve, as among so many primitive peoples, as a mainstay of the political system; the king's supreme authority, upon which the whole system rests, is not derived from any supposed supernatural powers or upon religious functions which only he could perform, but upon a tradition going back to the conquest of the country by his remote ancestor, in which the *lubule* [spirits or gods] have no part.

Everyone in Buganda was involved in dyadic relationships of *both* superordination and subordination; the Kabaka was an exception in that he was the only one who was always in a superordinate relationship to everyone else, including the gods.

Chiefs

Chiefs, here, constitute the king's ministers (*Katikiro* and *Kimbugwe*), the county chiefs and their subordinates (*bakungu*), and the Kabaka's

Melvin L. Perlman: Stratification Among Ganda and Nyoro

appointed officials (*batongole*). The hereditary heads of descent groups (*bataka*), a few of whom were also important chiefs, will be discussed later.

The first Kabaka, Kintu, is said to have established chiefs having territorial jurisdiction, among whom were the county chiefs. By the nineteenth century there were ten counties, usually with three levels of territorial chiefs, all appointed by the Kabaka. At every level the chiefs were ranked; each rank had a name, and often a position had a title in addition to its rank name. Even the ten county chieftainships were ranked in an order of precedence, and it was possible for a man in favor to move up in the hierarchy. Thus there were many gradations of chieftainships, and what mattered was not so much a man's class as his degree or rank, his precise position in the system. The chiefs were not a strongly institutionalized class, for they lacked both a developed subculture and a sense of common identity and interests (Southwold, 1961:9; Richards, 1960:49; M. C. Fallers, 1960:61–63, 64; Wrigley, 1964:19; L. A. Fallers, 1964:177).

Foremost among the chiefs was the Katikiro, who combined two distinct offices, those of prime minister and chief justice. He was an appointed official and his position was clearly never hereditary. Although a king could depose his Katikiro, this actually happened only a few times. All matters of state were taken first to the Katikiro in whom the whole hierarchy culminated. His authority and dignities were almost equal to those of the Kabaka himself. If a chief was suspected of plotting treachery he was tried in the royal council under the presidency of the Katikiro, who did not necessarily decide every case in favor of the king. One of the coveted powers of the Katikiro was his control over the approach of visitors to the king (Roscoe, 1911:234–35; Southwold, 1961:6; Mair, 1934:175, 177, 181, 182; Richards, 1964:275).

The next most important official in the country was the Kimbugwe, whose duties were mainly of a ritual nature, in particular the guardianship of the king's umbilical cord. The latter was called the "Twin" and was supposed to have attached to it the ghost of the afterbirth, of which the Kimbugwe was the guardian and priest. Also his position was not hereditary. By virtue of his office, he was a favorite of the king and was admitted to his presence at all times, and served as an important adviser. Both the Kimbugwe and the Katikiro had estates scattered over the country in each district, upon which no state taxes were levied. They levied their own yearly taxes and thus had private sources of revenue from these estates, in addition to the portion that they received of the taxes from the entire country. Both these high officials were important parties to the decision as to which prince would be made king, and which princess, the "queen" (Roscoe, 1911:189, 191, 235–36, 245; Southwold, 1961:6, 9).

The chiefs who served under the Katikiro performed many functions, the most important being the collection of taxes, adjudication of cases, maintenance of roads, and leadership in war. This last role was eagerly sought by a chief because a successful raiding expedition would bring him favor and promotion. In carrying out their duties to peasants, chiefs protected their men against unjust demands, accompanied them to plead a case on appeal, provided hospitality, and used their good offices to foster the advancement of their most faithful followers (L. A. Fallers, 1964: 107–8, 111; Wrigley, 1964: 19, 21; Richards, 1960: 50; Richards, 1964: 271).

By the latter part of the nineteenth century most of the chieftainships were open to talented men upon appointment by the king. No one was excluded by reason of humble birth, and social aspirations were central to Ganda life. But innate ability was not enough, and the best preparation for chieftainship was service as a page at the court of the king. This "school for chiefs" provided a common background of training for all those who would later serve the king, and when chieftainships were to be distributed, the Kabaka often thought first of his pages (L. A. Fallers, 1964: 69, 107, 170, 171; Wrigley, 1964: 19).

Sons of important persons were sent to be educated at the king's court, and sons of less important persons were sent to the courts of chiefs of differing ranks. But not all the sons of chiefs could move up in the hierarchy, partly because of their numbers; chiefs, through polygyny and through the provision of better diets for their children (especially more meat) were able to produce far more children than peasants were, and to keep them alive. This increased the degree of downward mobility. Leading chiefs and clan heads helped younger agnates gain entrance to the corps of pages, making the corps more accessible to their relatives than to those of the ordinary peasant. However, in the last analysis, promotion depended upon the royal evaluation of a man's performance. The most valued qualities were cleverness and loyalty (Richards, 1960: 66, L. A. Fallers, 1964: 161, 162, 170, 174–75).

Appointment to a particular chiefly position did not assure tenure. It was a competitive system; one chief might accuse another of treachery or incompetence. Meteoric promotions and demotions were common: appointment was revocable at any time. Quick and certain demotion awaited any chief who proved weak or cowardly in a military campaign. Chiefs might also be deposed for failing to attend the king's court. Although the Kabaka could depose a chief summarily, he usually trumped up some charge against him. Even some trifling circumstance might cause the king to put a chief to death. The Mugema, county chief of Busiro, was one of the very few who enjoyed a good deal of political immunity, and whose position was fairly secure (L. A. Fallers, 1964: 6, 96, 109; Wrigley, 1964: 20, 23; Roscoe, 1911: 238, 247, 259, 361–62).

As long as he remained in office, however, a chief had important powers and prerogatives. A county chief and his senior subordinates had

Melvin L. Perlman: Stratification Among Ganda and Nyoro

their own private estates, in which they appointed their own favorites to positions of authority. The most important chiefs could impose the death penalty. A chief could call at will upon the services of his people, who owed allegiance to him, as well as to the Kabaka. Senior chiefs formed an inner council which advised the king (Richards, 1960:49, 50, 53; Richards, 1964:290; Wrigley, 1964:21).

Chiefs could consume few goods and services not available to the peasants, but of course they consumed—and, more importantly, they controlled—larger quantities. They received tribute according to a rather elaborate system; for example, the county chief and his subordinates received 60 percent of the barkcloth collections. Chiefs who distinguished themselves in war received a commensurate share of the spoil. There were no doubt many other ways in which chiefs enriched themselves at the expense of their subjects, including the acceptance of bribes. Chiefs did no directly productive work; their business was leadership, and they enjoyed a political, social, and economic status markedly above the common man (L. A. Fallers, 1964:110, 182; Roscoe, 1911:263–64, 360; Mair, 1934:124, 184, 187; Wrigley, 1964:19).

Clans and Lineages

As we have seen, a few clan heads (*bataka*) were also chiefs, although of the ten county chiefs only one (*Mugema*) was also a clan head. Most clan and lineage heads—at least by the nineteenth century—were not chiefs in the sense described in the previous section, although they were overlords of the people living on their own clan lands. According to tradition, early in the kingdom's development clan heads held major positions of authority, the Kabaka occupying, perhaps, a *primus inter pares* position. Over the centuries there was constant diminution in the power and jurisdiction of clan heads and a corresponding increase of that of the Kabaka. The authority of the clan heads was limited more and more to the domestic affairs of their unilineal descent groups (L. A. Fallers, 1964:2, 89, 91).

Among the most important responsibilities of a clan head was the preservation and proper care of clan burial grounds. He also ruled over the peasants living on his clan land and had jurisdiction in clan courts over cases of succession, marriage, blood feuds, and other disputes between members. In addition, some national shrines were controlled by clan heads. Thus they enjoyed certain prerogatives and great prestige deriving both from their hereditary positions and from their association with the Kabaka. There was even a practice of speaking of the clan head as Kabaka, or, more cautiously, as "being like a Kabaka" (L. A. Fallers, 1964:71–72, 90, 96; Richards, 1960:44, 47).

All clan heads had ceremonial duties at the palace, which tied them to the court of the Kabaka by privileges and responsibilities. Such participation in court functions at the capital, plus the observance of common taboos and the knowledge of a common history, gave each of the thirty-odd clans a sense of unity. For the individual, however, the subclan was much more immediate, and this unit was further divided into lineages and sub lineages (M. C. Fallers, 1960:35, 52, 53).

Each clan, subclan, and lineage had estates on which their members were buried. These clan lands were not in a single compact unit but could be anywhere the Kabaka had allowed them the use of the land. Nor were the villages under clan heads composed entirely of clan members. Anyone could apply to a clan head, as to any other chief or headman, and be given a piece of land to use. Thus, a clan head played two roles: he was an overlord of a particular estate and the head of a scattered community of patrilineal kinsmen. The clans were not ranked in any way, although the members of a clan that had provided a queen mother or a prime minister would derive from that fact a good deal of material benefit and self-satisfaction, as well as a measure of prestige (M. C. Fallers, 1960:52; L. A. Fallers, 1964:72, 89).

Inheritance and succession were among the most important concerns of the clan. In addition to taking the property of the deceased, an heir succeeded to his social and political position. Although an heir had to be chosen from within the clan, there was a wide range of eligible candidates. As there was no birth-order rule it was not at all clear who would inherit. When an important clan head died, people might come from many parts of the country to participate in the decision. It is said that distant collateral inheritance was a good thing because it held the clan together. But no matter who was chosen he could not succeed until confirmed by the Kabaka, who, through his powers of confirming or withholding confirmation, could greatly influence clan leadership. He was head of all the clans and appellate judge in cases of dispute (L. A. Fallers, 1964:89–90, 164, 167; M. C. Fallers, 1960:64).

Palace Officials and Retainers

Kabakas of the seventeenth or eighteenth century started giving land as estates to their own favorites in return for such duties as collecting firewood or barkcloth or performing ritual services. The holders of these estates were known as *batongole*, and their successors have already been discussed under the general category of "Chiefs." Not all such servants of the king, however, were rewarded with large estates and political authority (Richards, 1960:50).

Servants who cannot be classed as chiefs were the palace officials and retainers, who included the king's tax collectors, secret policemen, guards, gatekeepers, cooks, the head of the herds, the head of the pages (and the pages themselves), the organizer of the royal wood supplies, and many other household officials. Many positions were hereditary, in particular clans such as the drummers, the keeper of the sacred fire, the brewer, the executioners, and blacksmiths. In addition, by the latter part of the nineteenth century the Kabaka had in his service a group of carpenters, potters, and smiths who had acquired skills that were still very scarce, and such people had high standing and a considerable measure of political influence (Roscoe, 1911:257; Richards, 1960:53; Nsimbi, 1964:27; Wrigley, 1964:25).

In addition to the king's wives and concubines, the main occupants of the palace were the pages. They came "to seek their fortunes," and formed a pool of eager talent from which the Kabaka, on the basis of personal observation, might choose men to serve him as chiefs and officials. The king's secret police included in particular two close relatives who were permitted to carry their weapons in the king's presence and to stand while they greeted him; they had to be on guard and ready to protect him and his mother at all times. Other secret servants had the duty of finding out what was happening in the country, and of reporting it to the Katikiro, who would take the messenger to the king. The king's chief cook had general control of the food supply for the royal table and had a vast army of cooks working under him. Gatekeepers had the right to detain even a chief, who then had to redeem himself, and in the same way they took a toll from each load of goods that was brought to the king either as tribute or as a present. Common to all these palace officials and retainers was the enjoyment of considerable prestige; they also had many opportunities for enrichment (especially the tax collectors) and for promotion (L. A. Fallers, 1964:106–7, 110; Roscoe, 1911:204–5, 206, 208–9; Wrigley, 1964:21).

Magico-Religious Specialists

It is difficult to reconstruct Ganda religious and magical practices, but in any case these most probably did not play a very prominent role and were quite remote from the working of the dominant political structure of nineteenth century Buganda (M. C. Fallers, 1960:69; Mair, 1934:242). There is considerable ambiguity as to which magico-religious specialists there were in traditional Buganda. It seems likely that the roles to be mentioned overlapped to some extent, and therefore they should not be distinguished too sharply. At any rate, according to Roscoe, among the most powerful, feared, and respected were the medicine men, of whom he writes:

> Medicine-men . . . , though not definitely connected with the temples and the gods, were yet regarded as belonging to the religious class in the country; they formed a most powerful body, and were greatly feared.

The priests and the mediums had but little power in comparison with the medicine-men. (1911:277)

They [the medicine men] were essential to all classes alike, and were feared by all; even priests and mediums paid them the greatest respect. (1911:278)

The major duties of the priests were in connection with the temples and shrines. The national shrines of major gods were large-scale affairs, and estates provided at least these important centers with economic support. A priest's son could inherit his father's office, but the clan had the right to reject him and appoint some other member of the clan if they had reason for so doing. In addition to the important centers, there were many local religious practitioners, most being part-time specialists (L. A. Fallers, 1964: 103; Roscoe, 1911: 296).

Mediums were said to have been chosen by spiritual intervention. A man or woman was suddenly possessed by spirits (*balubaale*) and began to utter secrets and to predict future events. *Balubaale* were spirits of people who were "known" to have had supernatural powers in their lifetime and who after death were consulted through their mediums. The major duty of a medium was to be the mouthpiece of the spirit whom he represented.

Another group of specialists were the sorcerers, who used magic for inflicting injury. Sorcery was considered to be an extremely common practice in the past, and sorcerers were greatly feared (M. C. Fallers, 1960: 69, 70; Roscoe, 1911: 274).

Peasants

The peasants (*bakopi*) were the undistinguished ordinary people who were *not* something else. They may be said to have constituted a general category, not a strongly institutionalized class; social and economic ties among the Ganda were vertical rather than horizontal. The category *peasant* included the vast majority who lived by the produce of small agricultural holdings, as well as others such as fishermen and barkcloth makers. These were the common people who did manual labor. In peacetime they performed all manner of tasks for their chief (especially building and maintaining his house and enclosures, and road-making); in war they fought under his command (L. A. Fallers, 1964: 68, 82; Wrigley, 1964: 21, 22).

These activities demanded a very great deal of labor from the peasants (L. A. Fallers, 1964: 83–84), and the sanctions for failure to work were severe. Roscoe provides the following description, for example, of how labor for clearing roads at the capital was provided:

This office [overseer for road-making] was always eagerly desired by the chiefs because there was profit to be made from it. The man appointed

Melvin L. Perlman: Stratification Among Ganda and Nyoro

could sublet it if he was a chief, and yet keep the emoluments from the office for himself. Every person called to do any State-work had to pay the overseer a sum of cowry-shells; during King Suna's reign the amount demanded was ten cowry-shells, in later times this was augmented to one hundred. If the workman had not the sum to hand, he was required to give something else, such as a barkcloth, or an equivalent in food or beer. Until this had been paid, no workman was allowed to begin his work, but unless he made a start within a given time, he was fined. If he was unable to obtain the amount by barter, or to borrow it, and still delayed making a start, his wife, or some other member of his family, would be taken as hostage, until he should bring the necessary sum; the woman or child thus taken would be required to work for the chief during the time of detention. This same custom held good with all State-labour. After the task had been begun, the workers had to bring food and beer from time to time for the overseer .... Any person who passed along a road, while it was being repaired, might be seized by the workmen, and forced to work for a time, before he was permitted to continue his way. (1911:241–43)

Besides these obligations, peasants had to provide tribute consisting of food, beer, firewood, barkcloth, and other products for their chiefs. And in addition there was an elaborate tax system organized at the capital which was quite unlike the casual tribute given to rulers in neighboring societies. The annual levy "included one in every twenty head of livestock, a vessel of simsim, a vessel of white termites and a bark-cloth from each homestead" (M. C. Fallers, 1960:51; Richards, 1960:49; L. A. Fallers, 1964:109–10).

In return for his services and tribute, a peasant received a piece of land allocated by the chief or by a subordinate village headman. He had reasonable security of tenure on his land as long as he gave tribute, labor, and military service to his overlord. But life and property were not always safe from the power of the king:

He [Kabaka Mutesa] had power of life and death over his people and maintained his authority by severe and brutal punishments, such as the destruction of houses and property, the selling of his subjects into slavery, mutilation, burning offenders alive or hacking them to pieces. (Richards, 1960:45)

Sometimes innocent people were caught and used as sacrifices. Roscoe describes the king's executioners in the following terms:

The party conducting these prisoners was one to be avoided; no sooner did they leave the royal presence, than they began to loot and plunder wherever they went. If they caught anyone, he would be added to the number of their victims, unless he promised them a reward for being set free; women would be enslaved, and property plundered on all sides. (1911:332)

Warriors also helped themselves to anything they found on route, even in their own country (Richards, 1964:271; M. C. Fallers, 1960:36; Wrigley, 1964:23; Roscoe, 1911:351).

Indeed, the ordinary peasant's share of the rewards of society was often meager. Chiefs took a "large portion" of any compensation paid for injuries such as theft or adultery, the rest going to the injured man (Mair, 1934:133). Mair states further that

> In the case of a very poor man, the injured party simply plundered his house and took anything they could find to the chief, who took out his share and left them (the injured man and the relatives who had helped him) to divide the rest. (1934:133)

There was some hospitality due from chief to peasant, but entertaining tended to be limited to favorites or to important clients. Moreover, peasants owed extreme deference and respect to their overlord, and they accepted punishment, such as beating, from him. They were his men and they had no redress from his demands except by moving to serve another lord. However, even if a peasant suffered at the hands of his overlord, it was at the same time useful to have a powerful patron whose clients were less likely to be seized by the king's executioners for human sacrifice, and more likely to be freed quickly from the stocks. It was only through war that the ordinary peasant—while remaining a peasant—had some opportunity to raise his standard of living. The booty was rather widely shared. Every warrior who had shown exceptional bravery was rewarded with either women or cattle, and peasants managed to hide things for themselves that were never accounted for to their chiefs (Richards, 1964:270, 271, 272; Richards, 1960:51; L. A. Fallers, 1964:112; Roscoe, 1911:360).

If most peasants did not have slaves to serve them, at least they had a secure food supply as well as the opportunity of moving up in the system to some position of authority. Service in the household of a local chief, or bravery in the war, could be the beginning of an important career. Although every young man aspired to a career in the service of the king, it has been pointed out that the ordinary peasant had less chance of gaining entrance to the corps of pages at the palace than did the son of a chief or a clan head. Nevertheless, it could and did happen that the sons of ordinary peasants attained important positions of authority, even at the higher levels. Opportunities for advancement depended, among other things, on such qualities as deference, loyalty, and efficiency. "The art of being

Melvin L. Perlman: Stratification Among Ganda and Nyoro

ruled," involving ostentatious humility, cleverly turned compliments, and the like, was particularly important (L. A. Fallers, 1964:6, 161, 175, 176; Mair, 1934:195; Roscoe, 1911:357; Richards, 1964:273; and cf. Wittfogel, 1957:364, quoted in Lenski, 1966:184).

Slaves

Slaves, mainly women and young boys, were almost all captives in war. Some were at the capital, and others were given to the temples and worked under the direction of the mediums. Some of the women slaves were given to priests in marriage; their children "were free to marry into any clan outside the temple area at will" (Roscoe, 1911:300).

The position of slaves in the households of chiefs did not really differ much from that of the chief's Ganda followers except that, lacking kinsmen, they were rather more completely in his power. Slaves were supposed to have been debarred from becoming chiefs, but this does not seem to have prevented at least some of them from attaining important government posts. Some chiefs and clan heads, afraid to send their own children to the king's court because of the Kabaka's fierceness, instead sent servants, who might be slaves and who were presented as their own children. Some of them served the Kabaka well and were rewarded with chieftainships (Wrigley, 1964:21; Mair, 1934:33; L. A. Fallers, 1964:176).

Still other slaves were found in the households of ordinary peasants who had received them as rewards for bravery in war. The essential difference between them and the rest of the household lay simply in the fact that they were not members of the clan or its head. It is true that slaves were specifically allotted certain duties, but by and large they shared in the ordinary life of the household and were described by the head as "his children" (Mair, 1934:32). Mair describes their position as follows:

> Captured women were taken at once as wives, and except that they had no relatives to go to in case of ill-treatment or their husband's death their different status ceased to have much importance. Girls might be married into their master's family or might marry other slaves; the latter on marriage set up their own houses, described themselves as members of their master's clan, and observed its practices. They differed from "free men" in that they could not leave him and that they could not inherit from a real member of the clan. (1934:33)

> The position of slave-women was different, since they had no relatives to go to, and they seem to have been obliged to marry any member of the clan who wished to take them. One of them might be claimed by the chief. The eldest son and the eldest son of a sister had each a definite claim to a slave who was still a virgin. (1934:219–20)

The lives of slaves were thus not very different from the lives of ordinary peasants, except where they were affected by the lack of kinsmen, and this did involve certain disabilities.

Social Inequality, Vertical Mobility, and Class Institutionalization

There was no conception of solidary classes or status groups, and little if any "class consciousness" in traditional Buganda. Fallers writes of the essential "classlessness" of nineteenth-century Buganda in the sense of the absence of cohesive and clearly delineated strata, but not, of course, in the sense of egalitarianism. Indeed, precedence was expressed in every aspect of Ganda life. It was the dyadic conception of inequality that was important in Buganda; the traditional view was of men arranged simply in dyadic relationships of superordination and subordination (L. A. Fallers, 1964:70, 163; Richards, 1964:273).

All those who occupied positions of authority clearly had "objective" political and economic advantages. "Cultural differentiation was traditionally limited to differential possession of material wealth and to . . . differences in courtliness of manners" (L. A. Fallers 1964:70). But even the latter could be learned by a clever peasant. All the necessities of high status could easily be acquired within a single generation, and there was a strong emphasis on ambition and advancement (L. A. Fallers 1964:163, 177). Wrigley describes the situation in the following terms:

> It was a society in which there was strongly marked differentiation of wealth and status but at the same time something like equality of opportunity. Ambition was general and unlimited, for no position in the state, except the supreme power, was in principle out of reach of the humblest youth. Inequality seemed natural to the Buganda; it aroused envy but not resentment; and this attitude reflected not (as in most of the neighbouring kingdoms) passive acceptance of immutable inferior status, but the knowledge that advancement was open to any clever and energetic man. (1964:20)

The Ganda had no developed notion of class—no notion that only chiefs' sons should become chiefs. Chiefs and clan heads were able, however, to give an added push to their abler progeny as well as to cushion the descent of their less gifted heirs. Mobility based on achievement was therefore not completely free; the talented poor could not always compete successfully in the general competition to get to the top because vacant positions were not always available. And, as already noted, the burden of downward mobility was increased by the higher reproduction rate of chiefs than of peasants. Thus, those men already in positions of authority were able to exert some measure of control over recruitment to appointive offices, especially at the higher levels (L. A. Fallers, 1964:162, 169, 176).

Melvin L. Perlman: Stratification Among Ganda and Nyoro

Nevertheless, a clever peasant could "rise in chieftainship" (*kuku-lakulana mu bwami*) by "attaching himself in loyal dependence to a superior" (*kusenga*), and faithful service was rewarded by at least the opportunity to acquire wealth and glory (L. A. Fallers, 1964:69, 74). Aspiration to upward social mobility was central to Ganda life, and most positions of substantial power were open to the talented man through appointment by the Kabaka. Buganda was a fluid society and became even more so through the extension of the authority of the Kabaka in the appointment of officials. Rising to a position of influence became ever easier and more acceptable in the course of the nineteenth century. Some positions were ascribed and some were achieved. But the historical trend seems to have been for the former to develop into the latter. And even those positions that were called "hereditary" were "in fact filled by selection from among quite wide ranges of eligible persons" (L. A. Fallers, 1964:76, 101, 159, 164, 176).

Although ability and diligence were quickly rewarded, failure was also quickly punished. Rapid promotion and demotion were common. There was a fierce competition for posts. To quote Richards:

> Each office holder, or set of office holders, struggled for the favour of the king by bravery in war, ingratiating behaviour to the monarch, the slandering of rivals, and the placing of kinsmen, clients or other loyal supporters in key positions at court. (1964:283–84)

The authorities concur in their emphasis on mobility in Buganda. Fallers states that there was mobility "on a very substantial scale" (1964:159). Richards writes that "it was a mobile system with constant chances of promotion from office to office" (1960:52). Mair describes the Ganda political system as "a social ladder which every man of ambition might hope to climb" (1934:173), and Wrigley describes the whole structure as "extremely fluid" (L. A. Fallers, 1964:110, 113, 121, 174; Wrigley, 1964:20; Richards, 1964:277).

THE NYORO

The King and other Royalty

The king and the princes were (and still are) members of the royal Bito clan of Nilotic origin; however, as kings frequently married Huma women, they were often of Huma descent on their mother's side. With one or two exceptions the king could take his wives from any of the clans, and a son of any of these women was eligible to succeed him. There was no fixed rule of succession; any son of a king could succeed except the eldest. Which one did depended upon the support he could command in killing whichever of his brothers was his rival for the throne (Beattie, 1960b: 105; 1964: 27, 32; 1960a: 27).

Succession to the kingship was based therefore upon a combination of ascribed and achieved factors. Only sons (excluding the eldest) of the king were eligible, but within this group personal attributes played an important role. For one thing, the son who could gain the favor of his father probably had some advantage, as Roscoe states that most of the chiefs would stand by this prince (1923: 123).

Even more important (at least when there was a succession war) were the political skill and military ability with which a prince could command support and eventually prove himself victorious in battle. It is important to note that the structure permitted a prince of strong personality or with a strong following to challenge even the favored son of his father, and we may assume that the considerable powers of the kingship provided sufficient motivation to a strong personality (if one existed) to fight for it.

It may be supposed therefore that where no battle took place, this itself was an acknowledgment of the strength and support of the late king's favorite son, and that any battles were probably between the strongest personalities, or those with the strongest following. Powerful backing may have been a reflection of the strength of a prince's mother's clan, as well as of the strength of his own personality.

Within the group of eligible princes the achievement factor was strong in Bunyoro as well as Buganda, where, at least in the nineteenth century, the highest chiefs virtually appointed the prince they thought most suitable. In any event, the importance of the element of achievement vis-à-vis ascription in determining who would be king was considerable for both the Ganda and the Nyoro, and they were more alike in this respect than might be supposed.

Members of the Bito clan, who had close and real genealogical links with the Mukama, were accorded special prestige, and they regarded themselves as a distinctive hereditary aristocracy. They were considered (and considered themselves) as being "born to rule" and as quite different from ordinary people. The most important Bito received large estates from the Mukama; they were thus important territorial chiefs. They were a wealthy and powerful group, claiming special privileges and in certain contexts they acted as a group under the authority of their head, the *Okwiri*, who was the Mukama's "official brother." Traditionally he was the eldest son of the late king and was formally appointed by the new Mukama after his accession (Beattie, 1960a: 25, 29–30).

The Mukama's "official sister," the *Kalyota*, was appointed as head of the Bito women or princesses. These royal ladies ruled as chiefs over areas allotted to them. Formerly they were not allowed to marry or bear

Melvin L. Perlman: Stratification Among Ganda and Nyoro

children in order to preserve the unity and exclusiveness of the king's lineage. The Kalyota was the chief lady in the land, a female counterpart of the king. She ruled as a kind of chief, and her appointment to office included the handing over to her of certain regalia. Also the king's mother had a position of considerable power and ritual significance; she had her own court and ruled her own estates. Roscoe states that she, as well as the Kalyota, had the power of life and death over the people on their respective estates (Beattie, 1960a: 30–31; Roscoe, 1923: 142, 147).

The king was, of course, the most important personage in the country. He was conceived of as being the "owner" or the "master" of all the land, as well as of everything on it, including especially the cattle and the people. Everyone had to give tribute to the king in the form of women, cattle, beer, and grain. At the same time, however, the Mukama was the center of an important exchange system. He gave feasts at frequent intervals, including one great yearly feast, and some of his special praise-names stress his magnanimity (Beattie, 1964: 31, 1960a: 34, 40; Roscoe, 1923: 51).

All political authority was seen as deriving from the Mukama; it was held subject to his approval, signified in a ceremony of "milk-drinking," which every candidate for political office had to undergo. Sometimes this meant little more than confirmation of the heir (as some chiefships tended to become hereditary), or confirmation of a chief's nomination but this ceremony was indispensable. Chiefships could be withdrawn at any time by the king, and sometimes they were, although his powers over the appointment and dismissal of chiefs were apparently not so great as British administrators later thought them to be (Beattie, 1960b: 103, 114; 1964: 31, and 1960a: 33, see also Roscoe, 1923: 54 and 1915: 20).

The Mukama was the supreme judge of the land and had the power of life and death over his subjects. At one time the poison ordeal was administered by chiefs as well as by the king, but it was later reserved to the king's court because too many people were being killed by this means (Roscoe, 1923: 8, 61, 70).

The Mukama's superiority to and difference from other people was expressed in royal ritual, which also stressed the identity between his physical condition and actions and the well-being of the whole kingdom. The Mukama was first and foremost a ruler, and the ritual surrounding him is best understood as a symbolic expression of his political preeminence and power. He was not a priest nor a rainmaker, though he had his priests and rainmakers. His importance and uniqueness were, however, expressed in the idiom of "divine kingship," as he was mystically identified with his kingdom. The king possessed a ritual potency, some of which he gave away when he delegated authority; even more, the grant of a crown to a chief implied the bestowal of some part of the ritual potency of the kingship itself (Beattie 1960a: 26–27; 1964: 30, 33–34).

Chiefs

Nyoro chiefs fell into two broad categories. There were probably no more than a dozen or so great chiefs who possessed political authority over definite named territories; most of them were of Bito or Huma origin, though it is probable that the king sometimes appointed an Iru of agricultural origin even to such a high position. Lesser chiefs did not fall into distinct categories, but may be regarded as having had positions on a graduated scale of importance. A chief's position on this scale depended upon the size of his territory, the number of his dependents, and the closeness of his relationship with the Mukama. Chiefships were not restricted to any one of the three clearly distinguished classes of persons, and there were no doubt a larger proportion of Iru among the lesser chiefs than among the great chiefs (Beattie, 1960b:104 and 1959:135; Roscoe, 1923:53, 56).

It is not clear from the literature exactly to what extent chiefships were hereditary, and this is probably a reflection of the absence of any fixed rule. It is worth quoting the authorities. Beattie writes:

> Advised by his formal and informal counsellors, he [the king] appointed his territorial chiefs to office, and their authority, down to the lowest level, had to be confirmed by him personally. Traditionally, political office was not thought of as hereditary, though it often tended to become so. A chiefship could be taken away by the king at any time, but often it would be passed on to the original chief's heir. Chiefship, then, was not just a formal administrative office; rather, it was a private and personal (though conditional) possession, which like any other private property was thought of as hereditable. (1960a:36)

> The usual ground (apart from inheritance) for appointment to a chieftainship was that the recipient had either by service or by gift earned the Mukama's approbation. (1960b:104)

Writing of the great chiefs, Roscoe states that "it was customary" for a son to succeed; and in the same paragraph he says that the king might, "if he wished," appoint someone else, but that this "was very seldom done" (1923:54).

It would appear, therefore, that although the king had the right to, and sometimes did, replace an heir with a man of his own choice, often (perhaps in most cases) he merely confirmed the heir; and unless he was very inept, probably the heir was basically secure in his position so long as he served well, remained loyal, and fostered a close personal relationship with and paid homage to the king, especially through generosity and servility. Furthermore, it was possible both to confirm many heirs and to appoint new chiefs so long as Bunyoro's territory was expanding, as it presumably was during the early part of its history. In the nineteenth century, new minor chieftainships were created within the boundaries of the large provinces. There was thus some proliferation of minor estates, which provided opportunities for mobility in the system. In any event, unlike the kings of Buganda, there is no evidence that Nyoro kings gradually replaced hereditary positions with their own appointees in order to increase their own power, though it may be supposed that a strong Mukama may have done so occasionally.

Chiefs received homage and tribute similar to that paid to the king (but on a much smaller scale), and within their areas they were accorded high prestige. This was partly because the power that had been delegated to them was not only political but also ritual. This was particularly true of those to whom the king had granted a "crown," which was the highest gift that the king could bestow. It was awarded only to those who had achieved conspicuous military success, or who had otherwise served with particular distinction. Crown wearers were thus specially honored chiefs who had been granted high dignity and prestige; they were also among the king's most influential advisers. Crowns were hereditary, although an heir would have to be confirmed in his succession by the king (Beattie, 1964:28, 33–34, and 1959:142).

The grant of a chiefship was essentially the bestowal of rights over a particular territory and the people on it. From these people the chief received tribute, a share of which he had to pass on to the king. At the same time it was expected that a chief should "enjoy the profits" of his estate, and thus it may be supposed that chiefs, especially the great chiefs, lived very well (Beattie, 1960a:37).

Palace Officials and Retainers

The king maintained a large body of palace officials, the two most important categories of which were those concerned with customary affairs and those who acted as his close unofficial advisers. Beattie writes that the first of these two categories

> . . . comprised all those who were formally responsible for the performance of ritual and domestic functions in the palace and for the custody of items of the extensive royal regalia. Many of these offices were and still are vested in particular clans, and their occupants often enjoyed close personal contact with the Mukama. . . . Even today it is sometimes said that [his close unofficial advisers] who have no place in the official chiefly hierarchy, are "nearer to the Mukama" than many of his officially appointed chiefs and advisers. (1960b:102–3)

The first category includes a considerable number of specialists such as water carriers, fuel-gatherers and fire-keepers, gatekeepers, cooks, brewers, herdsmen, bodyguards, pages, musicians, medicine men, regalia keepers, custodians of royal graves, "putters-on" of the royal crowns, potters, barkcloth makers, bath attendants, caretakers, and others. The more important ones had several assistants. Particularly significant for our purposes were the opportunities that these people had for upward mobility, especially to the class of minor chiefs, as they might be rewarded for personal service with a small chiefdom. Being the personal servant or adviser to the king carried a good deal of prestige, and, moreover, many of these officials had considerable political influence (Beattie, 1960b: 102–3, and 1960a: 31; Roscoe, 1923: 83–86).

Magico-Religious Specialists

Magico-religious specialists included rainmakers; "medicine men" or diviners; guardians of sacred snakes; hill, pool, and well spirits; sorcerers; and male and female priests or mediums, who were probably the most important. According to Roscoe the office of priest was "always hereditary." Beattie, however, doubts that priests were hereditary and says that they were certainly not "always" hereditary (personal communication). Each clan or lineage is said to have been associated with one or other of the 19 Chwezi spirits, and had its own priests and mediums.

Writing of one of "the higher class of medicine men," Roscoe states:

> So great was the power and fame of this man that no one under any circumstances dared to rob him or plunder his fields. Even the hostile Baganda stood in awe of him, and when they raided the country left his property untouched. (1923:38)

And some indication of the importance of rainmakers can be obtained from the following passage from Roscoe:

> In recognition of their services they had the right to levy certain taxes. They could demand twenty-five cowry-shells from each household and when harvest came they took toll of two heads of maize from each field. This toll of maize was seldom collected by a rain-maker in person, but by a deputy whom he appointed and who was repaid by exemption from paying the tax himself. If the people refused to pay the rain-maker's tax, he would threaten to send heavy rain, wind, or hail to destroy the crops, and the people, who stood in great awe of him, were glad to pay and to do anything they could to keep in his favour (1923:28)

These specialists appear to have been well paid for their services, and if they acquired great reputations they were no doubt paid very handsomely (as they are today), and were thus able to make large profits (Roscoe, 1923, Chap. III; Taylor, 1962:37–38; Beattie, 1960a:71).

Clans and Lineages

We have already noted that many of the palace offices were hereditarily vested in many of the clans, and represented them, and that this was a

Melvin L. Perlman: Stratification Among Ganda and Nyoro

source of prestige as well as opportunity for upward mobility. A somewhat similar source of prestige and opportunity was the tradition of polygyny among Nyoro kings. Any clan from which the king chose a wife was honored and acquired prestige. Furthermore, a girl given to the Mukama might possibly become the mother of the next king, and if so her whole clan would acquire extremely high prestige in the kingdom, as well as being rewarded by offices and estates (Beattie, 1964:32).

Although nowadays there is virtually no corporate lineage action above the level of the minimal descent group of a father and his adult sons, it seems that in the past there was some corporate action for a larger group of agnates. Also it appears that lineages were associated with particular territories and that almost all the men in any particular settlement were related by descent in the male line from a common ancestor. Of these matters Beattie writes:

> It seems, then, that organized agnatic lineages were dominant on particular [settlement areas]. Every such group had its head, . . . the senior or the most important member of the [lineage]. He represented the [settlement area] in its relations with other [settlement areas] and with the Mukama's fief-holding chiefs, and he was, in particular, responsible for the allocation of land for cultivation. He officiated in the ceremony of propitiation . . . of the paternal ancestors of the group. He claimed the right to settle disputes between members of the group and between members and their wives. No member of the [lineage] could marry without his approval, and he received one beast from the bridewealth paid for a female member of the group. (1957:323)

Thus, clan and lineage heads were men of considerable importance, and this was reinforced and expressed in the custom of ceremonial validation of their authority by the Mukama (Beattie, 1960b:100, 103, and 1960a: 49).

Ethnic Classes and Commoners

The three ethnic classes of rulers (Bito), cattle-keepers (Huma), and peasants (Iru) have always been clearly distinguished and even stressed in Bunyoro. Yet there is little of the rigid, castelike discrimination described for the neighboring kingdom of Ankole, apart from the exclusiveness of the Mukama and his lineage; even that exclusiveness was modified because, as kings frequently married Huma women, their offspring (i.e., future kings) were often of Huma descent on their mother's side. Moreover, it has always been at least theoretically possible for able peasants "to rise to the highest positions in the state" (Beattie, 1959:135, and 1960b:100–101, 105).

We have already discussed the Bito rulers. The Huma pastoralists were not *ipso facto* rulers, but herdsmen who had attached themselves to great chiefs. They have always regarded themselves as superior to Iru; they claimed and were accorded high prestige, and often became chiefs. Regarding the position of the Huma, Beattie writes:

> The fact that the Huma in Bunyoro lack the high political (as opposed to social) status accorded to the Hima in Ankole may, perhaps, be associated with the fact that the king of Ankole, unlike the king of Bunyoro, is himself a Hima and so is able to provide a symbol and focus for Hima political ascendancy in his country. (1960b:105)

Clearly there were differences among the Huma themselves, though these were mainly correlated with the distinction between chiefs and nonchiefs. Every chief owned cattle, though not all cattle owners were chiefs. If a pastoralist did not possess cows of his own, then he attached himself to a chief for whom he served as a herder. A cattle owner would always employ a Huma to herd his cows, though an Iru might herd sheep and goats. A Huma herder might own a few cows, whereas a great chief had large herds which he would divide into smaller herds of one hundred each. It is said that originally the Huma (and Bito) did not marry the Iru. In the course of time, however, some of the Iru became wealthy, and then the daughter of a poor herdsman "would be glad to exchange a life of poverty and shortage of milk for the more luxurious existence she would lead with such a husband" (Roscoe, 1923:176–78, 200).

Nyoro say that just as the Bito are "born to rule" the Iru are "born to be ruled" (Beattie, 1959:135). In spite of this belief (which has its origins in the complex history of the people), the conditions under which Nyoro peasants lived do not appear to have been oppressive, although peasants were despised by the pastoralists. The following passages from Roscoe are particularly relevant:

> [The agricultural people] were despised by the pastoral people, not because of their poverty, but because of their mode of life, for, in the eyes of a cow-man, anyone who ate vegetable food and cultivated the land, or worked at anything not connected with the cows, was low and mean. The serfs, however, were not slaves, for they were not bound to particular chiefs; they were free to move to other parts of the country and serve other chiefs without giving their former masters any indication of their intentions; nor indeed was a man bound to apply for permission to the chief in whose territory he meant to settle, though as a rule, he would present himself to his new chief and tell him of his desire to serve him. He was sure of a welcome from the chief, to whom each serf meant another labourer and an addition to his wealth, for besides doing building for him and perhaps herding his goats and sheep, each self paid him a

yearly tribute of grain and beer; this was not a compulsory tax but was regarded as a voluntary return to the chief for the land occupied (1923 :9–10)

> Peasants from generosity generally paid much more grain, without any demand being made by the chief for even the basketful to which he was entitled. (1915:26)

Although Roscoe has surely exaggerated where he implies that tribute was not compulsory but voluntary, these passages reveal the importance of the reciprocal gift-exchange aspect of the relationship between a chief and the people on his land. Beattie also emphasizes the mutual inter-dependence between ruler and ruled, and he notes that not only the king but also the chiefs were centers of systems of exchange. Although exactions for tribute, labor, and military service fell ultimately on the peasants, in return they looked for protection and security from their chiefs (Beattie, 1964: 31, and 1960b: 103–4). We may assume, therefore, that whatever the precise nature of the demands made on the peasants, they were probably not excessive nor enforced with too great zeal. It was very important that peasants had the right to move to other areas, which they would do if a chief became oppressive, and no doubt this sometimes happened. The Nyoro peasant, whose main crop was millet (which had to be replanted each year), could move to a new area more easily than could the Ganda peasant, whose major food source was the relatively permanent banana plantation.

Slaves

There is very little information available about the position of slaves among the Nyoro. Roscoe mentions them only a few times and all the important points he makes are contained in the following single paragraph:

> The possession of real slaves was, however, universal throughout the country, for even the poorest man night capture one or more during some raid or battle and afterwards be permitted by the leader to keep one. The wealthy people bought slaves when they needed them and a man's heir inherited his slaves along with the other property. Domestic slaves were regarded as superior to those who were used as laborers, and the domestic slaves whom a man inherited were regarded almost as members of his family and were not sold. A man might even marry a slave woman, and if she bore him a child she became free and was accepted by his clan, though her children might only inherit his property if he had no child by any other wife. The ordinary slaves, especially those who had been captured in battle, were bought and sold like cattle, and a man might kill a slave just as he might kill one of his cows and no one would question his action. (1923:11)

The position of "domestic slaves" as described by Roscoe seems not unlike that discussed previously for the Ganda. And although Roscoe makes a distinction between "domestic slaves" and "ordinary slaves" who were bought and sold, it may be assumed that once the latter were inherited they became, in effect, "domestic slaves."

Social Inequality, Vertical Mobility, and Class Institutionalization

One broad type of inequality was, of course, that based on the three different ethnic groups, the ruling Bito, the cattle-keeping Huma, and the agricultural Iru. In this sense Bunyoro was a strongly stratified society, the gap between the ruling Bito and the ordinary Iru being strongly marked and universally recognized (Beattie, 1964:30).

Bito interests have often conflicted with those of the people as a whole. These class differences were largely correlated with political power and wealth, but not entirely so because it was possible for a peasant to rise in the political hierarchy. In any event, the other main type of inequality was the distinction between the rulers and the ruled. Notions of superordination and subordination, of power and authority, especially characteristic of the political sphere, are ubiquitous and pervade the whole field of social relations (Beattie, 1960a:9, 30, and 1959:136). Beattie writes:

> . . . the idea that people occupy different social statuses, and that some kinds of people are "above" others, was and still is ubiquitous in Bunyoro . . . Most Banyoro see it as right and proper that some people should be "above" others, and the ruled see nothing to resent in this state of affairs. (1959:135)

These inequalities were not categorical, however. Several institutions bridged the gap and emphasized especially that the king was ruler and leader of all the Nyoro, not just his own group, the Bito (Beattie, 1964:29–32). One important mitigating factor was the very strong emphasis on redistribution; a reasonable share of the economic surplus, such as it was, certainly made life much more bearable for the low-prestige Iru than it otherwise would have been. Furthermore, it seems unlikely that the demands of most chiefs were either excessive or oppressive.

Political posts often tended to become hereditary, although the king had to confirm an heir in office. This means that opportunities for upward mobility based on achievement among the ordinary peasants were relatively limited. This is not to say that peasants had no opportunities at all; theoretically they could rise even to the highest positions in the state, and certainly had an even greater chance at the lower levels. Furthermore, a man could get a palace post, and then he had a fair opportunity of moving up to a minor chieftainship. Indeed, Beattie specifically states that "any person could attach himself to the court and might achieve high office regardless of his hereditary standing" (1960a:41). It was also possible for a man to move up within his own descent group, and clan and lineage heads had positions of some importance.

Nevertheless, there is no evidence that any considerable number of peasants ever attained political offices; and even when they did, such positions tended to become hereditary, thus further decreasing the chances of an able peasant of humble birth. Some positions of magico-religious specialists were probably hereditary. Finally, it seems a justifiable assumption that, as in Buganda, some downward mobility was inevitable because chiefs had more sons than there were posts available.

COMPARISON BY CLASSES

Having described the traditional system of stratification separately for each society, I now proceed to compare them briefly. First I will specifically compare each class, with particular attention to the three stratification variables. Then I will point out some broad similarities between the two societies as well as summarize the major differences, again by reference to the three stratification variables: degree of social inequality (X), rate of vertical mobility (Y), and degree of class institutionalization (Z).

The King and Other Royalty

In both societies, the king was considered the "owner" of all the land and everything on it, and he was the supreme judge in court cases. Both kings had the power of life and death over their subjects, though the Kabaka of Buganda appears to have used this power much more frequently than the Mukama of Bunyoro. Both kings obtained considerable wealth from their subjects, but again the Kabaka no doubt received and retained for his use much more than the Mukama. This was the result of a number of factors; the Kabaka imposed specific and relatively heavy taxes; his population was larger; he was more successful in war; he was less magnanimous than the Mukama, at least according to tradition; and the Ganda economy provided a more abundant food supply. The Kabaka was head of all the clans and had an important influence over appointments within them, whereas this was not true of the Mukama. Although both kings were said to be the source of all political authority, in Bunyoro this sometimes meant little more than confirmation of an heir, whereas the Kabaka attained extreme powers of appointment.

Both kings were surrounded by a great deal of ritual, but in Buganda the ritual act of killing men to make the king strong was considerably more frequent. Moreover, in Buganda, ritual ceremonies emphasized the king's despotic powers, and it is clear that the Kabaka was believed to control the gods. If one of the gods vexed him he might loot his temple and estate. There is no evidence that this ever happened in Bunyoro, where the less powerful Mukama clearly needed the support of religious beliefs more than did the Kabaka.

In both societies the kingship was restricted to the son of a king, though there was no fixed rule of succession. Although some kings were killed in office in both societies, there was very little mobility into or out of the position of king in either society.

The highest royal women—the king's sister and his mother—were given considerable and similar powers in both societies. The position of other royalty, however, was quite different. In Buganda there was no royal clan (as there was in Bunyoro), but only a royal dynasty, as children of the Kabaka belonged to the clans of their mothers. This is one reason why royalty as a class was less institutionalized in Buganda than in Bunyoro. Moreover, Ganda princes never formed a privileged class as did the members of the royal Bito clan in Bunyoro. Bito princes regarded themselves as a distinctive hereditary aristocracy and in certain contexts they acted as a group. They were considered (and considered themselves) as being "born to rule" and as quite different from ordinary people. They were clearly more strongly institutionalized as a class and had a much stronger "class consciousness" than the royal dynasty of Buganda.

Chiefs

In both societies senior chiefs formed an inner council that advised the king. All chiefs were granted rights over a particular territory as well as authority over the people on it. From the people on their land, chiefs received tribute, a share of which they passed on to the king; they also redistributed some of it to their subjects. It is possible that Ganda chiefs distributed largess less equally than Nyoro ones. Nevertheless, in both societies a chief was expected to enjoy the profits of his estate and it may be supposed that chiefs, especially senior chiefs, lived very well.

In Bunyoro a few chiefs were granted crowns, which meant that they were ritually accorded high dignity and prestige. In Buganda a county chief and his senior subordinates had their own private estates in which they appointed their own favorites to positions of authority, but there is no evidence of this for Bunyoro. The difference between the two societies in this respect may be explained by the hypothesis that ritual flourishes as a response to a condition of insufficient power (cf. Roberts, 1965:207). This same hypothesis applies to the two kings; that is, the Mukama was less powerful, and his position was also more strongly bolstered by ritual beliefs.

In Buganda there were usually three levels of territorial chiefs. At each

Melvin L. Perlman: Stratification Among Ganda and Nyoro

level the chiefs were ranked and they often had other titles in addition. Thus there was a strong emphasis on the order of precedence, and it was possible for a man in favor to move up in the hierarchy. What mattered most was a man's rank, his precise position in the hierarchy. In Buganda, then, there was a stronger emphasis on precise inequalities, as well as a greater difference in rank from the top to the bottom of the chiefly hierarchy, than in Bunyoro. This is particularly evident from the existence in Buganda (but not in Bunyoro) of two specific offices, the Katikiro and the Kimbugwe, who were the state's foremost chiefs, the authorities and dignities of the Katikiro being almost equal to those of the Kabaka himself.

Nyoro chiefs were often appointed from the Huma cattle-owning class, or from commoners of the Iru agricultural class, though the latter were usually members of families with a tradition of chieftainship. Some chiefships were given to maternal and affinal relatives of the king; minor chieftainships went to palace officials and servants. Although the Mukama had the right to and sometimes did replace an heir with a man of his own choice, many, perhaps most, heirs he merely confirmed. Thus both upward and downward mobility occurred much less often in Bunyoro than in Buganda where the king had extreme powers of appointment, which he often used. Indeed, meteoric promotions and demotions were common in Buganda, and a chief might be summarily deposed for even some trifling cause. When the Kabaka replaced such chiefs no one was excluded by reason of humble birth. Although there was a certain amount of downward mobility in both societies because there were not enough positions for all the sons of chiefs, on the whole the degree and rate of both upward and downward mobility were clearly greater in Buganda.

In Bunyoro most of the senior chiefs were of Bito or Huma origin. Yet, chiefships were not restricted to any one of the three ethnic classes. There was no doubt a larger proportion of Iru among the lesser than among the greater chiefs. The Ganda chiefs were not a strongly institutionalized class, for they lacked both a developed subculture and a sense of common identity and interests. Thus, in both Bunyoro and Buganda, the class of chiefs as a whole contained men from all segments of the societies. But the senior Nyoro chiefships were dominated by the two upper ethnic classes (members of which intermarried with one another), and therefore the degree of class institutionalization was probably somewhat higher in Bunyoro than in Buganda.

Palace Officials and Retainers

An office as a palace official or retainer carried considerable prestige and political influence in Bunyoro. It was sometimes said that such men were "nearer to the Mukama" than many of his officially appointed chiefs and advisers. Thus, in the distribution of rewards in society, at least some of the palace officials were relatively high in the scale. In Buganda the situation was similar. Skilled craftsmen (e.g., carpenters, potters, smiths) in the service of the Kabaka had a particularly high standing and a considerable measure of political influence. The king's secret police were permitted to carry their weapons in the king's presence and to stand while they greeted him. Common to all these palace officials and retainers was the enjoyment of considerable prestige as well as great opportunities for enrichment (especially the tax collectors) and for promotion. Thus, members of this class in both societies seem to have received a fairly similar share of societal rewards, with the exception that the Ganda members perhaps had somewhat greater opportunities for *enrichment* than the Nyoro ones had. Also, Nyoro palace officials may have been somewhat nearer to the king than Ganda ones were.

The rate of vertical mobility was probably lower in Bunyoro because there many offices were vested in particular clans. This meant that access to these positions was perhaps somewhat restricted because there were about 150 clans and it seems unlikely that each one had rights in a particular office. Those who did manage to obtain these positions, however, had good opportunities for upward mobility, especially to the class of minor chiefs.

In Buganda, as in Bunyoro, many of these positions were hereditary in particular clans, but as there were only thirty-odd clans, each had rights in particular offices at the palace. Thus, in contrast to Bunyoro, probably some palace position was available to members of every clan. Furthermore, the custom of sending young men to the palace as pages was strongly institutionalized in Buganda. Moreover, the Kabaka's corps of pages was like a "school" for chiefs, so there was a definite expectation of moving up in the hierarchy, which in fact was realized in practice, even to the highest chieftainships. On the whole, therefore, the mobility of the class of palace officials and retainers was more strongly institutionalized in Buganda than in Bunyoro and also encompassed a broader base of the population.

There is little or no evidence of class institutionalization for either society in regard to this class of palace officials and retainers.

Clans and Lineages

As the king in both societies could choose a wife from almost any clan, no one clan or group of clans had any priority over the considerable rewards that were obtainable in this way. However, because there were so many clans in Bunyoro, it seems unlikely that each one had hereditary rights in a palace office, as did each of the thirty-odd clans of Buganda. Ganda clans were more important also in other ways, especially because,

Melvin L. Perlman : Stratification Among Ganda and Nyoro

according to tradition, clan heads held major positions of authority early in the kingdom's development. Although by the nineteenth century their authority was limited more and more to the domestic affairs of their unilineal descent groups, still they were overlords not only of a scattered community of patrilineal kinsmen, but also of all the people living on their clan lands. Also, some of the shrines in Buganda were controlled by clan heads, who may even have been referred to as "Kabakas."

Descent group heads in Bunyoro were also men of considerable importance, but they could not have had the same degree of importance as the thirty-odd specific clan heads in Buganda, not only because there were about 150 clans in Bunyoro, but also because there was not a clearly defined specific head for each clan as a whole. Thus, the important descent group leaders were probably lineage heads, and of these there were probably many times 150.

For each of the Ganda clans there were also subclan and lineage heads in charge of estates on which their members were buried. The lineage heads would appear to have been the equivalents of the Nyoro descent group leaders previously described. It appears therefore that the Ganda had at least one more layer (clan heads) and perhaps a second one (subclan heads), in addition to the lineage heads that the Nyoro also had.

There seems no reason to believe that there was any significant difference between the two societies either in the rate of mobility or in the degree of class institutionalization of these lineage heads.

Magico-Religious Specialists

According to Roscoe, a member of the higher class of "medicine men" in Bunyoro was so powerful and his fame so great that no one dared rob him, and even the hostile Ganda stood in awe of him. Rainmakers had the right to levy certain taxes, and the people, who stood in great awe of them, were glad to do anything they could to stay in their favor. Such specialists were undoubtedly paid handsomely and made large profits.

In Buganda religious and magical practices probably played a less prominent role. Nevertheless, Roscoe reports that here also medicine men were very powerful and greatly feared. Sorcerers also were greatly feared, but there is no evidence that rainmakers had such importance in Buganda. The important national shrines were large-scale affairs economically supported through estates in Buganda, whereas there is no evidence that this was so in Bunyoro. Although religion seems to have been less closely related to politics in Buganda than in Bunyoro, the relative position of this class of religious specialists vis-à-vis others appears to have been very similar in both societies. Because the Ganda were wealthier, however, at least their most important magico-religious specialists appear to have had greater economic support from the state in the form of estates.

Although the office of priest has been said to be "always hereditary" in Bunyoro, Beattie doubts that this was true. The situation was perhaps very similar to that in Buganda—namely, that a priest's son could inherit his father's office, but the clan retained the right to reject him for any suitable reason. The rate of mobility into this class, therefore, seems to have been very similar in the two societies.

Again, there is little or no evidence on class institutionalization specifically concerning this class.

Peasants and Pastoralists

The conditions under which Nyoro peasants lived do not appear to have been very oppressive. The demands made upon them were probably not excessive nor made with too great zeal. There was an emphasis on reciprocal gift exchange and mutual interdependence between ruler and ruled.

By contrast Ganda peasants lived under more oppressive conditions. Roscoe's description of how labor was provided for making roads is particularly revealing of the severity of the sanctions used. Moreover, there were relatively heavy and specific demands in taxes, not just casual tribute. In addition, life in Buganda was not as secure as in Bunyoro; life and property were not always safe from the power of the king. Though it was sometimes useful to have powerful chiefs. Ganda peasants also suffered at their hands, and hospitality was probably shared unequally.

Ganda peasants may have had a higher standard of living than Nyoro ones in an absolute sense because of their secure food supply and greater success in war. But even this is not certain because of the fairly heavy demands made upon them. Relatively speaking, especially considering the large size of their society's economic surplus, they may have had a smaller share of the available surplus than their Nyoro counterparts had.

As to the rate of mobility, the evidence indicates that although the Mukama of Bunyoro did appoint some chiefs from among the peasants, this was more of an exception than the rule. Although in Buganda the ordinary peasant had less chance of moving up in the system than did the son of a chief or a clan head, nevertheless, some Ganda peasants attained positions at even the highest levels. The peasants clearly had greater opportunities for mobility, and their rate of mobility was faster in Buganda than in Bunyoro.

Ganda peasants constituted a general residual category of ordinary people, not a strongly institutionalized class. Nyoro peasants too—being the large majority of the population—were probably not overly "class conscious," at least in comparison with the Huma and especially the Bito. Nevertheless, they too accepted the Nyoro belief that they were "born to be ruled" and this—together with the fact that they were economically separated from the other two ethnic classes—surely fostered a stronger "class consciousness" than existed among the Ganda peasants.

There was no Ganda counterpart (excluding foreign herdsmen of great chiefs) to the Nyoro pastoralists, the Huma. It appears that the Huma constituted a small minority of the Nyoro population, and that some of them, perhaps many, were chiefs, although they were not *ipso facto* rulers. They regarded themselves as superior to Iru, and they claimed and were accorded high prestige. Still, there were differences among the Huma themselves, though these were largely correlated with the distinction between chiefs and nonchiefs. A Huma who was not a chief might possess only a few cows; the daughter of such a man probably welcomed the opportunity to marry an Iru who had become wealthy, although it is said that originally there was no intermarriage between these two ethnic classes (or between the Iru and the Bito). Thus the Huma *ethnic* class did not correspond to any single *power* class. Rather, it appears that although some Huma were chiefs, others were similar to the Nyoro peasants in their relationship to power, but were accorded higher prestige. Strong ethnic classes, then, may be one of the conditions under which prestige is not a function of power (cf. Lenski, 1966:45).

Slaves

Although there is very little information on the position of slaves, especially for the Nyoro, the evidence we have indicates that their position was not very different in the two societies. Their lives were very similar to the lives of ordinary peasants except where they had disabilities arising from their lack of kinsmen. Although Roscoe distinguishes between what he calls "domestic slaves" and "ordinary slaves" who were bought and sold, once the latter were inherited they became, in effect, "domestic slaves." The lives of all were generally less secure in Buganda; as slaves were at the bottom of the hierarchy, it seems likely that their position was even less secure in Buganda and that they more often lost their lives in sacrifices there than in Bunyoro. Although slaves were supposed to be debarred from becoming chiefs, some of them seem to have attained important government posts through the practice I have described of chiefs' sending slaves to the king's court in place of their sons. It is unlikely that this happened among the Nyoro, as there is no evidence that men were afraid to send their own sons to the palace.

SIMILARITIES AND DIFFERENCES

The two systems of stratification described in this chapter were broadly similar in several respects. For example, both societies had about the same number of classes, and with minor variations each class was broadly similar in its size, composition, complexity, and general importance. That is, the overall span and shape of the system of stratification was similar in the two societies. In addition to these broad similarities, there were many other specific similarities between particular classes, which have been previously noted. No doubt still other similarities have gone undetected because of lack of data. However, the special focus of this chapter has been on three stratification variables for which there are important differences between the two societies, and it is to these that I now turn.

X. Degree of Social Inequality

A few Ganda classes (palace officials and retainers, magico-religious specialists, and slaves) were not very different from similar classes in Bunyoro in the variable of the degree of social inequality. Other important and sizable classes, however, show marked differences. The position of royalty, especially that of the king, demonstrates these differences very well. The Kabaka received and retained much more wealth than the Mukama. The Kabaka was head of all the Ganda clans, had extreme powers of appointment, and was said to have controlled the gods. The Mukama, by contrast, had a greater need for the support of religious beliefs; in Bunyoro too there was a stronger emphasis on the distribution of wealth and power, not only to the common people but also to other royal princes. Important differences again existed at the level of chiefs. In Buganda, chiefs had their own private estates in addition to official ones); there was a greater emphasis on predecence and precise inequalities, and a greater difference in rank from the top to the bottom of the hierarchy than in Bunyoro. Furthermore, in Buganda, each of the thirty-odd clans had a very important head, whereas in Bunyoro there seem to have been many descent group leaders (probably lineage heads) in charge of particular settlement areas. At the low end of the scale, Ganda peasants lived under more oppressive, less secure conditions, and heavier demands were made upon them than upon Nyoro peasants. On the whole, therefore, the degree of social inequality was considerably greater in Buganda than in Bunyoro.

Y. Rate of Vertical Mobility

It is not surprising that there was very little difference between the two societies in the rate of vertical mobility for the three classes (royalty, clan and lineage heads, and magico-religious specialists), in which the hereditary principle clearly played an important role. There were very important differences, however, in the rate of vertical mobility of the remaining classes, for each of which both upward and downward mobility were clearly greater in Buganda than in Bunyoro. In Bunyoro there is no evidence that any considerable number of peasants ever attained political office; and even when this did happen such positions tended to become hereditary. In Buganda, the authorities agree that there was mobility "on a very substantial scale," and this meant that both rapid promotion and demotion were common (L. A. Fallers, 1964:159; Wrigley, 1964:20).

Z. Degree of Class Institutionalization

The evidence we have on this variable, which also includes "class consciousness," comes mainly from three important and sizable classes—royalty, chiefs, and peasants. All of this specific evidence points in the same direction, namely that at least these three classes were more strongly institutionalized in Bunyoro than in Buganda. Nyoro royalty especially was strongly institutionalized, and they even had a fairly strong degree of "class consciousness." Their interests as a class often conflicted with those of the people as a whole. By contrast, L. A. Fallers specifically writes of the "essential 'classlessness' " of nineteenth-century Buganda "in the sense of the absence of cohesive and clearly delineated strata" (1964:163).

In this chapter I have used the method of controlled comparison to elucidate a number of differences about the systems of social stratification of two Interlacustrine Bantu kingdoms, which are very similar in other ways. Explanations for the foregoing empirical generalizations noting differences in stratification can be made in terms of the major factors of difference mentioned at the beginning of this chapter. Due to limitations of space, however, it has not been possible to deal systematically with this problem.[4]

BIBLIOGRAPHY

Beattie, John   1957   Nyoro kinship. Africa, *27*:4.
——   1959   Rituals of Nyoro kingship. Africa, *29*:2.
——   1960a   Bunyoro: An African Kingdom. New York, Holt, Rinehart & Winston.
——   1960b   The Nyoro, in: East African Chiefs, A. I. Richards (ed.). London, Faber, for E.A.I.S.R.
——   1964   Bunyoro: an African feudality? Journal of African History, *1*.
Eggan, Fred   1954   Social anthropology and the method of controlled comparison. American Anthropologist, *56*:5.
Fallers, L. A.   1959   Despotism, status culture and social mobility in an African kingdom. Comparative Studies in Society and History, *2*:1.

4. Systematic explanations for these empirical generalizations will be found in a separate forthcoming publication tentatively entitled: *Systems Theory and Controlled Comparison: An Explanation of Stratification in Two Uganda Kingdoms.*

—— (ed.). 1964   The King's Men. New York, Oxford University Press, for E.A.I.S.R.

Fallers, M. C.   1960   The Eastern Lacustrine Bantu, Ethnographic Survey of Africa, East Central Africa, Part XI. International African Institute.

Lenski, Gerhard   1966   Power and Privilege: A Theory of Social Stratification. New York, McGraw-Hill.

Mair, Lucy   1934   An African People in the Twentieth Century. Baltimore, Routledge.

Nsimbi, M. B.   1964   The clan system in Buganda. Uganda Journal, *28*:1.

Oliver, Roland   1959   Ancient capital sites of Ankole. Uganda Journal, *23*:1.

Posnansky, Merrick   1966   Kingship, archeology and historical myth. Uganda Journal, *30*:1.

Richards, A. I. (ed.)   1960   East African Chiefs. London, Faber, for E.A.I.S.R.

—— 1964   Authority patterns in traditional Buganda, in: The King's Men, L. A. Fallers (ed.). New York, Oxford University Press, for E.A.I.S.R.

Roberts, John M.   1965   Oaths, automatic ordeals, and power, in: The Ethnography of Law, Laura Nader (ed.). American Anthropologist, Special Publication, *67*(6): Part 2, December.

Roscoe, John   1911   The Baganda. New York, Macmillan.

—— 1915   The Northern Bantu. Cambridge, Cambridge University Press.

—— 1923   The Bakitara or Banyoro. Cambridge, Cambridge University Press.

Southwold, Martin   1961   Bureaucracy and chiefship in Buganda. East African Studies, *14*, E.A.I.S.R.

Taylor, Brian   1962   The Western Lacustrine Bantu, Ethnographic Survey of Africa, East Central Africa, Part XIII. International African Institute.

Wittfogel, Karl A.   1957   Oriental Despotism: A Comparative Study of Total Power. New Haven, Yale University Press.

Wrigley, C. C.   1964   The changing economic structure of Buganda, in: The King's Men, L. A. Fallers (ed.). New York, Oxford University Press, for E.A.I.S.R.

WEALTH, INFLUENCE, AND PRESTIGE AMONG THE SHOA GALLA

BY HERBERT S. LEWIS

According to Ethiopian and Portuguese sources it was about the year 1537 that the Galla of southern Ethiopia began to expand to the north, changing the ethnic map of Ethiopia and being changed themselves.[1] The Galla peoples now number in the millions and occupy an area from northeastern Ethiopia to southeastern Kenya and from the borders of the Sudan to the borders of Somalia. From what were evidently a few small societies with one homogeneous culture have grown many Galla-speaking societies, cultures, and polities, some pastoral and egalitarian, others agricultural and monarchical, some Muslim or orthodox Christian, others still "pagan." The group to be described in this chapter is, therefore, by no means typical of the Galla of Ethiopia. No group is.

This study deals with inequality of wealth and influence among the Galla of western Shoa province, Ethiopia. It is concerned primarily with two levels of sociocultural integration: the single community and the district which integrates a number of these smaller units. At the local level we shall be concerned with landowners; at the regional, with religious leaders. It will also be necessary to take into account, but to a lesser degree, the presence of a higher level, that of the Empire of Ethiopia

This Chapter is based on fieldwork which was supported by the National Science Foundation and conducted in Ethiopia from September 1965 through July 1966. I wish to thank Professors Leonard Glick and Arnold Strickon for reading and criticizing the first draft.

1. Lewis, 1966:23–26.

and its government. That government set off important social and cultural changes when it established peace in the area, but at present its penetration into the countryside is slight and its officials are largely "invisible" to the local population.[2]

HISTORICAL BACKGROUND

From the time of their entry into western Shoa, probably late in the sixteenth century, until their conquest by the Amhara late in the nineteenth century, the Galla were independent. They were not ruled by kings, as were the Galla of Wellega to the west and of the Gibe region to the south, but were led by landowner-war leaders (*abba dula* or *moti*).[3] European sources from the nineteenth century and contemporary informants' accounts attest that there were men who successfully led their followers in war, obtained land and cattle through conquest and purchase, settled their followers on these lands, and gained considerable influence, even power, within relatively small areas. There were many such leaders in competition with one another, and war was frequent throughout the area.[4]

The followings of war leaders were not composed of descent groups or tribes with fixed and bounded membership, nor were the *abba dula* automatically filling prescribed leadership positions. Galla society allows individual residential mobility, and people are free to attach themselves to important men. Nor are there usually firm geographical boundaries to groups. *Abba dula* extended their influence as far as they were able from the core areas where they owned land. The evidence suggests that there was considerable scope for achievement; leaders could rise and fall rapidly depending upon their success in war and their ability to attract and hold adherents.

Late in the nineteenth century the Shoan Amhara, under Menelik II, expanded their empire, and at that time western Shoa was pacified and incorporated into the modern Empire of Ethiopia. Warfare was prohibited and the *abba dula* lost their *raison d'être*. Many also had some of their land expropriated. There was no large-scale settlement of Amhara

2. Slaves will not be dealt with here. Slavery ended several decades ago and freedmen today are treated like other people in everything but marriage. There is a feeling (not a rule) against marrying the descendants of slaves, but slave ancestry is no bar to other kinds of interaction or relationship.

  There are endogamous castes of smiths, tanners, potters, and woodworkers. (For a general discussion of caste groups in Ethiopia see Lewis, 1962:508–11.) These craftsmen represent a very small proportion of the population in most areas; there were hardly any in the districts discussed here, but see the last section of this chapter.
3. Knutsson, 1963:507; Lewis, 1964:26–35.
4. See, for example, the accounts of Massaja and Plowden.

on the land, but many Galla and some Amhara who had aided in the wars of consolidation were awarded eighty-acre land grants, and much of this land was obtained from the indigenous landowners. Many of the original residents evidently stayed on as tenants so there was not much dislocation of population.

The role of the *abba dula* has disappeared from Galla society and much of the system of inequality has changed, but the descendants of some of these former leaders are still prominent. Ancestry alone, however, confers few, if any, advantages, and landownership is not a sufficient condition for prominence. These men are not important today solely because of their antecedents, but because of the way in which they use their inheritance.

FAMILY AND KINSHIP

The patripotestal homestead, consisting of a nuclear family with possible extensions, is the basic residential group. It is an independent unit; family heads move freely and settle where they can find land for agriculture or agreeable social conditions, and it is quite common even for brothers to settle in widely separate areas. It often happens that small groups of agnatic relatives live near each other because they continue to dwell where their common ancestor did, but descent groups are not localized either in theory or in fact. Nor is common descent, except in special circumstances, a significant organizing principle.

The Shoa Galla are quite aware of agnatic relationship, and their "ethnohistoriography" views all Galla as connected through male ancestors into one great genealogy. (There is no agreement on any single genealogy, even at relatively recent levels, and it is clear that this is a way of conceptualizing the past rather than a probable reconstruction of it.) Some men can recite the line of their ancestry only as far back as three or four generations, but others can name as many as sixteen forebears before reaching Mec'a, the putative ancestor of many of the western Galla. They recognize their kinship with others descended from the same ancestors and can speak as though all the descendants of one eponym constituted a group as against the descendants of others, thus giving the impression of a segmentary descent system. To sum up their social system with those terms, however, would be entirely misleading, for the role of descent in actual behavior and activity is slight indeed.

Even closely related agnates often live far apart; they have no common leadership, own no joint property, and *may* never meet together as a group. For most social activities they simply do not think in terms of descent. Nevertheless, agnatic descent does exist as one potential basis for

Herbert S. Lewis: Wealth Among the Shoa Galla

joint activity and there are a few occasions for which some members of certain descent lines may come together. Occasionally they cooperate in the traditional courts to claim compensation for the murder of a relative or to aid in the collection of wergild for one of their own members. More commonly, several times a year agnates and their families may gather together to perform rituals and to propitiate spirits which are associated with their groups. Some descent groups have ritual leaders who are possessed by spirits; brothers and cousins come when in trouble to ask the spirits for help. Other groups lack such leaders; they simply gather at certain times of the year for an elder of their group to bless them. The size of these groups varies from just a few families to several dozen. As with much of Shoa Galla society there is a good deal of variation and looseness. Some groups of agnates have also formed associations based on the model of the voluntary associations; these are discussed later.

Aside from these few agnatically based group activities, obligations toward kinsmen are equivalent for maternal, paternal, and affinal kin. These consist primarily of some mutual aid, including help in farming, and attendance at funerals.[5]

Land, cattle, houses, and other property are owned by individuals, male or female. Most property can be willed away however the owner wishes, but land must be shared equally among sons (in theory, though rarely in practice, among daughters as well); thus several brothers or cousins may hold adjacent parcels of land derived from the single holding of their common ancestor. These holdings are in no sense joint property; each man can use and dispose of his land as he wishes. Membership in a descent group wider than the nuclear family confers no rights to property.

A man may say with pride that he shares a common ancestor with a prominent landowner and politician, but this in itself gives him no advantage and no prestige. Descent lines are not ranked relative to one another, nor do members of single groups share similar statuses. Each descent line contains rich and poor, landowner and tenant; there is no ideology demanding the leveling of the status of agnates. Inequality cross-cuts extended kinship.

THE COMMUNITY

Homesteads spread over the rolling countryside, singly and in clusters, with no visible boundaries between communities. There is no

5. See Knutsson, 1963. Knutsson reports a more highly formalized descent structure than I encountered in my area, but he comes to essentially the same conclusions about the bases for interaction.

The affect-laden term *firra,* denoting a person with whom one has a warm relationship, is applied equally to all consanguineals, affinals, and friends who have no kinship ties.

word for "community," and in the absence of clear-cut social or physical boundaries it is often difficult to tell where one begins and the other ends. But these communities, hamlets composed of dispersed homesteads, are the basic units for cooperation and mutual aid (in agriculture, house-building, misfortune); they are the locus of *rites de passage* (marriage, circumcision, death) and of much conflict resolution. Prestige and influence are manifested at the local level through leadership in the community activities, in voluntary associations, and in the settlement of disputes. In the following section we shall be concerned in part with the place of landowners in these activities.

Settlement and Landholding

Shoa Galla communities are open communities, easy for newcomers to join, composed of people who are, in the first place, cooperating neighbors, not kinsmen or lineage mates. New settlers are accepted if they are willing to participate in community affairs, especially if they attend and contribute labor and money to funerals and join in agricultural work parties. Members of other ethnic groups, such as Amharas, are accepted if they are cooperative. Of course, immigrants must also be acceptable to the landlord on whose land they settle.

In the part of western Shoa familiar to me (the area near Ambo [Hagere Hiywot]), most landholdings were originally granted in parcels of eighty to one hundred acres called *gasha*. These were given mainly to men who served in the armies of Menelik II or his war minister during the consolidation of the empire. A majority of the landowners in this region are Galla, although there are some Amhara among them.[6] Some landholdings, however, represent estates inherited from the former leaders, the *abba dula*, while still others, usually less than a *gasha*, were purchased more recently.

The pattern of inheritance introduced by the central government, which demands that all sons share a father's land equally, has resulted in increasing fragmentation of the original holdings, and by now many estates have been divided into four or more parts. This means that at present there are many smallholding farmers working their own land. But there are also only sons who have inherited full *gasha*, brothers whose father owned more than one *gasha*, and heirs who have bought more land on their own, who possess large landholdings which they cannot work themselves. These men (or women) cultivate as much of the land as they are able, perhaps leaving much of the actual labor to unmarried sons or hired men (slaves, as of thirty years ago), and rent the remainder to tenants.[7]

6. An Amhara landowner holds no special status or prestige due to his ethnic background alone.
7. The number of households a particular *gasha* can support varies, but it seems to average about four to six.

Herbert S. Lewis: Wealth Among the Shoa Galla

There are a few landlords who control several *gasha*, sometimes dispersed in different areas. A number of these people are direct descendants of Menelik's war minister, who was a Galla from a nearby region. Some of the large landowners have remained on the land and take part in local affairs; others have moved to Addis Ababa, send servants to collect their rents, and are virtually unknown to their tenants.

A majority of men are tenant farmers living on and sharecropping the land of resident owners or absentee landlords. Many work fields on the land of several owners and are thus not wholly dependent on one landlord. They pay their rents with a portion of each crop they grow on an owner's land. The main crops are *t'ef* (an indigenous grain), wheat, barley, sorghum, beans, chick peas, and oil seeds. The landlord receives one-half the crop if he also supplies the seeds or the oxen to draw the plow; he receives one-fourth if he provides nothing but the land. In addition, the tenant pays another one-tenth to the landlord to help pay the land tax, and he may be called upon for a few days' work for the owner per year.

Landlords are not *patrons* in Shoa. They do not provide special services for the tenant, nor does the tenant owe loyalty to the owner. There is no bond between owner and tenant; their relationship is a free contractual one and either party may terminate it, after the harvest, at will.

The Landowner's Style of Life

Even though a landowner may have an annual income several times that of his tenants, the difference in his style of life and that of the other members of his community is slight. A man who owns one or more *gasha* of land and chooses to live on and from the land is limited both in revenue and in the uses to which he can put it. An owner of eighty acres, working some of the land for the whole crop and renting the rest to four families for one-half the crop, might make from $200 to $350 profit from the sale of grain, after setting aside some for food and seed for the following year and paying his taxes. A landless tenant might make $50 to $100 for the year. Given this low income (in absolute terms) and the limited range of consumer goods available in the countryside, a landowner's life is different only in degree from that of his tenant.

With his cash income a man will buy livestock, most of which contribute more to his esteem and pleasure than to his economic capacity. A horse is almost a must for a leader in community affairs. Not only is it a status symbol, but it permits him to travel considerable distances to help settle disputes, attend meetings, go to the religious centers, and visit widely. However, since horses are relatively inexpensive, some costing as little as $10, they can be owned by many landless men as well as landlords.

The purchase of a cow adds to the supply of milk, butter, and cheese a man can serve to his family and guests and thus enhances his esteem and nutrition, but it produces little, if any, revenue. An ox, on the other hand, is a productive animal, for it can be rented to a tenant in return for a portion of his crop or used by a hired man to put more land under cultivation. But a good ox costs $40 to $50 and is thus a considerable investment. Cattle and sheep are sometimes slaughtered for meat. A wealthy man does not slaughter cattle for his family's use, however; he might give occasional feasts which will enhance his standing in a community, but feasts that are not connected with weddings or memorials for the dead are not at all common.

These people are not house proud and spend little on beautification, furnishings, or utensils. A wealthy man might build a rectangular house with a corrugated metal roof or build extra thatched houses for his family and hired man, but the life led inside his house is almost identical with that of his tenants. He is likely to possess a few more stools, porcelain coffee cups, whisky glasses, metal bowls, and there may be a saddle hanging on his wall, but little else distinguishes a wealthy man's home from that of anyone else.

The condition of a man's clothes marks his wealth and ambition. A rich man who cares about status wears jodhpurs and a jacket with few or no patches, and shoes or boots. The differences again, are only of degree. Good clothes are not the prerogative of any category of people in the society, and most have a good outfit for wear on special occasions. An important man dresses well more often than an unimportant one, however.

Most landowners do not control many people; nor have they great wealth or many economically productive uses to which to put their money. A landowner need not be a leader or a person of importance; it is common for an active and intelligent tenant cultivator to surpass in esteem and influence most of the landlords of his community. But a landlord who is ambitious and capable and wishes to be a leader in his district begins with a distinct advantage: he can have the time and the resources to participate in the activities that are most highly valued at the local level. Community leaders are men who devote their time to composing the disputes of others, take prominent part in the running of the community association and various voluntary organizations, and generally demonstrate wisdom, altruism, and oratorical skill in dealing with the affairs of their neighbors. By leaving the cultivation of his lands to a son or hired man, by riding here and there on his horse, dressed in good clothes, to help people settle fights, arrange marriages,[8] conduct com-

8. Marriage negotiations illustrate the importance of the community and of achieved leadership. Prominent men of each partner's community confront each other to discuss marriage payments and contracts. One man is chosen, ad hoc, to serve as chief representative for each side. Fathers are never the spokesmen, but otherwise relationship to the bride or groom is neither a qualification nor a handicap. A group of neighbours, led by an able negotiator, is expected to look out for the interests of each partner.

Herbert S. Lewis: Wealth Among the Shoa Galla

munity business, a man can become an important local leader. This is the path to respect and esteem, and landlords have the advantage, if they wish to take it.

The Community Association: Iddir

In the absence of physical boundaries, communities can be defined by the mutual-aid burial associations to which groups of neighbors belong. These associations, called *iddir*, are composed of from 50 to 150 male household heads, usually representing a continuous geographical area. They are voluntary associations, however, and some people choose to belong to groups farther from their homes, while others belong to two or more.

An *iddir* is a formal organization with written rules and records. If there is a literate member in the group, he may donate his time and skill to record-keeping and be excused from certain other work. A group with no literate member will pay someone from another community to keep its books. Each *iddir* has elected officers to see that the functions of the organization are carried out and that each member fulfills his obligations.

The chief officer (*hayu* or *dañi* ["judge"]) is the group spokesman, the chairman of all meetings he attends, and has precedence over all the other officers. The man elected to this position is often the most respected member of the community, but he is not necessarily a big landowner. The *hayu* of one large group is an elderly man who has acquired only ten acres of land through purchase but whose general leadership qualities and public spirit have led his neighbors to pay him great respect and to elect him also as their representative to the government. Because he owns some land and receives help from hired men and an adopted nephew, he is able to free himself from much agricultural work in order to devote time to arbitrating disputes, attending the religious court, or occasionally going to the government court. On the other hand, the *hayu* of a small *iddir* nearby is the son of a man whose immediate family controls about 400 acres (mostly inherited from ancestors who were *abba dula*) and whom the government appointed as its representative over about 4000 acres.

The second officer is responsible for accusing those members who fail to carry out their obligations to attend funerals, pay assessments, and do cooperative work. Below him are several men elected to direct the participation of groups of twenty to twenty-five neighbors. These officers collect money, announce all *iddir* activities, and report on those who refuse to help; they also organize the provision of bread and beer for the big monthly meetings. More often than not these positions are held by men who are tenant farmers, and a good-sized *iddir* may contain quite a few smallholders and some large landowners who hold no offices.

The members of an *iddir* must attend the funeral of any other member or a relative of a member. They must dig the grave and carry the coffin.

They bring grain and money for coffee for the meal after the funeral, and, on succeeding days, food for the mourning family. They pay twenty cents for a memorial feast. In addition, members agree to work one full day in the fields for a household in which a death occurred and to work one-half day for a man who has lost an ox. They rebuild and refurnish houses which have burned down. They agree, in the written rules, to give aid to the sick and to those in jail who are not thieves, adulterers, or habitual troublemakers. Finally, the *iddir* owns a tent, benches, tables, cups, and glasses which it lends out to its members for funerals, weddings, memorial feasts, and meetings of voluntary associations.

A member who fails to work or pay assessments is fined. One who consistently disobeys the officers and fails to pay fines will be thrown out of the *iddir* and may have to move from the community.

The rules apply equally to all members; the equality of all members is a basic element in the ideology of the community and I witnessed no exceptions. A big landowner and a poor tenant owe the same labor and money. A land owner might send a hired man to work in his stead, but a tenant farmer might send his son.

Iddir members frequently default in their commitments, and much time is spent in litigation arising from this source. Much of the litigation goes on at the monthly meeting when all the members are supposed to gather to discuss *iddir* problems. They then drink beer, eat bread, and hear community leaders ask the blessings of the spirits and *wak'a* (the Galla sky god). They may also have a Christian priest to ask the blessings of Jesus.

Other Voluntary Associations

Most men and some women belong to other types of voluntary associations. One of these is the *mhaber*, borrowed from the Amhara and adapted to Shoa Galla culture. The *mhaber* is a group of fifteen to thirty friends who gather monthly, at a different member's house each time, to eat and drink. Kinship or common residence is not a qualification for membership. Members are merely friends, and a candidate for admission must be admitted unanimously. Members agree to aid each other, to settle their differences within the group (an ideal they do not always maintain), and to look upon each other as "brothers." Indeed, the *mhaber* might reasonably be called a sort of fraternity. *Mhaber* have formal rules and presiding officers. The officers are either elected or chosen by lot.

The *ik'ub*, another voluntary association, meets to pool and redistribute small sums of money. Each time the groups meet (weekly, semi-weekly, or monthly) the members are assessed equally, and the total sum is given to one member chosen by lot. Both men and women may belong to a group. The *ik'ub*, too, has formal rules and elected leaders; it functions much the same way as a *mjhaber*.

Herbert S. Lewis: Wealth Among the Shoa Galla

The criterion for membership in a third voluntary association is agnatic descent from a common ancestor. Some groups of agnates have organized mutual aid associations which they hope will bring their dispersed kinsmen together so that they may know, help, and discipline each other. (Discipline consists of lecturing troublemakers and threatening to withhold assistance from them.) The organization of these associations is similar to that of the *ik'ub* and *mhaber*, featuring elected leaders, written rules, and fines for failure to attend the meetings which are held in a different member's house each month. And as with the *mhaber* and *ik'ub*, the elected officers are the most popular men or the most active leaders; they may or may not be the wealthiest.[9]

Membership in the *iddir*, *ik'ub*, and *mhaber*, as in the community itself, is based on universalistic criteria. All these associations may include Amharas and ex-slaves as well as free-born Gallas. They include both rich and poor. All are open to people who are considered friends, who are reasonably well liked or respected, and who are willing to abide by the organization's rules.

It is possible to see in the voluntary associations a twofold relationship congruent with the ranking system generally. On the one hand, the ideology of the associations stresses the equality of the members and the solidarity of the group. On the other, the associations provide settings in which leaders can exercise their talents. In these groups a man can gain a following and find activities to lead.

Community Conflict Resolution

The Shoa Galla are litigious people and a great many man-hours are spent in the arbitration of disputes. The lowest level of arbitration is within the community and involves gatherings of five to a dozen men in a convenient spot in the open air. The men listen to evidence from both parties, and the mediators reach unanimous decisions which they hope will be accepted by both sides. The men who actually speak and have the greatest influence are the same ones who lead in most other gatherings. They are not necessarily old men or rich men but are the ones respected for their disinterested attitudes, intelligence, concern, and willingness to devote the necessary hours. Landowners are represented out of proportion to their numbers, but they by no means dominate these sessions. Even a prominent landowner (and I have in mind an important man who owns eleven *gasha*) is but one of a company of equals.

9. One landowner and government official who had moved to town and changed his style of life called together his kinsmen to form such a group. His expressed aim was to make it an instrument for modernization as well as mutual aid. It is also likely that he hoped to use it to increase his own political capital. He is a forceful man, held in some awe in the countryside, and he dominated this association.

The Ideal of Equality in the Community

The word *k'it'e*, which means a meeting to settle a dispute or discuss problems of community interest, is an extension of the word for "equal." This stresses the ideal that, when they come together, all the members of the group are equal. In fact, some men have more influence and esteem than others; they speak more, they direct the flow of the discussion, and their words count more heavily than those of others present. But the ideal does reflect important aspects of the reality: Each member of the community is invited to and expected to take part in community affairs; each man can participate as an equal, limited only by his own abilities. His place in a *k'it'e* depends on his skills as a debater and leader. There is wide scope for individual achievement.

It is difficult to detect any condescension on the part of resident landowners toward tenant farmers. Deference is paid to a rich man (see later) but rich and poor visit each other's homes, eat each other's food, belong to the same associations. Those landowners who are held in the greatest esteem are also among the most polite of men. This is not a matter of *noblesse oblige* but of conformity to the general norms of conduct within the community.

It has not been my intention to deny that there are rich and poor in these communities or that the rich don't have more opportunities than the poor. A landowner who can evict a tenant from his land is in the superior position, and larger landholders are relatively often represented among community leaders. I am suggesting that a resident landowner's esteem comes primarily from its service to his community and that intelligent landless men will surpass in esteem and influence those landowners (and they are not rare) who do not play a leading role in community affairs. There is no feeling of status solidarity or status honor among landowners. I witnessed many disputes between landlords and tenants, but I did not see any tendency for the members of either group to side regularly with each other.

THE DISTRICT

There is no word for "district," as there is none for "community." And just as the dimensions of a community must be defined with reference to the patterns of interaction which pull neighbors together, so must the district or region be defined by the interaction which unites it. The integration of a district depends upon the institutions that center around the *k'allu*, the religious leaders.

Herbert S. Lewis: Wealth Among the Shoa Galla

K'allu and Their Ritual
Centers

K'allu are mediums who are regularly possessed by spirits (*ayana*). The spirits can directly affect all aspects of life. They can kill a man or cure him; slay his ox or increase his herd; make him mad or destroy his enemy. They can be vengeful toward the impious or benevolent to the faithful. And the spirits can be approached only through the *k'allu*.[10]

The following of a major *k'allu* is not necessarily drawn from a continuous geographical area nor from a particular descent group.[11] A *k'allu* tends to draw heavily from the districts around his ritual centers and attracts many members of the descent line with which he is associated, but decisions as to which *k'allu* to visit are not made on these bases alone. A person in trouble propitiates a spirit he believes can help him or which he believes is harming him. Some people believe they are called to the service of certain spirits. A man seeking satisfaction in a dispute goes to the ritual center where there are judges he trusts. As Knutson says, "On the whole . . . individuals are at liberty to choose their favourite k'allu."[12] Thus the congregation of a *k'allu* may fluctuate depending upon his ability to attract and impress people. Those who are most successful have considerable influence. One powerful man in the mid-1960's had nine ritual centers dotted across a fifty-mile area and had at least 30,000 followers.

A major *k'allu* maintains large and elaborate ritual centers. These contain several temples (*galma*), dining halls, sleeping houses for visitors, kitchens, storehouses, homes for the *k'allu* and his family, and houses for scores of servants. *Galma* are the only indigenous central places other than markets, so they serve for several types of gatherings. In addition, it is the *k'allu* who organizes most of the events that call people from different communities together. The spirits possess the *k'allu* there every fourteen days, and people come from many miles to appeal to them.[13] On days that the spirits appear, judges hear cases at the courts sanctified by the spirits. Hundreds of people come every other week to approach the spirits or engage in litigation; thousands come once a year for the annual *Mask'ali* ceremonies. And all who come are fed.

Major ritual centers are the sites of judicial activity several days every other week. At one *galma* there are often five or six cases going on concurrently, six or seven hours a day, Wednesday, Thursday, and Friday.

10. For a fuller discussion of the *k'allu* and Galla religion, see Knutsson, 1967.
11. There are lesser *k'allu* who serve, in part, as diagnosticians, directing troubled people to the spirits of the more powerful mediums. Some of these men and women are associated with descent groups, but most are freelance practitioners who serve any interested customer.
12. Knutsson, 1967:101.
13. For a fuller description see Lewis, n.d.

These sessions attract not only litigants but witnesses, spokesmen, community leaders, and judges as well. The *k'allu* is the highest judge, but other men are chosen by their neighbors to go to the court regularly to serve as judges (*dañi*). The *k'allu* formally invests them and admonishes them to judge wisely. Speaking through the *k'allu*, the spirits empower certain *dañi* to address them on behalf of the people. Other men are selected to act as sergeants-at-arms and as the representatives of the spirits in the countryside.

Once a year, usually in October or November, major ceremonies called *Mask'ali* are held at each *galma*. At these rites of intensification, the people of large districts gather to hear the *k'allu* and respected elders ask blessings for the district (and for Ethiopia and the Emperor). Five or six thousand people attend these ceremonies at the largest centers. People come as much for the fun and excitement as they do for religious reasons.

Mask'ali is an event filled with life and color. It begins with a great bonfire followed by drumming and singing in the *galma*. The next morning the elders of the district feast on raw beef with the *k'allu*. Men and women place bunches of yellow flowers around the circle of ashes left from the bonfire. As the distinguished men sit with the *k'allu* on the dais of a pavilion, horsemen ride back and forth in large parties, singing and boasting. Groups of young men with fighting sticks sing and dance. Possessed women cry, run, and leap on the ground before the *k'allu*, who bids the spirits to release them. Old women who live at the *galma* and are dedicated to the service of the spirits walk by, carrying flowers and singing. Thus, the statuses of the society are on display, in a holiday atmosphere.

Later, while the more adventurous horsemen take part in tournaments, the elders drink and eat. A minstrel sings praises of the ancestors of the prominent among them and of the *k'allu*. A single *k'allu* may direct such a show for as many as nine districts.

A *k'allu* is the center of many other relationships. Each has dozens of servants (some of them pledged for life to the service of the spirits), treasurers, majordomos for each *galma*, herders to care for his livestock, stewards to care for his lands. Each local community has men and women who announce corvée labor projects and levies of money or grain for the spirits, and who carry other messages from the *k'allu*. There are secretaries, boys with a few years of primary school education, who keep accounts and write receipts and, above all, write summonses to call disputants to court.

A man's comparative status in his own community is reflected in the treatment he receives at his district ritual center. Community leaders, respected elders, influential landowners, receive special recognition. At *Mask'ali* they not only sit on the dais with the *k'allu*, but are also invited to eat raw meat with him and to eat and drink in the best guest house.

In legal proceedings they sit with the judges and may be called upon to express their opinions. On all occasions the most respected men are ushered in to eat first; in fact, the usher may line them up in a rough rank order. Leaders are served higher quality food than ordinary people. The most impressive guests, wealthy ones who come from Addis Ababa or a large town, are given accommodations in special guest houses with separate rooms and beds. Unimportant visitors sleep on the floors of the dormitories.

The K'allu's Resources

Operations of the sort run by the *k'allu* demand economic means to sustain them and a *k'allu* has numerous resources to draw upon. Troubled people bring cattle, money, food, liquor, grain, clothing, pots, kerosene, and all manner of goods to the spirits. One great *k'allu* claims to receive the equivalent of $200 every fortnight. Sometimes landowners give portions of their land, often in the belief that spirits killed their fathers or other members of their families and that they are also marked for death. A *k'allu* may buy land with his other wealth. The *k'allu* just mentioned is said to own between 2400 and 3500 acres which he obtained as gifts, through purchase, and by inheritance. He has many tenant farmers and some of these lands are worked by corvée labor. The people of a district are called upon periodically to plow, plant, and harvest for the spirits, and they believe that if they refuse to do so the spirits will punish them. People also construct the buildings in the ritual centers.

Much of the income which these gifts and lands provide is used to run the *galma* and to feed the guests who stay, by the hundreds, for three or four days a week. One *k'allu* uses perhaps 1300 pounds of grain for bread and beer every week of the dry season. (As an elder said when urging people to pick a *k'allu*'s chick peas, "These are really *our* chick peas we are harvesting.") Some of the grain is given out as loans or gifts to the needy, and some is sold to support the *k'allu* and his family at a level above that of even the largest local landowner.

The K'allu's Position and Style of Life

Invariably, major *k'allu* are impressive figures, in fine clothes, followed by servants bearing their chairs, umbrellas, and cloaks. They are often big men physically, and they carry themselves with authority and dignity. *K'allu* are generally concerned with the traditional world rather than the modern world and live among countrymen rather than townsmen. But they are also wealthy and important leaders who need to impress as many people as possible, and they own gold watches, gold rings, leather boots, mules, and horses with fancy trappings. Some have radios and motor vehicles.

K'allu are the most important individuals in the countryside, even though their authority is unofficial and their influence often indirect and diffuse. As great landowners they have many tenants dependent on them. *K'allu* are constantly asked to settle disputes, and they frequently order individuals to fulfill obligations or pay debts to others. They cannot enforce these decisions, but they can authorize the plaintiff to curse his opponent before the spirits. The *k'allu* are not supposed to be able to call upon the spirits for their private purposes, but their nearness to the *ayana* is sufficient to guarantee them a great deal of respect. In addition, they may be genuinely helpful men who take an interest in their people's affairs and try to aid them when they can.

In some cases, the government has taken account of important *k'allu* and worked through them because they can reach the people with their communication networks and relations with community leaders. When collecting money to build several bridges, government officials approached one *k'allu* to direct the assessment of his followers. But, in addition, as a politically ambitious and astute man, he courts this sort of attention. He has taken an active part in raising funds for a school in a nearby town, and makes frequent calls to pay his respects to the local and provincial governors. Two of his sons have become minor officials, appointed by the government to serve in areas where they own land, while a third son is a district governor. These sons have also established connections with other important men through marriage. One married a sister of a powerful local leader and landowner who is also in the national parliament. Another married the sister of an army colonel. Thus the *k'allu*, although they are uneducated and owe their prominence to their ability to work in the traditional situation, are the heads of families which have increasing connections with the modern sector, and at relatively high levels.

The *k'allu* themselves do not constitute an interest group with common aims, an idea of status honor, or a style of life different in kind from that of their followers. Major *k'allu* are in competition with each other, and their success depends on how well they serve their congregations. They are not priests in a hierarchy who owe their appointments to superiors, but charismatic leaders who must work constantly at their jobs. The *k'allu* with nine *galma* centers is always occupied: traveling from *galma* to *galma* holding possession ceremonies, settling disputes, listening to peoples' problems, entertaining visitors, and directing building projects. The spirit sometimes stays on him for ten straight hours as people present petitions all through the night. The next morning, without having slept, he goes to listen to court cases. As a good politician he knows a great number of his followers by name and keeps informed of their doings. Furthermore, he identifies with them. It was not merely political oratory which led one great *k'allu* to tell a group of elders, "Don't be happy for

me when you see me going to see the Amhara officials in my suit. Be glad
when I am with my family and in my *buluko* [a blanket worn in the country-
side]."

A *k'allu* is not unlike a chief in a redistributive network. He acquires
land, livestock, money, and goods but he does not simply accumulate
this wealth; he distributes much of it in the form of food, shelter, and
entertainment. He also needs this wealth to obtain the robes, horses,
shields, headdresses, and other paraphernalia necessary for the spirits,
as well as the rings, boots, capes, and mules appropriate to his status as a
great man. His wealth provides the material means for him to fulfill his
functions. This is *not* to say that a *k'allu* may not become a rich man, but
rather, that the aim, the end that brings esteem and influence, is not
accumulation alone but successful organization and manipulation of
ritual, judicial, and social activity.

Patterns of Deference
Galla behavior toward high-ranking people contrasts sharply with
that of their near neighbors, the Amhara, who demand extreme deference
and obeisance of an inferior to a superior. The Amhara bow deeply,
kowtow, kiss feet, do not contradict or talk back to superiors.[14] Such
behavior is uncommon among the Galla. Normally one does not bow to
even the highest ranking Galla. They do kowtow to the *k'allu*—but as a
representative of the spirit. (Some of the *k'allu*'s servants even kiss the
hooves of a horse associated with a spirit.) But a man might shout his
disapproval of a suggestion or a judgment directly at a *k'allu*. Excited
litigants often argue with a *k'allu*; elders and judges may disagree with his
decision and try to modify it.

For the Galla of western Shoa, deference is indicated by greater
attention being given, by more people, to the common patterns of politeness and respect. There is a continuum from the respect given to any
household head to that accorded the highest ranking men or women.
Respect is shown most clearly by rising and greeting a newcomer who
joins a group. People don't rise for a youth or a young woman but they
do for an older man with a family, for wealthy mature men, and for older
women who are strong personalities and the wives or mothers of respected
men. The importance of an individual is indicated by how many people,
of what status, rise to greet him, and how much they interrupt their
business because of him. (A gracious man bids everyone to stay seated.)
The most respected person is directed to the best, perhaps only, seat: a
chair, a carved stool, a bench.

The ranking indicated in this way is largely based on an individual's
personal qualities rather than on his group or category ("class") affilia-
14. See Hoben, in the next chapter, for a vivid account of Amhara behavior toward superiors.

tions. A landowner rises for a respected elder; a respected elder rises for a major *k'allu*. The absence of marked patterns of obeisance is indicative of an egalitarian ideology which coexists with the reality of inequality.

CHANGE AND MODERNIZATION

It would be incorrect to assume that the system described here represents an untouched and original one. On the contrary, it is likely that a great deal of the current system is new. Incorporation into the Ethiopian state ended the importance of the war leaders. The *k'allu* seem to have risen to prominence only in this century, probably as the war leaders were declining, for there is no indication of any such important religious leaders in the nineteenth-century accounts of the Galla. The government replaced a system of inheritance by primogeniture with the equal inheritance currently in force, and it forbade slavery. *Mhaber* and *ik'ub* are relatively recent introductions, and although burial associations are old, the formal *iddir* organization is new. To admit all these changes, however, is not to say that the people of the countryside are subject at present to any great degree of "modernization" or integration into the national system.

At present the degree of penetration of the countryside by the central government, even within 100 miles of the capital, is very slight. The government makes few demands, requiring peace, order, and the payment of land taxes. It provides few services, and those it provides are mainly in the towns. (For example, there are courts in towns for those that want their cases heard by government judges.) The connections between the countryside and the government are, therefore, remote and intermittent. The main links between the two systems are the government's appointed representatives chosen from among the local Galla. The higher ranking ones are sometimes men who have moved into the modern sector and changed their styles of life. The lower ranking ones are generally traditional men, wedded to their communities. The appointees at both levels are usually landowners. Their official positions enhance their influence and esteem, of course.

K'allu may serve as intermediaries between the countryside and the modern world, both because of their direct relations with the government and because the children of some of them are becoming increasingly interested in the new ways of life. They listen to radios, sometimes wear Western clothes, and not infrequently go to school. Their wealth and contacts put them in position to take advantage of some of the new opportunities.

At present there are few opportunities for change and development in the countryside. There are virtually no new jobs, industries, schools, or towns off the main roads. Thus, people who opt for a new way of life invariably leave the community and usually have to move some distance away. Young men who become soldiers are generally transferred wherever the army sends them. There are some soldiers, however, who serve just a few months of the year and farm or lie idle at home the rest of the year. They generally live the same lives as their nonmilitary brothers but have shown greater interest in such material items as radios, metal frame beds, and Western clothes. A few people move to the towns and work in or own small shops. They tend to look in both directions, toward the community and toward Addis Ababa, but their numbers are small, and so far most are closer to their country cousins.

Some children manage to go to school and to stay long enough to be trained for new jobs. Most of them leave the towns where they went to school and go elsewhere in search of further schooling, training, and work. The ideal of most people who stay in the small towns and in the countryside is to get land and to have the time and money to be able to devote themselves to settling disputes and attending meetings; in other words, they follow the traditional goals.[15]

THE PATTERN OF INEQUALITY

Despite the apparent differences between the Shoa Galla and the majority of African systems with regard to such matters as land ownership, community organization, the role of descent in social organization, and the system of plow agriculture, Lloyd A. Fallers' generalization[16] about African values holds true here as well:

> It is perhaps not going too far to assert that the *emphasis* in African stratification is primarily political. The roles which are most highly regarded are usually authority roles, whether these involve the part-time political activity and adjudication of disputes which absorb the energies of the elders of a descent group, or the full-time exercise of authority engaged in by the rulers and chiefs of the great kingdoms.

15. The only "entrepreneur" I met outside of the towns was an industrious young man who farmed intelligently on rented fields, and saved enough money to buy a partnership in a small shop in a nearby town. He also bought several sewing machines which he rents to tailors. He lives in a thatched house in the country and spends many hours attending meetings and quietly suggesting solutions to disputes. He is respected for his diligence, his politeness, his good sense, and his public spirit.
16. Fallers, 1964:119.

This is certainly true at the local community level, only a little less so at the district level since the decline of the *abba dula* and the rise of the *k'allu*. Esteem goes to those who take an active part in organization and adjudication. The major portion of any meeting, whether of *iddir*, *mhaber*, *ik'ub*, marriage negotiations, or an ad hoc session in a field to settle a dispute. is spent in argument and conflict resolution. A leader, landowner or not, is no more than a *primus inter pares*. But the aim of an ambitious man is to be such a leader.

Although land is important at each level, it is not economic values that predominate. As important as land is in subsistence, its greatest value, in terms of stratification, is as a *facility*[17] which permits its owners to carry on political activities. For the *k'allu*, land is the means to carry out his many functions. Wealth is appreciated and worked for, but it is less of an end in itself than a means to an end; it alone does not bring esteem. To attain esteem and a position of leadership in a local community and its surrounding area it is neither necessary nor sufficient to be a landowner.

The contemporary social system of the western Shoa Galla contains considerable inequalities of wealth, influence, and prestige, in a setting featuring a high degree of universalism, achievement, and mobility. These inequalities are not distributed in a manner that allows us to speak (as yet) of "estate," "class," or *stand*, however. First, everyone may purchase and own land, even a former slave. Second, there is a tendency for landholdings to be fragmented so that the sons of a large landholder become smallholders, while industrious and ambitious landless men acquire land and pass them by on their way up. Third, except for those few landlords who own large holdings in several areas and live in town or Addis Ababa, the landowner is tied to a single locality and community, and usually has no special ties to landowners in other areas. (There is, however, a tendency toward intermarriage and interconnection between families at the highest levels in different areas. This appears to be an increasing trend.) Fourth, the style of life of the landowner, as we have noted, is the same as that of his tenant, and there is virtually no social distance between them. (With an increase in consumer goods and in opportunities for schooling and work outside the community there will be greater differences in style of life. This seems to be beginning now.)

The *k'allu*, too, are tied to their own localities for support and influence, even though they may marry women of wealthy families some distance from their own areas. Their influence depends upon the things they supply their people: access to the spirits; a center for authoritative adjudication of their disputes by men who are part of their own culture

17. Parsons, 1964:390, distinguishes " 'facilities,' i.e. means-objects relative to instrumental goal-attainment processes" and " 'rewards,' i.e. objects which are either objects of direct gratification or are symbolically associated with such objects."

(in contrast to the judges of the government courts); great rites of intensification which unite otherwise dispersed and acentric communities; a center of congregation for entertainment. To do this properly, a *k'allu* must be close to his people, live in the culture and know it well; if he does not, he can lose his following. According to informants, a great *k'allu's* importance does not depend on the power of the spirits he represents (as against those of another major *k'allu*) but on "what he knows." Achievement is prominent at this level, too.

There is, among the western Shoa Galla, an ideology of achievement and equality which is apparent in most activities and social relations. This is consistent with the relative unimportance of descent as a basis of organization and the prominence of neighborhood-based activity and voluntary association. It differs fundamentally from the pattern among their neighbors and rulers, the Amhara, among whom "most interaction . . . is cast in the form of superior-inferior personal dyadic relations."[18]

Modernization is frequently thought "to involve modes of social relationships in which there is a greater emphasis on universalism as distinct from particularism, on equality in contrast to elitism, on individual achievement rather than ascription,"[19] as well as an emphasis on the nuclear family, individual property, and a market system in which land and labor may be exchanged as well as goods. And yet, while the Galla of the countryside have all of these characteristics to some degree, they are in no sense "modern."[20] As economic development increases and the government extends its services more widely, it will be interesting to see how the Shoa Galla react and what direction change takes.

OCCUPATIONAL CASTE IN ETHIOPIA

If the term *caste* may be used for any phenomenon of social stratification outside of the Indian context, it can probably be applied as appropriately to the artisan groups of Ethiopia as to any other non-Indian case. Throughout the empire, artisanry and other craft specialization is carried on through distinct, named, endogamous groups which meet the criteria for "caste" suggested by such writers as Nadel (1954: 21–22) and De Vos (1966: 332–33), and show six of the seven characteristics of caste listed by Leach (1960: 2) (the seventh characteristic is the Hindu religion). Those charac-

18. Levine, 1965:219.   19. Lipset, in Marshall, 1965:viii.
20. It should not be assumed that these traits are new among the Galla, the result of the recent changes mentioned above. Comparative study of the literature on the contemporary Galla and those of the nineteenth century leads clearly to the conclusion that all of these traits are relatively old and typical, to some extent, of most Galla groups. Cf. Lewis, 1965, for example.

teristics are (1) endogamy; (2) restrictions on commensality; (3) status hierarchy; (4) concepts of pollution; (5) association with a traditional occupation; (6) caste membership ascribed by birth.

It is through these castelike arrangements that the peoples of Ethiopia and the Horn organize the specialization of labor. Although the system is perhaps more elaborate in Ethiopia than elsewhere in Africa, including a wide range of artisans and tasks, the pattern is similar in many ways to that described by Nadel for other parts of Africa.

> In many societies both in East and West Africa we find separate groups of blacksmiths which are endogamous, bound to their occupation by descent, and not only feared but distinctly despised, shunned and avoided. Yet they are a vital section of the tribes to which they belong, providing the tools for farmers and weapons for hunters or warriors. They are often also medicine experts, so that the physical welfare of the tribe lies in their hands. Finally, their position is mystically sanctioned and conceived of as preordained: in myths and cosmologies the blacksmiths are specifically mentioned among the first ancestors of man, already his benefactors and already bearing the stigma of their descent and calling. (Nadel, 1954:21)

Virtually every Ethiopian Cushitic- or Semitic-speaking society for which evidence exists contains within it at least one endogamous group of hereditary occupational specialists. The occupations of these groups include hunting, foraging, and the manufacture of items from forest products; smithing (iron, silver, gold) and such other artisanry as tanning, woodworking, pottery-making, and weaving; magical and ritual services, including burying, barbering, circumcising, the production and sale of ritual paraphernalia and medicines.

Societies differ in the number of such groups they recognize. The Galla of Harar distinguish two main categories: *tumtu*, blacksmiths whose wives are potters; and *watta*, hunters, feared for their magical powers, who also do leather work and make pots (they rely more on craft work where cultivation is dense and the hunting poor) (Brooke, 1957:73–74). Far more elaborate is the pattern in the Galla kingdom of Jimma Abba Jifar, where there are separate named groups of blacksmiths, silversmiths, potters, tanners, weavers, woodworkers, hunter-foragers, civet-cat hunters, beekeepers, horn cup makers, and magicians (H. S. Lewis, 1965:53–54). The Somali have three main groups: blacksmiths, who also make amulets and charms; and two groups of hunters who do leather work and perform ritual and personal services as well (I. M. Lewis, 1955:51ff). The occupational specialists of the Gurage, collectively known as *fuga*, are divided among themselves into woodworkers (who fell trees, chop wood, assist in housebuilding, and aid in burials and other important rituals), blacksmiths, and tanners (Shack, 1964:50–51).

Herbert S. Lewis: Wealth Among the Shoa Galla

It is said that members of these castes are ritually impure and that others may be polluted by contact with them. Above all, others will not willingly or knowingly marry them. They are not supposed to enter the houses of nonartisans, and if a Gurage *fuga*, for example, should do so, "the homestead must be ritually cleansed" (Shack, 1964:50). They are said to be forbidden to handle farm implements or deal with cattle, although in fact many do partly support themselves by doing some planting or keeping one or two cows.

Meat prepared by artisans and hunters is taboo to others, but it should be noted that in Ethiopia there are also bars to Christians, Muslims, or Falasha sharing meat. Low status caste groups, however, are often said to eat impure meat (wild pig, other taboo wild animals). Or, even if they no longer do so, it may be maintained that their ancestors once did, and that they still bear the stigma. This is probably partly a myth which validates their low prestige in this region of dietary proscriptions.

As a rule, members of these castes are associated with the supernatural. They are invariably considered bearers of the evil eye, are frequently suspected of being were-hyenas, and are believed to be capable of sorcery, magic, and the preparation of efficacious charms. (See I. M. Lewis, 1961:273ff., on the Yibir of the Somali.) They may also take part in ritual for the whole society. Shack (1966:11, 132ff.) has documented the participation of the *fuga* in Gurage ceremonies.

Members of these low castes are not allowed to own land and are normally disenfranchised from the regular political and judicial life of the societies at large. Among the age-grading Galla, the smiths and hunters were barred from participation in the important assemblies and were said to be under the protection and control of the elected assembly leaders. Members of the artisan castes among the Somali get protection by attaching themselves to "noble patrons" (I. M. Lewis, 1955:52). Gurage artisans also may depend on important hosts (Leslau, 1950–62), and they are forbidden to carry spears or go to war (Shack, 1966:9).

In the monarchical states there were special relations between the low status castes and the kings. In Jimma Abba Jifar they were directly under the control and patronage of the kings, who appointed representatives from among them to oversee their taxation and work service. They were not allowed to speak in the courts or serve as witnesses. In the kingdom of Kafa, members of the artisan-hunter group served the king as bodyguards and as the royal executioners. Their leader was an appointee of the king (see Cerulli, 1922:208).

These specialists are generally few in number in any given region. Their distribution is probably determined by the demand on their labor and the ability of others to make use of their work. They may also travel in search of work, and sometimes settle among new ethnic and linguistic groups. Within this century, Jimma Abba Jifar, which is a relatively prosperous region, attracted *fuga* from Janjero country and *watta* hunters from neighboring Kafa. This mobility undoubtedly helps to account for the great similarities in caste culture and organization throughout the empire and may also explain why some artisans and hunters are physically *somewhat* distinct from their current hosts.

It has long been argued that these artisan castes represented "remnants" of the earlier inhabitants of Ethiopia and the Horn. (See, for example, Cerulli, 1922:200ff.; Shack, 1964:50.) I have argued elsewhere that this hypothesis has no reasonable linguistic, cultural, or physical evidence to support it and that it is a highly improbable reconstruction (H. S. Lewis 1962:508–11). The thinking that produced this hypothesis is rooted in the sociology of L. Gumplowicz, in outmoded ideas of race, and in unacceptable ideas of waves of immigration into East Africa. Rather, the phenomenon of occupational caste in Ethopia must be looked at as a distinctive division of labor, a system for the production and distribution of goods and services which demand special skills and training. Caste in Ethiopia exists only in this context. As such it might profitably be investigated in the light of our knowledge of occupation specialization through caste elsewhere in Africa and Asia.

BIBLIOGRAPHY

Brooke, C. H., Jr. 1957 A Study of Galla Settlements: Hararge Province, Ethiopia. Unpublished Ph.D. dissertation. University of Nebraska, Lincoln, Nebraska.

Cerulli, E. 1922 The folk-literature of the Galla of southern Abyssinia. Varia Africana, *3*:9–228.

De Vos, G., and H. Wagatsuma 1966 Japan's Invisible Race. Berkeley, University of California Press.

Fallers, L. A. 1964 Social stratification and economic processes, in: Economic Transition in Africa, M. J. Herskovits and M. Harwitz (eds.). London, Routledge and Kegan Paul.

Knutsson, K. E. 1963 Social structure of the Mecca Galla. Ethnology, 2:506–11.

——— 1967 Authority and Change: A Study of the Kallu Institution Among the Macha Galla of Ethiopia. Goteborg, Etnografiska Museet.

Leach, E. R. (ed.) 1960 Aspects of Caste in South India, Ceylon and North-West Pakistan. Cambridge, The University Press.

Leslau, W. 1950 Ethiopic Documents: Gurage. Viking Fund Publications in Anthropology, No. 14. New York.

Levine, D. N. 1965 Wax and Gold: Tradition and Innovation in Ethiopian Culture. Chicago, University of Chicago Press.

Herbert S. Lewis: Wealth Among the Shoa Galla

Lewis, H. S.   1962   Historical problems in Ethiopia and the Horn of Africa. Annals of the New York Academy of Sciences, *96*:504–11.

——— 1964   A reconsideration of the socio-political system of the western Galla. Journal of Semitic Studies, *9*:139–43.

——— 1965   A Galla Monarchy: Jimma Abba Jifar, Ethiopia, 1930–1932. Madison, Wisconsin, University of Wisconsin Press.

——— 1966   The origins of the Galla and Somali. Journal of African History, *7*:27–46.

——— n.d.   Kud'arfan: A Multi-Functional Institution Among the Western Galla. Paper read at the Third International Conference of Ethiopian Studies, Addis Ababa, April, 1966. To be published in the Journal of Ethiopian Studies.

Lewis, I. M.   1955   Peoples of the Horn of Africa. International African Institute. London, Oxford University Press.

——— 1961   A Pastoral Democracy. London, Oxford University Press.

Marshall, T. H.   1965   Class, Citizenship, and Social Development. Garden City, New York, Doubleday.

Massaja, G.   1885–95   I Miei Trentacinque Anni di Missione nell'Alta Etiopia. 12 vols. Milan, Pontificia S. Guiseppe.

Nadel, S. F.   1954   Caste and government in primitive society. Journal of the Anthropological Society of Bombay, n.s., *8*:9–22.

Parsons, T.   1964   A revised analytical approach to the theory of social stratification, in: Essays in Sociological Theory. London, The Free Press of Glencoe.

Plowden, W. C.   1868   Travels in Abyssinia and the Galla Country. London, Longmans Green.

Shack, W. A.   1964   Notes on occupational castes among the Gurage of south-west Ethiopia. Man, March-April, (*54*):50–52.

——— 1966   The Gurage: A People of the Ensete Culture. London, Oxford University Press.

SOCIAL STRATIFICATION IN TRADITIONAL AMHARA SOCIETY

BY ALLAN HOBEN

The traditional pattern of social stratification among the Amhara of Ethiopia is atypical of societies in sub-Saharan Africa. Indeed it has struck many European observers as reminiscent of their own medieval past. The object of this chapter is to describe Amhara stratification, and the relevant features of its institutional setting, in terms that will make possible more meaningful comparisons of this order, though such comparisons will not be undertaken here.

The way in which Amhara classify one another as better and worse, as of higher and lower degrees of honor, can best be understood in terms of a single cultural paradigm—an indigenous theory of human nature—and its implications for the ways men can be tied to one another. Following some introductory remarks on the concept of stratification and on the ethnographic setting, I will examine the diverse ways in which this cultural paradigm was traditionally institutionalized in the local peasant community, the nobility, the clergy, and the monarchy. Though there are significant differences in the way fundamental Amhara ideas of ranking are contextualized in the role expectations of these diverse segments of the population, one important respect in which the Amhara pattern of

This chapter is based in part on fieldwork supported by a grant from the Ford Foundation Foreign Area Fellowship Program and a grant from the Wenner-Gren Foundation for Anthropological Research. I am also heavily indebted, as I shall indicate in the text, to Donald N. Levine and Wolfgang Weissleder for their penetrating analysis of aspects of Amhara social stratification. For their very great help with the clarification of issues and organization of the presentation I would also like to thank, in particular, Robert Merrill and Arnold Green.

stratification can be distinguished from those of later European feudalism is the relative sameness in Amhara society, of the ideals and standards in terms of which all Amhara of all classes rank one another.

THE CONCEPT OF SOCIAL STRATIFICATION

Social stratification, as it is understood here, has its roots in the fact that people in every society not only categorize each other for significant social purposes but differentially evaluate some of these "categories of persons" as more and less worthy and desirable (Fallers, 1963, 1964; Parsons, 1954a, 1954b).

Thus conceived, social stratification has its roots in social structure and culture—in social structure because people do not rank one another directly as whole and unique individuals but rather in terms of standardized categories of "social person" or social identity (Goodenough, 1965); in culture because the evaluative standards in terms of which categories of person are ranked are themselves a part of the whole system of ideas and symbols through which a people apprehend their relationship to one another and their world.

A description of social stratification, to be meaningful, must have a behavioral referent. It must be based on expectations about the treatment of people as superior, inferior, or equal to one another in recurrent types of specific social scenes.

One consequence of this is that when the stratification patterns of several social scenes in the same society are compared, the rank order of the same individuals may vary. In an Amhara community, for example, the relative rank, as indicated by deferential behavior, of a poor priest and a well-to-do farmer is reversed when they move from a sacred to a secular setting. In what sense, then, is it meaningful to speak of social stratification in a community or a society as a whole? In the context of the present discussion there are two dimensions—the structural and the cultural—in terms of which it may be possible to distinguish an overall pattern of stratification.

The structural dimension concerns the extent to which certain categories of person, certain key identities, are crucial factors in establishing ranking patterns in a great many different social settings. From a structural point of view the holders of these key "identities," who are very frequently given high position, may be said to have high status in a generalized sense, provided it is remembered that their position vis-à-vis others may vary somewhat situationally and that there may be more than one "parallel" structural hierarchy.

The Concept of Social Stratification

The distribution and differentiation of these highly ranked key identities in a population provides one of the axes in terms of which classifications and comparisons of structural patterns of stratification can be made cross-culturally. Questions as to the number of stratified hierarchies, such as church and military elite; the existence, number, and size of ranked groups or strata; and the nature of the boundaries of these groups, all fall along this axis.

The cultural dimension, in terms of which it may be possible to distinguish a general pattern of stratification, concerns the extent to which ranking in many types of social settings is justified by similar evaluative standards or, at a higher level of generality, supported by the same cultural image of ultimate existential reality.

Highly evaluated positions are inevitably a focus of interest and anxiety for both individuals and groups.[1] It is therefore appropriate to examine the processes through which people are recruited to valued positions and to find out what ideas they have concerning this process and its justice or injustice. In studying recruitment it is particularly important to determine the ways in which and the extent to which ordinary individuals can and do achieve high status, and conversely, the ways in which and extent to which other individuals are allocated to highly evaluated identities on the basis of nonvolitional or ascriptive criteria. The two aspects are, of course, not mutually exclusive. In the study of traditional states the first question usually leads to a substantive investigation of the economic, political, or ecclesiastical systems in relation to recruitment; the second question usually leads to an investigation of the ways in which relationships of kinship, descent, inheritance, and succession facilitate access to high status.

The ideas held by the members of stratified agrarian societies such as the Amhara concerning their system of stratification, and the process of recruitment within it, must take into account the fact that the number of people with highly evaluated positions is very small in comparison with the agricultural population that supports them. Even if a high proportion of the elite is recruited from the farming population in each generation, the proportion of farmers that can achieve elite status is very low. Ideological solutions to this dilemma range between two poles. At one extreme are the elitist ideologies of relatively closed ruling groups which assert that their members deserve their high positions because they have unique qualities, often acquired through descent, inheritance, succession, or

---

1. Some of the forms that secondary cultural aspects of stratification can take are discussed by Fallers (1963: 164–66). The basic problem involved here, that of the acceptance of a position that the actor himself considers to be low, has been long recognized. It is a central theme in Marx (Bottomore and Ruble, 1956: 78) and plays an important part in Durkheim's discussion of anomic suicide (Durkheim, 1951: 250).

Allan Hoben: Traditional Amhara Society

family ties which enable them alone to successfully direct the affairs of their fellow countrymen.

At the other end of the continuum are traditional societies in which there is relatively little cohesion amongst the holders of high rank, relatively little elaboration of an exclusive elite subculture, but there is an ideology of upward social mobility for all able individuals. The important point here is not that there need be a high rate of upward mobility but that there is a wide diffusion amongst that agricultural population of the ideals and aspirations associated with the highest positions in the land. It will become evident in the following discussion that the traditional Amhara ideology of stratification fell toward the second pole[2] with regard to both the internal structure of the elite and the relative homogeneity of life-style, social organization, and evaluative ranking standards throughout Amhara society.

THE SETTING

The Amhara, numbering perhaps five million, today occupy a central position on the great plateau that rises between the Somali desert and the hot lowlands of the Sudan. At present the Amhara live mainly in the Ethiopian provinces of Begemdir, Gojjam, Shoa, and Wallo.

Since their emergence as a self-conscious ethnic and linguistic group in the beginning of the second millennium A.D. the Amhara have been the main political heirs of Axum, the ancient Semitic kingdom that dominated the northern plateau, the Red Sea, and occasionally sections of the Arabian Red Sea coast, from several centuries before Christ until well after the rise of Islam. From the restoration of the Solomonid Dynasty (1270) until today there has been but one Ethiopian Emperor, Yohannis IV (reigned 1872-89), who was not an Amhara, and the presence of a British expeditionary force under Lord Napier was instrumental in his rise to power.

Of paramount importance in the heritage of Axum were a plow-based mixed farming agricultural pattern, the Ethiopic Christian church, and the venerated tradition of the Imperial throne, standing above and symbolically uniting the great regional rulers and their lower lords.

The vast majority of Amhara are farmers who live in sprawling hamlets and cultivate their scattered plots for the major part of their subsistence. From a fourth to a tenth of these farmers are members of the local Coptic clergy. A small fraction of the population, not more than

2. The Amhara were not, however, as far toward this end of the continuum as certain East African societies were. See, for example, Fallers' discussion, "Despotism, Status Culture and Social Mobility" (Fallers, 1959).

5 percent, belong to endogamous, low status artisan groups. Most of these artisans also farm, though exclusively as tenants. In the past, non-Amhara slaves were kept in the households of important men (*tiliq sawoch*) and nobles. The latter categories ranged from local lords who controlled only a single estate with less than 100 resident farming families, through more important title-holding lords with several estates, to great regional governors who held numerous estates and received tribute from the lesser lords within their districts. Far above the greatest regional lords in prestige stood the semisacred throne which was located at most times in a military camp, a mobile city of tents, for, in traditional Ethiopia, there were no major and lasting cities.

Traditional Amhara political organization was primarily structured by a branching, pyramidal network of personal, diffuse, and contractual ties between patron and client. Each of these ties was conceived of by the Amhara as a personal bond between "whole" men, not as a clearly delimited and circumscribed set of rights and duties between officeholders. A superior might, therefore, in Amhara theory, call upon one of his men to render him any type of personal or administrative service. Despite its personal and diffuse character, however, the patron-client relationship was basically contractual and voluntary. In return for his service and support the client expected protection, clothing, and feasts at his lord's table, and he ultimately hoped to be rewarded with rights in land. These land rights might take many forms, and they varied with both period and place. Those that were of greatest significance at higher political levels and were most eagerly sought after were a class of rights known as *gult*, which involved the granting away of "sovereignty" (Amhr.: *gesat*) to the recipient. Generally included in grants of *gult* were the right to judge, tax, and lead in war those farmers who resided on the land concerned. In Amhara political theory such rights, indeed all secular authority, ultimately derived from the throne; but in fact, at most times in most parts of the empire, the holder of *gult* or his local representative enjoyed a large amount of autonomy.

It would seem then, that insofar as the term *feudal* is detached from its historical setting and used to describe a type of societal organization in which the polity is based on a hierarchical network of personal, diffuse, and contractual ties between patron and client and in which sovereignty is bound to rights in land, the Amhara pattern may be called a feudal one.

Similarities between traditional Amhara and European feudalism go beyond these similarities in the pattern of political and land relations. There are similarities in the ideology of social stratification also, in the ways that people conceptualize and justify the major divisions or "estates" that make up society. The Amhara frequently speak of the nobility (*mekwannint*), the clergy (*Kahanat*), and the farming population (*gebaroch*)[3] as basic and complementary social categories. Indeed the image of the Amhara peasant plowman following his oxen down a strip field in the local lord's "demesne," or of the great "baron" and his retainers feasting upon beef washed down with drafts of honey "mead," while an itinerant minstrel recounts their deeds of valor to their greater fame and glory, or of the solemn priest, silver cross in hand, intoning the Lord's Prayer at a baptismal ceremony in the churchyard, all create a comforting impression of familiarity to one steeped in the traditions of our Western past. But this impression is in part misleading, for these similarities in political organization, life-style, and religious forms mask very significant differences between the overall pattern of traditional Amhara social stratification and those most characteristic of medieval Europe.

These differences had to do with the relatively low degree of differentiation in life-style—i.e., forms of social organization ideas and ideals—between the Amhara "peasantry" and the overarching military and ecclesiastical elites. The Amhara farmer and his lord did not consider themselves to be of different breed or blood. Often they claimed descent from a common ancestor and acknowledged bilaterally traced ties of kinship. Nor were their aspirations so very different, for the Amhara military ethos, with its promise of rewards of land and title for daring conduct in battle, was shared by all. There were differences in life-style and etiquette to be sure, but they were more of degree than kind. The peasant-farmer, like the lord, tried his best to gain control over land (particularly over usufructuary rights known as *rist*) and to build a large household of dependents who would serve him, show him respect, and give him honor. His well-being, like that of the lord, depended primarily on his success in the art of managing his relationships with his dependents, rivals, and superiors, and not on the number of his children, or his position in solidary local groups based on kinship or vicinage.

This sameness or continuity in social relations among Amhara of all ranks is not the result of recent trends. It was remarked astutely more than a century ago by the British adventurer-diplomat Walter Plowden who wrote:

> The Abyssinian soldier or servant must not be viewed in the same light as with us: it must ever be remembered that between the chief and the most ragged of his followers there is no distinction, save that of wealth or good fortune, . . . There are none of those real and essential differences of education, of language, or of breeding, and consequently of thought and feeling, that elsewhere prevent the servant and his master, the soldier and

3. There are great regional differences in the connotation of the Amharic term *gebar* (pl. *gebaroch*). In Gojjam it simply means a taxpaying farmer. In the southern provinces it seems to have the pejorative implication of landless tenant or even serf.

his officer, from meeting on a footing of intimacy, however much respect and affection may be mutually felt and entertained. . . . If, on the morrow, by some freak of fortune not unfrequent, they should reverse positions— partly from their natural versatility, partly from this absence of any solid separating traits—there is scarcely one of those who stand humbly to serve to-day, that would not to-morrow grace the seat of honour and issue commands as well as his nobly-born master, who in his turn would find no awkwardness in handling the mead-horn, or saddling the horse, of his quondam domestic. Their education, if it may be so called, fits them for this. (Plowden, 1868:60)

In an important sense, then, the same cultural conception of human nature and social order, the same image of excellence and merit, the same understanding of authority, and the same sense of honor and ranking pervade all levels of Amhara society, from the humblest tenant-farmer to the highest lord.

Throughout their period of ascendancy, the Amhara were frequently engaged in warfare with their Islamic or pagan neighbors or among themselves. This frequency of warfare contributed to the continuing primacy of the political and, above all, military orientation of Amhara culture and the dyadic ties of subordination and superordination which it supported.

The remoteness of the Ethiopian plateau from the rest of Christendom and its rugged terrain also doubtless retarded the development of an Amhara "high culture." Mile-deep chasms and tortuous trails contri- buted to political fission in inhibited centralization. They also made transportation difficult and expensive. Trade was limited to relatively small regions and to higher-cost merchandise such as gold, salt, and civet.

Perhaps because of the limited development of trade, perhaps owing to continual strife, the Emperor usually lived in his shifting military camp. Urban centers never developed in Ethiopia. Whatever the reasons may have been, the absence of cities with their doubting intellectuals, their scholastic skeptics, and their intricate webs of horizontal economic relations and classes of people with market-defined common interests, left the feudal military structure of Amhara society in unchallenged supremacy.

Today most of this feudal structure has been replaced by a system of government ministries, a parliament, a well-disciplined modern army, and a formally bureaucratic central administration. Modernization, however, has been an uneven process. Many of the attitudes, standards, and senti- ments characteristic of the old order still persist, as do many of the local institutions on which it rested, particularly in rural regions. In order to avoid endless qualifications with regard to period of reference I have chosen to use the past tense wherever I meaningfully could, even though much of what I report is still to be found today.

The battle of Adowa in 1896, at which the Ethiopian armies decimated an Italian expeditionary force of 20,000 men and thereby gained diplomatic recognition from the major European powers, may be taken as a convenient if arbitrary cutoff date for the "traditional" period with which I am primarily concerned. It should be remembered, however, that the "traditional period" is itself only an abstraction, a convenient approximation, for there were innumerable variations, of institutional detail and significant differences in the interplay and balance of power from region to region throughout Amhara history.

THE PATTERN OF TRADITIONAL
AMHARA STRATIFICATION

The elaboration and pervasiveness of deferential behavior in the social scenes of Amhara life is striking. Whether it is at a church service or at court, on the trail or in the privacy of the homestead, decorous and elaborate forms of speech, dress, and gesture are employed by the Amhara to express toward one another appropriate degrees of subordination and superordination. In virtually all of these situations it is possible (with adequate knowledge) to discern a pattern of ranking, an ordered difference in the amount of deference that people give and receive. An accidental or transitional lapse in this orientation causes the Amhara discomfort or embarrassment. There is a moment of confusion or deliberate "not noticing" while people rearrange their positioning and their clothing so as to satisfactorily reorder the scene with regard to the main sources of secular or sacred authority.

This constant concern with the etiquette of deference is not primarily oriented to membership in ranked segments of society, descent groups, or the nexus of kinship relations. It is rather defined, at least in secular scenes, by personal, dyadic, hierarchical social ties between persons who have access to political office and land, and those who depend upon them. The Amhara concern with these social relationships is related to their central integrative role in Amhara social organization. It is manifest in the pattern of ties that bind men to one another and shape their interests. It is consistent with the image offered by Amhara culture of man's nature, man's relationship with his fellowmen, and his relationship with his God. It is a fundamental postulate of Amhara culture, evidenced in each of these dimensions of the Amhara "world view," *that social order, which is good, can be created and maintained only through hierarchical, legitimate control, a control that ultimately must be authorized by God.*

The Amhara postulate that ordered social relations depend upon the existence of legitimate regulatory control reflects a fundamentally Hobbesian view of human nature. As Donald Levine has succinctly put it, the Amhara

> . . . suffers from no illusion about *homo sapiens* at his best—unless they are dark illusions. . . . The Amhara believes that unformed human nature is pure raw material, and that without strict punishment (I would prefer discipline) throughout childhood a person will grow up to be rude and offensive toward others. As an adult, moreover, he must constantly be kept in check. (Levine, 1965:80)

Without control there is thought to be constant danger that man will become aggressive toward his fellows. This assumption is explicit in the Amhara concept of *tegebenga*, a person who, being satiated, is no longer dependent on anyone and hence has become insulting and aggressive.

To some extent, the Amhara think that this "natural tendency" to be aggressive and disruptive can be restrained with stern discipline, training, and the frequent and arduous round of feasts prescribed by the Ethiopian church. To some extent they think its expression can be contained through adherence to an elaborate, formal code of etiquette governing interpersonal relations, and to some extent it is recognized that aggression can be channeled into legitimate military activity. But above all it must be contained by the surveillance and regulation of an authority figure with whom the person has a diffuse and personal relationship of dependence.

From an Amhara point of view it is natural and reasonable that the individual, left to himself, will be aggressive and self-seeking and will pursue his own narrowly conceived interests—interests that, because of the Amhara "zero sum" view of available rewards and the near absence of collective or communal goals, must inevitably lead to interpersonal conflict.

The basic Amhara pattern of group formation which constrains these potential conflicts involves two types of relationship: those between patron and client, and those between clients by virtue of their common allegiance to the same patron. Patron-client ties are voluntary and personal in nature and diffuse in scope. They are expected to be mutually beneficial, but are predicated on an asymmetric upward flow of deference, loyalty, and support and a downward flow of protection, material rewards, and delegated authority. It is also thought appropriate to the relationship that the client assume a formal (titled) or informal position in the patron's household entourage, regardless of whether or not he (the client) is himself the master of a similar, autonomous group.

The relationship between the clients of a patron is characterized by mistrust, suspicion, and malicious rivalry. Their ability to cooperate, to

Allan Hoben : Traditional Amhara Society

the extent that they do, rests on the constant efforts of their patron to restrain them from quarreling rather than from a sense of purposive solidarity in his behalf. Indeed, a patron spends a good deal of his time managing relationships between his followers, usually through secretive audiences first with one and then with another.[4]

In the Amhara view, then, society consists, to a very large extent, of a pyramiding network of these interlinked, vertically structured groupings. Order at any level or in any group depends on the effective exercising of leadership. Through the regulatory control exercised by legitimate holders of authority, inherently destructive human tendencies are held in check and social order established. This belief in the efficaciousness of legitimate controlling figures is self-fulfilling. The expectation that bloody anarchy will prevail in the absence of a strong ruler, for example, has often been validated during interregnums and more recently in the period of turmoil that accompanied the reconquest of Ethiopia from the Italians.

The Amhara postulate that order is made possible only by legitimate control is evident in the selection and elaboration in Ethiopic Christianity of hierarchical ordering aspects of the Biblical tradition, which receive far less attention in contemporary Western Christianity. Though the general cosmogony and cosmography of the Ethiopian Orthodox Church is similar to that with which Western Christians are familiar, Amhara cosmological emphasis is quite distinct. Western Christian doctrines emphasize the New Testament, the humanity of Christ, the ubiquity of God, and the direct confrontation or even intimacy possible between man and God. Ethiopic Christianity stresses the Old Testament, the divinity of Christ, formalized in adherence to the monophysite doctrine,[5] the remoteness of God, and the necessity of dealing with him through a multitude of hierarchically ordered angelic messengers, agents, and deputies. In time of trouble, an Amhara makes representations to a number of saints and angels, who take his pleas to higher authorities; he seldom appeals directly to God, nor does God deal directly with him.

There is disorder in the cosmos, to be sure, for not all spirits are in the service of God. A vast multitude of spirits (Amhr.: *zar*), devils (Amhr.: *ganil*), and ogres (Amhr.: *chiraq*) roam the earth, undisciplined,

4. An excellent analysis of integration based on vertical rather than horizontal ties is to be found in Chie Nakane's as yet unpublished manuscript entitled *Univalent Society*. It appears, on the basis of this work, that a comparative analysis of Japanese and Amhara stratification patterns would be most productive.

5. The monophysite doctrine, which arose in extreme reaction to the Nestorian heresy, asserts that the two natures of Christ, the divine and the human, are fused into one, not merely combined as the leaders of the Greco-Latin church claimed. The final split over this issue took place at the Council of Chalcedon in 451. The Monophysites included the Syrian, Armenian, and Egyptian Churches. The Ethiopian Church was not involved in the controversy but followed the lead of its parent church in Egypt.

capricious, malicious, ready to fall upon the unwary man and to derange his mind or blight his body. There is also constant danger from that greatest of all rebels, *Dabilos*, who was cast out of heaven where he once ruled second only unto God. The crucial point, then, is not that the universe is completely ordered, but that whatever order is to be found is created by divine hierarchic control.

The routine happenings of the Amhara world are not thought to be dictated by God (though they are foreknown to him) or effected by his angelic host. The control exercised by God is regulatory, not dominating. In this respect it is like the control exercised by human "masters." It is a control that orders the world, to the extent that it is ordered, by making certain minimal demands, by establishing certain formal standards—by setting boundaries to legitimate action and by setting punishments for those who willingly transgress these boundaries.

The concept of order-giving, legitimate control is central to the evaluation of standards that underlie Amhara social stratification. *Kibur*, which I will gloss as "honor," the attribute that commands deference and determines rank order, derives above all else from *the legitimate control or influence over people or their destinies*. The pervasive pattern of deference and ranking in Amhara social life is thus closely related to the pyramidal network of patron-client ties that structure the Amhara polity. It is closely related but not identical. Social stratification is not political organization and honor is not power. Honor or *kibur* is distinguished from power (Amhr.: *hayl*) by its transitivity and its sources.

Power in the Amhara polity is intensive. A man of high rank has virtually no power over people unless they have bonds of personal dependency on him or his followers, and his control over his followers' followers is tenuous. Indeed, a man has no political relationship, per se, with other men unless they are his immediate superior, his follower, or are bound as client to the same lord.[6]

Honor is transitive. The legitimate control over men, to the extent that it is known and acknowledged, entitles the holder to well-defined degrees of deference and an appropriate rank vis-à-vis others, regardless of the personal political bonds that exist between them. A lord is not without honor in another district and among another lord's people, but he may be without power.

The principal sources of power are control over men and control over the land rights required to support and reward these men. A great man or governor at any level must rely on the support he personally

6. This generalization, like most generalizations, is not completely accurate. Powerful emperors did attempt to establish a rudimentary administration—particularly for purposes of tax collection—in areas over which they had a high degree of control. Such attempts were only temporary successes and seldom outlived the reign of the ruler.

controls, not on that at the command of his superior. In this sense power flows upward in the Amhara polity. Honor derives from power or control only to the extent that that power is considered to be legitimate. The source of legitimacy in this context is authorization or delegation from above, through a chain of links which ultimately leads to God, either directly or through the church or through the emperor. Honor, or rather the legitimacy from which it follows, thus flows downward. In sum, honor is transitive, flows downward and is continuous. Power is intransitive, flows upward, and is discontinuous.[7]

Though ultimately all authorized control which gives *kibur* flows from God, there are two major immediate sources or channels through which it is usually delegated to concrete individuals: through the emperor to the secular, military administrative hierarchy, and through the church to the clergy. The character of legitimate control is differentiated according to the channel through which it is legitimated. There are, thus, in traditional Amhara society, two partially independent and incommensurate stratificational scales and correspondingly two partially distinct ranked hierarchies.

The dichotomy between the secular and clerical "estates" in Amhara society is made explicit in Amhara concepts by the dichotomy between *bet kahinat* (literally, house of clergy) and *bet mengist* (literally, house of government) or *bet negus* (literally, house of the king). It is a dichotomy that involves differences not only in the specific hierarchies concerned but also in the character of the qualities and performances appropriate to recruitment to these identities, and proper to the enactment of their roles. In short, below the most general and unifying cultural perspective there is a fundamental difference between the ethos of the military elite and the ethos of the church, a difference that is evident in the standards by which members of church and army are ranked, and which permeates the images of the "ideal man" associated with these two institutions.

STRATIFICATION IN THE LOCAL COMMUNITY

The most important social groups to which members of a local community belong are households. Each household consists of the people who occupy a single homestead of one to three wattle and daub

---

7. This statement of the relationship among power, honor, and authority in the traditional Amhara polity is a highly condensed version of a central theme in Max Weber's writings on traditional domination, particularly as this theme has been set forth in relation to the political organization of the Alur by Southall (n.d.).

huts and who are subject to the jural and economic control of the house-hold head. The membership of a household normally includes the head, his spouse, perhaps an aging parent of either, and as many of the head's and his wife's respective children, collateral kinsmen (reckoned bilaterally), poor dependent retainers, and slaves as are useful in the exploitation of the economic resources at the head's disposal. The household may include a recently married son and his wife, but by the end of their second year of marriage they will move out and establish an autonomous household of their own. "Extended" or "joint" family households are not found.

The idiom of the household is not primarily an idiom of kinship as it is in so much of sub-Saharan Africa. It is rather the idiom of politics and clientship.[8] The Amhara term *betiseb* (literally, house people), which I have glossed household, denotes a co-resident group, not a kinship unit. In this sense there is no economical Amhara gloss for the English term *family*. The members of a household address one another by name rather than by kin terms. The head, however, is addressed with the honorific plural form "masters" (Amhr.: *getoch*) or "my master" (Amhr.: *getay*). Membership in the household is not determined in Amhara theory or practice by kinship ties, for all members except infants and small children can move from household to household, provided, of course, that the new household's head is willing to take them in and that the calculated cost of abandoning the old household's head is not too great. In a small sample gathered in Gojjam province, for example, household size corresponded more closely to size of landholding than to the number of living offspring claimed by the head.

Household interactional roles also evince little regard for kinship. The primary definition of social relations is between the head and those who serve him and hence are supported by him. It is difficult for a casual visitor to distinguish the head's children from his young dependent relatives or servants. Furthermore, the head is obligated to provide marriage-gift cattle and a wedding feast for all the boys and girls he "raises" and who "serve him," not just for those of them who happen to be his offspring.

Though the authority of the household head is thus relatively inde-pendent of kinship ties, the land-use rights on which the household as an economic unit relies are not, for plots of land and potential rights to additional plots are inherited bilaterally—that is, by sons and daughters (or their husbands or children) through both parents. In Amhara theory these actual and potential rights, both of which are termed *rist*, are rights to a share of the land first held by an illustrious ancestor (a principal ancestor or *wanna abbat*) whose name the land still bears. The arable lands in older Amhara regions are these ancestral blocks which vary from one

8. This same point was made by Beattie with regard to the Bunyoro.

half to two or three square kilometers in area. In Amhara legal theory *rist* rights in these lands are the inalienable and inextinguishable birthright of all the first ancestor's descendant's in all lines, regardless of whether or not the rights were utilized by intermediate lineal ancestors in the claimant's pedigree. In fact, most claims are forgotten. Nevertheless most adult men claim to have *rist* land rights in a half dozen or more of these "founding first ancestor's" blocks of land. Whether or not and to what extent a man can obtain strip fields, by virtue of these claims, in each of these blocks from the other co-descendants who happen to be sharing it depends on (1) whether his parents or grandparents or wife's father held fields in the block; (2) the proximity of his homestead to the block; and (3) his political influence. The detailed workings of his tenurial system are complex (Hoben, 1963, 1968). Two of its facets are particularly relevant to the present discussion: though *rist* land rights are "hereditary," the amount of land a man can control by virtue of these rights is dependent, above all, on his political influence; and land use rights over plots are considered to be held by individuals.

As the head of a household, a man must manage not only its members but also their combined economic resources, the main parts of which are cattle and land. The cattle, which are essential for cultivating the land, are contributed by the parents or guardian of the bride and groom in equal value at the time of the marriage and should be divided in case of divorce. The land includes (1) the scattered strips that the head has acquired from his father and mother or through litigation in which he cited a pedigree traced through one of them; (2) the strips he has acquired from his wife's father (or brother if the father is dead) or through litigation in her name; (3) the strips he may hold rent-free from an important man whom he supports; (4) the strips he holds in sharecropping tenancy; and (5) the strips that technically belong to other dependent members of his household.

In terms of authority and support the structure of the household conforms to the general Amhara model. While the head must be shown the utmost deference and outward submission by all the members of his household in all social interaction, in fact all of them have the option of leaving if they are not satisfied with his leadership, and many of them have rights in resources which they can take away with them. It is this mutual sanction of expulsion or departure rather than semisacralized or mystical notions of kinship which guarantees reasonably proper conduct in social relations between the household member and its head. Satisfactory relations between members are maintained only through internal ranking by age and sex, and the vigilance and mediation of the "master."

Thus even in this most elementary co-residential and socialization group of Amhara society, the household, order is maintained by the authority and managerial talent of a personal leader rather than by a sense of publicly upheld and ritually sanctionable group unity or spiritual solidarity.[9]

The pattern of local social organization and stratification above the household level is also consistent with the basic Amhara principle that deference is due those who maintain order through the exercising of legitimate control. Members of the local community are ranked when they gather on all formal occasions, and on all occasions when food is served, in accordance with the control they exert over others by virtue of their office, their lands, and the size of their households and their personal following.

Not all aspects of local social organization are based on vertical, dyadic, personal bonds to be sure. Indeed, there are a great many other kinds of social relationships in terms of which an Amhara farmer interacts with, is grouped with, and divided from his fellows. His homestead, along with 20 to 100 others, is part of a sprawling hamlet that may have occasional and minor administrative functions. The homesteads of several hamlets fall within a parish, a territorial unit a few square miles in area which is the building block of ecclesiastic organization. As a resident of the parish, a farmer must baptize his young and bury his dead at the parish church, must pay a small wheat tax, and must contribute labor and money to the maintenance of the church buildings. Each parish comprises the land blocks of from one to a dozen or more "first" ancestors. Tax rights over some of these blocks have been granted to the local church. Priests and ordinary farmers who hold fields as *rist* in these blocks pay no tax to the local lord but must support the regular mass by service or other contribution. The peasant's sense of identification with his parish is weakened by changes of residence (over 50 per cent of the adult males surveyed in rural Gojjam were not living in their natal parishes) and the many other ties he has which crosscut parish lines. Among the latter are his memberships in religious feasting associations (Amhr.: *mahabaroch*) and his reciprocal plowing, harvesting, housebuilding, wedding feast and trade relationships with various and varying constellations of his kinsmen, neighbors, and friends. Finally, a farmer's bilaterally traced kinship ties and affiliations with the landholding "corporations" mentioned previously are predominantly with people of other parishes.

This multiplicity of affiliations might seem to contradict the generalization that horizontal ties based on group membership are weakly developed in the social organization of the Amhara local community. In fact it is precisely this multiplicity of ties—their voluntary character, their wide and variable distribution, and the concomitant specificity of activity

9. The most comprehensive discussion of the Amhara household as an economic and political unit is to be found in Weissleder (1965: 22ff.).

and interest in each—that precludes an individual's committing himself very strongly to any of them. Every Amhara peasant has a unique constellation of potential and activated rights and interests. He may be united with people upon one occasion and in terms of one type of affiliation only to be opposed to some of these same people on another occasion in terms of another type of affiliation. His attitude toward his own and other peoples' fulfillment of role obligations is, consequently, in comparison with reports of other African societies, pragmatic rather than moralistic or ritualistic. This is particularly striking in the areas of kinship and descent (Hoben, 1963).

The high degree of structural individuation in Amhara social organization is consistent with the observed low degree of individual commitment to any of the groups of which he is a member. This low degree of group solidarity is evident in the paucity of group symbols, in the very limited amount of ritual activity specifically associated with any group except the parish, in the near absence of group-imposed sanctions, and, above all, in the inability of groups to undertake or bring to fruition cooperative activity unless their members are individually exhorted to action by an authority figure who characteristically exerts his influence, not as a leading member of the group, but through a role unrelated to group membership.

Perhaps the most striking example of this type of organization is to be seen in the way parishioners rebuild their churches. Despite the common belief that the collective and individual welfare of the parishioners is bound up with the ritual functioning of their church, parishioners are virtually never able to overcome their mutual suspicions and fears and organize the work without the intervention and assistance of an important man or noble. Most often this man is the local lord, the holder of the *gult* rights over the "estate" or seigniory within which the parish church happens to be located. Indeed, lord of the seigniory provides the main axis of organization and ranking within the local community.

As the judge, recipient of tribute (often one fifth to one fourth of the crop), leader of the militia, and representative of the government in all matters, the local lord enjoyed great authority over the peasants who lived in his seigniory. *Gult* rights do not include rights of cultivation, but if he could trace descent from one or more of the "first ancestors" of the land blocks within his seigniory, the lord was also able to control more fields as *rist* than any of his subjects. Some of these fields were farmed for him by the peasants of the seigniory, who were all obligated to give him a fixed number of days of labor during each crucial agricultural season. Other fields he might give rent-free to his favorite retainers or artisans, while still others were given to tenants.

The seigniory-holder thus had sufficient power to exceed his authority with respect to peasants who particularly displeased him.[10] Nevertheless it was in his own interest to maintain amicable relations with most of the peasants resident in his seigniory most of the time, for unlike the villeins of the thirteenth-century English manor, the Amhara peasant had both the *rist* land rights and the legal right which enabled him to move from one seigniory to another. Except in periods of political turmoil when there might be a rapid succession of *gult*-holders and in non-Amhara regions, the seigniory-holder could ill afford to be a despot, for land without people on it was of little value.

Regardless of their feelings or the actual state of their personal relationship with their lord, the peasants resident in the seigniory always showed him the utmost deference as befit his authority. Not only did the lord outrank the residents in all secular settings, but in a very real sense his physical presence defined the setting. The appropriate spatial arrangement of other persons present as well as the meaning of other types of deferential behavior was defined in relation to his presence.

On any occasion a great man had to be addressed with properly respectful speech forms, had to be approached with appropriate genuflexions and with the cotton cape draped in the required style. The lord could not take off his honor among his own people—not even when he entered a situation defined primarily in sacred, rather than secular, terms. In church, though he was clearly a layman and hence was not allowed to enter the mysterious sanctum sanctorum during the service, he was honored with a special seat in the outer vestibule and was the first layman to be offered the book or the cross to kiss.

Through deferential behavior was focused above all on the lord there were also important distinctions in rank between the other household heads in the seigniory. These differences in degree of honor corresponded quite closely to degrees of control over land and people. The resultant ranking pattern was expressed in many social settings but was nowhere more clear than on occasions when food was served. The major cleavages in rank in these terms were between (1) slaves; (2) low status artisans or *tayb*; (3) landless squatters or *tesengya*; and (4) *rist* right holders or *ristenya*.

Slaves having neither control over themselves nor land were the lowest group of all. The terms *shankalla* and *barea* by which they were known both refer to the darker tribal people who inhabit the lowlands to the west of the Ethiopian plateau. The terms have pejorative racial and ethnic implications. Though it would be inaccurate to say that the Amhara had an articulate racist doctrine, there can be no doubt that they had a low estimate of the potential ability of the tribal peoples they enslaved.

The *tayb* (also known as *tabib*), or artisans, varied somewhat in com-

---

10. A fascinating description of this situation is to be found in a novelette by Ras Imru, himself a former governor of Gojjam.

Allan Hoben: Traditional Amhara Society

position regionally, but generally they included the endogamous groups tanners and smiths, and in some areas weavers (Gojjam and part of Begemdir). The low status of these peoples is attributed by the other Amhara to their reputation as necrophagous witches (Amhr.: *Budda*), who kill their victims with the evil eye, and to their having no *rist* rights. While informants lay stress on the former quality—indeed *tayb* were formerly forbidden to eat with others for fear of the evil eye—it is striking that without *rist* rights it was impossible for any Amhara to build an estate and attract dependents. Besides plying their trades, *tayb* generally cultivated some land as rent-free tenants of the local lord for whom they, in return, worked without charge.

Tesenyas status depended on their presumed origin and their success in obtaining land. They were not *ipso facto* assumed to be possessed of the evil eye, but as strangers they were suspect. They suffered the same political liability as the landless *tayb* except that they might contract a rather disadvantageous type of uxorilocal marriage with a local woman and thus gain somewhat precarious control over her land.

The *rist*-holding group included most of the population, well over 90 percent in the older Amhara regions in northeastern Gojjam, Begemdir, northern Shoa, and western Wallo. In more recently occupied or re-occupied lands the *rist*-holding class might include only the households of the lord, his favorite soldiers, and the priests of the newly established church.

There were many distinctions of rank within the *rist*-holding class. These were evident in the seating arrangements at the feasts which accompanied weddings, memorial services for the dead, and major holidays. Guests were seated strictly in accordance with their honor on all of these occasions regardless of their roles (other than guest) in the proceedings. The main factor contributing to honor once again was the control derived from land, followers, and perhaps a close service tie with the local lord. Amhara often describe the important men of their community as big men (*tilliq saw*) or wealthy man. The latter appellation is misleading since it is only the wealth that comes from controlling land that gives honor. Even today a rich merchant is accorded little honor. Finally, all other factors being equal, age was an important criterion in the local community ranking pattern.

The *rist*-holding peasantry was also sharply divided into clergy (*Kahanat*) and laity (*Choa* in Gojjam dilaect). While this distinction was of great importance in sacred settings, as will be discussed, it did not affect ranking in most secular interaction. Priests might be poor or rich, "tired" or "strong," or high or low status just like anyone else.

At the apex of the ranking system stood the lord with his mandate of delegated authority from a still higher lord and his *gult* rights over the land. In an important sense the local lord "faced two ways," for his seigniory was not merely the most important single local unit of secular administration; as a grant of *gult* land it was also the fundamental building block on which rested the overarching military and ecclesiastic elites.

THE NOBILITY

The Amharic term *mekwannint*, in its most general sense, comprehends all those men who hold or have held office (Amhr.: *Shumat*) in the secular or ecclesiastic elite at the national, provincial, or subprovincial level. Ideally it was the desire of members of the secular elite, who will concern us here, to have (1) a governorate over a part of their lord's region: (2) a high military rank; (3) a court title entailing a service relationship to their lord; and (4) *gult* rights over as many seigniories as possible, especially over seigniories in which they also had *rist* rights and that lay within the districts they governed. Few men achieved all of these goals.

In spite of the great authority, special privileges and high honor enjoyed by the nobility, its members' consumptive tastes, their ideals, and their outlook on life were, in comparative terms, not very sharply differentiated from those of the general populace; nor did the nobles develop an *esprit de corps*, a sense of common purpose or an articulate notion of their common interests, as opposed to those of the peasantry or the emperor. This weak development of vertical cultural differentiation and of group solidarity is related to (1) the prominence of, one might almost say preoccupation with, dyadic and personal relationships which unite superior and inferior and set those of equal station against one another in their mutual competition for the favor of their common lord; (2) the participation of both nobles and landholding commoners indiscriminately in the same descent system; and (3) the wide diffusion of military ideals.

It is difficult to describe the formal structure of the Amhara polity concisely, not only because it is imperfectly known below the highest echelons but also because it was not rigidly fixed or standardized (Perham, 1948). Below the monarchy were a number of provinces defined largely by natural barriers, such as the mile-deep Blue Nile gorge that bounds Gojjam on three sides. These provinces in turn were subdivided by similar geographical factors into districts. While units on both levels and still smaller subdistricts and their constituent seigniories maintained their ethnohistorical identity through time, they were grouped and divided in various ways according to the vicissitudes of provincial politics and the ebb and flow of imperial power (Perham, 1948).

Allan Hoben: Traditional Amhara Society

At the turn of the century Gojjam, for example, was ruled by Negus Tekle Haymanot, a powerful lord who also ruled the newly won province of Kafa in the southwest. Gojjam itself was divided into a half-dozen districts. Each district was under the control of an appointed but often "local" governor who was himself a military lord with a large retinue and a mobile tent camp. Under each district governor were several hundred seigniories, many of which were held by the district governor himself, his superior, or his retainers. There were also several large monasteries embedded within most districts which were administratively autonomous and which themselves held the *gult* rights over up to one fifth of all the seigniories in the district. The secular seigniory-holders were, at that time, appointed by Tekle Haymanot, for whom they performed guard duty several weeks each year. After Tekle Haymanot's death Gojjam was divided among several contenders, each of whom acquired the right to grant seigniories as *gult*.

I have spoken of *gult* rights and the seigniories over which they extended as if they were all of one kind. This oversimplification is not unreasonable in relation to the local community, for it usually made little difference to peasants whether their local lord was a minor court official, an abbot or his appointee, a steward of some great lord, or even a representative of the provincial ruler who might hold the seigniory for his personal support. From the point of view of the provincial or district lord, however, there were many types of *gult* rights. These varied with the conditions under which they were given, the duration of the grant, and the identity of the recipient. Thus, for example, in Gojjam *gult* was termed *rist-gult* if given for life to a man who had acknowledged *rist* rights in the seigniory; or *maderiya-gult* if it was given on a temporary basis to a court official; or again *ganegeb* if it was retained by the *gult*-giving governor himself. There are numerous other specialized terms in other regions which reflect differences in the term of tenure and types of tribute.

There were also variations in the size of seigniories, in their relationship to other local territorial units such as the ancestral *rist* land blocks, and in the terms by which the local lords were known. In Gojjam, where about two thirds of all parishes were coterminous with seigniories, the average seigniory was from three to five square miles in area. Its holder was called a *gult-gej*. In the more recently occupied region around Ankober in Shoa, Weissleder (1965:105) reports that there are several hundred seigniories in a region of seventy-nine parishes. There the local lord was called a *melkenya*. In Gondar to the north of Lake Tana and Agau Midir (which was not completely Amharacized) to the south, there were from five to fifteen seigniories in a single parish. The holders of these small *gults* were termed *feresenya*, or horsemen. Significantly, in these latter regions there were the beginnings of bureaucratic office, and the local *gult* holders, whose power was small, might be little more than soldiers.

The *mekwannint* constituted the structure around which military activity in Amhara society coalesced and through which it was sustained. It is in keeping with this martial orientation that the most prized Amhara titles were in origin and reference positions of leadership in the army. The more important of these were:

ras	head (of any army)
dejazmatch	commander of the doorway (to the "palace")
fitawrari	commander of the vanguard
qerrazmatch	commander of the right wing
gerazmatch	commander of the left wing
balambaras	commander of a citadel

These titles were given by the emperor or, at times, by independent provincial rulers themselves of the rank of *rases* and *dejazmatches*.

A title-holding lord might have another title which signified his special sphere of responsibility at his liege lord's court. These court titles, which usually described personal services given to the lord, varied somewhat with time and place. At the imperial court of Iyasu I (1682–1706) they were:

behtwedded	chief counselor and confidant (two)
bilatten geta	chief administrator of the palace (greater and lesser) (two)
raq masere or	
wist azazh	majordomo, master of ceremonies
tsahafi tezaz	royal scribe; keeper of the seal (two)
zhandereba azash	chief of the eunuchs
bejirond	guardian of royal property, treasurer (two)
liqa mekuas	king's double and keeper of the king's mule (Levine, 1965:159–60)

Positions mentioned at other times include chief of honey-mead making, chief of beer-brewing, chief of bread-baking, chief of the lord's horses, chief of the lord's cattle, and even chief chaser-away-of-hyenas from the imperial tent! The specificity of the tasks referred to in these titles is misleading. What was required of the incumbent was that he command and control the people who performed the job, not that he have any particular technical competence. In all instances, these job-descriptive titles stressed the personal service performed for the lord within his household-military camp. The men who held these titles were not the heads of differentiated, functionally specific hierarchies through which the lord administered his domain. When there was a job to be supervised at some distance from the lord's camp, any of the high officials might be

Allan Hoben: Traditional Amhara Society

assigned the task of overseeing it to completion. In battle, the essentially unspecialized nature of the court officials became abundantly evident, for, one and all, the members of the lord's camp, from cook to brewmaster to majordomo and general, were warriors.

It was thus the ambition of every lord to have a military title, a court title, and, above all, *gezat*, or governorship, especially a land grant of the type previously referred to, so that he could establish his own military camp and his own court, complete with a set of personally loyal appointed officials. As Levine has remarked, the ideal type of the *mekwannint* was at once governor, soldier, and courtier.

The high status of an Amhara lord was made tangible in all social settings through numerous forms of deferential etiquette. The dominant theme expressed overtly and symbolically in all these forms of deferential behavior was one of unlimited and personal dependence on the lord. At feasts the great lord sat at the head of the table with his guests to the right and left of him, in order of their honor. Thus seated, sometimes behind a curtain, the lord issued a constant stream of commands to those serving the food and drink, many of whom were not his normal household servants but men who sought his favor. The lord saw to it that his guests at table were replete and, then, that their retainers, who were seated or standing at some distance, were given food in turn. The lord or one of his honored guests might call in a lower-ranking favored man, woman, or child and stuff a large roll of Amhara bread and sauce into his mouth as a sign of special affection.

Outside his compound the lord was shown deference in other ways. There were, almost invariably, people waiting for him at his gate ready to wail for his attention and present him personally with their woes—usually a court case. When the lord appeared, this throng fell into an ordered, crescent-shaped group. The lord was at the center, men of higher honor were near him to his left and right, and lesser men were out toward the forward-curving tips of the formation. In effect, everyone's field of vision was focused in the same direction as the lord's, yet all could see the lord and be seen by him. When the lord turned to one side, which he did with measured gravity, the entire entourage had to realign itself, one wing falling back and the other moving forward.

When the lord traveled, he always rode on a finely caparisoned mule. Around him were as many gun-bearing followers as befitted his means and station. If he was of high rank he was accompanied by a prescribed number of mounted kettledrums (Anhr.: *negarit*, literally, announcers) which announced his glorious approach. Ordinary travelers had to dismount, if they were riding, rearrange their white cotton shawls in one of the deferential styles, and bow to the great man as he approached. If a lord was passing through his own territory, peasants would leave their plows in midfield and accompany his procession as far as the parish boundary or even farther.

The symbolic importance of personal service relationships was evident in the great multiplication of personal retainers. Similarly the propensity of even the humbler retainers (for there are still no servants, in our sense of the word, in Amharaland) to engage retainers on their own initiative has been remarked by every traveler and social scientist who has written about Amhara society.

The importance of the personal bond is well illustrated by the two customary ways of establishing the relationship with a powerful lord: *dej tenat* and the *baldaraba*. *Dej tenat*, "gate waiting," involves literally waiting at the gate of the lord's compound each day until the lord takes notice, makes inquiries, and grants an audience. *Dej tenat* is synonymous with seeking a position in the lord household or other office.

When a man went to a lord to seek advantage against someone or to lodge a complaint there was no prescribed social or political identity in terms of which he could have a direct audience with the lord as citizen or subject. Unless he did *dej tenat* he had to find a court official of lesser rank with whom he could establish a bond on the basis of kinship, vicinage, or a gift, who would be his introducer and affair-tender. This person becomes his *baldaraba* and court.

The extensive deferential etiquette that governed interaction between superior and inferior in Amhara political relations might well suggest a deep-going authoritarianism in Amhara society. In a sense this is correct, but only provided it is remembered that authority is not power. It is true that, as Weissleder (1965:165) has put it, "status differential between two members of any social group [is] thought of and expressed as a leadership/follower relation." There are, however, three factors that serve to limit the effective power that could be exercised by the leader: the personal nature of control; concomitant subinfeudation; and customary expectations concerning the legitimate normal limits of control.

Because loyalty and deference were to the lord and not to an impersonal principle of administration or law, it was extremely difficult for a big man to have his command implemented unless he was physically present. A lord's power was almost unlimited within range of his vision and very great throughout his military camp. It dropped off very quickly, however, outside the confines of his camp—much to the frustration of many a traveler and anthropologist traveling in the Amhara countryside. The obverse of this limitation on the range of the lord's command was that if he was to exercise control over people to whom he was not highly visible, he had to delegate his authority to someone who was, but who thus became, if he was not already, the focal point of allegiance and loyalty to the local population concerned. In other words, the lord had to give away

Allan Hoben: Traditional Amhara Society

his authority in order to gain power, but his power thereby became conditional and subject to the agreement of his appointee.

Since the personal power base of the higher lord in troops and land was seldom large in comparison with the combined power of even a few of his major vassals, the power relationship between each vassal and the lord was subject to a secretive bargaining relationship. The vassal seldom undertook to mobilize his retainers and other resources on his superior's behalf unless it was to fulfill one of his time-honored expectations, such as tribute payment, or unless he stood to gain some immediate advantage from the lord in return—an advantage that he might have to partially relinquish, in turn, in favor of his own retainers to ensure their support. But then this is simply to recognize with Southall (n.d. 249ff.) that in the Amhara type of polity power flows up and authority down the political hierarchy, or to say with Weissleder (1965:324) that "a feudal leader recognizes power and tames it by clothing it with authority."

Recruitment and succession to the highly valued positions of the secular elite must be understood in relation to this pattern of political process, for there was in traditional Amhara society no rule of descent or succession through which any of a great nobleman's progeny were assured of attaining noble status. Every member of the nobility in every generation had to be raised to, not merely confirmed in, his father's glory.

In regranting high office or bestowing titles, the effective ruler had two kinds of considerations: that the recipient be capable of commanding a following, and that he be loyal. It was not normally possible to give equal weight to each consideration. Indeed the process of recruitment was affected by which of these factors was of paramount concern to the ruler. If he thought that he could control the governorate in question with his personal following, he might grant it to one of his loyal retainers as a reward for past service and in anticipation of future loyalty. Such an appointee might well be a commoner who had become a page boy at court in his youth and who had risen to rank in the ruling lord's retinue. The figure of the "self-made" lord was, at all times, a familiar one, though not a common one, on the Amhara scene.

If, on the other hand, the superior ruling lord was unsure of his ability to control a region personally, it was expedient for him to grant control over it to a leading contender who was already powerful if not dominant there.

The death of the lord in such a region normally fragmented his power base because neither the land rights nor the dyadic interpersonal political ties on which his power rested normally passed intact to a single heir. The lord's senescence and death were regularly followed by an intense rivalry among his sons, sons-in-law, and collateral kinsmen, each of whom hoped to reconsolidate that part of the deceased's power base to which he could lay claim and, if possible, to add to it. The children of the lord usually had the initial advantage of having "inherited" a share of the father's land and with it a share of his following; but it was their position in a "field of political opportunity," their de facto control of men and land, rather than a rule of succession to office, which gave them this advantage and made them the most likely candidates for appointment by the ruler to the vacant position. When this pattern of competitive succession was followed for several generations it created what are somewhat misleadingly referred to in the English literature as "leading families."

Yet another path to glory, and one that illustrates the dynamics of recruitment to high position well, was that of the commoner outlaw or *shifta*. After rising through a career of brigandage and extortion, the outlaw might convert his precarious power over his region into more stable authority by accepting office and title and thus reincorporating his remote or unsettled territory into the wider Ethiopian polity.

Such men fared best in troubled times, such as the first half of the nineteenth century, the "age of princes," when any able brigand leader might hope to have his power "clothed with authority." Indeed the Emperor Theodore, who put an end to this unhappy period of Ethiopian political turmoil, was himself such a self-made man.

Regardless of his road to success, however, a nobleman could hope to gain a vast estate of *gult* land to rule, judge, and tax, and thousands of acres of *rist* land to further supply his household's needs. All of this he would likely claim as his hereditary right, for any member of the *rist*-holding class could trace (or find some expert to trace) pedigrees not only to numerous "first ancestors" but through them to illustrious if remote ancestors (Hoben 1963). The rich tapestry of founding myths, the images and beliefs associated with each land block, parish, and seigniory, and woven into legends relating to district, province, and nation, are thus the means by which newly achieved political authority was cloaked with antiquity and bolstered with a readymade hereditary estate. At the same time these myths served to some extent to commit the *rist*-holding peasants to their lord should he have a local pedigree.

To these free Amhara in their traditional homelands the lord of the seigniory was not the hated representative of an alien elite or a member of a culturally distinct and superior social class. He was one of themselves, often a kinsman to some and a descendant of the same founding ancestor as many. There was an aura of pomp and authority surrounding him, but it was to a great extent an attribute of the order-giving authority he held, and not of the incumbent himself, who might even be of humble birth.

There was, to be sure, an authoritarian cast to the social interaction between the lord of the seigniory and his peasants, but this very quality was considered proper and appropriate by all concerned. The peasants might grumble about the burdensome obligations placed upon them, but they also took great pride in the munificence of the lord's feasts, the the size of his household, and in the gifts, titles, and rank he received fom his lord. There was no assumption that the holder of any office had superior moral worth. On the contrary there was rather a tendency to suspect that the great will always abuse their power. This attitude is summed up most pithily in the oft-aired proverb to the effect that "the wise man bows low to the great lord and silently farts."

The myth of common descent with the nobility thus provided an ideological counterweight to the burden of secular authority that rested upon the peasantry. It told every farmer that he, too, had great and noble ancestors but a few generations back, and that he, too, or perhaps his seed, could once again rise to office through military service and claim a share of his rightful hereditary estate and seigniories.

The farming population's sense of participation in and continuity with the Amhara polity was also strengthened by the diffusion of military ideals and values throughout the landholding peasantry, for this military ethos set before lay farmers an image of opportunity for all through military service. It was characterized by its pervasiveness and its essentially unspecialized nature. It entailed a way of life, a mode of achievement and a state of soul which was held appropriate not to some of the people (the elite) all of the time, but to all of the people (except the clergy) some of the time.[11] As Levine (n.d.:6) has remarked:

> They [the Amhara armies] came quickly into being, performed erratically and dissolved in a moment. Their potency was due, not to the perfection of a specialized institution devoted to the art of warfare, but rather to the extent to which Ethiopian society as a whole was pervaded by military skills, virtues, and ambitions.

There was, of course, a considerable amount of reality behind the myth of mobility through seizing the military moment. Every able-bodied free male Amhara farmer did have a certain degree of knowledge of and competence with arms.

The peasant or lord who took down his rifle, packed his provisions and marched off to war with his local leader did so with the expectation of getting a more substantial reward than glory. Participation in a successful campaign might supply a man with ample booty in livestock, slaves, or other goods. Most importantly, however, as has already been remarked, success on the battlefield brought political benefits.

Though it was by no means infrequent (campaigns were often renewed annually in the dry season), warfare remained throughout most of Ethiopian history a part-time vocation. Its ideological or motivational impor-

11. For a further treatment of this theme see Weissleder (1965:61–62).

tance should not, for this reason, be underestimated. There is a sense in which the Amhara are oriented in their aspirations, not to the daily or yearly routines of administration or farming, but rather to the great military moment, to the exceptional time of crisis when fame, political fortune, and honor are to be won or lost. This orientation is evident in the content of poems and songs heard by the fireside or at public festivities in the Amhara countryside as well as in the courts of local lords. It is evident in discussions of how particular men gained office and why they merit it. It is evident in the matter-of-fact assurance and detail with which the visitor is told what will be done when, once again, the call of arms is issued and the militia mobilized, and it is evident in the obvious excitement with which men anticipate this return of the extraordinary military moment.

The pervasive ideal of military glory, coupled with the dogma of bilateral descent, validated the conviction that upward mobility was possible, a conviction that helped commit the peasantry to a social system in which their rewards and prerogatives were comparatively small. At the same time it diverted the energy of unusually able and potentially disruptive individual peasants into legitimate military activities.

THE CLERGY

It is not possible to distinguish in the clergy, as it was in the secular elite, a single rather simple pattern of social stratification. Though the clergy as a whole contrasts with the secular elite, there is, within its ranks, a more situationally differentiated system of ranking than is found in the secular sector of Amhara society.

The crucial positions that form the structural framework of stratification in the secular elite constitute a single hierarchy. This is because they are functionally undifferentiated, primarily political positions in a nominally unitary, fully articulated, political hierarchy. At the same time, the cultural basis and the nature of the control or authority in terms of which they are ranked are essentially the same for all identities.

The crucial clerical identities in terms of which ranking is ordered cannot be said to constitute a unified hierarchy. Behaviorally this means that the relevance of a "clerical" identity to ranking varies with the type of setting involved. In other words, the ranking of the same identities is different in different social scenes. From an analytical point of view, this means that clerical identities do not constitute a single institutional hierarchy, are functionally differentiated, and derive their honor from legitimate control which derives from God via diverse routes.

Allan Hoben: Traditional Amhara Society

Concretely, it is useful to distinguish three kinds of identities within the clergy: high ecclesiastical officials, local clergy, and monks. These three types of identities are distinguished by the scenes in which they are highly ranked, the source of the control or influence which gives them *kibur*, and the qualifications required of the incumbent. The *kibur* of the high official rests largely on his secular administrative control. The *kibur* of the local clergy rests on its control of routine access to the sacred symbols and services of the church. It is attained through learning and requires adherence to certain standards of ritually pure conduct. The *kibur* of the monk, in instances where it is manifest, derives from the direct contact he has with Heaven by virtue of his rigorous ascetic piety. It must be kept in mind, however, that there is considerable variation within each category and that the same individual may have more than one type of identity.

Traditionally, the high ecclesiastical officials of the national level included the *abuna* or bishop; the *ichege*, second in rank but first in secular command of the clergy; several clerical imperial court officials; the *alekas* and *memhers*, who were abbots of the great landed monasteries; and provincial officials known as *liqekahenat*, who controlled the provincial (nonmonastic) clergy.

With the exception of the *abuna*, these officials owed their high rank primarily to their secular control, a control that derived directly or indirectly from imperial appointment, and only secondarily to their ritual functions and minimally to ascetic piety. Like their secular counterparts, the nobles, from whom many of them were recruited, high church officials were shown honor in most secular social settings.

From the fourth century until 1949, the *abuna* was appointed from the monastery of Saint Anthony by the Patriarch of Alexandria. As a foreigner who took little active interest in the customs or language of his new home, the *abuna* normally exercised virtually no authority in his own right. He has been described as a "tool," a "prisoner," and even as a slave of the emperor.

Nevertheless, he was ritually indispensable, for, as the Egyptian church refused to appoint suffragan bishops, he was the only official in Ethiopia who could anoint and crown the emperor, ordain the clergy, bless the arks essential for each church and, in accordance with the emperor's wishes, excommunicate. Ritually important as he was, however, the *abuna* did not enjoy autonomy in doctrinal matters. Forced by his own holiness to live in relative seclusion, the *abuna* had to content himself with the comforts afforded by his generous endowment in benefices, the outward sign of highest deference shown his august person, and whatever satisfaction he might derive from sitting in "his 'solemn insignificance' upon the emperor's right hand at all public occasions" (Perham, 1948:106).

The second-ranked *ichege* was appointed by the emperor, usually from the monastery of Debra Libanos of which he became, in any case, the abbot ex-officio. As the administrative head of all Ethiopia's monasteries and of the provincial *liqekahenat* as well, the *ichege* enjoyed rather more power than the *abuna*. He was, of course, subject in all matters to the throne.

High churchmen of the imperial court owed their influence, and hence their *kibur*, very largely to their proximity to and familiarity with the highest secular officialdom. Like secular courtiers, their positions were defined in terms of the services they performed for the king—in this case, services of a ritual nature.

The laymen appointed as heads of great secular monasteries (Amhr.: *deber*, sing.) and the monks who served as the heads of more purely religious monasteries (Amhr.: *geddam*, sing.) enjoyed high honor and received great deference within the territories they governed. Provincial and subprovincial *liqekahenat* also enjoyed high honor and considerable secular authority over the clergy they controlled. At great public festivities they are still found at the right hand of the secular governor of their territory.

The "working" or local clergy includes the priests (Amhr.: *qes*, sing.), deacons (Amhr.: *diakon*, sing.), more marginally teachers (Amhr.: *meregeta*, sing.), and canons (Amhr.: *debtera*, sing.) associated with the common parish church. All of them are usually also full members of the local farming community enmeshed in ties of kinship, descent, regular landholding and voluntary associations with their lay neighbors. The interests of the clergy are thus, in many respects, congruent with those of the lay population. With respect to their shared interests in the land rights, movable property, income and other prerogatives of the local church corporation, usually referred to as "the ark," however, the clergy have a distinct and, upon occasions, conflicting position which sets them off from their fellow parishioners. It is primarily in relation to their religious duties that the local clergy receive deference, and it is in primarily religious "scenes" that they enjoy higher rank than men of equivalent secular standing.

In a general sense all the clergy are servants of the lord. They all enjoy *kibur* from the control they have as dispensers of church benefits, but they are internally differentiated according to the nature of their ritual services, the degree of their education, and the purity of their way of life.

Priests and deacons are the most essential members of the local clergy, for they alone can celebrate the mass upon which the welfare of the community is thought to be mystically dependent. At least two priests and three deacons must take part in each service.

The deacons, who have the secret privilege of preparing the host, are prepubescent boys who have been trained in the Ethiopian syllabary characters, excerpts from the gospels, the psalms, and a number of other sacred texts, including Paul, and the first part of the readings used in the church service. Finally, they must have been ordained by the bishop, of whom there was traditionally but one in all of Ethiopia. This practical difficulty was met at times with the practical expedient of ordaining en masse babes in arms and young boys who were only subsequently trained in the mysteries of the church.

The deacon is schooled in a strict regime while living at one of the local churches, begging for his food, enduring physical hardships, and memorizing Geez texts and chants he does not understand.

With the approach of puberty a deacon should not assist at the mass, for it is doubted that he will keep his sexual purity. If he is to become a priest, he must marry and have his marriage consecrated in a double communion church ceremony which binds him to one woman for life. He must also complete additional studies and journey to the bishop for ordination.

As a priest, an Amhara enjoys a number of material and jural benefits as well as a certain amount of prestige. At the same time he suffers several disabilities. If his wife dies the priest may not remarry if he wishes to keep his ordination, nor may he have extramarital intercourse. Even within marriage his sexual activity is restricted by ritual requirements. In addition to this sexual restraint, the priest should observe moderation in drinking and avoid becoming embroiled in brawls. The priesthood is not, however, noted for its great success in living up to these latter ideals. In fact, the extra honor shown to the priest is quite clearly deference to the ritual sanctity entailed in his identity and not to any illusions about his holiness of heart or purity of motivation.

Except in specifically religious settings, such as those associated with the normal service and the great cycle of church holidays and festivals, the priest receives special deference only when he is wearing his distinctive white turban and carrying his cross.

The other principal members of the local clergy are the teacher and the canon. The teacher is usually distinguished from the priest by his years of advanced church studies at one or more of the famed regional or national monasteries. Unless he is also a priest he need not, however, maintain the ritual purity or monogamy expected of the latter. The teacher is least likely of all the local clergy to be of local origin. It is perhaps due to his peripatetic life (who knows who his father was?), as well as to a deep Amhara mistrust of excessive arcane learning unaccompanied by ascetic piety, that the teacher is often the least-honored member of the clergy.

The canon is a man who is, educationally, at least, qualified for the priesthood but who has not preserved his ritual—particularly his sexual—purity. Indeed many canons are more learned in the vast esoterica of the Ethiopic religious tradition than are most priests, for while the status of the priest is significantly dependent on his church functions as chorister, dancer, and poet, the canon must supplement his minor influence as a member of the church corporation with a private trade in charms, amulets, spells, and curses.

The influence a canon may derive through his reputation for manipulating the forces of evil and trafficking with the devil is suspect. It may yield him some power; but it is a power based on fear, not *kibur*. The same is true of a number of other practitioners who deal with the supernatural through illicit channels, including the astrologer (Amhr.: *kokeb qoteri*), the book-revealer (Amhr.: *mesahaf gelatch*), and the spirit medium (Amhr.: *bale zar*).

In general cultural terms, the identity "monk" (Amhr.: *menewske*) contrasts with all other Amhara religious and secular identities, since it entails an explicit renunciation of earthly pleasure, possessions, power, and legal obligations. Any person, man or woman, who wants to become a "monk" must receive religious instructions, give up his rights and obligations in property, and undergo a ceremony in which his body is declared dead (Levine, 1965:170). There are, however, a number of ways in which this generalized ideal of withdrawal from wordly concerns is institutionalized. These relate to both the qualities of the people who become "monks" and the paths they choose to follow after they have done so.

The commonest type of "monk" today is the feeble old man (or woman) who wishes to retire from the normal responsibilities of peasant life and to live out his last years in contemplative preparation for the next world. Such monks often continue to live with kinsmen. An old man without close kin may derive sustenance performing menial tasks at the local church. Widowed priests, in particular, frequently become monks, as indeed they must, if they want to keep their ordination and continue to serve the mass.

It was not only men of humble status who chose the monastic path. Famed warriors, great noblemen, and even emperors became monks when oppressed by years or evil times. Finally, and least commonly, unmarried deacons and young widows might take monastic vows.

Except for the rare instance of the monk who "leaves the world only to rejoin it at a higher level" (Levine, 1965:171) as the abbot of a great monastery, the Amhara monk renounces the world in deed as well as word. The success with which he is judged to have succeeded in breaking his bonds with this secular life and to have established communication with the next is directly related to his prophetic and mystic powers and

Allan Hoben : Traditional Amhara Society

to his associated *kibur*. Monks who seek more seclusion than normal parish life can afford them may attach themselves to monasteries, where they follow a stringent schedule of fasting, prayer, and service. Others wander from parish to parish and district to district (some even go to Jerusalem) as mendicants, receiving alms for their food and sleeping in churchyards amid the graves. Such are the monks who occasionally settle in a parish long enough to successfully exhort the parishioners to rebuild or repair their church buildings, an organizational task normally achieved only by men of considerable political standing or unusual economic means.

Most withdrawn of all, and most awesome, are the hermits who dwell in the "caves and the forests," eating only what vegetable matter they can forage and subjecting themselves to painful vigils and self-mortification.

The legendary archetype of these monks is St. Tekle Haymanot, who is believed to have stood praying on one leg so long that it fell off and rose to heaven. It is the same saint who is believed to have established the present institutional relationship between church and state—ordering the complementary division of land and powers in each parish as in the Empire. More recently the prophecies of noted monks have more than once played a vital ideological role in the politics of national and regional succession. In the present decade I witnessed an occasion in Gojjam province when a naked, anchoretic monk walked into the house of a district governor unobstructed by a multitude of guards, violated all the normal rules of etiquette and respect for secular authority, and openly criticized the emperor of Ethiopia for permitting the local weekly market to be held on Saturday.

THE MONARCHY

The emperor stood alone, far above all other Amhara in authority, legitimacy, and *kibur*. In his person the secular and ecclesiastic hierarchies culminated and were united. His order-creating control rested, according to Amhara political theory, on his sole right to grant high office in church and state, his titular "ownership" of the land, and the direct mystical influence his social personality was thought to have on the peace, prosperity, and fertility of his realm. The dual nature of the emperor's control was legitimized by belief in his descent from King Solomon and his election by God. These two sources of legitimacy are expressed in the conventional honorific, "The Lion of the Tribe of Judah has Conquered, the Elect of God, King of the Kings of Ethiopia," and symbolized at his coronation when the archbishop anointed him with oil and crowned him. They are also clearly evident in the ritual and symbolism of deference which surrounds his court and person, and in the image he presents to his people.

Throughout the greater part of the period of Amhara ascendancy the seat of the imperial court was a mobile military camp. At the center of this circular city of tents were the emperor's personal tents and the tent that housed his chapel. Arranged in a fixed pattern around the royal tents were the tent establishments of those of the emperor's great retainers who were at court, each surrounded in turn by his followers and would-be followers. On the outer circumference of the camp was a horde of ragged followers.

Though the legitimacy and formal prerogatives of the throne were always great, the actual power that the monarch exercised over his lords and through them over his outlying provinces varied considerably. The ideology of absolute imperial authority was set forth eloquently by Sir James Bruce, a visitor to Ethiopia during the latter half of the eighteenth century:

> The kings of Abyssinia are above all laws. They are supreme in all causes, ecclesiastical and civil; the land and persons of all their subjects are equally their property and every inhabitant of the kingdom is born their slave; if he bears a higher rank it is by the king's gift; for his nearest relations are accounted nothing better. (Bruce, 1790: Vol. III: 280)

As head of the nation's defense force, head of its church, and highest judge in the land, the emperor had very substantial rights to wealth and control if he could but enforce them. He had rights to tribute in grain, livestock, slaves, honey, horses, civet, ivory, and gold from the various regions in his empire. He also had the right to control and tax long-distance trade, to receive judicial fees, to levy and collect market fees, and to grant monopolies over certain high-value commodities such as salt and gold. Many of these rights were not exercised directly even by the most powerful emperor but were granted away by him to his favorites at court or in the regions where these rights were of use.

The ruler had several means by which he could attempt to enforce his rights. Important among these were the small army he maintained personally, his ability to monopolize a high proportion of firearms in the land (after their introduction in the sixteenth century), and his ability to appoint and recall, promote and demote his major followers. The ability of the emperor to exercise this last prerogative was the best index to the extent of his actual power.

Historically, the power of the throne was at its height before and during the early part of the sixteenth century prior to the Moslem invasion. During this time the emperor easily was able to appoint and dismiss governors, at least in some northern regions, and was able to force them to wait for months at court in abject submissiveness for a new governorate.

Allan Hoben: Traditional Amhara Society

It is clear, however, from the accounts of early travelers, that even when the monarchy was at its greatest strength the absence of a differentiated governmental service restricted the emperor's power to the realm of tribute and tax collection and the recall and replacement of higher officials. It did not extend to most areas of civil or communal affairs. Nor was the emperor's "passport" sufficient to assure his guests tranquil passage through his domain.

Imperial power reached its nadir in the first half of the nineteenth century, in an epoch characterized by short-reigned rulers, powerful kingmaker lords, and rival monarchs. In part this erosion of imperial power seems to be the result of Moslem and Galla incursions, but equally important was the long residence of the throne amid the elegant court life at the Portuguese-inspired stone castles at Gondar to the north of Lake Tana. The Ethiopian emperor, like the early Irish kings, could not expect his sovereignty to long remain intact unless his authority was periodically manifested in each corner of his kingdom by the presence of his royal person and his rapacious following.

There were also great changes in imperial power associated with the succession and the maturation in office of a new monarch. Succession, if a word so laden with connotations of orderly progression may be used, to the crown was not determined by a highly restrictive rule such as primogeniture or even immediate royal parentage. Indeed, succession from father to son was the exception, not the rule. To be sure, a candidate for the crown had to be accounted of the Solomonid line, but this could, like all Amhara pedigrees, be traced "ambilaterally" through a number of unillustrious generations. There was no rule limiting the number of nonruling generations through which a legitimating royal pedigree might be traced. As in the case of the great provincial noble, however, a successor was best able to marshal support if he was not too far off the ruling line. At times all of the major potential contenders were imprisoned on an inaccessible mesalike mountain whence they were summoned by factions of would-be kingmakers.

Regardless of the power of the emperor at a particular time, his honor was always immense. On all occasions, the deference to him was elaborate and formal. Not only did the forms of deferential behavior associated with the role of the ruler prescribe that he be shown respect through forms of speech, rules of dress, and modes of genuflexion, but they tended to make him "invisible" as well—to remove him as a man from the purview of his subjects. Few could have audiences with him, and those who did had to approach him with their bodies prostrate upon the ground, their foreheads on the earth, and their eyes downcast. Furthermore the emperor, especially in earlier times, was partially veiled or secluded in a "kind of box" when he appeared for state functions or duties.

The image of sanctity conveyed by medieval Amhara monarchs, the combination of quiescence and stationary power, has never been described more vividly than by Father Francisco Alvares writing of the audience he had with Emperor Lebna Dengel on November 20, 1520:

> In front of this dais [inside the royal tent] were other curtains of much greater splendour, and while we were standing before them, they opened them, for they were drawn together, and there we saw the Prester John [a term always used by Alvares, who was convinced that he had found the Prester John of legendary fame] sitting upon a platform of six steps very richly adorned. He had on his head a high crown of gold and silver . . . and a silver cross in his hand; there was a piece of blue taffeta before his face, which covered his mouth and beard, and from time to time they lowered it and the whole of his face appeared, and again they raised it. . . . The Prester was dressed in a rich mantle . . . and he was sitting as they paint God the Father on the wall. (Alvares, 1961:303–4)

SUMMARY AND CONCLUSIONS

Traditional Amhara society may be classed usefully as feudal inasmuch as its polity and ranking system rested on a hierarchical network of personal and contractual, vertical ties between whole men, and on a conjunction of sovereignty with rights in land. At the same time the pattern of Amhara social organization and stratification differed from those of most European feudal orders in the relative absence of social and cultural differentiation between the farming and the ruling groups. The difference between farmer and local lord was largely of achieved rank, not "blood," ideals, or basic style of life. Peasant and noble shared similar military aspirations, the same ancestors, and above all the same vertical principles of social organization and ranking. The fundamental cultural postulate upon which this ubiquitous vertical principle rests was that *social order, which is good, can be created and maintained only through hierarchical, legitimate control deriving ultimately from God.*

The structural correlate of this postulate was the integrative emphasis at all levels of Amhara society on dyadic vertical social relationships rather than on membership in corporate groups based on qualification or on common purpose. In almost all situations social ties between subordinate and superordinate had greater economic, political, and affective importance than ties between people of approximately equal status. The economic aspect of such ties took the form of tribute and reward rather than market exchange. The political aspect took the form of personal service and protection rather than coalition and cooperation. The affective aspect took the form of loyalty and support rather than corporate solidarity.

The Amhara system of stratification and ranking was closely related to this vertical pattern of integration, for "honor," which commanded deference and determined rank order in all social scenes, derived from legitimately authorized control over people. The partially independent secular and ecclesiastical hierarchies were differentiated by the source of this legitimate control. The ranking of people in scenes defined by the secular order corresponded quite closely to the distribution of official authority in the quasi-feudal polity. Wealth, education, sanctity, or other attributes were of little independent importance in this order. Ranking in the religious sphere, on the other hand, involved greater internal institutional differentiation; thus there were three partly discrete religious scales of ranking distinguished according to the source of their legitimacy.

Crosscutting the secular and ecclesiastical hierarchies were horizontal strata distinguished by major differences in types of authority and control over land. At the top of both hierarchies was the emperor with his (ideally) unlimited authority and his (theoretical) control over all the land. Next in honor were the *makwannint*, or nobles, comprising all titled members of both elites and distinguished from lower strata by their possession of the authority entailed in grants of *gult*. Below the nobility in the secular hierarchy were the taxpaying lay farmers who were subdivided into *rist*-holders and cotters. In the ecclesiastic hierarchy the counterpart of the lay farmers were the clergy. Still lower in honor were the endogamous artisans' groups, suspected of the evil eye, forbidden to eat with other Amhara, usually landless and without hope of ever attaining title, *gult*, or honor. Lowest of all—in a sense not fully Amhara—were the slaves who had neither land nor authority over anyone.

During the present century a permanent capital city of half a million population has grown up at Addis Ababa. With its growth the old Amhara feudal order has been changing at an ever accelerating pace. A centralized modern army and police force have replaced the scattered, ragtag peasant armies. A differentiated, centralized, and formally bureaucratic administration has been established. The authority once held by the *gult*-holding lord of the seigniory has been gradually taken from him and now is exercised by a tax collector, a judge, a police chief, and a governor at the local district (*werrede*) level. At the same time the belief that upward social mobility was possible through military activity has been largely replaced by a similar faith in government school education. The church, which has lost many of its local judicial and economic powers and has not developed new and rewarding occupational roles, offers much less opportunity for advancement than it did in the past.

The growth of administration and the increase in modern commercial activity has produced a great multiplication of occupational roles and of social scenes in which their incumbents must interact. Along with these structural changes there have been changes in the attributes in terms of which men rank one another, though these have generally lagged behind. Technical skills that require physical work are still regarded with disdain. Education, particularly through or beyond the twelfth grade, carries great prestige but largely because it guarantees a person government employment, salary, and authority.

Wealth has also become a more significant factor in ranking, though if unaccompanied by title or authority it is still viewed with suspicion. The modern businessman, like the courtier of old, should pay periodic visits to the imperial court, for the symbolic demonstration of personal dependence on the throne has not lessened.

If anything, the pattern of personal dependence on the emperor has been strengthened, as the present emperor, Haile Selassie I, has converted much of his traditional, often theoretical, authority to effective control and has introduced innovations which were, at first, little understood and not always appreciated by his people. The vertical principle of social integration and the view of human nature it reflects are thus still very much in evidence today. Indeed it has contributed greatly to the speed and the minimum of disturbance, disorganization, political discontinuity with which innovations have been accepted. Yet paradoxically it appears to some observers, particularly Levine (1965), that this same principle— this same emphasis on personal, dyadic vertical ties—is the greatest hindrance to the institutionalization of bureaucratic norms and the further modernization of Ethiopian society.

BIBLIOGRAPHY

Alvares Francisco   1961   The Prester John of the Indies: A True Relation of the Lands of the Prester John. Published for the Hakluyt Society, Cambridge.

Beattie, John   1960   Bunyoro: An African Kingdom. New York, Holt, Rinehart & Winston.

Bottomore, T. B., and Maximilien Rubel   1956   Karl Marx: Selected Writings in Sociology and Social Philosophy. Watts & Co.

Bruce, James   1790   Travels to Discover the Source of the Nile, vol. 3. Edinburgh, J. Ruthven.

Durkheim, Emile   1951   Suicide: A Study in Sociology. New York, The Free Press.

Fallers, Lloyd A.   1959   Despotism, status culture and social mobility in an African kingdom. Comparative Studies in Society and History, 2(1): 11–32.

———— 1963 Equality, modernity, and democracy in the new states, in: Old Societies and New States: The Quest for Modernity in Asia and Africa, Clifford Geertz (ed.). New York, The Free Press.

———— 1964 The King's Men. London, Oxford University Press.

Goodenough, Ward H. 1965 Rethinking "status" and "role" towards a general model of the cultural organization of social relationships, in: The Relevance of Models for Social Anthropology. A.S.A. Monographs 1. New York, Frederick A. Praeger.

Hoben, Allan 1963 The role of Ambilineal Descent Groups in Gojjam Amhara Social Organization. Doctoral dissertation, University of California, Berkeley. University Microfilms, Ann Arbor, Michigan.

———— 1968 Land tenure and social mobility among the Damot Amhara. To be published by the Journal of Ethiopian Studies, Proceedings of the Third International Conference of Ethiopian Studies.

Imru, Haile Sellassie (H. H. Ras) 1962 Fitawrari Belay. Ethiopia Observer, 5:(4):342–60.

Levine, Donald N. 1965 Wax & Gold: Tradition and Innovation in Ethiopian Culture. Chicago, University of Chicago Press.

———— n.d. The Military in Ethiopian Politics. Unpublished manuscript.

Nakane, Chie n.d. Univalent Society. Unpublished manuscript.

Parsons, Talcott 1954a An analytical approach to the theory of social stratification, in: Essays in Sociological Theory, rev. ed., Talcott Parsons (ed.). New York, The Free Press.

———— 1954b A revised analytical approach to the theory of social stratification, in Essays in: Sociological Theory, rev. ed., Talcott Parsons (ed.). New York, The Free Press.

Perham, Margery 1948 The Government of Ethiopia. New York, Oxford University Press.

Plowden, Walter Chichele 1868 Travels in Abyssinia and the Galla Country. London, Longmans, Green.

Southall, Aidan W. n.d. Alur Society. London, Heffer & Sons.

Weissleder, Wolfgang 1965 The Political Ecology of Amhara Domination. Doctoral dissertation, University of Chicago.

SOCIAL STRATIFICATION IN BORNU

BY RONALD COHEN

A MODEL OF SOCIAL STRATIFICATION

In order to describe and analyze a society from the point of view of social stratification, some overall theoretical framework is necessary. Yet, given the present lack of agreement in this field, such theoretical tools are not easily come by unless the researcher has (a) a logical means of preferring one approach over another or (b) some means of testing which theoretical concepts can adequately explain his data.[1] On the other hand, the primary goal of this chapter is not so generally theoretical in nature, which means that we must have a set of concepts that do justice to the complexity of the case material to follow and provide an adequate basis for submitting this data to analysis and explanation.

As a starting point, let us define social stratification as an aspect of social systems. Social stratification may be a system in and of itself, but it is, empirically, always embedded in the social system such that it is in effect an attribute of the role structure. Thus, on definitional grounds alone we should start our theoretical analysis by stating that social

Fieldwork in Bornu was first carried out in 1955–57 under the auspices of the Ford Foundation Area Training Program. I returned to the area in the summer of 1964 under a small grant from NIMH and again in the summers of 1965 and 1966 with the financial assistance of NSF. I am grateful to all these agencies and to the Program of African Studies at Northwestern University for making these trips possible. I would also like to thank Professor John Middleton, who read and commented on a previous draft of this chapter.

1. See Lasswell, 1965.

stratification is a function of social structure. This means that any understanding of stratification depends on an understanding of the basic outline of the social structure in which it operates. In operational terms we can expand this definition by saying that social stratification refers to the means by which the members of a society are able to rank the roles in their society and the activities that make up these roles. This is due to the fact that social stratification always refers to the way in which scarce values are allocated. Societal members then rank roles in terms of how much the desirable ends are available in different parts of the role structure of the social system. A theory of social stratification then must explain how this ranking is carried out, how it is perceived, how people may change from one rank to another, how ranking procedures change over time, and how much agreement there is about the ranking criteria throughout the population under study. The reason why these are the crucial questions will become clear as I discuss the four elements that make up a working or processual model of social stratification.

Status Distinctions

The first aspect of social stratification is embedded in what I call status. By status I mean the ordinal rank given to a role when it is compared to others by members of a society. Thus a role may be higher than, lower than, or equal to others for any given perceiver when he is asked to rank them in sets or by paired comparisons. Such distinctions result from the fact that role differentiation of any kind is almost always associated with some form of differential evaluation of the activities in each role when roles are compared. Thus the more complex the activities of a society are, and the more they are differentiated into separate roles, then the more complex are the status distinctions. Evaluation of roles is carried on in terms of a set of criteria or status determinants, some of which cut across many societies, others of which are more peculiar to one society. Examples of more generally applicable status determinants are such things as age, sex, descent group membership, wealth, and occupation. Examples of less general ones would be number of coups counted (Plain Indians), number of heads taken (Ifugao), which suburb one lives in (modern America), and shaministic power (Eskimo). Whether general or less so, all such status determinants are arranged into ordinal scales such that they can be thought of not only as determinants but also as gradients running from high to low for any particular society or group within a society. Although it is not universally the case, the possibility also exists that there is some ranking of status gradients amongst themselves, when they are compared with one another. Thus occupation may be more important than descent group membership in one society, and the opposite might be the case in another place. Smith claims that there is no dominant status distinction among the Hausa that he was able to find when comparing the set of gradients used to determine status among men with those used for the same purposes among women.[2] It should also be remembered that such ranking among the status determinants may change over time so that what was one a very important determinant may be of little importance today, when evaluating someone's *social position*—i.e., the sum total of rankings he received on all gradients in terms of which he is being judged by others and himself. A person may be ranked high on all gradients, or low, or high on some and low on others, etc. In any of these cases he would have a different resultant social position. Theoretically we may summarize this basic element of the model by saying that status distinctions are defined by a set of determinants, each of which is a gradient. The number of such determinants and the size of their gradient scales is a function of the degree of role differentiation in the society.

Status Consensus

Unfortunately the real world is even more complicated than the concepts of status distinction, status determinant, gradients, and their derivation from one another would suggest. This is due to the fact that people may agree, disagree, or only partially agree with one another about the exact nature of a set of status determinants and their arrangement into gradients, and ranked (or unranked) sets of these. To explain the degree of agreement among the members of a society, we must have some concepts to describe such variance so that this lack of agreement can become an attribute of the system being described. I label such a condition *status consensus* and define it as the degree to which all members of a society agree on the status determinants, their ranking and their relative importance to one another. Such variance can theoretically range from perfect agreement, in which there is completely consistent evaluation of status among all members of a society, to total disagreement, in which there is virtually no agreement from person to person about how different roles should be ranked. Two propositions result from this formulation: First, it follows that the greater the role differentiation, the higher the probability of less status consensus. This follows from the fact that it is easier to institutionalize and maintain a consensus about a few roles than about many. In the latter case people may not be aware of the total role set for their own society, and therefore find it more difficult to agree on ranking comparisons they do not ordinarily or customarily make in their everyday lives. On the other hand, in very simple societies—for example, traditional Eskimo—there is generally very high consensus, although not perfect, about what constitutes high and low status.[3]

2. Smith, M. G., 1959:250.
3. Work carried out by Merwyn Garbarino (1966) on decision-making among the Seminole

Ronald Cohen: Social Stratification in Bornu

Second, it also follows from the definition that status consensus will vary inversely with the rate of social change. This is due to the fact that social change never affects a total population in the same way.[4] Some people accept change more readily than others or have greater opportunity to do so, while the reverse is the case in other segments of the society. This means that when the evaluation of status is changing, some people will be using new status determinats for judging themselves and others or changing priorities among an older set of determinants, while other people may still be using the former set of determinants and/or the customary (for them) set of priorities among status determinants. This makes for less consensus than in situations of less rapid social change.

The foregoing concept unfortunately complicates the model by contradicting an often implicit, sometimes explicit, assumption in much anthropological research. This is the idea that the anthropologist can and should provide us with a uniform and consistent picture of the society. Thus Smith, in his article on Hausa social stratification, claims there are two "orders" of status, male and female, and a set of socially recognized status determinants for each, which have a "common basis" or acceptance by the population at large.[5] However, we cannot really confirm or disconfirm this statement, because Smith never discusses how much agreement there is among the Hausa with regard to the stratification system he has presented us with. I only choose Smith's work because the Hausa are very similar to the Kanuri, but the criticism could, I believe, be just as easily leveled at much of the work in Africa or elsewhere.[6] In other words, a generalized or abstract picture of a social stratification system may be useful for purposes of obtaining an outline, but is it in fact a good explanation or theory of a particular society's ranking system? I would say it is not. The people themselves do not act in terms of it. As a concept, status consensus is designed to do this job—to relate a generalized picture of social stratification often found in anthropological accounts, to the actual behavior of the people in more or less complex role situations and during situations of more or less rapid social change.

Social Class

Our model can now account for differential ranking of roles in a society and the degree of agreement among members of the society about such rankings. However, the final picture is still more complex because people tend to have similar rankings on a whole series of status gradients and also

4. Rosman, A., 1959.   5. Smith, M. G., 1959:39.   6. Cf. Sahlins, M., 1958.

Indians indicates that for this isolated group with very simple role structure there is extremely high consensus concerning who is an influential person in the community. On the other hand, similar work done in more complex societies generally indicates varying degrees of disagreement.

tend to have more in common with one another. Such common ranges of intercorrelated rankings provide the basis for similarity among large sections of society. Thus people who are ranked by themselves and others as high on all gradients—i.e., they have consistently high social positions —tend to be thought of as an upper class, while people who are consistently low or lower on all gradients might be considered a lower class. This is a way of roughly summarizing the complicated evaluations across many status gradients that are made about people in the society. However, such groups tend to become differentiated into semi-separate sections of society because they share more with those of similar social position. This semi-separation provides an opportunity for the development of somewhat different values—clothes, language, house furnishings, etc., i.e., a style of life correlated with the range of ranks on the status gradients. However, over time these products of a different style of life carried out by each social class in a society can in turn become status determinants in and of themselves. In other words, social class is here theorized to be a resultant of status distinctions as these are indicated by the status determinants (operating as gradients or scales), but then as a product it is theorized that class in and of itself becomes another status distinction that can lead to the use of class identifiers as status determinants in their own right. Thus different language patterns, dress, social manners, using special means of transportation, etc., may all be associated with social class as higher or lower. However, the cultural attributes of social class are semi-separate from the higher or lower ranges of the other status gradients, and to imitate or acquire such attributes is easier than many other social and economic bases of rank such as wealth or another sex (if your own is lower in status). Thus we may define social class as a section, or large grouping of people within a society, divided into a socially recognized, and often named, category possessing a common style of life and *supposedly* sharing similar ranges of status. I say "supposedly" because it may be possible for people who wish to raise their social position to do so by obtaining these easier or culturally symbolic attributes of class membership. It is not easy to make as much money as Rockefeller, but at least one could with some money buy suits from the same tailor, comb one's hair the same way, drive the same kind of car, etc. However, "real" upper or lower or any other social class membership is not based in the end on these unstable markers of class distinction. A person must eventually show that he or she can rank similarly to his fellow class members along all gradients necessary to class membership in order to obtain a more stable place in the class one aspires to join.

Eventually class is also a simple means for identifying a person's social position in a "shorthand" way. It would be too difficult to analyze then weight the results of a whole set of questions about alter that ego must

Ronald Cohen: Social Stratification in Bornu

settle for each status gradient before he can assign a special position to alter. As we have seen, the interesting thing about class is not only that it is an institutionalized oversimplification of a complex set of judgments based on status determinants and their arrangement into gradient scales; besides this, class develops its own markers, and these become in themselves another and imitable status gradient among the set being utilized in the society.

Finally it should be noted that as status gradients change in their number and relative importance, so do the basic underlying determinants of class, so that class, then, is a function of positive interconnections among status gradients and the rate of social change.

Social Mobility

The final element in this set of concepts is that of social mobility. This refers to changes that may occur in status distinctions such that a person may change his overall social position. This comes about through (a) modifying social roles, i.e., actually changing the nature of the activities traditionally subsumed within the role, or (b) taking on new roles, or (c) dropping roles. It is assumed that most persons desire to rise in status if possible, although it is always conceivable in low consensus situations that a person or a group will react to, or reject, cultural values and regard lower status or downward mobility along some status gradients as being desirable.

Another means for obtaining social mobility is imitation. People whose social position is low and who wish to raise their position tend to take on easily acquired aspects of behavior from those higher in position than themselves. Thus there is the constant strain or tension toward vulgarization or leveling of differences that is in conflict with the actual distribution of scarce resources and values in a society exhibiting status distinctions.

These then are the basic concepts I wish to use to describe social stratification among the Kanuri—status distinction, status consensus, social class, social mobility, and how these are related logically to one another through time to provide a framework upon which the rest of this discussion depends.

THE EVOLUTION OF KANURI SOCIAL
AND POLITICAL STRUCTURE

As a culture, Kanuri influences extend over a great territory of the Chad basin, Hausaland, and up into the central Sahara. As a society it is very clearly delineated by its political boundaries—that of the sovereign territory of Bornu and the hegemony of its rulers. The system of social stratification is tied closely into the social structure and its political hierarchy, so that in order to understand the context we must first outline the social and political system in which the stratification elements are embedded. I have described both the historical background and its contemporary setting more fully elsewhere and will therefore simply outline it in its present context.[7]

The roots of Kanuri society and culture as evidenced by linguistic and historical data tie its orgins to the central Sahara and the ancient kingdom of Kanem to the northeast of Lake Chad. This early kingdom was founded probably in the first millennium A.D. or earlier by nomad peoples of the desert who retreated with the great Chad basin water courses from the desert toward the present attenuated area of the lake. They probably had a patrilineal clan organization, and as they increased in density in the Chad area, social heterogeneity and competition over the control of trade routes produced tendencies toward stratification and bilateral kinship organization.[8] One clan, the Magumi, and one lineage within that clan, the Sefuwa, drew away from the others and came to be regarded as a chiefly or royal group. Oral traditions indicate that the kingdom was not a highly centralized one to begin with. The monarch was most likely a *primus inter pares* among the leaders of the major clans and lineage groups, and the entire ruling group formed a council of nobles.

Only after the breakup of Kanem and the flight of the Magumi Sefuwa and their followers to present-day Bornu in Nigeria *circa* A.D. 1400 can we speak of a highly centralized kingdom. In the new situation the Kanuri, as they now called themselves, conquered the local pagan groups, absorbed them, and set up a capital city from which they ruled Bornu and subdued older neighbors such as Kanem, Zinder, and several of the Hausa states. The main point, however, involves the great increase in centralized control which the move from Kanem to Bornu occasioned. This development occurred because in Bornu (a) they were not in a political alliance with peoples of similar social and political organization and cultural background, (b) they were conquerors who set themselves over the local population of Bornu, and (c) the monarch decided to maintain all leading nobles of the realm in the capital under his surveillance.

The second historical event which provoked even more centralization of control was the change of dynasty that occurred in the early nineteenth

7. Cohen, R., 1962, 1965, 1966a, 1966b, 1966c.
8. Jack Goody (n.d.) has recently suggested that the Sudanic societies all have strong tendencies away from unilineal descent toward bilateralism as a result of the practice of "open connubium" in which upper class intruders or conquerors in an area marry women from among subordinated ethnic groups so that distinctions due to matrifiliation become important status indicators to succeeding generations.

century. Shehu Laminu (or El Kanemi, as he is sometimes called), a Kanembu chief, saved the Bornu kingdom from the expansionist tendencies of the Fulani Empire of Sokoto whose rulers had stimulated local Bornu Fulani to revolt. At the same time, however, Laminu was able to gain effective control of Bornu. But to accomplish the take-over he had to organize the kingdom with many new titles for subordinates loyal to him and not the ancient dynasty, whose royal descendants remained as puppets while he carried out the functions of effective monarchical leadership in the state.

These two historical events have been aided and abetted by forces of growth and centralization at the social structural level. The most important of these is the basic principle of recruitment. Succession to political office, or to almost any role, has always been accomplished by choosing from a group of eligibles. Sometimes these eligibles are limited to the members of a lineage, as in the case of the monarchy, sometimes to members of a household or a larger residence group, and sometimes to members of a particular grouping such as religious practitioners or eunuchs. Whatever the limitations, the principle has always resulted in two important consequences for the system. First, it concentrates control in the hands of superiors and ultimately in the hands of the monarch, since he can always appoint people who are most loyal to him. In the case of the monarch it means that he is never totally restrained by any person's traditional right of political office. Second, it has always meant that personal achievement is possible as long as the upwardly mobile person thoroughly understands the potentialities of deference and loyal subordination to superiors. Third, it has provided throughout Bornu history for factionalism in the state, since contenders for important positions all have their own followers who stand to gain if their particular superior is chosen for a powerful office. It involves factions whose ultimate loyalties center on segments of the royal lineage.

Added to this is the historical development of the fief organization which, from the time of the flight from Kanem in the fifteenth century and the setting up of the Bornu kingdom, has always been a centrally controlled one.[9] Thus all fief-holders, with one notable exception, always lived in the capital and were not allowed to consolidate their holdings which were instead fragmented throughout the kingdom. Fiefs were administered through loyal subordinates of the fief-holder who worked with local settlement leaders in the rural areas. This has always meant that Kanuri society has stressed a difference between the capital city with its courtly life, as opposed to rural life, in which there were only a few representatives of the ruling class present.

9. A fief is a political unit within a state over which a superior has rights of tribute collection and political leadership (not necessarily exclusive rights) given to him by his, or his ancestors', relationship to a monarch.

All of these factors of centralization have also meant that throughout Bornu history higher positions in rank on all status gradients have been closely tied with the political structure of the realm. Wealth, power, prestige, and a host of other valued activities all flowed from the structure of the political offices and the dynamics of political conflict.

Within the social system as a whole the basic unit of social, economic, and political organization is the household.[10] Households link together to form wards, hamlets, villages, and cities. Traditionally a village head had under him ward heads, and hamlet heads in the area surrounding his settlement. If a settlement developed and enlarged, its leader could be brought to the capital by the fief-holder through his representative in the rural area. The monarch bestowed the title of *Lawan* upon him at this time, thus allowing the ward heads and hamlet heads in the fief the possibility of becoming local leaders with their own subordinates. If it continued to grow, he could be taken in again to the capital and given another title (*Ajia*), giving his political subordinates the chance to become *Lawans* if their own settlements flourished. Anyone wishing to start a settlement of his own could do so by moving to empty land. Through patrilocal marriage and clientage he could build up a small settlement with himself and his heirs as the local political leaders. This emphasis on the household as the basic unit from which wards, hamlets, villages, and even cities are constructed, plus a high frequency of patrilocality, has produced constant tendencies in Bornu history for households having similar occupations to reside in one ward or hamlet. Thus the head of the ward is also the leading person in the occupational grouping. In other words a correlation between settlement growth, and political leadership on the one hand, with patrilocality and localized occupational homogeneity on the other, has tended toward the formation of craft guilds, for the wards tend to become in fact political, social, and economic units. In the state as a whole the occupational grouping in the capital city, and its particular headman—again often the headman of a ward in which most of these occupation members worked and lived—was considered the head of the entire occupational group of the state and was the person to whom all the occupational members throughout the society gave deference, tributes, and support. In turn, the head of the national guild could be relied upon for some support in the capital despite the other political obligations and subordination a person might be involved in as a result of the fief system and the basic administrative organization of Bornu.

Two other aspects of Kanuri historical development have had consequences for the system of social stratification. The first of these is the combination of high divorce and continual warfare, which has meant that divorced women were available as a work force to provide for the needs

10. See Cohen, R., 1966c.

234

Ronald Cohen: Social Stratification in Bornu

of armies on the march. Thus divorced women in each town or village had a head woman, and the women of the state as a whole had some organization of their own outside of household life and marriage. Secondly Kanuri society, like many Islamic kingdoms of the Sudan, engaged in slavery and the slave trade. Slaves, just like clients, were additions to households and could be used both as extra labor and loyal subordinates. They varied in status and sex—males were for the most part born into the status or captured as children in a raid on a neighboring pagan group. A few were made into eunuchs and lived exclusively among the women as household servants; they were also used as loyal political subordinates, especially by the monarch. Traditionally a number of the most important administrative offices in the realm were reserved for eunuchs. This gave the monarch the ultimate in powers of appointment, since the eunuch as a subordinate had no descendants of his own who might make claims on the basis of a family or lineage link to the superior. Female slaves add an extra work force to the household. In wealthy powerful households this can prove to be extremely important, since there are often very large numbers of people eating in such households each day, and the Islamic limitation of four wives makes the catering problem insurmountable without extra female members of the household. Traditionally they also worked in the fields and served to produce more issue for the household head in the way of possible heirs.

The twentieth century has seen a number of significant changes in the system of organization, although much of it has remained intact. The greatest change has come in the political structure.[11] The British consolidated fiefs into twenty-one districts, then sent out fief-holders to live in these areas whose administrative center came to be called the district capital. From the personnel of the Shehu's royal court a council was chosen which developed into a formal, appointed cabinet whose members under a Waziri, or chief minister, administered a local native authority civil service organization with representatives in each district capital. Thus in the twenty-one villages throughout the emirate there are district heads and local representatives of the Native Authority department. These men and their families make up an urban group of administrators living throughout the rural area of the state. As soon as these changes were put into effect, district capitals began to grow in importance; they increased in size, developed important markets, and were soon tied to the emirate capital by a system of motor roads. The colonial, and now the Nigerian, government administered the emirate under a group of officials whose responsibility covers all of Bornu province, of which Bornu emirate is the major subdivision. Administrative officers looked after taxation, judicial affairs, etc., for the province, while technical personnel—e.g., educational

11. See Cohen, R., 1966b.

officers, veterinary officers—advised the Bornu Emirate Native Authority (among others) on specific technical matters.

The inception of cash crops, Western education, and the slow, but steady, incorporation of Bornu into a wider Nigerian polity has broadened the horizons for many Kanuri men and women and has provided new avenues of mobility for those willing and able to take advantage of them.

THE STRUCTURE OF KANURI STRATIFICATION

The historical development of Kanuri society previously discussed has produced a well-ordered complex system of social stratification. Before dealing analytically with the determinants of social status, it is necessary to obtain an overview of the entire society and its various subsections as these relate to one another in terms of higher and lower amounts of status. In general terms, the society has a two-class system, traditionally, complicated by internal divisions within each class and divided across classes by the institution of slavery. As we shall see in discussing status distinctions such as ethnicity, age, sex, rural/urban residence, and occupation, as well as contemporary social change, the stratification is further subdivided by ranges of status distinction within each separate status group in the society.

At the top of the traditional society is the nobility (*kantuoma*, translated literally as "the important people"). This group is divided into royalty, on the one hand, and the free and slave nobles, on the other. The royal family is formed by the patrilineage of the monarch; status within this group is divided by sex and genealogical proximity to the throne. The monarch, or Shehu, is a cut above everyone. He symbolizes the kingdom in his person and is held in awe and reverence by the people, who address him as "master," the term used traditionally by slaves to address their owners. In precolonial Bornu, the Shehu had life-and-death power over his subjects and wielded it when necessary. All matters of state were carried out in his name, and he had the right to revoke all decisions or all offices and to make war on neighboring states and rebellious tributaries. In practice power could be obtained by his advisers, and he had, at all times, to keep a wary eye on rival claimants to the throne who would benefit from his death. Nevertheless, ultimately, all privileges resulted from his favors, and what he gave he could take away. Some indication of his central position in the state is shown by the fact that traders from foreign lands were not allowed to enter the capital city unless he was in residence. Or again, half of all booty taken in war or in raids was automatically the property of the king. His powers were enhanced by the belief that he was capable of controlling supernatural forces, even of becoming invisible when in danger. Shehu Laminu (1910–35) is said to have been able to adjudicate very difficult legal disputes by simply waving his hand in the air. At such times, law books in Cairo would appear to him, and he could read of similar cases in other parts of the Islamic world. Even today with the growth of a complex civil service, whose leaders in the Native Authority Council handle most of the decision-making and administrative tasks of the state on a day-to-day basis, the monarch is, unquestionably, the central and most important figure in Bornu.

All men of the royal lineage whose fathers were monarchs are held to be eligible for succession, and, as such, they are considered to be *maina*, or princes of the realm. A man whose father is a *maina* has the status of *maidugu*, or grandson, of a king. Of these, those whose fathers are still alive have higher status, since they still have, theoretically, the chance of becoming *maina* if their fathers inherit the throne. On the other hand, *maidugu* whose fathers are dead (i.e., whose fathers never became monarchs) are, in fact, deroyalized. Their children have no royal status, although the memory of such ancestry is kept for a number of generations in the patrilineage.

Women of the royal patrilineage have noble status, and several hold titled positions in the state. The king's mother and one of his female agnates—whether a sister or his father's sister—and the king's senior wife hold the three senior female titles of the kingdom. All daughters of a monarch have the status of *nana*. Their high status stems, primarily, from the fact that marriage with one of them puts the husband into a close, affinal relationship to the royal patrilineage.

The royal court is made up of the *maina*, some of whom hold leading titles of the realm, plus the holders of leading free and slave titles. In the nineteenth century the free nobility stemmed from five original, close subordinates of the first Shehu, whose family names are now honored titles in Bornu, plus those of the pre-nineteenth century who espoused the cause of the Shehu against that of the previous dynasty. Along with these free nobles were those of slave ancestry who came to special prominence in the nineteenth century because the Shehu had to create a bureaucracy and did not have enough trustworthy supporters among the free nobility. These slave nobles were divided into several groups. First, there were the eunuchs, most of whom lived in the palace as close, personal attendants to the monarch; second, there were house slaves, who were non eunuchs but were also part of the king's titled slave following; and third, there were the titled military slave leaders (*kachella*), who formed the most important element of the slave nobility. They reached this prominence in the nineteenth century because each *kachella*, or military leader, kept a constant, armed force available to the monarch for military purposes. Previous (pre-nineteenth century) rulers had only very small, standing military forces and thus had to rely, for the raising of militia, on the nobles and their control of fief settlements.

A group of nobles, semi-separated from those already described, are the religious-legal leaders of the state. These holy men, expert in Muslim law and theology, hold a number of titles in Bornu. There are a limited number of patrilineages in Bornu who supply the members for these leading religious titles, and they have done so for a long time. Such stability has persisted even when dynasties did not. Thus the present holders of the chief religious and legal titles in Bornu have held these and similar offices in their agnatic groups from well before the time of the present dynasty. In this case their special training and the high status accorded Islam, as well as their legal and supernatural utility to rulers, has ensured them their status.

This titled top echelon of the upper class had to remain in the capital city of the realm, as previously mentioned, and made up the core of the royal court. They served as a central bureaucracy of the emirate government, and the state was administered through their own chief subordinates working with the local headmen in each fief. These latter, the local village heads and the client and slave-followers of the titled courtiers, formed a lower segment of the upper class through which contact with the ordinary people was maintained on a day-to-day basis.

Crosscutting this upper-class segment of the society are the factions, and incipient factions, that stem out of the realities of competition for power in the state. Contenders for the throne each have their own following among the nobles and among those of their followers who hope one day to achieve noble titles and the prerogatives that go with them. Generally, the leading faction is that of the reigning monarch, since he can control appointments to titled offices as well as distribute, or redistribute, fief-holdings traditionally; thus he rewards followers more thoroughly than his competitors. However, at times of interregnum, or of revolution, or when a ruling monarch is extremely old, such factionalism becomes important, since the royal office is the goal of competition at that point and the winning faction stands to gain control of the most effective authority position in the state.

Today the old royal court still sits; the title holders still attend the Shehu and place themselves in positions in front of the throne in the traditional manner with the higher status titles closest to the throne and those of lesser status sitting farther away. However, the bureaucracy has, as already noted, proliferated into a modern civil service. To mesh the new and the old, the Kanuri have multiplied the number of titled people so that all senior Native Authority personnel receive titles. In practice this

Ronald Cohen: Social Stratification in Bornu

means Native Authority Councillors and each Native Authority supervisor receives a title from the Shehu which enables the holder to attend the court of the monarch.

Titles are emblems of nobility and status. They do not, however, nor did they ever, in Bornu history, totally define status. It is well known in Bornu what actual powers any particular title holder has in the state. It is these real, underlying bases of power that produce the ultimate, rather than the honorific, title held by the person himself, and this was certainly the case traditionally as well. Thus titles can rise or fall in status; this has been well documented for several of the leading titles during the nineteenth century. In some cases titles fell out of use and disappeared. This happened with the title of *fufuma*, or headman, of the pre-nineteenth century capital of Bornu. On the other hand, the title of *kaigama*, or war leader, which was a free, noble title of the pre-nineteenth century, was dropped during the early part of the nineteenth century. Later it was resuscitated and given, or taken, by the leading *kachella*, or slave war leader, under the Shehus. The present holder of this title traces his ancestry to these slave-holders rather than to the free nobles who held this title in pre-nineteenth century Bornu. The general feeling in Bornu today is that it is easier to get a title and that there are many, many more titled persons than there were traditionally. In some cases slave and free have even become mixed. Thus, one informant has been given a slave title although his ancestry has always been free. Nevertheless, this proliferation of titles simply refers to the increase in the size of the bureaucracy and the number of government activities being carried out in the modern emirate as opposed to the traditional one. The fact that there are more titled people today can also be interpreted to mean that such emblems are still honorific and have value to the people of Bornu.

Below the upper class ranges the broad base of the *tala'a*, or common people. Traditionally they were the farmers, craftsmen, and traders who lived in the cities, towns, and villages of the state. At the top of this class were, and are, the wealthy traders and craft specialists who live in the capital city of Bornu. They catered to the needs of the wealthy upper-class rulers and were able to become influential if they associated closely with particular upper-class members. Unlike the upper class, such men had clients or slaves (traditionally), on farms in the rural areas. In contrast the upper-class holders of titles obtained agricultural produce from their fiefs; commoners either had to purchase their needs in the market or obtain farms in outlying areas. Many of the less wealthy traders and craftsmen in the city also farmed in the surrounding area, which made the capital more like the rural settlements than is the case in more industrialized states.

In rural areas the peoples were, and are, farmers and part-time specialists in trade and craftwork. Higher status was gained by wealth, household size, and proximity, in social terms, to powerful political leaders. Mobility within this class was, however, often more possible in these rural areas. A man could, if he wished to, go off and found a new settlement and thereby found a headman lineage for the new village. Kanuri informants claim that this still is a good way to raise one's status in Bornu society.

Slaves in Bornu cut across all class and status lines. As we have seen, some of the nobles were slaves of the monarch. They, like the other nobles, generally had large numbers of their own slaves. Male slaves (*karliya*) could be bought and sold in the market, while female slaves (*chir*) were purchased privately from their owners. Slaves were also obtained by capture through both politically sponsored warfare and through the efforts of private slave raiders who engaged in the trade. When in the slave status, they carried out all Bornu occupations practiced by the freemen and formed a significant portion of the population. Thus, in all likelihood, most people had at least a few slaves as extra male and female help in the household. Male slaves could be recognized on sight because they were not allowed to wear the ubiquitous cap of the Muslim population. Female slaves were used as laborers on the farms and as concubines among the wealthy and noble of the society. These latter households had onerous catering problems in food preparation, and the Muslim limit of four wives was often not enough to prepare meals for the large numbers who regularly ate at an important person's house. Undoubtedly sexual appetites, the desire for more variety and for more absolute control over women also helped to perpetuate slave concubinage, although it is falling into disuse today.

Slaves are absorbed in the population in a number of ways. If a person with a slave mother is born of a free father, then he or she is free although of lower status in the family compared to offspring both of whose parents are free. Owners of slaves might leave directions that, at their death, the slaves, or certain of them, should be freed. Thus there is a constant attrition of the slave population within the society which is replenished through the slave trade.

Today, holders of royal slave titles are proud of their ancestry, since their high positions result from the fact of their slave relationship to the monarch. Slaves of leading men tend to keep their status as well, since their owners have some obligation to maintain them as dependents. In general, however, for the population at large, slavery has disappeared as a significant aspect of social stratification.

For the common people of Bornu today the status situation has become more complicated than it was traditionally because of the large number of new occupations, especially those having salaries or leading to high profits that are now associated with Westernization. In the capital city a group of very wealthy entrepreneurs has sprung up who, although not noble, are thought of by everyone to be "big men." These people are beginning to form an urban, middle class between the commoners and the nobles, but only in a very preliminary way, as yet, can we begin to speak of a solid, separate middle class who are neither commoners or nobles but something in between. Thus, when questioned as to whether they are commoners or nobles, these wealthy men respond immediately and claim they are commoners.

In summary, then, these are some of the main categories of stratification for Kanuri society as a whole. However, it is important to remember that the Kanuri themselves do not cut their society into a neatly stratified structure with Group A here and Group B below it and so on. Instead, they see a series of criteria and think of these as their way of assessing a person's status. When a Kanuri meets a stranger, he observes, first, not what stratum a person belongs to but from what tribe this person comes; next, he might ask, is this man powerful or important; is he wealthy; is he from a city or rural area? Often he asks who the person's father is or in whose household the stranger grew up, what occupation did the person practice, and who are his friends and protectors? These questions tell a Kanuri about another person's rank and thus form an underlying basis for differentiating persons and groups. It is, therefore, to these distinctions that we now turn for a more detailed analysis of Kanuri stratification.

KANURI STATUS DISTINCTIONS: ETHNICITY

The Kanuri take a great pride in their culture, its religion, language, and social and political organization, as well as in their history, some of which is known by everyone. The large majority of marriages are within the ethnic group; the most notable exceptions are between Kanuri men and Shuwa or Hausa women. During 1957 in a small, rural sample of seventy households, there were six marriages in which one partner was non-Kanuri; four of these six were between households of Shuwa woman and Kanuri men; one was between a pagan man and two rather pariah Kanuri women; and one was between a recent Muslim convert (originally pagan) and a Kanuri woman. A more recent sample, taken in 1964 and 1965 in both rural and urban areas, indicates similar results for the rural area and slightly more interethnic marriages between Kanuri and non-Kanuri in the city.

When 146 Kanuri school boys (aged thirteen to nineteen) were asked (in 1957) who they would most like to marry among a number of ethnic groups including "Europeans," they tended to agree with one another that Kanuri, Arabic, European, Shuwa, or Hausa wives would be the most preferable. Below this most highly ranked group came a category of other Muslim tribes: Fulani, Yoruba, Babur, Bolewa, Kanembu, Mandara, Tubu, Magari, in the middle range of choice, and finally a group that consistently came lowest of all including Tuareg, Tiv, and Cameroon pagans such as the Banana and Gwoza peoples. These evaluations agree with informally obtained rankings from other informants concerning the status of ethnic groups. In other words, the Kanuri seem to have a tri-partite division of rank categories for various ethnic groups. First there are the high status groups including themselves, then a middle range category below this, and finally a very low status category who the Kanuri feel are socially very distant from themselves.

The explanation for this set of rankings can be seen in the historical contacts between the Kanuri and other ethnic groups. Throughout the history of the emirate there have been constant contacts with other ethnic groups both within and beyond its borders. Almost every village over 1,000 population (i.e., 70 percent of all named settlements) has a pagan ward; slightly larger villages generally have a Hausa quarter, and often politically dependent Fulani or Shuwa hamlets nearby. Larger centers, such as Maiduguri, Nguru, Geidam, Dikwa, or Damaturu, have Ibo, Yoruba, and many other Nigerian ethnic groups present as well as a few Europeans. Maiduguri, the capital, also has a large Arab-speaking population from the Sudan and the Near East, and the largest group of Europeans (including Americans). It is not surprising that in such a long established contact situation, evaluation of status by ethnic membership takes place.

It is probably a measure of their cosmopolitanism rather than from any profound feelings of inferiority that some Kanuri do not rank their own group as having highest status. Often Arabs, Europeans, or both are said to rank higher, although many other Kanuri place their own group first then mention these other high status peoples. Certainly there is very widespread agreement that these three ethnic groups should rank at the top. The European derives high status from his dominance in the superior authority position occasioned by colonial rule as well as his superior economic position associated with the establishment of European trading companies in Bornu. The degree of consensus concerning the high status of Europeans varies with the possibilities for social contact. In general those having greater contact do not rank them as high as those having little or no social contacts. Thus Europeans are said to be "kings," "true Muslims," "the greatest people," when the question is asked in a small rural hamlet, but in the city among junior officials who interact every day with Europeans, the ranking is lower, and often Arab and Kanuri are ranked higher.

Ronald Cohen: Social Stratification in Bornu

Arabs from the Sudan and the Near East interact very little with the Kanuri except in commercial transactions. However, Arab facial features, skin color, and general appearance are regarded as the most pleasing physical features. Thus almost universally Kanuri men find Arab women extremely attractive. Finally, the place of the Arabs as the original Muslims gives them added status in the eyes of the Kanuri, who specifically mention this point themselves when speaking of Arabs. These views are quite widely held, although there is some antagonism to Arab commerce by Kanuri political and business leaders and a growing attempt in the past few years by this element to limit Arab commercial activities in order to make room for increased opportunities by Kanuri entrepreneurs.

Similar historical experience and much contact over the centuries have produced a feeling of social proximity to other Muslim groups in the Sudan with whom the Kanuri have had friendly relations. The two highest ranking among such groups are the Hausa to the west and Shuwa (Arab-speaking) nomads from the east. The widespread use in northern Nigeria of Hausa as a lingua franca, plus much cultural similarity between Hausa and Kanuri, has meant an ease of contact between these two ethnic groups. The Shuwa are considered to have beautiful women and to be friendly and unthreatening as nomads.

In a large sample of marriages taken in 1964–65, Shuwa-Kanuri marriages turned out to have the largest frequency of intertribal unions.[12] Their Arabic language as well as the ease with which they acculturate to Kanuri society when they settle in Bornu helps to make the Shuwa a highly ranked ethnic group. Kanuri individuals with Shuwa mothers are proud of the fact and often incorporate it into their own name. To take a name signifying connection to one's own mother is quite common in Bornu, but not so widely practiced when this connection indicates matrifilial connections to a low status group.

In the middle category are other Muslim tribes who are significantly different from those in high status rank because of some feature that has created social distance. These are people like the Fulani, Yoruba, Babur, Bolewa, Kanembu, Mandara, and Tubu. Kanuri men admire the beauty of Fulani women but in general they share feelings of mistrust and even fear of the Fulani as an ethnic group. This results from interaction between Fulani nomads and settled Kanuri, which often produces clashes between

12. Among 100 Kanuri men chosen equally from rural and urban areas, there were over 400 marriages. Of these there were no non-Kanuri marriages for the rural men, while 7 percent of the urban unions were interethnic. These included 11 with Shuwa women, 2 with Hausa, and 1 with a Fulani. Twenty-five divorced urban women had married 89 times. These included 5 Hausa men, 5 Shuwa men, 5 Fulani men, 2 Mandara, 1 Kanembu, 1 Babur, and 1 member of an unidentified pagan tribe. The total, however, of 23 percent indicates that women in urban areas marry outside their ethnic group more than men. Comparable data are now being collected for women in rural areas.

the two over pasturage and cattle damage to crops, as well as from the well-remembered history of past warfare between the two groups during the nineteenth century. In a rural village people often say, "Lock your doors tonight; there are Fulani nomads in the village area." The Kanuri also find the public dancing and flagellation ceremony of the Fulani, often carried out in Kanuri markets, to be strange, frightening, and barbaric. With the other groups there are also strong and positive as well as negative reactions. Yoruba are poorly known. The people say of them, "They are only half Muslim," referring to the fact that there are pagan and Christian elements in this particular tribe. Babur to the south of Bornu are the same in this respect and besides were at one time a group from whom the Kanuri took slaves. Bolewa, Kanembu, Mandara, and Tubu are all felt to be friendly surrounding Muslim peoples, but it is also known that they were traditionally hostile peoples against whom the Kanuri went to war.

There are many Ibo in Kanuri urban centers—and all Kanuri have some image about "Niamali" (Ibo). Like all Muslim groups except the Hausa, Shuwa, and Arabs, the Kanuri are ambivalent about Ibo. In general Ibo are disliked, mistrusted, and even despised as in the case of Cameroons pagans whom they often are grouped with. Yet Kanuri grudgingly admire Ibo for their Western education, salaried jobs, and higher standards of living; thus the Ibo generally get ranked within the middle status category somewhat above pariah groups.

At the very bottom are those groups such as the Cameroon pagans, Tiv, and rather surprisingly the Tuareg, whom the Kanuri rank lowest and most distant socially from themselves. Most Kanuri have had firsthand experience with members of pagan Cameroon tribes such as the Banana and Gwoza peoples. Members of these tribes are water carriers, laborers, brewers of millet beer; and women from these groups serve as prostitutes in Maiduguri. Historically they were taken as slaves by the Kanuri, and many of their men were operated on to produce eunuchs, a process in which over 95 percent of those involved died as a result of the operation. When speaking of these people, Kanuri always mention their aboriginal nakedness and then comment that such groups have no shame, no religion; indeed several informants went further and remarked that they were akin to animals. Tiv are considered to be very similar to the Cameroon pagans, even though most Kanuri have never had any personal relations with them. However, stories about their appearance, their behavior, and especially their ferocity are widespread in Bornu. Thus they are considered to be in a similar social and cultural category to the Cameroon pagans and murderous as well. This last point goes a long way toward explaining the rather odd grouping of a Muslim people, the Tuareg, along with the other pariah ethnic groups all of whom are non-Muslim. Tuareg raided and pillaged Kanuri towns and caravans well into the present century,

Ronald Cohen: Social Stratification in Bornu

and even today they are considered a violent and murderous group whose behavior cannot be sanctioned or predicted. The few Tuareg that appear in Bornu are often pointed out to children as something frightening and dangerous; certainly these tall veiled men who walk silently through a Kanuri village, or down a city street, seem strange, and at the very least (to a Western eye) mysterious. But to the Kanuri they are more—they mean danger, conflict, and unaccountability. It is believed that there is no adequate control available when dealing with Tuareg, since they can run away to the desert whenever they wish, which means ultimately that the safety of a jural society does not apply (in the minds of Kanuri) to relations with Tuareg.

In summary, Kanuri rank ethnic groups into three broad categories. First are those whom they consider as highly, such as the Arabs, Europeans, Hausa, Shuwa, as themselves. These groups are not all judged by the same criterion; Europeans are powerful while Hausa and Shuwa are friendly Muslims. They are all, however, positively and highly judged on those criteria utilized. Second, there are groups that are both positively and negatively judged, with both elements quite strong. This results in feelings of ambivalence for such groups and an overall lower status compared to own-group or other highly rated groups. Third, there are groups rated consistently low on all criteria, such as the Cameroon pagans. The Tuareg are a special case here in that they are positively rated for being Muslims but their negative attributes are so strong that Kanuri unanimously feel there is an unbridgeable gulf between themselves and such peoples and therefore rank them among the lowest when comparing ethnic groups.

The degree of status consensus applied to ethnic status is quite high. Thus rural peasants and Western-educated school boys seem to agree on these three categories. A few more highly educated Kanuri men and women have spoken to me of Nigeria or Africa as an identification unit and suggested that the rankings described here are old-fashioned, but this group is as yet negligible in size and influence. The greater proportion of women marrying outside the ethnic group also suggests that ethnic status consensus is conditioned by sexual status.

AGE, SEX, AND RURAL OR
URBAN RESIDENCE

Within Kanuri society itself the easily visible factors of age, sex, and rural urban residence provide a gross set of status distinctions that crosscut all others; that is to say, they condition and are conditioned by the other status distinctions. As in many societies, status increases with age and is tied to the age-grading system of infant, child, young adolescent, maturity, old age for men. It is the same for women except that young adolescent status (boys) is replaced by young married status, since girls marry eight to ten years earlier than men and spend their adolescence as young married women or divorcees. Children are taught to respect all older people and that it is proper to apply the kin terms for father and mother to any older person with whom one has contact. Men look forward to the rising status that comes with advanced years and feel that the age period of 35–40 is a turning point of life. Frivolity is excusable before this age, but beyond it they consider themselves senior people. This means they should divorce less often, appear less in public, and take on leadership responsibilities in their households and local communities. The situation is more complicated for women. The best way to illustrate this point is to examine bridewealth payments over a life-span. In general such payments rise as a man grows older and fall as a woman goes from marriage to marriage.[13] Thus, although a woman should increase her status as she ages in accordance with the general rule of the culture, the high divorce rate reverses this aging effect so that a woman's worth in her own eyes and that of the community in fact decreases. This does not apply so much to those very few women who never divorce, but such cases are relatively infrequent. Later, when a woman reaches into very old age, she overcomes this divorce effect and becomes a respected person in accordance with the aging norm, often in a son's, brother's, or other kinsman's household. People in the household come to her for blessing before *rites de passage* or before going on a trip, since her old age is considered to give her supernatural powers to bestow good fortune upon those around her. The status consensus of old age as a distinction is very high, and everyone accepts the reverse effect for women as caused by the high divorce rate.

When sex is isolated as a status distinction on its own, then the general Muslim rule that all men are superior to all women holds powerful sway among Kanuri. Women receive only half a man's share in inheritance. Traditionally they were not allowed to sit in a courtroom, but had to remain in a side room reserved especially for that purpose. They must not eat with men, they must walk behind them in public, and they must be obedient within marriage. The Kanuri believe that gonorrhea may result if a woman lies on top of a man during intercourse. As already mentioned, traditionally the very high divorce rate, plus the well-developed militarism of the state, which involved it in many campaigns against rebellious tributary states, produced a woman's organization in the society.

13. The divorce rate in Bornu varies from 85 to 99 percent of all completed marriages depending upon (a) fertility of the woman, (b) socioeconomic status of the husband, (c) rural/urban residence, and (d) number of wives in a polygynous union.

Ronald Cohen: Social Stratification in Bornu

There are always divorced women in every Kanuri settlement. These women are looking for husbands or liaisons with men. They cook for the men, sometimes sleep with them, and are free and independent until they remarry. Traditionally such women in the *zower* (divorced women) status had a head woman for each town who could organize them to cook food for a large visitation from the capital, or to help when an army on the march came by. Today the divorced women of Bornu are asked to come out to political meetings and other public events to which wives cannot go. They dance for the men and thus provide entertainment for the event as well as some personal advertisement for themselves.

As I have written elsewhere, the difficulty with sex as a status distinction whereby women are considered inferior to men, and subordinate to them in marriage, is the lack of status consensus on the part of the women.[14] Traditionally they subverted male dominance in a number of ways, because many of the men were highly dependent on women's labor contributions to the welfare of the household. Modern secondary-school girls discuss marriage and their relations to men in terms of equality, independendence, competitiveness; and they complain of a lack of such qualities in the traditional culture. Secondary-school boys seem not to accept these views of the school girls and instead agree with the traditional non-Western-educated men who say that these girls are "spoiled," i.e., they will not accept a lower status relative to that of men.[15] What is important here is the fact that Kanuri society has always had problems, and still does today, over the culturally defined status distinction between men and women because women have never fully or necessarily accepted their inferior position. Western education is aggravating the problem so that this particular status distinction is, in fact, an unstable one.

The long history of an urban administrative center that has served as an administrative capital for the Bornu state has led to a well-entrenched distinction between rural and urban life in Kanuri culture. Since this results primarily from the type of life lived by wealthy and powerful people in the capital, it is a distinction made more sharply by them than by others. City dwellers consider themselves to be more sophisticated, better informed, and more able to move upward in status than rural peasants, or "bush" people, who are judged to be ignorant, dirty, and relatively poor economically. Rural people make fewer distinctions between rural and urban residence, although they admit universally that there are many "wonderful" things in the city not to be found in the rural areas, such as

14. See Cohen, R., 1961, 1965.
15. This evaluation means a number of things all at once. First, it refers to their lack of respect and obedience to men; second, to their widely rumored, but unproven, lack of virginity before marriage because they are beyond the usual age of marriage; third, to their understanding, and desire for, a high standard of material wealth and Westernization in their married life.

the big market which is open every day, the royal palace, and many modern innovations from the Western world such as the cinema. Everyone in both rural and urban areas admits that housing is more comfortable and more permanent in the city, and that water is easier to obtain.

In general, then, rural-urban distinctions center around the different quality of life to be found in both places. Since aspects of this quality can be diffused, we can also speak of urbanism in the rural areas and ruralism in the urban areas—both of which exist in Bornu. Civil-service workers, chiefs, and others import urbanism in the form of house styles, radios, style of dress, and other material and nonmaterial items from the urban centers out into the bush areas. The cities, however, have for centuries housed people who lived a life not far removed from that of rural peasants. They have farms, do craftwork, or trade, and have close relations to kinsmen in rural villages. Unfortunately it is difficult to assess from present data how much status consensus there is on rural-urban status distinctions. However, in general, wealthy, powerful, and/or Western-educated city people make these distinctions and judge rural and urban life as very different. Within this context, urban is rated high and rural is rated low in status.

On the other hand, rural people and poor people in the cities tend to see these differences as not being nearly so great.

OCCUPATION

Occupation is a major status distinction in Kanuri society, and always has been. Bornu social life is complex, and one of the major indications of this is its multitude of economic, political, and religious specializations. These may be full-time specialities, and often are in the urban areas, or they may only be part-time in which a man works his farm during the short growing season and looks after his trade or craft during the dry months. Women have fewer economic specialties, and thus their role as married women in the household or as single divorced women who may maintain themselves by having liaisons with marriageable men is their most common occupational one.[16]

Traditionally the Kanuri rank occupations into three categories: high status jobs, ordinary jobs, and pariah occupations that are somewhat shameful and create a low status for persons carrying out such work. Within these categories distinctions are also made; there is wide agree-

16. Pottery-making, hair-dressing, embroidery, selling cooked and uncooked foods, and basket-making are the predominant female specialties in traditional society. Western-educated women are in a very few cases taking up schoolteaching, nursing, and secretarial work.

ment about the top and the bottom of the occupational scale but much less consensus about the wide range of occupations in the middle.

In precolonial times high status was attached to any and all jobs associated with the political organization of the kingdom, and status was measured grossly by the place in the administrative hierarchy of the particular office. The attributes of a political title and the history of success of the titleholder and the previous titleholders also provided gross measures of status, since the titles were divided up into categories— one for royalty, one for officials of the royal court, titles for free nobles of the court, titles for slaves of the court, several of which were reserved for eunuchs, and titles for religious functionaries of the court, and heads of occupations in the capital. There were also titles for rural chieftaincies and titles for followers of powerful men. As we shall see in the discussion on mobility, more exact measures of status distinctions were, however, made on the basis of a man's achieved prerogatives in the political systems, so that holders of particular titles varied greatly through time as to the status position they were accorded in the overall society.

In contemporary Bornu this background, plus the fact that the vast bulk of salaried jobs are in the administrative structure, has maintained the high status of political jobs, although it has changed their nature in accordance with the modern political system. High status is afforded higher paying positions and the more powerful ones. Thus persons holding traditional titles but who do not have a position in the salaried hierarchy of the contemporary emirate or the Nigerian government obtain little recognition from the population at large. Informants often joke about such titles as being empty and meaningless since the incumbent cannot use it to gain anything for himself as he could in the precolonial era.

The Muslim concept of *baraka* (Kanuri: *barka*), or holiness, is a status distinction that cuts across occupations in some respects. However, it may also define a fully specialized or semispecialized occupational role. The general principle is that religion is good and confers power and prestige upon those that practice it professionally. Traditionally, and today as well, there are religious functionaries at the top of the political system who serve as legal and religious advisers to the state. Below them in status come full-time *mallams* or religious specialists who officiate at *rites de passage* and lead their local communities in other annual religious ceremonies, provide prayers and charms for the sick, ward off evil, and practice divination. Finally there are men who have other occupations but who spend much of their spare time learning the Koran by heart; they also help officiate at ceremonies. Many people, whose primary place in the economic system is that of farmer, craftsman, or trader, when asked for their occupation reply that they are *mallams* (religious practitioners).

Only when the question is pressed or they are observed for some time does it become clear that they are only part-time *mallams* who have chosen religious activities as a means to increase their status.

In the middle category are the large numbers of occupations that "ordinary" people carry out. Basic to all of them is farming, since most Kanuri men are craftsmen and farmers, or traders and farmers, etc. Such roles are differentiated primarily on the basis of wealth. The highest status is accorded to wealthy traders, since people who practice this occupation seem to be the largest group in the middle range of status to achieve higher standards of living. Low-paid salary jobs are not in this category, since there are still so few of them in relation to the population as a whole that they have generally higher status because of the secure cash income they provide, unless they involve some kind of "dirty" work such as motor mechanics and paid laborers.

At the bottom of the occupational hierarchy are a few jobs that have been defined traditionally as shameful. People go further and say that it would be extremely shameful for anyone whose father held office in the political system, or whose father was a *mallam*, ever to consider doing such work. On the other hand, many thoughtful informants, when pressed on this point, often made a functional analysis of their own occupational system and admitted that such services were needed if society was to operate although they personally would never fill such a role. People who do carry on these activities manifest feelings of social inferiority resulting from their own awareness of their low status in the society as a whole. The occupations and some of the most often repeated reasons for their low status are as follows:

 a. *Butcher*: a butcher cuts animals; he takes life away for money; he smells of blood (the Kanuri equate blood with life, soul, and personal power, and in general ascribe supernatural significance to it as a substance).
 b. *Blacksmiths*: they made weapons for the enemies of the Prophet.
 c. *Tanners*: they smell badly; their work smells unpleasant; only a man with no proper sense of shame could do such work.
 d. *Barbers:* They are ignorant; they know bad things (the word "bad" refers here to sorcery which is also attributed to hunters, medicine sellers, and some *mallams*. However barbers also deal with blood by performing surgical operations such as circumcision, removing the uvula, marking the faces with cutting tribal marks, and so on).
 e. *Petty brokers*: they take property to sell at the market that belongs to someone else, but they can never be trusted to return the right amount; they can never be trusted because they work on their own and not as someone in one's household or the household of a person one knows and can trust.

Ronald Cohen: Social Stratification in Bornu

    f. Moneylender: people who do this are bad Muslims. (It is widely known that usury is against the edicts of Islam. However, there is ambivalence about the practice when it is discussed with someone intimately because of the high wealth status it very often occasions.)

    g. Drummer-entertainers: they are shameful people; they beg money in public.

    The foregoing ranking of occupations was obtained using interview material, mostly from rural peasant farmers. The consensus seems quite high across both sexes and up and down the status position.[17] Table 1 gives the ranking of 55 occupations taken from 81 Kanuri secondary-school boys in 1957.[18] The boys were instructed in Kanuri to rank all occupations from 1 to 55 and to choose as if God had given them the power to do anything they liked. The large number of judgments did not seem to bother them. This is attributed to the traditional Kanuri practice of numbering things and people according to rank from one on (one being the highest in status). The fact that they gave high ratings to such offices as Emir (*Shehu*) of Bornu, an office totally unavailable to any of them, indicates that the instruction helped them to evaluate the ranked position of these occupations in a socially recognized manner, and less so in terms of personal preferences and ambition.

    The results showed that high status traditional jobs only maintain their relative position when they have been absorbed into modern government and carry a salary. Thus salary-supported, traditionally high status, occupations when averaged together obtain a rank of 11.9, while non-salaried ones ranked 31.9. White-collar jobs of all kinds rank high (11.3); next came European-type manual labor (28.7), then lowest of all Kanuri forms of manual labor (44.3). When Western jobs were compared as to employer relations, self-employed jobs ranked lower (27.2) than those in large bureaucratic organizations (14.4).

    Although these data were gathered nearly a decade ago, recent experience in the field leads me to believe that for the population at large these occupational ratings are still valid. However, I am impressed with the rapidity with which those receiving Western education have changed their notion of job status in accordance with the changing opportunities in a modernizing state. A decade ago almost all of the school boys evaluated white-collar administrative jobs very highly, reflecting the views of both the Kanuri and the colonial officials in Bornu. Today they are aware of (*a*) a much larger social field, viz., Nigeria as a whole, or its northern provinces, (*b*) the utility of university education in gaining better jobs

17. Cf. Mitchell, J. C., and S. C. Irvine, 1965.
18. The questionnaire was also given to 67 senior primary-school boys on the same occasion. Although the results are slightly different, and the sample not entirely a Kanuri one for the younger boys, it showed a rank-order correlation of .90 with the ordering in Table 1.

Table 1. *Occupation Ranking of Maiduguri Secondary-School Boys (1957)*

Cardinal Choice	Occupation	Mean Choice	Average Deviation
1	Shehu of Bornu	5.21	4.7
2	District Officer	6.03	5.0
3	Waziri of Bornu	7.15	5.2
4	Member of Northern House of Assembly	7.72	4.4
5	Government Service	9.21	5.4
6	Koranic Mallam	9.26	9.4
7	Agricultural Officer	10.66	6.7
8	Native Authority	12.06	6.2
9	Chief Scribe of the Capital City of Maiduguri (salaried)	12.19	5.8
10	Medical Officer	12.19	6.2
11	District Head (*Ajia*)	13.69	5.0
12	Alkalai (Muslim judge)	17.02	9.3
13	Kaigama (a District Head today, traditionally a high status title)	17.88	7.9
14	Bank Clerk	18.40	8.1
15	Engineer	18.51	9.2
16	Clerk in a European Trading Company	19.71	6.2
17	Bank Manager	20.10	9.3
18	Radio Announcer	20.76	7.6
19	Farmer	20.97	9.4
20	European Company Manager	21.70	8.3
21	Journalist	21.76	7.4
22	Owner of Retail Store	22.65	5.9
23	Trader with Credit from European Companies	22.73	8.0
24	Rural Village Head (salaried)	23.94	7.3
25	Male Nurse	24.45	10.4
26	Hotel Owner	25.57	6.7
27	Truck Driver	25.93	7.3
28	Mechanic	27.77	9.8
29	Traditional Trader	29.49	10.9
30	Member of Native Authority Council	29.61	9.4
31	Truck Owner	30.68	9.5
32	Kachella Shehube (traditional title, unsalaried job in present system)	31.88	10.1
33	Building Contractor	31.90	9.6
34	Carpenter	31.94	7.8
35	Tailor on Sewing Machine	32.34	7.6
36	Scale Man (cash crop buyer in bush)	32.91	9.2
37	Rural Hamlet Head (unsalaried)	33.46	7.3
38	Small Retailer at Roadside Table Selling Sundries	33.66	6.8
39	Mudhouse Building (traditional)	34.82	9.4
40	Seller of Charms	37.52	8.8
41	Horsed Servant (traditional political position unsalaried)	38.62	6.1
42	Hunter	38.88	7.4
43	Kola-nut Seller	38.90	6.3
44	Shoemaker	39.86	6.8
45	Hatmaker	40.00	6.6
46	Shehu's Slave (unsalaried)	41.03	9.1
47	Laborer	41.54	5.9

Table 1. (continued)

Cardinal Choice	Occupation	Mean Choice	Average Deviation
48	Blacksmith	42.05	8.5
49	Barber	42.15	6.1
50	Weaver	42.44	6.9
51	Calabash Maker	40.03	6.5
52	Petty Broker	45.15	6.5
53	Drummer-Entertainer	47.08	5.6
54	Butcher	47.33	5.5
55	Moneylender	47.96	7.7

(which they hardly knew about in 1957), and (c) a much wider range of possible occupations starting with commercial corporations and stretching across the entire gamut of government service. They also seem to know something they were totally unaware of a decade ago—that highly trained technicians are in charge of modernization, have much of the real power to get things done, and have greater security of status than those in purely administrative, nontechnical roles.

WEALTH

The Kanuri have well-established social rankings for differences in wealth. These can be translated into a four-part scale with "destitute" at one end, then "poor" above this, then "not rich, not poor," and finally "wealthy." Starting from the top the Kanuri define a wealthy man as anyone who has a highly lucrative occupation, who can afford more than two wives, and who lives materially in a manner set apart from, and above, that of his neighbors. Next to this are those who would be described and judged by others as being "not rich, not poor." This is the person who is in some ways similar to the poor man but has more material wealth, and a slightly higher status occupation than the poor man. He is also successful financially to the extent that he can afford more than one wife and provide the members of his household with sufficient clothes and money to keep them satisfied enough to remain under his roof. A poor man is one who is judged to have very few possessions, no liquid capital, not enough money to afford any luxuries or an extra wife and/or one who has a low status occupation. Finally a destitute man (*ngudi*: literally, an unfortunate man) is one without any property, and no claim to land, or material possessions. He cannot even wear good clothes on religious festivals, or return gifts to his friends and relatives at ceremonies. Thus he cannot maintain his network of social relations through the obligatory reciprocity of gift-giving. Reciprocal gift-giving is part and parcel of membership in a network of social relations. Thus to be poor is one thing, but to be destitute (*ngudi*) is quite another, since it means the person so judged is outside the normal network of social relations and is consequently without the possibility of successful membership in ongoing groups, the members of which can help him if he requires it. The Kanuri say that such a person is not to be trusted. Thus to call a man "poor" is to describe his economic condition, to call a man *"ngudi"* or destitute or to refer to him as such is to insult or negate his sense of legitimate membership in the community and his commitment to its moral standards.

In general, all Kanuri agree that wealth is desirable and provides higher status to those who have it. It is good to have fine clothes to wear and give away, to have a good horse, or bicycle, or motorbike, or car, a big house, many wives, and so on; conversely, it is undesirable not to have these things. Many people suggest that wealth is really not so important as holiness or religiosity, but given the choice, this turns out to be a form of lip service to religious values. Besides, this wealth can increase piety. The wealthy man has more time to pray; he can hire religious practitioners or take them into his household as clients to pray for him and advise him on religious matters; he can be generous with charity and take the pilgrimage to Mecca more easily than other people. On the other hand, women seem more unidimensional in their interests in wealth as a status distinction. Thus they claim that the best husband is a wealthy one regardless of his occupation. Men, on the other hand, feel that powerful, influential occupations are more important than wealth alone, since material wealth comes with such occupations anyway.

This difference in status consensus is probably due to the fact that women and men live in different social words. Men have many of their meaningful social relations outside the household, and thus the type of social relations from which wealth is derived becomes important to them. A woman, however, lives in a social world of relations with her husband, co-wives, and kindred. The wealthier her husband is, the better off she is, but she derives very little, if anything, from her husband's social life outside the household and is therefore much less interested in it than he is when she judges the importance of wealth as a desirable status distinction.

CLASS

Generically in both traditional and contemporary terms the Kanuri have a two-class system, although this overall categorization must be seen in the light of the status distinctions which support its continuity and the subdivisions within it which have both traditional and modern provenience. The two classes are the commoners (*talaa*) and the upper class or "important people" (*kəntuoma*). Traditionally, as well as today,

Ronald Cohen: Social Stratification in Bornu

everyone not connected by office to the centralized political system was automatically a commoner. These people are engaged in the productive sector of the economy, wear a different style of dress for everyday work, have dialect distinctions in their speech, and are dependent upon the upper class for protection and the adjudication of disputes. Through their connections along hierarchical chains of political relations they link themselves to upper-classs members.

Upper class people dress more elaborately in long flowing robes, and their speech is different in that they do not drop *g* and *s* as consonants in the middle of words—a widespread, lower-class custom.[19] The most important distinction is one of power and authority. Upper class people hold office in the political system of Bornu. They can exert power over others in many ways because Kanuri society is identifiable primarily as a political unit. Thus a very wealthy trader who has never had any political office describes himself as a commoner, even though many of the people he regards as upper class members are much less wealthy than he himself.

Within the upper class tradition there has always been a distinction between (*a*) royals and nonroyals and (*b*) slaves and freemen. Royals are people who are connected by descent to the royal patrilineage of Bornu. Although some Kanuri are not clear on this point, it also means that royals should be the issue of nonslave wives of members of the royal lineage. Certainly, though all claiming cognatic ties to the royal lineage can, and do, call themselves *dur maibe* (family of the king), those agnatically related through nonslave mothers have the higher status. Within this high status group of royals, distinctions are made by the Kanuri on the basis of sex and father's status. Women of the royal family are (*a*) sisters of the king, (*b*) the king's mother, (*c*) the wives of the king among whom the senior wife is the most important, (*d*) daughters of the king, and (*e*) grandchildren of the king. Of these the Shehu's mother and his senior wife have the highest status, both traditionally and today, since they are the highest female authorities in the palace. Men of the royal family are divided into (*a*) those whose fathers were monarchs, i.e., heirs to the throne and the princes of the realm (*maina*), and (*b*) those whose grandfathers were monarchs (*maidugu*), i.e., those whose fathers are or were princes. These latter have higher status if their fathers are still alive, since this means their own chances of becoming monarchs are still at issue.

Free nobles are traditionally the sons of nobles who have gained either their father's title or been given one by the monarch. Traditionally they held fiefs in various parts of the kingdom and lived in the capital city. In addition, various slaves of the monarch, including eunuchs, were titled officials in the administration. They could be very powerful men, but were

19. Upper class persons say *musko* instead of *muko* for hand, or *gabagaa* rather than *gaba'a* for a roll of cloth.

always of lower status than free nobles. At the local village level town heads and representatives of the fiefholders, under whose administrative responsibility the town was governed, formed a local upper class in the rural areas.

Today, the same principle still applies, but not necessarily with the same title. Men in important positions in the emirate government form the upper class in contemporary Bornu. Since a number of officials are now present in the district capital, each district has residing at its major town a local group who are urban, upper class people living in the rural areas. A large new group, not totally allied to either the upper class or the broad band of the commoner class, is made up of low-paid clerical staff, primary schoolteachers, lower echelon civil servants, and a number of others, *"mallams"* or educated people. They earn salaries, yet hardly enough to live like the wealthy upper class people. On the other hand, their Western education, their ability to subsist without recourse to trade, craftwork, or farming, and their attachment to the political system give them higher than commoner status, thus they form a middle group or class differentiated from both of the two traditional classes of Bornu.

Perhaps the best method of illustrating the Kanuri class system "at work" is to let an informant speak for himself. One young farmer in a rural area when asked about wealthy people in his own village replied that there were none, although in the next village to the east there were about a dozen who could be called "rich." When asked why they were rich, he said they had very large farms (fifteen to twenty acres) and one was a successful kola-nut seller who turned over at least four to six *kwando* per month (one *kwando* equals approximately seven to eight thousand nuts). When asked why he had not thought of mentioning a number of people in his own town who were far richer than these men, he looked very puzzled and exclaimed, "That is different—the men you speak of in my own town are different people, and we [including the rich man in the next town] are *talaa* [commoners]." The men in his own town were salaried officials of the emirate government, thus defined as upper class members— which the informant interpreted to mean "outside my range of judgment." The informant, like most other Kanuri, sees two separate ranges of status distinctions, one for "us," the common people, and one for "them," the upper class people. This same view of society can be obtained from upper class members, who see *talaa* as "them." All these people are the same ethnic group, but still there is a feature perceived and understood by everyone that cuts across these other distinctions—this I would call "class."

As indicated by both the data and our theoretical discussion, we must also view class differences as another status distinction in and of itself, since it is such a broadly inclusive feature and is, therefore, in a number of senses a multifaceted variable instead of a dichotomous category when it is actually utilized by the people themselves to judge and generalize about someone else's or one's own high or low status in the society. This is spelled out in greater detail in the following discussion on social mobility.

MOBILITY

Like many societies, especially more complex ones, the Kanuri recognize that status comes from both personal achievement and ascribed characteristics obtained by birth into a particular family in the society, and this is a long-established feature of their culture. Although Kanuri reckon descent bilaterally, there is an emphasis placed on the agnatic group for purposes of inheritance and in terms of legal responsibility to the community. Therefore a person's status is much affected by the status of his agnatic descent group and its leading members. One of the first questions asked of anyone, or about them, is "Who is his father?" This point became very clear during the collection of genealogical information. A very ambitious man who had, it was rumored, risen from extreme poverty to become the trusted political subordinate of a district head, gave a trumped-up genealogy including among his ancestors a number of clients of well-known Kanuri nobles. Later it was discovered this man was the son of humble parents and he had started his own career as a gatherer and seller of bush grass or horse fodder. He had faked his genealogy in order to give a newcomer to the society the impression that his forebears were all close associates of the Bornu nobility, a position he was hoping to achieve for himself.

The Kanuri explain why some men succeed or go ahead on the basis of indwelling supernatural causes in the human personality (to be discussed) and also as a result of a person's birth. Thus when judging someone's rise or fall, success or failure, or any other quality capable of evaluation, the Kanuri are quick to refer to a man's birth. One chief remarked that the dishonest behavior of another chief was very understandable if it were remembered that this particular chief being gossiped about was the son of a slave, i.e., he was really of lower status background and could not ever behave as well as a freeman noble. Among commoners people always ask questions about a person's birth into a particular agnatic descent group when trying to gauge the possibilities of success or failure for that person. Many peasants, when asked what occupation their father had, replied "*mallam*" or religious practitioner because it gives them higher status than to say their father was simply a farmer, craftsman, or a trader.

Birth into a particular descent group limits mobility, and thus most higher status people in Bornu are from high status backgrounds. Western education and a plethora of new jobs are opening up because modernization has increased mobility. But these schools were first filled by sons of upper class people who were the first to perceive the value of the new schools in the future of Bornu. Consequently large sections of the Western-educated are the sons of traditional leaders.

At the commoner level it is not difficult to find craftsmen who, when questioned about their occupational history, remark that they come from a kin group that has practiced this occupation "*duk*" (far back into the unremembered past). This is only partially true, however; many informants holding very low status occupations claim the excuse of *kna nzukko* (hunger pushed me into it). That is to say, they claim that they were not actually born into families whose status was that of blacksmith, or builder, or butcher, etc. Rather they were forced by unfortunate circumstances to go into the occupation in order to maintain some form of livelihood. Birth into a particular group is important, then. So are the events of a person's life which permit him or her to rise, or force them to fall, with respect to that which is normally expected of them.

With regard to other status distinctions there is some ability to achieve higher status, and there always has been in the past, so that Bornu culture and society contain a constant tension between achieved and ascribed status. It is possible for individuals of neighboring ethnic groups, for example, to assimilate to Kanuri society and thus move from a lower to a higher status vis-à-vis Kanuri judgments. For Muslim groups this simply means settling in Kanuri towns, learning the language, and marrying Kanuri women. Many Kanuri villages have people of Fulani, Hausa, Shuwa, or Kanembu backgrounds who have assimilated into the local community. Their own personal histories are known and remembered, but there seems to be very little discrimination against them once they decide to live a Kanuri way of life. Non-Muslims have a somewhat more difficult time, but they do enter Kanuri society in a fairly steady stream. If they are women, they simply learn the language, profess Islam, and take on the dress and distinctive coiffure of the Kanuri. Men must be circumcised, and they arrange to do this at Kanuri circumcision ceremonies. Sometimes as many as five to ten of these non-Muslims (ages fifteen to thirty-five) may ask to be included in a large urban circumcision ceremony that could involve as many as thirty to forty Kanuri boys who range in age from seven to fourteen. They are still thought of as members of their old tribal group after the circumcision, but they are also thought of as having improved themselves by taking on the Muslim religion and going through the ordeal of circumcision. In a few cases they eventually marry Kanuri women, but this is quite rare.

As already noted, perhaps the most important status distinction in Bornu is occupation. Mobility along this gradient is achieved primarily through clientage, and always has been. The basic unit of Kanuri social

258

Ronald Cohen: Social Stratification in Bornu

organization is the household. Occupations are learned and to a large
extent carried on in households. Thus to enter a higher status occupation
requires that the person obtain some relationship to a household either as
an apprentice who lives and works in the household of his master, or as a
client who lives elsewhere, usually close by. In every case these relations
are based on mutual trust in which the superior helps the subordinate to
achieve the occupation by training him while the subordinate supplies a
large range of services for the superior. It is difficult to overemphasize
the importance of this mobility technique. Ask any Kanuri how he con-
ceives of getting ahead in the world, and he quickly replies in terms of
obtaining a working client-patron relationship with a big, powerful, rich
person, in which the patron will help him to achieve a worthwhile occupation.

Traditionally, and today, people wishing to set up profitable social
relations like this deliver presents and pay their respects constantly to
those whom they feel can expedite favors designed to help the giver gain
status and perhaps, hopefully, in the end to establish a client relationship.
One man told me recently that although he had never held political office,
nor had any of his forebears, he feels confident that one day he will be
appointed to the headship of a particular village nearby. He reports that
he regularly visits all the major decision-makers in the Native Authority
and gives them presents, pays them his respects, and tries to show them
and everyone else that he is a proper, respectful person who is loyal to the
present political hierarchy. Someday this "investment" may pay off, and
he will be appointed to a village headship because he will have established
himself as a worthwhile candidate. This quality of continually searching
for profitable client-patron relations gives all Bornu society a labile quality
such that that people negotiate with their own subordination in order to
achieve a promise of greater status for themselves in the future.[20] Again
this is a very old feature of the society and is tied closely to the historical
development of Bornu as a system of feudal social relations.[21]

Today Western education is entering the society, and more and more
it is becoming a new means for achieving occupational mobility. However,
it still affects a very small percentage of the population and is only significant at the elite level for those few going into government positions or
the large, private companies. The important point, however, is that such
mobility also includes a strong possibility of obtaining an occupation
anywhere in Nigeria, not just in Bornu, thus creating a new set of horizons
in which, not Kanuri society, but the nation as a whole becomes the
referent for making status distinctions. This mobility factor, however, is
still embryonic in Bornu, and for most of the population traditional modes
of mobility are the only ones practiced.

20. See Cohen, R., 1965.   21. See Cohen, R., 1966a.

The utilization of wealth is also used to raise or lower status in the society. Certainly, as already noted, wealth should be used to live well. But the primary use of wealth is to create dependent relations, obtain more wives, and generally keep many people dependent, so that the dispenser of wealth has many supporters. People who are judged to have wealth and not give it out to wives, relatives, clients, and would-be clients are considered to be stringy or miserly. Men who give too much away are spendthrifts, although the literal translation of "spendthrift" is instructive; it means "the man who goes to too many ceremonies." Giving ceremonies and going to those of one's friends and relatives is obligatory among the Kanuri, as with many other people the world over. Great and powerful men always go to very many, and/or send gifts to friends and relatives who are giving ceremonies. A spendthrift, then, is a man who goes not only to those ceremonies he is obliged to go to, but to many others as well. Besides this he gives more than he receives to those with whom he does have reciprocal obligations. This means that his gift-giving relations to others for ceremonial purposes tend to become redistributive, like the men in positions of political leadership, rather than reciprocal as it is with most people.[22] If a man has adequate means to give larger and more gifts than others, he can be spoken of as being socially mobile; if not, then he is considered foolish, imprudent, and unable to withstand the temptation to be thought of as better off than he really deserves.

The optimum use of wealth is described as "wise generosity." This type of person uses his wealth to support himself, his family, his clients, neighbors, friends, to the extent that he can afford it, and no more. But he does not go into debt to achieve this generosity, and he is wise enough to balance his actual assets against the requirements of his social position. This is, however, an ideal. Since there is always pressure from others in the community to dispense wealth well beyond what one can afford, and this is reinforced by a desire to use wealth to raise one's status, it takes a strong self-confident person, or a very wealthy one, to fit the ideal of Kanuri generosity associated with the use of wealth and its relation to status validation and status mobility. This is one of the reasons Kanuri men become tense and anxious over ceremonies. They are always afraid that the ceremony will cost much more than they bargained for or can afford.

Class, as we have defined it, is a consistently high or consistently low position along many status distinctions which tends eventually to unite large sections of the population. From the point of view of the people themselves, class is a generalization about stratification which expresses their understanding of the correlations among status gradients. However,

22. See Cohen, R., 1965.

it should be remembered that the separation of these classes produces differing styles of life in language, dress, housing, and a host of other cultural traits.

In Bornu, language, dress, house style, numbers of dependents, clients, and supporters are the most apparent and visible symptoms both traditionally and in the contemporary society of one's class position. These qualities are, however, imitable. Members of the commoner class can buy the voluminous robes worn traditionally by the upper class, and everyone has at least one such robe for festive occasions. A more mobile person acquires many of these robes, and of a variety and style well known to be associated with upper class membership, if he wishes to take on the features of upper class subculture. Furthermore he tries to be seen not wearing anything but the long robes of the upper class, since the short sleeveless work shirt of the lower class signifies immediately the class position of its wearer. The same is true of language, both in pronunciation and in content. An upwardly mobile person can with some effort pronounce words as the upper classes do, and drop from his conversation the ribaldry and slightly profane exclamations that color and punctuate the speech of peasants and lower class people in general. If he has the means, the mobile person can, if he will, live in a larger better-built house with more dependents and more clients; he can possess horses and today a motorcar that automatically advertises his wealth to everyone.

Political power, the traditional avenue to upper class membership, is, however, not so easy to acquire. Traditionally, a man without any such power could acquire it in several ways. First he could, if he were living in a rural area, found his own settlement and in time become the leader of a growing and successful village. This entitled him and his descendants to the headship of the settlement and to the possibility of a title bestowed by the Shehu upon successful rural leaders. Over the years if his settlement succeeded, he could add a title derived from the village itself. Thus the head of Titiwa not only received an ordinary title of village head (or head of a group of linked villages) but could also call himself the "Titiwama." There are traditions of such rural men who continually visited the rural court and capital during the nineteenth century hoping to obtain some recognition for their title, not simply in terms of its being rurally based, but as a part of the courtly titled group around the monarch. This involved efforts by such people at integrating themselves with the monarch and his chief advisers by a constant giving of tributes.

Today it is still possible to found one's own settlement and produce a local headship for oneself and one's agnatic descendants. Both traditionally as well as today, this method has some insecurity, since superiors in the system have the right, most often used at times of succession to office, either to recognize a proper agnatic heir or to give the office to one of their own favorites either locally or from somewhere else in the kingdom. Another method, and one more commonly used, is to become the client of a powerful man, often spending some time in his household in order to prove one's loyalty and continuing obedience to the superior's interest. This method, both traditionally and today, is still the primary mode of access to, or recruitment into, the politically powerful class in Bornu if one is not born into it. As we have said, this is now not the only way, since Western education has become more common and a number of the politically powerful jobs in the emirate require some degree of technical competence. However, even among Western-educated aspirants to powerful positions, decorous behavior, loyalty to the power structure, and general upper class Kanuri values are extremely important criteria for acceptance into top jobs in the Kanuri emirate civil service.

For those who do not aspire to political power, the acquisition of wealth in the commercial sector is the most common way up the status ladder. Traditionally, there were always wealthy traders in Bornu who were not in the important positions of political power. However, many of the powerful political leaders engaged in commerce. Today this is still true of many political leaders. Members of the Kanuri political elite have, as of 1966, bought up small farms and are planting citrus orchards; they are financing construction enterprises, buying up houses in the capital city, and charging rents, as well as financing the export-import trade. However, local entrepreneurs, through connections to political leaders, as well as on their own or in conjunction with commercial interests outside Bornu, have expanded enormously in the last decade and a half. It is now possible to speak of an incipient business class in Bornu who share many of the same interests and have a desire to stay out of politics, but they do actively seek wealth through commerce. This nonpolitical group and their values form a new upper class sector for the upwardly mobile that was never so clearly demarcated as it is now becoming today.

Mobility combines with social structure to create a highly unified society in Bornu. This results from the fact that Kanuri social stratification mitigates class conflicts (*a*) because there are and always have been avenues of mobility for many who strive to obtain higher status, and (*b*) because the social structure provides for vertical and hierarchical sets of social relations through household membership, clientship, and the basic nature of the political and economic systems of the society. Relations with fellow lower class members may be friendly, but every Kanuri knows that his relations with persons of superior status are the most important and meaningful activities of his entire social life in Bornu. In such a situation class solidarity is cultural but not social, i.e., lower and upper class members share common cultural understandings, but each has multiple sets of social relations cutting across class lines that maintain whatever social position they have and create the basis for status they hope to have in the future. Thus Bornu society crosscuts its class divisions by social mobility and the nature of its social relational networks.

STATUS ANXIETY AND THE USE
OF SOCIAL NARCOTICS

One final point about social mobility that is important and perhaps unique for this area is status anxiety and its cultural expression, which I would call a social narcotic. As we have seen, Kanuri society has always been hierarchical, and this arrangement of roles into superior-subordinate sets has always been expressed in class terms and differential ranking for many activities connected with the role structure. Upward mobility has always accompanied this social system as its desirable end or a social value. Achievement of higher status may be accomplished through the potentialities offered by deference and subordination, i.e., client relations, and such achievement certainly is a value to be striven for whenever this is possible.

Unfortunately there has never been enough access to upward mobility to meet the demand, and this has called forth a cultural response that satisfies this demand artificially. I am referring here to the institution of the praise-singer.[23] Traditionally in Bornu important men have their own praise-singers who travel along with their superior and blare out his praises, his accomplishments, and those of his ancestors for all within earshot. The loudest and most complex musical instrumentation among praise-singers was that of the monarch himself. Indeed even today each district head still has his own group of praise-singers, as does the Waziri of Bornu (the chairman of the Native Authority Council). Thus praise-singers are a well-known attribute of upper class status associated particularly with high status distinctions—i.e., those of high political office in the emirate.

For the masses there are nonaffiliated praise-singers who wander about markets, play at ceremonies or public meetings, or often simply come into a town to stay for a while. Upright Kanuri have told me that it is silly to go to hear such "beggars," for one may waste money and get nothing in return. However, large crowds gather at such concerts, and many succumb. They give money to the players, who then loudly announce the bequest and sing the praises of the donor who stands silently showing no expression, which is the way upper class persons behave in similar situations. Unlike

23. Cf. Smith, M. G., 1957.

his upper class counterpart, however, he is treated to a *momentary* increase in his status, whereas the upper class person obtains such praise as an aspect of his status.

For many people who have strong desires for upward mobility it is difficult to maintain composure and control during such praise-singing concerts. One young man related how he became enraged one evening because he had only one pound to give the praise-singers (his salary was seven pounds ten shillings per month). He spent his pound quickly, then the singers were taken over by other men while he remained as an onlooker listening to the praises of other men. Before the evening was over he had spent fourteen pounds that did not belong to him and which he was frantic to replace the next day. I have recorded many other cases where men spent more than they intended while attending praise-singing displays. All felt to some extent out of control, or angry on such occasions because they were not about to give the praise-singers as much as they would have liked. In one of these cases a man spent several months' savings in about two hours. He had been promised a young virgin bride. The girl's parents at the last minute returned the bridewealth and married her to someone else. The man came to the festivities the night before the wedding, and in the presence of the family he took over control of the praise-singers hired to sing the praises of those concerned in the marriage. Instead the entire village heard nothing but praise for the jilted suitor, while he spent the entire amount he had intended as bridewealth in order to obtain this balm to his hurt pride.

It is the momentary quality of status enhancement by praise-singers that makes it a social narcotic. Certainly, as Smith[24] suggests, for the Hausa it validates status for those who already have it. But for those who do not have high status, and who desperately want it, the praise-singers provide a momentary sense of public acclaim. To keep the sense of accomplishment, the person desiring the status must give again, and again, each time getting only a moment or two of the players' time. It is like a narcotic in other respects as well. Praise-singing does not give any real increase in status to those who do not derive the grounds for such status from other sources, i.e., with respect to the real and recognized status distinctions already discussed. Instead, giving money to praise-singers only alleviates, again momentarily, for as long as the praise-singers play, the desire for higher status, and in order to fake satisfaction one must keep paying for their services. That is why people get angry; their turn is over, their moment of status has been lost, and they are back where they started, indeed worse, because the whole thing cost them money and the status gained by it was not real but theatrical in its quality.

24. Smith M. G., 1957.

THE KANURI THEORY OF SUCCESS
AND ITS RELATION TO STRATIFICATION

While the analytical social scientist may attempt to explain a phenomenon such as social stratification, this does not mean that the people he is studying may not themselves have some theories about their own behavior that can shed light on the subject from the analyst's point of view. The Kanuri know full well the meaning and effect of the various status distinctions, status consensus about these, and mobility factors that have been previously described. However, they feel that there is more to explain than this. Why are there status distinctions to begin with? Why do some men playing the same role succeed in differing degrees? Why are some men born with higher status than others?

To explain this—the ultimate causes of stratification, mobility, and success in achieving status—the Kanuri use the widespread Sudanic concept of good fortune, or indwelling spiritual aspect of personality that produces success or failure for each person. This quality is an essential and variable aspect of human nature, essential for success and variable from person to person and within the same person through time. If an individual moves up in terms of occupation, amasses wealth, harvests a good crop, is lucky in gambling, wins judicial decisions, obtains power and authority over others, or makes what power he has work well for him, avoids illness, poverty and derision, or does anything that can be measured in terms of achievement, then the degree of his success is the proof as to how much *arẓiyi* (good fortune, personal degree of success) he has in his *hal* (his nature, his being, his essence). Like Calvinistic predetermination, *arẓiyi* is hoped for before the fact, and indicated or substantiated after the fact of success in life.

In answering questions about *arẓiyi*, informants from all classes of society are generally agreed that no matter how much success a peasant has with his farm, his wife, at cards, or at his craft work, he can never possibly come close to having as much *arẓiyi* as even a bad political leader in the capital. When finer discriminations are asked for, however, disagreements sometimes arise. Thus informants, when questioned as to who has more *arẓiyi*, a trader in the city who recently bought a big truck and has a large compound of wives and followers, or a somewhat effete district head who has failed badly at his job, they answered according to how they ranked wealth alone as compared to political power alone, although they were not used to thinking of these things as being separate. Since both of these status distinctions are usually congruent when ranked high, the discrimination is often a difficult one. Nevertheless there is at any one level of the society a large measure of agreement about the amount or *arẓiyi* of the various social roles in the society at any one time. People from different levels of society give somewhat differing pictures of the distribution of *arziyi* in the society. This is all from different vantage points, and therefore different opportunities for perceiving their own social structure. Thus, although many lower class people find it difficult to decide whether or not the effete district head has more *arziyi* than the rich city trader, those close to the chief, including himself, feel that the rich trader has more.

This brings up an interesting observation. The judgment of any individual about the distribution of *arziyi* in society at any one time is his particular notion about the arrangement of social roles in the social structure. Furthermore his estimation of the distribution of *arziyi* at any one level of the hierarchy—i.e., for example, comparing the behavior of one district head with another—is his judgment of the success that occupants of similar roles are enjoying relative to one another at any particular time.

Arziyi, then, seems to be used in two related ways in Kanuri society. Firstly, in an enormously heterogeneous society, it gives a satisfactory answer to individual variations along one of the most important dimensions of behavior, success in achieving immediate and long-range goals. Secondly, it is used as an explanation for the nature of the social structure itself, especially for that aspect of the social structure which deals with rank—i.e., its stratification system. Those people who have higher status along any gradient of status distinction have more *arziyi*, which accounts for their ability to maintain such a role in the social organization. These two ways of using *arziyi* as an explanation for differentiation are related so that what results is a Kanuri theory of their own society that at once validates its structure and explains the changes in personnel which accompany a system where personal fortunes may rise and fall rapidly. Thus a high status position in the structure indicates that the person has that particular amount of *arziyi*. If his performance of the role required by this status shows him to have even more *arziyi*, then he will outstrip others who occupy the same status and seek the same goals. On the other hand, he may do badly, which will indicate a loss of *arziyi* and a loss of status. *Arziyi* is also, besides being a theory of society, a theory of causation which integrates social and individual differentiation under one simple mystical force—personal good fortune—which is continually being validated since its presence is indicated after the fact of its operation in behavior.[25]

CONCLUSIONS

I have tried to describe Kanuri social stratification by first summarizing its sociopolitical structure and the development of this structure in Bornu.

25. For a fuller account of *arziyi* and its place in the Kanuri world view, see Cohen, R., 1966d.

Ronald Cohen: Social Stratification in Bornu

The points of major importance in this respect are (1) that the Kanuri have had a centralized preindustrial state in the Bornu area for centuries, and (2) that this state has given the social system a strong emphasis on its hierarchical role relations in which high status has always been associated with higher position in the political structure of the state.

Because the state has had contacts with other ethnic groups and absorbed many of them over the centuries there has developed in the local culture a standardized attitude for judging ethnicity as a status distinction along with strong ethnocentrism in marriage choices. Occupation, wealth, age, sex, and rural/urban status are also important status distinctions and have been described in some detail along with the degree of status consensus exhibited by each one of these for the population as a whole. Class differences are derived from the status distinctions, but tend to become more complicated as style of life features elaborate the overall differences between the two major classes in the society.

Social mobility is present in the society along each status distinction (except that of sex), and the wide ramifications of class distinction mean that the attributes of class membership can be imitated by those wishing to obtain recognition for higher status in the society. Anxiety about mobility and the lack of enough access to increase status has produced a tension in the society that finds an outlet in praise-singing, in which the ambitious but frustrated may obtain momentary satisfaction for their desires of enhanced status. The data also indicate that the Kanuri have their own theory of social stratification which utilizes a concept concerning the quality of human personality to explain both their system of role differentiation and social structure on the one hand, and individual success on the other. Finally from the theoretical point of view, the concepts of status distinctions, status consensus, class, and mobility as herein defined and used seem adequate in describing and helping to explain Kanuri social stratification.

Status distinctions as variables are, of course, dependent upon each other (among other things); thus wealth is a function of occupation, sex, and rural-urban residence, and so on. The gradients of status form a network of forces that all work in an interrelated fashion to maintain the system of social stratification at any particular point in the history of the society. The stability of Kanuri (or any other) system of social stratification depends upon the numbers and kinds of interrelations among status distinctions and the means available in the society for social mobility. If nonpolitical occupations come to have higher status than political ones in Bornu, then the social order will have changed radically. The same is true for any number of changes that might occur in terms of the status distinctions enumerated in this chapter.

The change most likely to occur in Bornu is the increased emphasis placed on the Western educational system as a means of mobility rather than the traditional system of birth into a particular family, or clientage. As this occurs it will create a much higher status for Western education itself than is now accorded to it, and it will begin to break down the uniformity of Kanuri social stratification and mobility patterns, since entrance to high status roles will not come through the traditional system of hierarchically arranged political offices and the traditional means for recruitment into such roles.

BIBLIOGRAPHY

Cohen, Ronald 1961 Marriage instability among the Kanuri of northern Nigeria. American Anthropologist, *63*:1231–49.

——— 1962 The analysis of conflict in hierarchical systems: an example from Kanuri political organization, in: Power in Complex Societies, Ronald Cohen (ed.). Anthropologica, *4*:87–120.

——— 1965 Kanuri exchange relations. Cahiers d'Etudes Africaines, *5*(19): 353–69. Reprint #4, Program of African Studies, Northwestern University.

——— 1966a The dynamics of feudalism in Bornu, Boston University Publications in African History #2 (in press).

——— 1966b From empire to colony: Bornu in the nineteenth and twentieth centuries, in: The Impact of Colonialism, V. Turner (ed.). Stanford, Hoover Institute (in press).

——— 1966c The Kanuri of Bornu. New York, Holt, Rinehart & Winston.

——— 1966d Power, authority, and personal success in Islam and Bornu, in: Political Anthropology, M. Schwartz, A. Tuden, and V. Turner (eds.).

Garbarino, Merywin 1966 Decision-Making Among the Seminole of Florida. Unpublished Ph.D. dissertation, Northwestern University.

Goody, Jack n.d. Incorporation in northern Ghana. To be published in: Tribe and Nation in Africa, Ronald Cohen and John Middleton (eds.).

Lasswell, T. E. 1965 Class and Stratum. Boston, Houghton Mifflin.

Mitchell, J. C., and S. C. Irvine 1965 Social position and the grading of occupations. Rhodes-Livingstone Journal, *38*:42–54.

Rosman, A. 1959 Social structure and acculturation among the Kanuri of Bornu Province, Northern Nigeria, Transactions of the New York Academy of Sciences, *21* (7):620–30.

Sahlins, M. 1958 Social Stratification in Polynesia. Seattle, University of Washington Press (published for the American Ethnological Society).

Smith, M. G. 1957 The social functions and meaning of Hausa praise-singing. Africa, *27*:26–45.

——— 1959 The Hausa system of social status. Africa, *29*:239–52.

THE MODERN AFRICAN ELITE OF JOS, NIGERIA

BY LEONARD PLOTNICOV

CONCEPTS OF CLASS IN AFRICA

In the view of many scholars it would be premature now to speak of the existence of social classes in Africa. Lloyd states that classes, in the Marxist sense of propertied and nonpropertied groups, exist neither in traditional nor in modern African society (1966: 56). Mitchell and Epstein reject the notion of class in the modern context because corporate political behavior is absent (1959: 35–36). Banton sees the seeds of class consciousness (1965: 143), but both he (1965: 145) and Lloyd (1966: 14, 53, 58) find that tribal loyalties have inhibited this development. Lloyd does, however, point out that the modern elite have special interests that would provide the basis for a class consciousness (1966: 59), and that they do possess a self-awareness[1] manifested in cultural traits that make a marked contrast between them and the remainder of the population (1966: 58). Forde (1956: 43) and Southall (1956: 574) note the presence of multiple ranking systems—involving traditional and modern criteria—that blur, rather than define, class categories. Banton adds that social class segregation has not occurred in such critical areas as residence, marriage, and life-styles generally (1965: 144 et passim); and Little, for the reasons mentioned so far and for the fact that members of the modern elite interact intensively

---

1. Lloyd suggests that a distinction be made "between class awareness and class consciousness—the latter implying consciousness of the special interests of the class and activity directed towards preserving these interests" (1966: 57).

with traditionalists in terms of traditional ideals of status and etiquette, would concede only embryonic formation of social classes (1959).

Because Fallers believes that these factors will continue to operate even with the modernization of economies, and because "welfare state policies in education and other fields . . . will militate against the solidification of the new elites into hereditary estates or castes," he predicts that for the immediate future African states will remain relatively classless, just as they have been in the past (1964:130). Lloyd also reminds us that classes tend to be hereditary groups, but that while there has been an insufficient passage of time for classes in the modern sense to develop, "the well educated and wealthy elite is tending to become a hereditary group" (1966:57). Southall states the general consensus of one position, that "it is more useful to envisage elites as dynamic and flexible categories rather than as groups, as persons in process of becoming rather than as actually achieving corporate definition" (1966:347).

There are others, however, who see some sort of class system appearing in Africa—at least on the basis of occupational criteria—although my impression is that they too would only with great caution apply the concept of social classes derived from Western societies.[2] Van den Berghe, for example, states that "whatever system of social stratification is taking shape in various parts of Africa, it is not likely to resemble closely that of Europe, Latin America, or even the other new states of Asia" (1965:162). On one point there is a general agreement: if any segment of the modern society approaches resemblance to a social class it is the modern elite.

> The peasantry still think in terms of ethnic units, with descent and age as the main criteria of stratification and social divisions. The sub-elite of clerks, primary-school teachers, and skilled artisans are perhaps slightly less ethnically oriented, but actively aspire to elite membership. The urban labourer remains ethnically oriented, often relying on his ethnic association for his social security. Trades unions, which might otherwise protect his interests, are weakly developed, especially among the least skilled. . . . One of the advantages of the term elite in describing the affluent western-educated African is that its counterpart, "the masses," vaguely implies a lack of structure, or at least of dominant structures among the non-elite. This is certainly generally appropriate in the African context. In other respects, however, the components of the class concept seem more useful in describing the African elite. (Lloyd, 1966:60)

Is it possible that a social group—in this case the modern African elite—can possess all the characteristics of a social class and still not be considered a class because there are no other classes in the society with

2. For an appreciation of some of the complexities that observers have faced in defining modern African social classes, the reader is referred to two examples of such classifications, Horner (1965:171–72) and van den Berghe (1965:161).

which it can be in political and economic competition? We tend to think of a social class as one layer in a system of stratified groups. To speak of one class is to imply the existence of others. Lloyd states that "a social class can exist only in a system of classes. In their homogeneity, hereditary characteristics, and class consciousness, the classes should resemble one another. But if the African elite forms an upper class, where are the lower classes?" (1966:60).

In this chapter I shall argue that despite the absence of lower classes, the modern elite do form a social class and that they do show corporate political behavior as a class. Their political energies are not always expressed within the society, but are more often directed externally. If only one class is now present, it is because a system of class stratification cannot appear at once full-blown, but requires an initial crystallization at the top, further developments proceeding downward. These remarks stem from my research in one northern Nigerian urban community, Jos, a middle-sized city, and therefore are intended only to suggest that, under similar conditions, the same processes may occur elsewhere.

My reasons for devoting attention to the formation and role of the modern African elite in a provincial urban center is not merely to counter the prevailing tendency to view the modern African elite as a product only of the capitals and major urban areas. If a modern class system is developing in the new nations, its representative persons (and their subcultures) will also be present in the smaller cities and larger provincial towns, and this is surely the case in a nation as large as Nigeria, where there are dozens of urban areas with populations of 50,000 or more.

GENERAL CHARACTERISTICS AND THE SOCIAL SETTING OF JOS

No city in Nigeria can be regarded as typical, but Jos may be taken as representative of those of middle size. It is a mining, commercial, and administrative center that has experienced rapid growth, particularly since World War II.[3] In 1930 its population was about 2,500 and in 1962 it had grown to about 60,000. The people come from all areas of Nigeria, and almost all the ethnic groups of the country are represented in proportions that are remarkably close to those for the nation as a whole. There are similar parallels in the ratios of Muslims, Christian, and pagan believers. Persons from other West African countries are also present in Jos, and

3. My research was carried out from 1960 to 1962 with support from the National Institutes of Health, which is gratefully acknowledged. The present description of Jos pertains to the period of fieldwork, but conditions have changed considerably since the political riots there during 1966.

Leonard Plotnicov: Modern African Elite of Jos

there are also the ubiquitous Levantines, a few Indians, and a large permanent and transient European population.

While Jos owed its inception to the mining of tin ore, its commercial stability today stems primarily from transportation enterprises and secondly from government administrative activities. The growth away from economic dependence on mining is one reason for some sharp contrasts between Jos and mining communities in other parts of Africa. Migrant laborers, for instance, are insignificant in Jos itself, and census data also show that there has long been a stable balance in the sex and age ratios of the African population. The presence of a very large proportion of children of primary school age may also be taken as an indication of the population's residential stability.[4]

Throughout most of its existence, Jos has been free from the problems afflicting other African urban centers, such as overcrowding and slum housing. Since squatting was never permitted, and the tax rates on house plots were low, Jos also lacked the problems of peri-urban shanty towns, insecurity of tenure, and property speculation reported for other parts of the continent, particularly East Africa.

The cooler climate of Jos (with an elevation of 4,000 feet), and the early establishment of a variety of modern amenities—electricity, schools, churches, hotels and rest houses, hospitals and clinics, social clubs, tribal union halls, markets, banks, missionary headquarters, an airport, a railroad link with southern Nigeria, a national museum and zoo, bars and cinemas—have made Jos attractive to Europeans and Africans alike.

When Jos was officially established, around 1915, as the administrative center for a rapdily growing tin-mining industry, streets and building plots were carefully laid out on a modified grid pattern, and the colonial policy of separating commercial and residential areas was put into effect. Peoples and institutions alien to northern Nigeria, such as southern Nigerians, non-Nigerian Africans, Levantines, and Europeans, administration offices, and nonindigenous business enterprises, were assigned to Jos Township. There Africans were settled in the *Sabon Gari* ("New Town," in Hausa), and colonial expatriates lived in suburban "European reservations." People and institutions (such as mosques and markets) native to northern Nigeria were located in Jos Native Town. Thus a residential and administrative division was imposed on Jos from the start. The more culturally conservative northern Nigerians developed their community in the Town under a modified system of traditional rule, while skilled African artisans and clerks, who were invariably nonindigenous to northern Nigeria, resided in the Township and came under a separate administration.

4. Further information about Jos will be found in Plotnicov, 1967, especially Chapters II and III.

Building codes and sanitary regulations were distinct for these two areas. Regulations were more lax in the Native Town where, for example, houses built of mud brick and thatch roof were always allowed, whereas in the Township concrete building blocks and galvanized iron sheet roofs were minimally standard construction materials. Within the Township higher values were set on house plots, and a building code inappropriate for the traditional Islamic practice of wife seclusion (*purdah*) was enforced. Muslim northerners were not prevented from settling in the Township, but since their generally lower incomes precluded their meeting the more stringent requirements, economic as well as cultural factors tended to make northerners, whether Muslim or not, residents of the Native Town. Immigrants to Jos were inclined to settle among people of their own ethnic group, area of origin, or religion, and so there was a tendency for such clustering in both the Town and Township. While most southern and "educated" Africans resided in the Township, some moved very early into the Native Town and eventually formed a large minority there. Since around 1960 some modern elite Africans, as well as wealthy Levantines, have come to reside in areas formerly exclusively European.

Within these established settlement patterns Africans of high and low rank, both wealthy and poor, live as neighbors. Two-story, concrete block, iron-roofed houses of the prosperous are situated alongside humble dwellings and the contemporary African equivalent of tenements. The quantity, quality, and style of interior furnishings are consistent with these architectural differences. For the wealthy and modern-oriented, appointments are European, although wealthy traditionalists may furnish their reception rooms with mats and cushions rather than upholstered chairs and sofas. Piped water, flush toilets, and electrically wired houses, while far more common in the Township, are now desired by wealthier Africans wherever they might reside and regardless of their cultural leanings. Even the poorest persons own some kind of radio, and phonographs are possessed by a considerable number, but only the wealthiest among the modern elite possess telephones in their homes. Except for refrigerators (for chilling beverages and providing ice cubes), modern household labor-saving appliances generally have little value in Jos among the modern elite because servant labor is plentiful and can be cheap. Uniformed cooks and stewards, who command high wages, are to be found only in the homes of wealthy, modern elite Africans, but boys and girls who are called servants are associated with households at all income levels. These youngsters may receive no wages, but are provided with room and board, support to see them through primary school, and perhaps a small allowance. Only the wealthy—by Nigerian standards—own automobiles; only the wealthiest retain servants as chauffeurs. The bicycle is the most common form of mechanical transport in Jos, but many bicycle riders would prefer, if they were able, to own a motorbike for its convenience and its somewhat greater prestige.

TRADITIONAL AND MODERN ORIENTATIONS

There is no one overall system of ranking or stratification in Jos. Banton points out that groups in Freetown are accorded different degrees of esteem on the basis of religion and ethnicity (1965:139–40), and Fallers reminds us that all communities will make such differentiations among individuals on the basis of age, sex, kinship, and other distinctions (1964:115). All of these distinctions are present in Jos, and social ranking of groups and individuals is based on a variety of criteria. However, these criteria fall on different dimensions or scales so that they have little or no reference to one another. What does it mean to a Hausa that his Ibo neighbor has acquired a traditional society rank or honorific title? How can one judge the relative prestige of traditional amd modern occupational roles or of the persons holding them? There are just as many systems of stratification or ranking in Jos as there are traditional ethnic communities. And in addition to these there is one other: a modern system of ranking modeled after that of Western societies.

People in Jos have no difficulty determining whether an individual is a traditionalist or a modernist for the cultural indications are many and clear. They know the precise ranking of traditionalists within their own ethnic group, and for other groups they have a general notion of what the rankings are; people in Jos are primarily evaluated and ranked according to criteria that are either ethnic and traditional or national and modern. This does not mean, however, that persons who are designated traditionalists and modernists are exclusively one or the other. What distinguishes the two is the basic orientation by which a person seeks to gain prestige and esteem. Thus a man who lives according to his tribal norms is a traditionalist, though he may work for a modern commercial enterprise; a man who leads a European way of life is a modernist, even though he will occasionally wear native clothing and interact with his own tribal traditionalists according to their standards. Of course, some designates of social worth, such as wealth, material possessions, beauty, exceptional skills or abilities, etc., are universal and independent of cultural restrictions.

ELITES

An occupation in an industrial society provides a person with one of his most important forms of social identification, determines his style of life, and sets the conditions for his mobility within a stratification system. Because of these associations with a career, the analysis of social stratification in Western societies has been largely based on occupational roles. However, those who have attempted to use occupation as a primary index of class identification in Africa have met with only partial success because, as Banton indicates, "occupation prestige does not have the significance in other social contexts which the Westerner would expect" (1965:144).

The Western model fits Africa imperfectly but there is some correspondence, at least among those persons who seek to achieve success primarily through Western or modern institutions. In Jos most of these are bureaucrats (government officials, school directors, managers of large firms), some are independent professionals (mainly lawyers), and a few are wealthy entrepreneurs (such as contractors, hotel proprietors, and middlemen). Those politicians in Jos who operate on a national level would also be included in this category, although most Jos politicians, because of their local and restricted arena, should be classified in a lower stratum, such as that of the subelite of Lloyd (1966:12). I call this latter group the incipient middle class, and include in it the bulk of white-collar workers below the managerial level, skilled workers, schoolteachers, clergymen,[5] and most traders who have had some formal education. With the exceptions of traditional elite persons and prominent persons who are neither clearly traditionalist nor modernist, the remainder of the Jos population is a residual category that is essentially traditionalist. These people are poorly educated or uneducated and have few or none of the skills needed for employment in modern business or industry. Because of these deficiencies they could not hope to achieve higher social status through the medium of modern occupational institutions. Some politicians, traders, and entrepreneurs have been able to overcome the handicaps of illiteracy and a poor command of English, but have expressed their success in these activities through a traditional style of life. This is the general outline describing the categories of social stratification in Jos. To describe and analyze the modern elite in Jos I must briefly indicate the position and some of the activities of elites who are not entirely modern, in order to provide a picture of the social setting in which the modern elite act.

In Africa studies, the term *elite* has been used flexibly (Herskovits, 1962:289–91) to designate persons controlling political power, those who are wealthy, and those who possess great social influence. We generally

5. The upper echelon clerics of wealthy churches in large Nigerian cities should be classed among the modern elite, and perhaps some prominent pastors in Jos should be so designated. Most, however, have about the same amount of formal education as schoolteachers, and comparable salaries.

Leonard Plotnicov: Modern African Elite of Jos

mean by elite the leaders of society and those persons who are emulated, but it is sometimes difficult to distinguish between the modern elite and the traditional elites, especially where they overlap. The differences between the modern and traditional elites are of more than academic interest, for their orientations are basically dissimilar. The traditionalists are primarily conservative and parochial, while the modern elite are progressive and cosmopolitan, and these differences have profound political and social implications.

TRADITIONAL ELITES

The traditional elites are primarily oriented toward their own ethnic communities and cultures. Their position strongly influences them to be conservative, for the position itself depends on the maintenance of the traditional system. As the leaders of their communities they set the example of ideal traditional behavior, they settle disputes, give advice, render assistance, and participate in making decisions that affect their communities. In the wider municipal society, they act as ethnic representatives and protect the interests and the integrity of their communities. However, the circumstances in which they must act prevent them from being absolutely parochialistic. Their own ethnic followers desire some changes that would provide them material or other benefits, and would withdraw their support if their elite persistently attempted to prevent such developments. For concrete instances of this we may look to the tribal unions, which are basically traditional institutions.

Tribal unions preserve traditional forms of entertainment, recreation, dispute settling, and decision making, and they render assistance to members where the ethnic community is distant from the homeland. Because the tribal unions must operate in an alien and modern setting, the traditional elite (who hold prominent positions in the unions) must relinquish some of their power to modernists and make some concessions toward change (cf. Lloyd, 1966:31). In arranging funerals, burials, and celebrations, seeking jobs for members, building union meeting halls, or investing the union's funds in a commercial enterprise, the traditional leaders must depend on those members who have the skills for dealing with municipal and other authorities. To protect their tribal members the traditional elite must also attempt to make accommodations with the heterogeneous population of Jos as a whole. When receptions for visiting tribal dignitaries and important ethnic celebrations are to be held, the tribal unions send special invitations to modern elite persons and traditional leaders of the larger or more important ethnic communities of Jos.

Traditional ethnic leaders also counsel their followers to show exemplary behavior toward members of other ethnic groups so that the tribe in Jos will not develop a bad reputation and thereby be discriminated against. Tribal union halls and facilities are provided to other ethnic groups lacking these for their celebrations or special meetings, and many of the traditional elite will themselves set examples of peaceful interaction with other tribesmen. For instance, a Christian sends gifts of food on Muslim holy days to his Hausa neighbors. Informants, particularly traders, hinted that such neighborly gestures (including loans of money to nontribesmen that would probably never be repaid) bought goodwill, and these practices could be considered economic investments.

Traditional leaders also make accommodations to the plural social conditions of Jos by participating in modern institutions. Such participation strengthens their leadership within their own ethnic groups for it demonstrates that outsiders recognize their prominence. They sit on the Town Council and are assessors (experts on tribal law and custom) in the Native Courts. Some traditional leaders lend their support to national political parties; others show civic responsibility without partisan politics. For instance, the manager of the foremost Islamic school in Jos (the acknowledged leading Koranic scholar in the community) sat on the Board of Governors of the R.C.M. Blessed Murumba College alongside prominent Roman Catholics, Protestants, and other leading members of the traditional and modern Jos communities. This man could speak no English, but he felt it his civic duty to participate in modern contexts when called upon to do so. Perhaps the best example among such persons is the Chief of Jos, whose official duties require him to participate at functions that demonstrate the modern development of Jos. He holds his position on the basis of traditional criteria, yet, like a city mayor, he must give the customary municipal blessings at the opening of new schools, medical clinics, social welfare recreational facilities, social club halls, or church buildings. He is also called on to lend formal dignity to special events, and sometimes he is invited to address cultural groups such as the Jos Literary Society. Since he speaks English poorly, his addresses on these occasions are in Hausa.

MODERN ELITE

Europeans and European culture have provided the models for modern African elite emulation. Most modern elite Africans in Jos had learned European behaviors and values prior to their arrival and settlement there, and some had been enculturated almost entirely there from infancy. In either case, Jos offered ample opportunities for the modern elite living there to observe and practice European ways.

A European community had settled in and around Jos during the second decade of this century, and almost as early had established European physical and social amenities. English women began to accompany their mining husbands to Jos from around 1912 and brought with them something of a European family life and the need to develop polite social activities. Their increased presence transformed the European commercial and administrative population from a settlement to a community. By 1921, less than ten years after the founding of Jos, the Annual Provincial Report for Plateau Province described an established European social life of clubs and dancing, and subsequent reports noted the presence of horse racing, polo, tennis, golf, and special shopping facilities for the European housewife. Educated and skilled Africans were brought to this area as soon as mining and colonial administrative activities had commenced, so it comes as no surprise that the 1925 Annual Report indicates the establishment in Jos of the African Sports Club. Since then the modern elite have found Jos attractive, for it compares favorably with other major Nigerian cities in offering them the kinds of social and cultural activities they desire.

Prior to the disruption of 1966, Jos had a large and socially active modern elite stratum. I estimate that this group formed about 1 percent of the Jos population.[6] Aside from the fact that the modern African elite in Jos are recognized by their modern and prestigeful occupations and greater wealth, they also display cultural features that are European. They tend to wear European clothing except for those occasions when they

6. This estimate is based partly on a count from elite organization membership lists, and also on the assumption that persons are designated modern elite by virtue of holding certain occupations. Harbison has estimated that Nigerians holding managerial, professional, administrative, and political posts, together with highly qualified teachers and technicians, form slightly less than 0.01 percent of the nation's population (1962:206). This is rather low when compared with highly industrialized countries (about 5 percent), or even other African countries (0.03 per cent for Ghana and 0.05 for Egypt). The reason my estimate for Jos is one hundred times higher than that for the country as a whole is because peasant cultivators, the bulk of Nigerians, are absent in Jos, and because it is only in the cities that the modern elite can find occupational opportunities.

   My use of the figure 1 percent is intended merely to show the relative proportion of this group to the rest of the city population, and must be taken with caution. Based, as it largely is, on occupational categories, it would alter considerably if certain occupations were included or others excluded. Many occupations that I have classified within the modern elite stratum could just as easily have been classified a lower stratum, and the reverse is also true (see footnote 5). The social status evaluations I have made for Jos (which is, after all, a minor city) would not be entirely applicable for other areas of the country and its major cities. For instance, the degree of education attained by many modern elite in Jos would not provide them with as much prestige in Lagos, the federal capital, as it does in Jos where the number of highly educated persons is much smaller. The same would be true for other scales, such as wealth; a relatively wealthy person in Jos is relatively less wealthy in Lagos.

wish to express their ethnic identity or their Nigerian or African national-ism. Many of them have lived abroad, and almost all of them speak English with little or no trace of an "African accent," one that is marked by tonal patterns and misplaced stress and accentuation. Even those who have learned English and acquired Western cultural behaviors solely from Nigerian schools do, in time, perfect these qualities by means of intensive and extensive association with modern elite persons. These European cultural traits include not only preferences in food, drink, dress, speech, and recreation habits, but also intellectual tastes and standards of etiquette. That an African dinner host is usually more solicitous than his European equivalent in his regard for the comfort of the ladies, and in other matters such as the arrangement of silver and china and the performance of his servants, has been noted by several observers.

Polite and gentlemanly behavior, often approaching a stiff Victorian formality, is characteristic of the Jos modern elite. Social grace and elegance, and highly stylized—even Victorian—speech patterns (with a display of erudition and an impressive polysyllabic vocabulary) may be regarded as manifestly functioning to establish and maintain social boundaries between the elite and the rest of the African population.[7] These serve not only as marks of common identity among the modern elite, but also, I suspect, as a demonstration to Europeans that they can master European culture just as well as, if not better than, the original culture bearers. For instance, invitations, preferably on commercially printed embossed cards, are sent by post or messenger for almost any social occasion. Parties and dances are arranged with elaborate detail, which includes seating arrangements, designated hosts, hostesses, dis-tinguished guests (perhaps honorific sponsors), and masters and mistresses of ceremonies. I share an impression with other observers that African men command a greater repertory of ballroom dances than Europeans and perform these with greater skill and embellishment. Lawn tennis offers some of the Jos modern elite an opportunity to compete directly with Europeans. Friendly matches are arranged between the recreation clubs of predominantly European and predominantly African membership, and the African players (so the latter tell) usually fare better than their opponents, perhaps because these African players practice on their own club at every available opportunity.

Club life, with its various forms of social and recreational activities, is

7. The more relaxed behavior of the modern African elite in other large Nigerian cities would seem to indicate that those in Jos may be more sensitive about the second-rate or pro-vincial status of their city and thus try harder. A younger generation of modern elite, associated with centers of intellectual and cultural (in the colloquial sense) activity, demon-strate their contempt for those who ape Victorian mannerisms. Expressing their rebellion with beard, book, and sandals, they most closely resemble the young intellectuals and artists of Paris, London, and New York. Except for brief visits, they do not appear in Jos.

one of the prominent interests of the modern elite, and they regularly go out in the evening to meet friends at a club or at a bar. Movie-going has also become popular, but the elite will only attend the cinema on what is known as "European night," when the higher entrance fee, which ostensibly covers the higher cost of showing European or American productions (and which also provides a cushion to pad the metal chairs), effectively bars the attendance of the poor and illiterate, who attend the same theater when Indian films are shown.

Most of the Jos modern elite are Christians and regularly attend church services, sometimes joining congregations that were formerly exclusively European. They are usually members of the "established" and wealthier denominations—Anglican, Methodist, Roman Catholic—whose church buildings clearly show the greater wealth of their congregations.

All these behavioral qualities that together constitute a common modern elite style of life are strong and clear enough to have inclined Little (1959:10) and Goldthorpe (1961:150) to regard this group as possessing a distinctive class culture.

The distinctiveness of the modern elite is recognized by the wider community; respect and deference are shown them. They are given the foremost seats at church services, formal dances, and athletic events. They are secular leaders of church congregations, the patrons or masters of ceremony at social events, and they officiate and judge cultural and athletic competitions.

A handful of modern elite persons in Jos have acquired, by inheritance or other means, traditional offices or titles of high rank. This may require their participation in traditional ceremonies without otherwise altering their modern elite style of living. Some of these persons are formally addressed as "Prince" or "Chief," but even close friends will use these titles as expressions of intimacy and affection. It would appear that the traditional and modern ranking systems are mutually influential—a successful career in the modern world will facilitate the achievement of traditional titles, and a traditional title enhances the prestige of a modern elite person.

MODERN ELITE SOCIAL NETWORK

The modern African elite in Jos are few enough in number for most to know one another personally. By belonging to the same churches, civic organizations, international fraternal orders, social clubs, and professional groups, and because of shared special experiences—such as overseas education—they interact more frequently with one another both by choice and through structural determinants such as occupational activities. Thus they share both a sense of identity and a common social network (cf. Lloyd, 1966:58). In contrast to traditionalist persons who are oriented toward their own ethnic groups and their tribal homelands, the modern elite develop strong interethnic ties through friendships and colleagueships. The mixed tribal memberships of the modern elite social clubs and quasi-secret fraternities in Jos (Royal Freemasons, International Order of Oddfellows, Reformed Ogboni Fraternity) indicate the modern elite's contrast with the prevailing parochialism in Jos. Modern elite persons count among their acquaintances and friends persons whose way of life is similar to their own, whether they be Nigerians of other tribes, other Africans, Indians, West Indians, Levantines, or Europeans, the ties that develop being based on a shared set of ideological, cultural, occupational, and recreational interests. The result is that the same people are seen together at clubs and churches, visiting one another, and attending the same parties. These shared interests and activities have resulted in a solidarity that is manifested not only on these occasions but also in visits to sickbed or hospital and in attendance at funerals. There is a sense of duty displayed in these expressions of loyalty and concern, even where the acquaintanceship has been slight.

The social network of modern elite persons in Jos extends to communities throughout Nigeria and is based on personal ties that have a variety of origins—e.g., common ethnicity or hometown, friendships from school days, business or occupational connections, professional associations and activities, mutual acquaintances, or membership in the same elite associations. Common school ties appear to be especially strong and are exploited by fellow alumni for acquiring jobs, business contracts with government, and other special privileges. Informants generally indicated that membership in the modern elite usually assures them of hospitality when they travel to other parts of the country. Reciprocally, this also means that modern elite persons in Jos will put up friends or mutual friends when they visit Jos. Even in a relatively small city, such as Jos, members of the modern elite are in the mainstream of national affairs. The extent to which they are related to or have close friendships with lawyers, magistrates, doctors, journalists, university administrators, high-ranking police and army officers, top government officials, and the most prominent politicians in the federal and regional capitals and the larger cities is surprisingly great and could be illustrated by numerous examples. In short, they are intimately associated with the national policy and decision makers. Since many of the modern elite in Jos have lived abroad, their social networks also extend even beyond the boundaries of Nigeria.

If members of the modern African elite contrast with the rest of the Nigerian population through their participation in a broad national and international social network, they also contrast in their free movement between two major social networks. The modern elite, while they are cosmopolitan and antiparochial, have not severed their ethnic and kinship links. They are neither "detribalized" nor "lost sons," but have maintained their ethnic affiliations. They take pride in their tribal histories, and cite the achievements of their fellow tribesmen in modern occupational, political, and artistic fields. They frequently participate actively in their tribal unions—usually in the top echelons—and not only are they admired by their ethnic communities for their professional and social achievements in the modern world, but they are also embraced for their loyalty and their willingness to assume positions of leadership among their own people.[8] Furthermore, they observe traditional ideals of respect and decorum when interacting with their more conservative tribesmen, and they are also respected for this. As noted earlier, Little regards the extent and intensity of these ethnic and kinship associations as the structural factor that prevents the modern elite from being regarded as a distinct social class, but it must also be noted that the modern elite manifest no difficulty in shifting between modern and traditional social contexts, and show no emotional conflicts as a result.

MODERN ELITE NORTHERNERS

Southern Nigerians and other West Africans predominate among the modern African elite of Jos. Northern Nigerians not only are few, but are also poorly integrated with the rest of the modern elite. An examination of the peripheral position of the northerners aids in an understanding of the modern elite as a whole, and also provides some insights into the circumstances surrounding the centrifugal political developments of 1966 in Nigeria.

There have been fewer northerners among the modern elite in Jos and elsewhere because European education was far less extensive in northern Nigeria than in the rest of the country. Since the 1950's, however, considerable numbers of northerners have received university degrees and assumed senior civil service positions. Yet these young northerners, who hold prestigeful occupations, and who have the requisite wealth, speech, and cultural skills—who, in other words, are eminently eligible for membership among the modern elite—have tended to form separate cliques among themselves.

Religious differences only partially account for the separation between

8. Several observers have commented on the modern elite's continued close association with their traditional societies. Cf. Hodgkin (1956:87), Lloyd (1966:14), Sklar (1963:503), and Smyth (1960:167).

the southern and northern elements of the Jos modern elite. While some northerners are Christian, most are Muslim and the bond of common church membership is absent. Convivial drinking is one of the main reasons for belonging to a social club, but whereas many Muslims may drink alcoholic beverages privately with friends, they will not do so in public. For the same reason of religious pride, these persons will observe the month-long Ramadan fast. They are also sensitive to the fact that their public behavior is carefully observed and reported to the fanatically devout Muslim northern political elite. These young northerners are beholden to the rulers for the advantages they have received (their education and their favored occupational positions). Stories circulate about northern modern elite young men who were called before the Premier of the Northern Region, the late Sir Ahmadu Bello, Sardauna of Sokoto, and given a tongue lashing, or worse, following reports of their irreligious behavior. They must be, and are, circumspect. As a result, they are ambivalent toward the southern modern elite, neither rejecting them as peers nor being overly friendly.

Southern and northern modern elite individuals will describe one another as friends, particularly if they work in the same office. They may be seen together in the late afternoon, after office hours, "cooling down" over a beer and soft drinks at a bar. They may do this again later in the evening, and nibble on roasted groundnuts, goat meat or chicken. However, in contrast to the usual pattern among Africans who are friends, they rarely eat at one another's homes. Northerners said that most of their southern friends would not eat at their homes because they could not tolerate northern cuisine, and that they themselves felt somewhat uncomfortable on the few occasions when they visited the home of their southern friends. It appears that the camaraderie of friendship is dampened by the presence of the southern wives, who demonstrate a stiff formality and politeness at these meetings. Southerners would not admit that their wives affected snobbish attitudes, but would explain that their northern friends were reluctant to invite southerners to their homes because the northern wives were uneducated and therefore embarrassed in the presence of strangers with European manners.

The situation takes on added significance when one understands the important role wives play in establishing and cementing ties between the men of the southern modern elite as, in many instances, the wives have attended the same girls' secondary schools and colleges. There are many social occasions when southern modern elite men and women come together, such as at dinner parties, ballroom dances, and church services. An educated wife, and one who demonstrates social skills and graces, enhances the prestige of her husband, while one who lacks these qualities does the opposite. Southern modern elite women lead active public lives

Leonard Plotnicov : Modern African Elite of Jos

and participate in social institutions and organizations that are nonparochial. In contrast, northern wives, even when they are not secluded by the Muslim practice of *purdah*, tend to be traditional and parochial, seeking as friends and companions kinswomen or women from their home areas. Most of them, even if they have had some education, do not speak English, and few of them have had even a primary school education.

Among the southern elite, men who cannot or will not have their wives accompany them to modern elite social functions carry the stigma of an improper conjugal arrangement. The absence of a wife either indicates marital discord or implies that the husband would be ashamed of her crudeness or timidity in polite company. Some Muslim northern modern elite who have educated wives and do not practice *purdah* may nevertheless hesitate to bring their wives to the mixed company of Christians because they believe they will appear disrepectful of their religious convictions. Since the practice of appearing in public without one's wife, but with a mistress or girl friend, is deprecated by the modern elite, northern men appear at modern elite social gatherings unaccompanied by women. They look out of place and feel somewhat uncomfortable.

The southerners who dominate the modern African elite clubs in Jos continually invite their northern friends, acquaintances, and office colleagues to join their organizations. The northerners visit the clubs, have their beer or soft drinks, chat and joke, but do not become members. The usual excuse is that they cannot afford to pay the initiation fee, but it is easily within their reach. That the southerners sincerely want the northerners as members is indicated by the idiom of speech used when northerners are present. Except when two or several members of the same tribe are together, all the club members use English in their conversation with each other; when northerners are present, however, the conversation and joking take place in Hausa. Northerners speak English as well as the southerners, and for many northerners Hausa is as much a second language as it is for the southerners. "We are in the north, so we speak the language of the north," was the reason southerners gave, but the use of Hausa was deliberately intended to establish a sense of common identity, a way of expressing Nigerian nationalism and denying parochialism.

Southerners also invited northerners into their clubs with the hope of gaining specific immediate benefits (other than the increased revenue that would result with new members), although these reasons were not overtly expressed. Because the government of the Northern Region of Nigeria was discriminating against southern Nigerians, the latter among the modern elite believed that the inclusion of northern members in their organizations would facilitate receiving government loans, grants, and building plots for the improvement and expansion of club facilities,

which were otherwise not forthcoming. In one elite club, certain southerners holding positions in the local administration were under the constant
threat of being arbitrarily dismissed and replaced by northerners, in
accordance with the aims of the government's northernization policy, and
they hoped that their northern friends would exert political influence on
their behalf. Less immediately, many southerners who were affected or
threatened by the northernization policy hoped that stronger ties of
friendship with their northern peers might assuage the northern government's fears of southern domination and would eventually bring a
relaxation of the restrictive practices against them.

Those northerners who did join clubs cast their membership where
the southern Nigerian element was not prominent. Some joined clubs
associated with large mining enterprises, where the companies had, under
government pressure, been reducing their southern staff and upgrading
their northern employees. These same persons would visit but not join
the southern Nigerian modern elite clubs, and they must be distinguished
from another group of northerners who did not visit the African clubs,
but joined the formerly exclusively European clubs.

While Africans have been welcomed at the European clubs, especially
since Nigeria's independence, the white members have made little effort
to integrate the Africans into the club's social activities or friendship
cliques. When northerners who had joined these clubs complained to me
of token integration, and I asked them why they remained members,
the several reasons offered indicated that national and racial pride was
involved. In the United States and Britain they had experienced racial
prejudice, and now, by their education and occupational achievements,
they wanted to demonstrate their equality with Europeans. The presence
of Europeans in their own country was, they felt, a privilege that they
now extended to foreigners and no longer a condition imposed by colonial
domination. They would not tolerate racial discrimination by Europeans
against Africans on Nigerian soil, and they partly regarded it as an ideological duty to join the European clubs, despite the antipathy of the European
members, in order to demonstrate that Africans were above harboring
resentments.

These northerners also claimed that European clubs possessed special
facilities that they desired, such as billiard tables. But they would not
avail themselves of the same facilities at the African clubs, with excuses
that the latter were inadequate or that not all the members of the African
clubs were congenial. This group of northern Nigerians forms a single
social network that has little overlap with that which visits the African
clubs, and several reasons may be offered for their cliquish behavior.

There is a marked occupational and educational difference between
the two groups, the European club northerners holding professional

occupations or very high positions with the federal or northern government, the others tending toward senior civil service positions in the local
government of administrative positions in local firms. The former also
hold university degrees, whereas the latter tend to lack university training
and have not lived for any extended time in England or America as the
others have. There are comparable differences in wealth and in ethnic
composition—the European club northerners stem mostly from prestigious northern Muslim ethnic groups (Hausa, Fulani, and Kanuri)
while the others derive from a greater variety of northern peoples, many
of whom were not traditionally Muslim and today include many Christians.

It may well be that the European club northerners wish to maintain
a social distance between themselves and other northern modern elite
persons by emphasizing the status differences between them, reflected in
part by the higher initiation fees of the European clubs.

At the time of my study the southern and northern Nigerian modern
elite shared the same democratic political ideologies, and both recognized
that the traditional elite in control of the northern government was too
inflexible to alter its conservative and parochial policies, and too firmly
entrenched in power to be readily removed. The southern Nigerians
expressed the hope that the young Western-educated northerners would
someday gain control of the northern government, and that they would
join with the southern modern elite as a progressive vanguard that would
lead a truly united nation toward the political and social goals that were
the ideals of the movement for Nigerian independence. The Northern
modern elite were well aware of the southerners' difficulties in the north,
and would sometimes express sympathy for them. They also hoped that
the balance of political power would change for the better in the future,
but at that time it was a practical matter for them to avoid showing an
overly friendly attitude toward southerners.

Since 1966 political conditions in Nigeria have changed radically. It
now seems certain that the old northern political elite has lost its power,
and that there is the real possibility that young educated northerners will
increasingly become socially integrated with their southern peers.

AMBIGUOUS ELITE

There is a range of persons who might be regarded as modern elite
yet who lack certain qualifying criteria that would enable them to fully
receive this social recognition. Often they are persons quite prominent
in Jos, but they cannot be classed as traditional or modern elite for they
belong to both at once, yet not quite fully to either. Many of them are

tribal union leaders, but their lack of traditional tribal lore, ascribed high tribal status, or other qualities of traditional superiority disqualify them from being the topmost traditional elite. Similarly, their lack of formal education, their poor command of English, and their unprestigious occupations prevent their being fully accepted and recognized as modern elite. Such persons are elite, but hold ambiguous positions. Since they are quite diverse in characteristics, no general description is possible, but the following example will illustrate many of the factors that account for this ambiguous status.

Madam S is of mixed southern Nigerian tribal origins and reflects her dual cultural heritage by being an active member in two ethnically distinct tribal unions. A woman in her late fifties, she no longer wears the European gowns and dresses shown in the large personal photographs that hang on the walls of her sitting room. She lives in one of two adjacent houses that are alleged to have been acquired for her by a European miner with whom she lived for several years as a common-law wife. Renting the living quarters of these houses provides her with a steady and comfortable income. If Madam S holds any occupation, other than that of landlady, it is a traditional one which she performs more out of a sense of duty than the need for additional income. For a nominal fee she gives a series of baths and massages which help to restore to proper functioning the internal organs of women who have recently given birth. Occasionally she receives gifts of money from European miners who were friends of her "husband." In past years she had served many of them as a procuress. In fact she earned considerable sums by arranging temporary "marriages" between British miners and Ibo girls whom she brought from the impoverished Niger Delta area, after making financial arrangements with their parents. Europeans and Africans who knew Madam S during the 1930's and 1940's agree that she was an accomplished hostess, skilled in the European etiquette, and an excellent ballroom dancer. She was much sought after as a dancing partner by the modern African elite.

While the years may have slowed her down a bit, Madam S has remained active in public affairs. She has long been a member of the Jos Township Advisory Council and is often asked to serve on special civic committees. She is a leading member of her church congregation and of the women's wing of a national political party, for which she sometimes serves as a delegate to national conventions. Recognition of her position as a foremost resident in Jos was demonstrated at the ceremonial opening of the new quarters of the Plateau International Club (the most elite of the modern elite social clubs), when she was one of those asked to cut a ribbon opening one of the entrances. The other ribbons were cut by the Provincial Resident, the Chief of Jos, the first African lawyer in Jos, another woman who is one of the leading market middlemen, and the general manager of the leading tin-mining company in the area.

Despite the accomplishments of Madam S, her lack of formal education and her pidgin speech are definite liabilities. She is also unmarried and unmarriageable. Without a husband who is a member of the modern elite she cannot be drawn more fully into their circles and social activities, as are other women through their husbands. Unlike young spinsters and divorcees, she cannot be drawn into these activities through male escorts and the prospect of marriage to a modern elite man. All these factors prevent Madam S from being fully accepted into the ranks of the modern elite and foreclose any such future possibility.

In Jos there are many persons who fall into the ambiguous position of Madam S, although in each case the circumstances that make them prominent citizens and those that prevent them from attaining full traditional or modern elite status are different. The choice of a female example of this category is intended to illustrate in addition that women are not barred, simply because of their sex, from entrance into the modern elite.

COMMUNITY–INTEGRATIVE ACTIVITIES OF THE MODERN ELITE

The elite, whether modern or traditional, have greater social responsibilities to the community (however that be defined) than ordinary folk. These responsibilities range from rendering personal assistance—such as advice, money, or employment favors—to assuming political or organizational offices. While both elites are civic-minded, there is a distinction between the traditional and the modern in their definition of the community. The former regard their main responsibilities as being toward their own ethnic communities, in Jos and at the tribal homeland, and will discharge their duties through traditional institutions or tribal unions. The modern elite, on the other hand, are oriented to the modern, multiethnic community. As private but prominent individuals they may feel obliged to express their civic responsibilities by writing letters to the editor of the local newspaper, accepting patronage of youth clubs and athletic associations, presenting lectures to schoolchildren, clubs, and the local literary societies, planting public gardens, or donating their professional skills for community development projects (e.g., civil engineers or contractors may estimate the cost of projected local works and may even offer to do the work at cost or near cost). It is a duty as well as an honor for such people to sit on government, school, and church boards that will consider and make recommendations for conditions of the community such as street drainage and lighting, juvenile delinquency, crime, prostitution, noise and other public nuisances, motor traffic, the market of Jos, school curricula, local hospital and prison conditions, etc.

There is a good deal of overlap in the personnel of these committees, which sometimes serves to conceal the fact that protests or appeals for some community action from several different organizations actually originate with the same persons. For example, the Plateau African Trader's Union and the Rates and Taxpayer's Association, after the traffic death of a woman pedestrian, complained of the lax enforcement of traffic regulations to the Jos police. The same man was then president of the two organizations, both of which also worked closely with the Jos Township Local Authority in bringing public grievances to the attention of the administration.

As valued members of their ethnic associations, the modern elite have been able to involve their tribal unions in Jos community affairs. The larger and better organized unions have at times been critical of local administrative authorities on civic issues, made proposals for public development, offered the services of their members for such community projects as the assessment and collection of taxes, and provided facilities of their meeting halls for civic functions, frequently free of charge. These otherwise parochial bodies have shown such public spirit partly because they are sensitive about their image as an ethnic group and make efforts to project a favorable one, and partly because leadership in them is shared between traditionalists and the modern elite. The latter play vital roles, for they have the skills for dealing with government and the wider community. Their knowledge in legal and economic matters, secretarial and bookkeeping procedures, and their general sophistication in modern and urban affairs is indispensable. Their value to the ethnic group, and their superior status in the modern social setting, are recognized through the granting of high union offices (cf. Lloyd, 1966:32) and sometimes traditional titles as well, which further reinforce the modern elite's powers within the tribal group. Their opinions and views carry as much weight as those of the traditional leaders and, quite often, the modern elite are the only persons capable of healing serious breaches between intraethnic factions.

Tribal unions frequently display community-mindedness when they stage public ballroom dances. The traditionalist members see this as a quick way of raising funds for the union, while the modern elite members also view the occasion as an opportunity to play host to the public at large. The modern elite members, because they are knowledgeable in such tasks, assume responsibility for all the arrangements, and play the parts of hosts and masters of ceremonies, sharing these duties with modern elite persons of other ethnic groups. Individuals of all tribes, having connections with members of the hosting union through friendship or occupation, are eager to attend, thereby expressing both their friendship and their cosmopolitan values—this is one of the ways in which respect is shown for an associate's ethnic identification.

Another expression of interethnic community identification occurs in the annual church bazaars. The modern elite of the congregations, not usually tribally identified, are responsible for the organizing and running of these affairs, which are well attended. They are festive occasions taking place outdoors, over several days around harvest time. People of different tribes and church congregations participate, dancing, singing, praying, gambling, enjoying homecooked food, buying craft work, and pledging church funds.

CORPORATE POLITICAL ACTIVITIES OF THE MODERN ELITE

Examples of modern elite corporate activity in Jos go back almost to its founding, and although many of these efforts benefited the community at large, they could also be interpreted as demonstrations of class self-interest. For example, in the early 1920's the African clerks and skilled workers in and around Jos repeatedly petitioned for a government school to be located in Jos so that they would not have to send away their children to southern Nigeria—where the nearest available boarding schools were. Government records show that these parents applied continuous pressure until they were able to achieve their goal in 1925.

The activities of the modern elite in Jos range into areas that are clearly political: the history of relations with the colonial administration and other European corporate institutions is marked with efforts (some-times fierce conflicts) to achieve privileges and rights for the African community (or for the modern elite itself, in the name of the African community). These protests were largely reactions against the blatant racial discrimination against Africans, to which the modern elite were the most acutely sensitive. They fought what they regarded as affronts and insults to their dignity.

One particularly fervent African nationalist, Kusimo Soluade, a lawyer and one of the original founders of the West African Students Union in London, led the battles with the colonial administration. From the time he arrived in Jos in the late 1920's, he contested discriminatory restrictions against Africans and invariably won. He refused to doff his hat when addressed by a European, and he refused to build his house *facing away* from the European section of the Township, as all Africans were required to do until the 1940's. The practice of racially segregated seating at the Jos horse races and other public events was discontinued at his insistence. When night soil, to form compost, was being dumped near the African section of the Township, and his complaints about the offensive odor were met with derision, he had the satisfaction of conducting administration officers through the area (to their discomfort); they removed the dump. Around 1935 he complained to the Legislative Council in Lagos of what he regarded as an unjustified use of Native Administration funds: the printing of the *Gazetteer* of Plateau Province, which, he felt, could be of no benefit to Africans. Finally the administration sought to retaliate against his persistent crusading by revoking one of his privileges: his liquor ration was taken away.

Liquor restrictions in Jos were imposed on all Africans at an early period, but they essentially applied only to the educated Africans of the Township who had a taste for and the means to buy European alcoholic beverages.[9] The basis of this legislation lay in the administration's policy of indirect rule and its view of the Northern Provinces as an Islamic area within which the traditional rulers should not be offended, despite the fact that the indigenous peoples of the Jos Plateau and the majority of the African immigrants to Jos were not Muslim. Africans were allowed to purchase liquor only with a permit obtained through the administration upon showing a doctor's certificate that testified to the applicant's need for liquor for health reasons. Since (until the late twenties) all doctors were European, an African's ability to purchase liquor through these regulations largely depended on the personal benevolence of Europeans.

Soluade obtained 1600 signatures from Africans all over the north to a petition that was forwarded to the Lieutenant-Governor in Kaduna and the Governor-General in Lagos, with the result that all Africans could henceforth purchase four bottles of spirits a month without a permit. Despite this concession Soluade was determined to remove the restriction entirely, and succeeded, by enlisting the efforts of influential Africans in Lagos who were his personal friends. Many of these were lawyers like himself, but one of the most effective was Ernest Ikoli, then editor of the *Daily Times*, who conducted a relentless agitation in his newspaper.[10]

These are several instances of what I regard as corporate political behavior by the modern African elite. It was not directed, in the Marxist sense, *within* the society to other and competing classes; rather, it was directed by a classlike group to a target regarded, by the modern African elite, as outside its own society.[11]

9. These restrictions were regarded by modern elite Africans as an affront to their dignity and led directly to the founding of an African social club. As a legal corporation, the club could purchase liquor with no restrictions, and it was through club membership that the early African elite in Jos could freely imbibe with a measure of self-respect.

10. Protests against expression of European racial discrimination continued to occur even after Nigeria's independence, and almost invariably these came from African lawyers.

11. Balandier has observed that "the stronger the antagonism felt toward the colonial (European) community, the less will be the friction between the socially unequal elements of the African population" (1956:501).

UPPER STRATUM CRYSTALLIZATION AND
INCIPIENT MIDDLE CLASS DEVELOPMENT

One dimension of modern societies is a class system of social stratification wherein groups are ranked according to their differential degrees of social worth and political and economic power. These strata, or classes, are also identifiable by their subcultural differences. Compared with other forms of social stratification, the modern system is said to be "open" for status mobility. That is, modern societies hold the ideology that positions of prestige and esteem must be merited through a person's own efforts. High social status may be achieved by an individual in his lifetime or, if he was born to a superior position, he must, by appropriate means, protect this advantage by demonstrating that he deserves it. It is not his as a birthright. The ideology holds that status in a superior stratum is both an indication of, and a major form of reward for, social accomplishments, and this value orientation provides the motivation to acquire or retain the positions of merit. Under these conditions people compete for superior positions; however, an individual's class position determines his perception of what he can realistically hope to achieve in terms of greater social worth. I hold that Nigeria is moving toward a modern class system, as outlined above, and that, in Jos, part of the population seeks to identify with the modern African elite and strives to be accepted into its ranks. This is, of course, untrue for most of the population, who sorely lack even a modest amount of modern elite qualifying attributes, and who adhere to traditional systems of prestige. But it is true for those persons in the immediate social vicinity of the modern elite—for example, junior officers in the civil service and in businesses, schoolteachers, nurses, skilled workers, and literate traders of modest wealth (Lloyd makes this a generalization for Africa as a whole, 1966:60). Such modern oriented persons seek modern elite status, but few will be accepted as peers by the modern elite. Since this group has not yet fully developed a corporate character, I would refer to it as an incipient middle class.

It may appear that this distinction, based on quantitative differences— the modern elite having more of what it takes to be elite—is merely analytical and arbitrary. I would not draw a sharp line dividing the two groups, but these empirical differences of degree are also associated with important structural aspects in the clustering of social relations. There is an intensity of personal and professional interaction among members of the modern elite that marks this group as a distinct entity, and while there is more interaction between modern elite persons and those of the incipient middle class than there is between the elite and the residual mass, there nonetheless remains a threshold, in the level of interaction between the two groups, that separates them. Furthermore, as will be seen, the modern

Upper Stratum Crystallization and Incipient Middle Class Development

elite in Jos are institutionalizing recruitment into their ranks, being as much concerned with rejecting as with accepting aspirants.

The modern elite hold social power not only because they are respected and to some extent emulated, but also because they are able to reject those who seek their company. As style-setters, the elite have defined the rules of etiquette, dress, and other behavior demanded of candidates to their society. Since formal ballroom dancing ability is regarded by the incipient middle class as one of the necessary qualifications for further upward mobility, Jos has a lively trade in dancing "schools" (unregistered and unlicensed) and private dancing tutorials. Anyone can "highlife," but only the elite and would-be elite learn to fox trot and waltz.

The Smythes indicate that elite "provide an arrangement through which the younger generation develops with the class patterns they value" (1960:169). In Jos they not only sponsor, work with, and address youth clubs, they may go so far as to attempt to institutionalize recruitment among the younger generation of potential elite. For example, the foremost African modern elite social club conferred special membership status on members of the Jos Literary Society for a token initiation fee and small dues, and with an arrangement for performances of plays and other literary entertainments by the members of the Literary Society. The latter are a group of ambitious young people, often attending college or university, who are most likely to meet the highest standards of eligibility for modern elite membership.

The process that forms the modern elite equally involves the formation of an inferior stratum, the incipient middle class; one cannot occur without the other. The growing acceptance of the elite's values and standards by aspirants to that group is part of a developing moral system that serves to bolster the distinctiveness and superiority of the elite. That people seek and strive to achieve modern elite status in part creates the stratum of the modern elite. The stratum is also in part created by the modern elite in their effort to differentiate themselves from persons who most closely resemble them but do not fully qualify for acceptance. They do this in various ways, and many instances of snobbery can be given. One of the clearest illustrations, involving the formation of a new social club in Jos, shows how the modern elite closed ranks to set themselves off as a distinct group when faced with an infiltration of persons they considered socially inferior.

The first, and for a long time the sole, African modern elite social club in Jos was founded in the early 1920's, when no similar recreational facilities were available to Africans and it was difficult for them to purchase liquor. Called the African Games and Sports Club (its name was later changed to the Recreation Club, but people continue to call it the African Club), it was started by literate Africans from southern Nigeria,

Sierra Leone, and the (then) Gold Coast, who were employed as administrative and mercantile clerks. Up until around 1953, the club remained
financially sound on the basis of revenues from memberships, rental of
the club's facilities for social dances, and also its own sponsoring of
ballroom dances, for which admission was charged. Profits came mainly
from liquor sales.

Up to that time only two commercial bars with dance floors existed
in Jos. During 1953 and 1954 people connected with the mining industry
suddenly came into huge sums of money because of the high price of tin
ore and columbite. This prosperity brought the opening of many bars in
Jos and a serious loss of revenue for the African Club. To restore the lost
income the club increased the number of dances open to the public and
accepted as new members persons with inferior qualifications. At the public
dances there was little effort to bar the entrance of rough young men, who
were unaccustomed to having much spending money and frequently got
drunk and created unpleasant incidents. As one modern elite man said:

> Some of the commoner Africans used to do some very objectionable
> things. They would spit on the floor, shout across the room. . . . Some
> of us were self-conscious of being among people who were very unlike
> ourselves. For example, how would you like it if at a dance an artisan,
> who is a complete stranger to you, comes to ask your wife for a dance in a
> most unbecoming manner? It was a most unharmonious group of people,
> ranging from the more couth persons with culture and letters to men
> without letters. The situation was unsuitable for certain classes of Africans.
> Quite hopeless! People like myself would not want to associate with
> unlettered persons.

Many of the "lettered" and "couth" members of the African Club
ceased attending its functions, but retained membership. No consideration
was given to forming a second club until around early 1956, when it
became clear that the European clubs would not lower their racial bars.
There was an incident at one of the European clubs involving the assault
of an African lawyer who entered for some refreshment. Then another
African lawyer in Jos interested his close friends in establishing the
Plateau International Club.[12] Their initial effort to be highly restrictive in
membership showed them that the club could not become financially
viable unless they made some concessions in this regard. They then brought
in affluent persons of inferior education, and they also recruited some
Levantines, Indians, and a few liberal whites. Most of the persons who
formed the Plateau International Club, who had been members of the
African Club, retained their membership in the latter club for a while

12. It is significant that most of the small group of the original founding members are Roman
Catholic and as such are constrained from joining the prestigeful fraternal societies.

Upper Stratum Crystallization and Incipient Middle Class Development

and steadfastly insisted that they did not intend the new club to be in competition with the old. They claimed their outlook was indeed international and that was why they wanted non-African members in a new club. But none of these persons attended African Club functions, and most eventually dropped their membership.

The establishment of the Plateau International Club resulted in a clear drop in the prestige of the African Club. The withdrawal of most of the wealthier members to the rival club, the increasing competition with commercial bars, and an economic recession in mining created a financially desperate situation for the African Club, which sought to alleviate it by attracting more new members. But to do so it had to lower its standards of recruitment even further. If one now compares the membership lists of the two clubs for educational attainment, prestigeful occupations, and wealth, there is a marked status difference between them, with the African Club having an inferior position. Membership in one of the clubs, or intimate association with the members of one of the clubs, now serves as a status marker.[13]

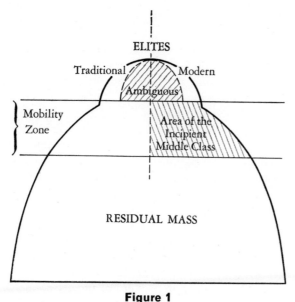

Figure 1
The Form of Social Stratification in Jos

The modern African elite in Jos is a distinct social group which serves as a model for emulation for part of the population and which, for its wealth, power, knowledge, and modern social sophistication, is admired

13. Lloyd indicates that the movement of top elite to a new club when the old has been diluted with inferiors is not uncommon (1966:37).

Leonard Plotnicov: Modern African Elite of Jos

and respected by all. It has its own subculture and a strong sense of common identity for the reasons previously indicated and briefly reviewed here.

Modern elite persons have shared experiences that other Nigerians wholly or largely lack, particularly in their extensive Western education. They have become strongly oriented to Western culture. Many of them have lived in Western countries for long periods, many possess a speaking or reading facility in European languages other than English, and to an undetermined degree they are culturally alienated from their fellow tribesmen. They have acquired cultural needs, or tastes, that can only be satisfied among themselves or with Westerners. These common tastes and other shared interests thrust them upon one another so that they form their own social network.

Their greater exposure to Europeans, along with the acquisition of European cultural tastes, has made them acutely sensitive to European discrimination against Africans. In part, then, their emulation of European behavior patterns can be viewed as acts directed at Europeans. Demonstrating that they can meet the cultural standards of Europeans is not only intended to dispel the image of African inferiority, it expresses the ambivalence of the elite in wishing, on the one hand, to be accepted as equals among Europeans and, on the other hand, in attempting to outdo Europeans at their own skills (as superior hosts, tennis players, and dancers, as Christians of a greater integrity), and thereby demonstrating an African superiority. At the same time, the skillful command of European behavior patterns is directed toward other Africans. It not only confers prestige on those who hold the requisite qualifications, it also serves to prevent entrance to and dilution of the elite stratum by parvenues and unacceptable elite aspirants.

All these factors help create a sense of corporateness and solidarity among the Jos modern elite which is further strengthened by their efforts to counter the parochial and centrifugal tendencies pervasive in Nigeria. While the modern elite have more to gain from maintaining and strengthening Nigerian unity, and more to lose from its partition into small states (an ever present danger), it is not solely on the basis of pragmatic advantages to themselves that they assume this posture. They take pride in the great size of Nigeria and in its cultural and economic developments relative to other African countries. For Nigeria to succumb to division, and thus to fail politically in the eyes of Westerners, would be shameful and disadvantageous for Nigeria's role as a leader among African countries, as well as a serious deterrent to further economic developments. The integrative ethos of the modern elite, while expressing nationalistic aspirations, is also an expression of the democratic ideologies acquired through Western contact.

IMPLICATIONS FOR COMMUNITY AND NATIONAL INTEGRATION

Let us examine the role of the modern Nigerian elite in community and national integration. That the new African states are fragile compositions of diverse ethnic aggregations, and that their political viability remains threatened by the divisive primordial (tribal, regional, parochial) sentiments[14] of their citizenries, are common observations (Fallers, 1963: 216; Kuper, L., 1965:120; Little, 1959:10). In Nigeria, as in much of Africa, tribalism has been the outstanding factor threatening national unity. Political leaders as well as scholars seek a formula that will allow an "integrative revolution"—a reconciliation among groups holding divergent primordial sentiments so that parochial identifications and ties are superseded by national allegiance—but precisely how this may come about remains a matter of speculation (Geertz, 1963:155). Fallers has written that the new African states "tend to be congeries of traditional societies in varying stages of modernization, held together by the leadership of elites[15] whose common culture is largely alien to the traditional cultures and discontinuous with them" (1963:216). The modern elite, having greater awareness of the social problems associated with parochial and particularistic allegiances, including the potential threats to their own advantages, have acted vigorously to counter the primordial values held by their compatriots.

Nigeria's economy and many essential services are regionally interdependent, and the modern elite are cognizant of the unfavorable economic consequences of regional separatism for themselves as well as for the country as a whole (cf. Lloyd, 1966:59). With a disruption of national economic and political institutions, most Nigerians could relatively easily revert to traditional subsistence activities or become dependent upon the aid of kinsmen—their way of life would change relatively little. The modern elite, however, would suffer. And just as this group would not wish their material advantages to be jeopardized, they would not want to have their social position diminished through the division of Nigeria into several small independent states. Ideologically, too, they could not easily tolerate being restricted to a parochial context, for their educational and professional experiences orient them toward a Pan-Africanist as well as a nationalist stance. Therefore, they have preached the message of national

14. For a fuller explanation of this terminology introduced by Clifford Geertz, see his paper, "The Integrative Revolution: Primordial Sentiments and Civil Politics in the New States" (1963).

15. Many scholars have made the same suggestion regarding the integrative functions of the modern elite in new nations. For Nigeria see Smythe, H. H. and M. M. (1960:118, 169), for other areas see Apter (1963:275), Eisenstadt (1952:226), Liebenow (1965:49), and Reissman (1964:181, 188).

and community integration. Of course, to be effective, this message must have power behind it and channels of transmission. The power of this group lies in their position as an elite—emulated and respected by others. The channels of transmission lie in the social networks of the elite which extend in two directions.

One is horizontal, consisting of social ties across the stratum through friendships, associational and professional connections, and of other close links among peers in the local community as well as with members of the status group around the nation. In the other direction, "vertical" if you wish, modern elite persons have maintained their parochial affiliations, and are embraced by their ethnic communities for the reasons outlined earlier. These two dimensions of the modern elite social networks put the elite in the most favorable structural position for direct and continuous communication with all elements of the population.[16] No other segment of the society is so favorably situated.[17]

THEORETICAL DISCUSSION: THE FORMATION OF CLASSES

On the basis of the information available, can we regard the modern elite as forming a socioeconomic class similar to those of industrialized

16. According to my explanation, the modern elite should have been able to prevent or greatly curtail the extent of the tribal riots of 1966, which resulted in the mass return of Ibo to Eastern Nigeria, and shook the political and economic foundations of Nigeria to the core. My investigations in Nigeria the following year convinced me that modern elite and traditional leaders in the north did try to stop the riots and were instrumental in saving the lives of many Ibo (also see Aluko, 1967: 497–98). That northern modern elite were not successful in halting attacks of northern tribesmen on the Ibo, once they began, was partially due to their lack of integration with the southern modern elite. However much the northern modern elite may have deplored the situation (and they did), the Ibo who were being attacked were not their close friends and associates. The relatively small number of the northern modern elite, and their lack of influence with the mass of northern tribesmen, was also significant. Yet, one must not exclude the likelihood that the northern modern elite viewed the situation as an opportunity to be rid of rivals and competitors. Full analysis of these events must await further research.
17. There have been suggestions that in the new states of Africa the military will serve as the bridge between the divided ethnic factions of the society. The military do hold great power, but it must be recognized that this group best functions at a national and not at a local community level. Professional military people have always and everywhere maintained a social distance in informal interaction with civilians, and there is no reason to believe that British-trained Nigerian officers will behave otherwise. In addition, in the present Nigerian situation, the garrisons have become regionalized, with troops and officers deriving from the regions in which they are stationed. Compared with the modern elite, the Nigerian military establishment appears poorly suited to perform community integrative functions, although their power may go a long way toward maintaining the political unity of the country.

societies? The arguments against the existence of social classes in contemporary Negro Africa, cited at the beginning of this chapter, offered three main objections: (1) multiple ranking systems and parochial allegiances blur class outlines; (2) classless residential patterns and intimate interactions between relatives and tribesmen regardless of socioeconomic rank indicate that class social segregation has not occurred; and (3) corporate political behavior does not revolve about class issues. The Jos data uphold the validity of these objections—there is no class society there. Nonetheless, the stratum of the modern elite exhibits all the characteristics of a class, and I think that it should be so regarded. If it is a class, how then does it express its corporate character in political action, and thus meet Mitchell and Epstein's criterion? It surely is not through class conflict, unless we regard the latent antagonism against traditional elites as such. Unlike the class antagonism in classical Marxist theory, the modern elite's corporate political action is not directed *within* the society (it cannot be, for other classes and class interests have not formed); rather, the modern elite's political efforts are directed *outward*, in an attempt to combat threats to the national integrity and Nigerian dignity.

If the criteria designating a social class do indeed apply to the modern African elite of Jos, we are then faced with the apparent paradox of the presence of a modern social class within an otherwise classless society (cf. Lloyd, 1966:60). The paradox remains only so long as we assume that the presence of one social class implies the existence of an entire social class system. To assume this would also require us to accept ipso facto an inability to deal with process, to describe and analyze the conditions under which a class system develops. We tie our hands by a circular definition—there is no social class system without classes, there are no classes without a social class system. What warrants the assumption that a social class system must appear full-blown when it emerges within a previously classless society? May we not assume, with perhaps more justification, that it develops part by part, class by class?

Leaving aside conditions such as conquest (although this is not without relevance to African colonial and precolonial experience) whereby an alien group, by military and political domination, superimposes itself as a ruling stratum, let us consider how a society may generate a system of social stratification. There are two logical ways in which a society can develop from a classless state into a class society. Either one part of the population is depressed to form a stratum below that of the rest (as with the development of despised groups or slaves), or a part of the population is elevated to form a superior stratum. (Conceivably, in a third case, part of the population rises while part falls, but this possibility is logically subsumed under the previous two.) Whatever may have occurred elsewhere and at other times, the evidence from Nigeria suggests that a class system will develop from the top down, and that initially an upper stratum will exist without lower, supporting strata.[18]

A necessary condition for the development of social classes is an expanding economy under which there is a general rise in the wealth and standard of living of the society as a whole, but there must also be differential access to the increased material wealth that is being generated. Since we regard a class system as based on free social mobility contingent upon achievement criteria, we should expect a priori that elite positions will appear first. These positions are socially valued and coveted (a class system requires a consensus from the society of what statuses are attractive) and the system also requires enlisting the people's motivation to achieve these higher statuses. The process of an emerging class system should show an initial bifurcation of an elite from the general mass, after which additional strata could be generated from the midsection of a rising pyramid as more and more persons seek identification with the upper stratum. But members of the elite seek to avoid having their valued position debased through the increase in membership. (It is hard to conceive of a social group holding an advantageous position or having access to most of the limited quantity of material, cultural, and social valuables— in occupation, wealth, prestigious statuses, and political power—that would not strongly attempt to maintain its position.) In order to maintain a position superior to an upwardly mobile middle section, members of the upper stratum would become more selective in the recruitment of new members and would also assume new cultural characteristics to further differentiate themselves.[19] The generation of new or additional cultural forms at the top, serving to distinguish that sector from the rest of society, must be perpetuated, since the new fashionable behaviors are eventually adopted by those who strive to emulate the elite. This "treadmill"[20] effect is quite common wherever there are systems of social stratification.[21]

It is reasonable to conclude that Nigeria, along with the rest of Africa, will develop a class system as it undergoes modernization of its economy, and now that a modern elite upper stratum has formed, we can expect the crystallization of a middle class. The general mass, as a residual category, will continue to form the base of the pyramid.

18. I have not made an extensive review of the literature to test the general validity of this hypothesis, but it is of interest that the Lugbara of Uganda show this development (Middleton, 1965:91), and E. E. Bergel notes that social stratification in ancient Rome "came into being by a separation of the top from the rest" (1962:15).
19. A similar point of view has been expressed by Epstein (1961:59).
20. See Fallers (1954).
21. In contemporary India this is called "sanskritization." For other examples of this in European history, see Brown's comments on the dissemination of upper stratum polite forms of speech (1965:57).

BIBLIOGRAPHY

Aluko, S. 1967 Displaced Nigerians. West Africa, *2602* (April 15):495–98.

Apter, D. E. 1963 Ghana in Transition. New York, Atheneum.

Balandier, G. 1956 Urbanism in west and central Africa: the scope and aims of research, in: UNESCO, pp. 495–510.

Banton, M. 1965 Social alignment and identity in a west African city, in: Kuper, H. (ed.), pp. 131–47.

Bergel, E. E. 1962 Social Stratification. New York, McGraw-Hill.

Brown, R. 1965 Social Psychology. New York, The Free Press.

Eisenstadt, S. N. 1952 The place of elites and primary groups in the absorption of new immigrants in Israel. American Journal of Sociology, *57*:222–31.

Epstein, A. L. 1961 The network and urban social organization. Rhodes-Livingstone Journal, *29*:29–62.

Fallers, L. A. 1954 A note on the "trickle effect." Public Opinion Quarterly, *18*:314–21.

––––––– 1963 Equality, modernity, and democracy in the new states, in: Geertz, C. (ed.), pp. 158–219.

––––––– 1964 Social stratification and economic processes, in: Herskovits, M. J., and M. Harwitz (eds.), pp. 113–30.

Forde, C. D. 1956 Introductory Survey, in: UNESCO, pp. 11–50.

Geertz, C. (ed.) 1963 Old Societies and New States: The Quest for Modernity in Asia and Africa. New York, The Free Press.

––––––– 1963 The integrative revolution: primordial sentiments and civil politics in the new states, in: Geertz, C. (ed.), pp. 104–57.

Goldthorpe, J. E. 1961 Educated Africans: some conceptual and terminological Problems, in: Southall, A. (ed.), pp. 145–58.

Harbison, F. 1962 Human resources and economic development in Nigeria, in: Tilman, R. O. and T. Cole (eds.), pp. 198–219.

Herskovits, M. J. 1962 The Human Factor in Changing Africa. New York, Alfred A. Knopf.

––––––– 1964 Economic Transition in Africa. Evanston, Ill., Northwestern University Press.

Hodgkin, T. 1956 Nationalism in Colonial Africa. London, Frederick Muller.

Horner, G. R. 1965 Selected cultural barriers to the modernization of labor, in: Lewis, W. H. (ed.), pp. 166–75.

Kuper, H. (ed.) 1965 Urbanization and Migration in West Africa. Berkeley, University of California Press.

Kuper, L. 1965 Sociology: some aspects of urban plural societies, in: Lystad, R. A. (ed.), pp. 107–30.

Lewis, W. H. (ed.) 1965 French-Speaking Africa: The Search for Identity. New York, Walker and Company.

Liebenow, J. G. 1965 The one-party state in West Africa: its strengths and weaknesses in the nation-building process, in: Lewis, W. H. (ed.), pp. 45–57.

Little, K. 1959 Introduction to special number on urbanization in West Africa. Sociological Review, 7:5–14.

Lloyd, P. C. (ed.) 1966 The New Elites of Tropical Africa. London, Oxford University Press.

Lystad, R. A. (ed.) 1965 The African World: A Survey of Social Research. London, Pall Mall.

Middleton, J. 1965 The Lugbara of Uganda. New York, Holt, Rinehart, & Winston.

Mitchell, J. C., and A. L. Epstein 1959 Occupational prestige and social status. Africa, 29:22–39.

Plotnicov, L. 1967 Strangers to the City: Urban Man in Jos, Nigeria. Pittsburgh, University of Pittsburgh Press.

Reissman, L. 1964 The Urban Process: Cities in Industrial Societies. New York, The Free Press.

Sklar, R. L. 1963 Nigerian Political Parties. Princeton, Princeton University Press.

Smythe, H. H. and M. M. 1960 The New Nigerian Elite. Stanford, Stanford University Press.

Southall, A. 1956 Determinants of the social structure of African urban populations, with special reference to Kampala (Uganda), in: UNESCO, pp. 557–78.

—— (ed.) 1961 Social Change in Modern Africa. London, Oxford University Press.

—— 1966 The concept of the elites and their formation in Uganda, in: Lloyd, P. C. (ed.), pp. 342–66.

Tilman, R. O., and T. Cole (eds.) 1962 The Nigerian Political Scene. Durham, N. C., Duke University Press.

UNESCO 1956 Social Implications of Industrialization and Urbanization in Africa South of the Sahara. London, International African Institute for UNESCO.

van den Berghe, P. L. (ed.) 1965 Africa: Social Problems of Change and Conflict. San Francisco: Chandler.

RACE, CLASS, AND STATUS IN SOUTH CENTRAL AFRICA

BY J. C. MITCHELL

SOCIAL ORDER AND PLURALISM

Malawi, Rhodesia, and Zambia, the countries which together
constitute the region of Central Africa and with which we are here concerned, have been and are, to different degrees, typical "plural" societies.
Plural societies may be thought of as political units that include socially
delineated ethnic groups having comparatively few contacts with one another apart from commercial and administrative relationships (cf. Furnivall,
1948: Mitchell, 1960c: Smith, 1960). In these Central African societies, as in
most plural societies, the significant ethnic groups are defined primarily
by racial characteristics. The particular interest, however, in the Central
African societies is that two of them, Malawi and Zambia, by 1966 had
undergone extensive constitutional changes through which political
power had shifted from an economically and socially dominant white
minority, racially defined, to a formerly subservient African majority,
while in the third, Rhodesia, the ruling minority had if anything further
consolidated its position. The problem raised by these events is the nature
of the basis of a social order in which a substantial proportion of the
population, while being allocated an inferior social standing and severely
restricted access to life-chances, nevertheless performs tasks essential for
the operation of the society as a whole. It is evident that a unified protest
of the subordinate racial group against their underprivileged position—

I acknowledge gratefully the stimulus I have received with consequent development of the ideas set out here from discussions with Mr. Bruce Kapferer and
with Hilary Flegg Mitchell, who accepted it to be part of her sponsorial duties to
clarify my expression as well.

303

by refusing to perform their occupational roles, for example—would throw the social system into disorder. Yet this has not happened on a widespread scale. Furthermore the political changes giving the subordinate racial groups a larger role, say, in the allocation of rewards and resources, have taken place in two of the societies concerned, although all three were set up under similar circumstances at the same time in history.

This problem of the relationship between the social order and the allocation of positions in society has been a topic of lively sociological debate for many years. Broadly the opposing points of view may be conveniently classified into "order" or "consensus" and "conflict" or "coercion" theories (Horton, 1966; Adams, 1966). The approaches of Parsons (1954), Davis (1948), and Davis and Moore (1945), for example, could be considered attempts to seek an explanation of the differential ranking of people in a social system as constituting a necessary condition for the continued operation of that system. Under Parsons' formulation, a dominant value orientation of the society leads to ranking of persons in terms of that value and provides an overall consensus in terms of which social actions are organized toward major societal goals. Davis and Moore argue that a system of differential rewards impels the more capable elements in a population to perform functions and undertake responsibilities which are essential for the continuance of the social system as a whole. Dahrendorf, on the other hand, takes an opposing point of view and argues that coherence and order in society are founded on force and constraint: "on the domination of some and the subjection of others" (1959:157).

The Solomonic judgment delivered by Williams is, of course, that: "Actual societies are held together by consensus, by interdependence, by sociability, and by coercion. This has always been the case, and there is no reason to expect it to be otherwise in any foreseeable future. The real job is to show how actual social structures and processes operating in these ways can be predicted and explained" (1966:721). (See also Dahrendorf, 1959, and van den Berghe, 1963.) The emergence, growth, and change of the several plural societies in Central Africa, particularly in respect of the status, class, and power relationships of the groups involved, provide one illustration of the way in which coercion and consensus have operated within actual social structures in the past, and how under changing political circumstances the balance between coercion and consensus varies.

THE ORIGINS OF PLURALISM

The idea of pluralism implies an overarching social order in which culturally distinct and partially autonomous soical groups coexist, for differentiation becomes patent only when the different units are placed in juxtaposition within a framework of comparison. Social differentiation, thus, as the Wilsons have noted, is a correlate of an increase in the scale of a society where formerly independent groups are brought within the compass of a single social order (G. and M. Wilson: 1945). A small-scale society is likely to be characterized by multiplex and close-knit face-to-face social relationships. In these circumstances cultural heterogeneity would be minimized, since the intensity of social relationship interaction implied by the scale of the society would require a considerable degree of consensus of ideas, values, and beliefs.

Before the absorption of the indigenous African peoples of Central Africa into the British Empire in the last two decades of the nineteenth century, the population was distributed in a plethora of small-scale autonomous social units of considerable cultural diversity. Ethnographically the region includes representatives of all four major divisions of the Bantu—i.e., Western Bantu in the northwest region of Zambia, Eastern Bantu in Malawi and the northern fringe of Zambia, Central Bantu in Zambia, and Central and Southern Bantu in Rhodesia. There is, therefore, wide heterogeneity in the region including agricultural and cattle-keeping people, matrilineal, bilateral, and patrilineal descent, uxorilocal and virilocal marriage, centralized chieftaincies and acephalous societies, militarily organized states and stateless groups, people with and without male circumcision and female initiations and with many different languages. A total of 150 separate groups based on ethnographic criteria have been identified,[1] and amongst these, 27 languages involving 50 dialects are spoken (Fortune, 1959).

This ethnographic diversity was an element in the relationships among neighboring chieftaincies in the period before British rule and remains so in some social situations in present-day affairs. A chieftaincy might easily have been, but was not always, composed of people speaking a dialect or even a language and following a set of customs different from its neighbor. Ethnic distinctiveness in these circumstances helped to stress the separateness of the chieftaincies and to emphasize their autonomy from each other. Descriptions by explorers like Livingstone or missionaries like Coillard, Laws, or Macdonald of conditions before British rule tell how villagers thought it unsafe to venture farther afield than the confines of

1. Mitchell, 1960a:179–81. General accounts are to be found in Colson and Gluckman 1951s Brelsford, n.d.; and Mitchell 1960a. For descriptions of particular groups—Bemba: Richard; 1939; Bisa: Kapferer, 1967; Luapula Lunda: Cunnison, 1959; Mambwe: Watson, 1958; Ambo: Stefaniszyn, 1964; Ndembu: Turner, 1957; Luvale: White, 1959, 1960; Lozi: Gluckman, 1941, 1955b; Plateau Tonga: Colson, 1958, 1962; Gwembe Tonga: Colson, 1960; Shona: Holleman, 1952; Gelfand, 1956, 1959, 1962; Garbett, 1960; Ndebele: Hughes, 1956; Chewa: Marwick, 1965; Fort Jameson Ngoni: Barnes, 1954; Lakeside Tonga: van Velsen 1964b; Yao: Mitchell, 1956a; Gomani and Mbelwa Nguni: Read, 1956; Ila: Smith and Dale, 1920; Lamba: Doke, 1931; Ngonde: Wilson, 1939.

the chieftaincy they lived in for fear of being taken into bondage. Apparently slave-raiding against neighboring chieftaincies was common even when they were of the same ethnic and linguistic group.

The social units varied in size and complexity from the elaborate kingdoms of the Barotse, the confederation of Bemba chieftaincies, and the military states of the Ngoni and Ndebele at the one extreme, to small village communities linked to each other by many diverse social ties, the headman of which acknowledged no superiors amongst their fellows at the other. The majority of the population appeared to be distributed in autonomous political entities involving perhaps five to ten thousand people intermediate in organization between these extremes. The leaders of these units were later called "chiefs" by the British administrators. Their positions were inherited within a defined kinship group. This group may have shared a clan name with others who, though excluded from succession to the title, nevertheless looked upon themselves as superior in social status to those bearing other clan names. Thus amongst the matrilineal Bemba people the clan name of the paramount, the Chitimukulu, was "Crocodile." Commoners who were of the "Crocodile" clan were accorded higher prestige than, say, those of the "Elephant" or "Lion" clans. The distinction between "royal" and "commoner" clans in this way was a differentiation in terms of invidious comparison and therefore involved social stratification of a rudimentary kind. The access of commoner clansmen to the life-chances of royal clansmen and to their style of life, however, was almost equal to that of royals, whose prestige amounted therefore to little more than social precedence in public gatherings. In much the same way the descent group of a village headman in a village might have had slight advantage over descent groups related by less direct links to the headman, but these differences were slight in comparison with the advantages of groups placed in especially favorable ecological circumstances or possessing enough men and weapons to make their presence felt.

The basis of subsistence throughout the region was crop cultivation, but this was supplemented by fishing and hunting where feasible or by cattle products where stock could survive. A lack of the facilities for long-term storage of agricultural produce meant that for most groups surplus crops had little value in differentiating people in terms of wealth. Land was relatively plentiful but it could only be rendered fruitful by the expenditure of labor which was a comparatively scarce commodity. The use of poles and mud and thatch and the lack of other materials for the construction of houses, except amongst the Shona-speaking peoples of Rhodesia, placed a limitation on differentiation in the levels of habitation. Similar restrictions applied to clothing and the possession of weapons and implements. It was only cattle-keeping people—the Shona, the Plateau

Tonga, the Ila, the Barotse, the Mambwe, and allied people of the northern border of Zambia and the people descended from the Zulu (the Ngoni and Ndebele)—who had a means of accumulating wealth in a form that could constitute the basis of what Veblen called "invidious comparison" (1954: 37).

Status depended rather on the command over followers. It was the size of his following that distinguished an important village headman from a prestigious lineage elder. The connection between status and power here was direct, since force was often the means whereby groups, even within chieftaincies, maintained their rights. Contemporary accounts tell how villages often took reprisals against other villages to protect their land rights or to avenge the murder of one of their number (see Colson, 1958, and Mitchell, 1956). Through the judicious distribution of surplus crops either as food or beer, or the loan of cattle, a person could build up ties of dependency among his peers and so extend his power and increase his standing in their eyes.

The clearest form of status distinction was that between a slave or bondsman and a freeman, a distinction that has survived in some rural areas and still serves to justify the restriction of some villagers from positions of authority and economic advantage (see, for example, White, 1957; Tuden, 1959; Mitchell, 1956a; van Velsen, 1964a; Douglas, 1964). Bondsmen or bondswomen may have been captives taken in war or in raids on neighboring communities; refugees from other communities who had offered their submission to powerful leaders; persons who had been proffered as compensation for homicide or who had simply been purchased with food, ivory, or cloth. The bondsmen or bondswomen were allocated tasks in the villages which relieved their master and his wives of the burden of subsistence activities. Bondsmen were also required to carry arms in defense of their captors. Female serfs usually bore children by their masters and sometimes by other men to whom they had been given by their former masters. In matrilineal societies bondsmen might have become the consorts of women from free lineages. In patrilineal societies they could have taken wives from among other serfs. In each case the children were aligned with the master's group so that the bondsmen and serfs became media by means of which the following and power of leaders could be increased.

Bondsmen and bondswomen were under the direct control of their master, who could sell them to slave-traders. In certain circumstances he could take their lives, as, for example, by causing them to undergo the poison ordeal on his behalf. But their primary value was to increase the master's status and power, so that it was unusual for him to cause their death. The master was in fact dependent on his slaves, making him a slave to his slaves. The position of the serf was approximated to that of a child or grandchild, and it is clear that through time a close personal link between masters and serfs developed. This was particularly so when bondswomen had borne children by their masters so that they became linked to their masters by being the mother of their children.

But the distinction between a freeman and a bondsman was clear-cut. The characteristic that marked bondspeople from free was a lack of supporting relatives—"no people behind their back," as the Lakeside Tonga would say (van Velsen, 1964a: 262)—people who could defend and ensure their rights and autonomy of action. The ultimate sanction a master had over bondspeople was his freedom to kill them without invoking retribution from the kinsfolk of the bondsman. Coercion was thus the ultimate basis on which the master's control over his bondsmen rested. The efficacy of this sanction was demonstrated when it was removed by the *pax Britannica* at the turn of the century. Many bondsmen took advantage of the loss of power of their masters by breaking away from their villages to found new settlements of their own. Elements of both coercion and cooperation characterized the link between bondsman and master in preconquest circumstances, but coercion arose only when cooperation failed.

Coercion and cooperation also characterized the internal structure of the autonomous chieftaincies before they were brought under British rule. Each chief was an autonomous ruler over a number of subjects who acknowledged his superiority by the payment of tribute and by the recognition of his ritual influence over the success of their agriculture and hunting. As with masters and their bondsmen, the chief usually had at his command more force than his rivals and could subdue them, but in the last resort support from his subjects legitimized his office. Yet the security of the chief's subjects depended directly upon their cooperation under the chief in defense against enemies among themselves, such as believed witches, or from outside, such as hostile neighbors or slave-raiders. The relationship between political office and follower was based on coercion and cooperation, but coercion was resorted to only when the interest of the rulers was threatened by a breakdown in cooperation. Some chieftaincies were organized specifically on the basis of the incorporation of groups into subservient strata within the polity. The most notable examples were the Ngoni kingdoms which had their origin in the Zulu Empire in present-day Natal in South Africa. Under Zulu leaders, particularly Chaka, neighboring Ngoni-speaking peoples were subjugated by force of arms and the women and cattle appropriated by the Zulu king. The captives taken in these raids were allocated in subservient positions to regional governors, though the young men could elevate their positions by serving in the army. Several dissident groups leaving Zululand in the 1820's found their way into Central Africa. They incorporated captive groups from foreign tribes as they moved northward or from neighboring tribes when they settled in any region. The Ndebele, for example, incorporated Sotho and Tswana people on the way north from the Transvaal and later Kalanga and Roswi people in what is today Rhodesia. The Ndebele aristocrats of Ngoni origin call themselves Zansi, while the people of Sotho origin are called Enhla, and they form a middle stratum in the community. The lowest stratum comprised the local Shona-speaking people called Holi or Tjabi. These strata were endogamous units in a hierarchical system (Hughes, 1956:52–62). In a similar way among Mpeseni's Ngoni in Zambia captives incorporated during the early stages of the migration had higher prestige than those of more recent incorporation, while those of local origin had the lowest of all (Barnes, 1954). Read's description of Gomani's and Mbelwa's Ngoni in Malawi confirms this. Below the ruling Zulu clans those incorporated south of the Zambezi River were accorded greater honor than those incorporated after crossing it to the north (Read, 1956). These were military kingdoms which had come into being through military conquest and continued to expand by it. Subject peoples were incorporated into what Barnes has called a "snowball state," and even when the kingdoms were settled in one place they continued to raid neighboring people for cattle, slaves, grain, and other loot. Coercion was the basis of the polity.

Yet at the same time captives incorporated into the system were able to ameliorate their inferior status by success in military exploits and by taking captives and cattle on their own account. The low status to which they had been ascribed could be partly, though not completely, offset by successful achievement in terms of the major values of the society itself. Thus we find references in the early literature to the way in which Ngoni captives out-Heroded Herod in their pursuit of Ngoni values of warfare and conquest (Read, 1956:24).

Other devices served to counterbalance the low prestige of incorporated groups in some other political systems. The Barotse kingdom was another polity established on the basis of conquest, this time by a Sotho group in 1836. The conquerors themselves were overthrown in 1860, and the dominant Luyi people set up a political system in which they maintained control over a large number of ethnically distinct groups by an elaborate system of courts and administration. Underlying the unity of the system, however, as Gluckman points out, was a complex economic interdependence among the various ethnic groups. The administrative and legal system which maintained the political system guaranteed the rights of the various minority groups involved, but at the same time both administrative and legal systems were linked at the top in the person of the Litunga—the paramount chief—who represented the coercive power behind the courts and the state (Gluckman, 1941, 1955).

J. C. Mitchell: Race and Status in South Central Africa

In other societies, and perhaps more generally than by legal and administrative arrangements, the low secular status of conquered groups was balanced by their high ritual status. This is illustrated particularly by the relationships of the different ethnic groups included in the Lunda state in the Luapula Valley of Zambia. Here the invading Lunda people accepted the ritual ascendancy of the conquered Shila people in respect of the agricultural and fishing activities upon which both groups were vitally dependent. Myths purporting to explain how the relationships came into being at the time of the invasion provide a validation for their present-day status relationships (Cunnison, 1959). The ritual ascendancy of the original inhabitants of a region over their secularly dominant conquerors by reason of their special relationship to the land is also characteristic of at least the Bemba, the Yao, and some Shona groups (see references in Mitchell, 1961). In these societies the coercion inherent in conquest was reduced by the interdependence in ritual activities of the groups of unequal status.

Conflict was implicit in the autonomy of chieftaincies, since their independence was maintained only by armed resistance to the depredations of hostile neighbors. But the hostility between neighboring groups had of necessity to be overcome, partly because of their reliance on trade for at least some commodities they considered essential. Most people in pre-European Central Africa consumed at least some commodities which could only be obtained by trade with neighboring groups or with itinerant traders (see Miracle, 1960). Where links into neighboring but hostile groups were needed, it seems that the protection of common clanship was invoked, since a similar system of clan names existed over a considerable part of central Africa. Arab, Bemba, or Yao trading caravans, however, were well armed with muzzle-loading firearms and were capable of warding off hostile attacks. On the whole it seems that the mutual advantage accruing to both trader and customer meant that in general these caravans could pass from one hostile chieftaincy to another with little let, or hindrance.

From time to time larger political units came into being which incorporated considerable populations into a single polity. Some, like the "empires" under the Shona potentate, the Monomotapa, the Malawi empire of Chewa-speaking peoples under Undi and Mwase, the Bisa kingdoms of the early nineteenth century, all referred to in early Portuguese writings, have since disintegrated into smaller units. Others such as the Barotse kingdom, the Lunda under Chief Kasembe, the Bemba confederation of chieftaincies (Werbner, 1967), and the military kingdoms of Zulu origin were all in active existence at the time of the establishment of British rule at the close of the nineteenth century. At this time the smaller and less centralized groups were at the mercy of their larger and more powerfully armed neighbors. Contemporary reports describe how raiding parties periodically ravaged villages in search of cattle, crops, and slaves. To protect themselves from these depredations some groups paid an annual tribute in crops or cattle to powerful neighbors, such submissions serving to exonerate them from destructive raids. These tributes, however, did not imply a patron-client relationship, since the payment of tribute did not entitle the payer to expect protection from the payee against other predators. Rather it purchased simple immunity from raids by the payee only. Some peoples, as, for example, the Kaonde of the Kasempa district, paid tribute to both the Lunda under Mwata Yamvo and to the Barotse under Lewanika.

At the time of the appearance of the British in Central Africa the region seemed to be dominated by a few powerful chieftaincies who were periodically at war with one another. Interposed between them were a large number of smaller and relatively weaker chieftaincies subject to periodic raiding and constant tribute paying to their more powerful neighbors. In the field of intertribal relationships, therefore, although trade provided some basis of independence, in general relationships were characterized by hostility and conflict.

THE ESTABLISHMENT OF RACIAL STRATIFICATION

It was on this scene from 1859 onward that first British explorers, and later missionaries, began to appear. Although the Portuguese had been settled at Sofala near Beira since 1505 and had made several journeys into the interior to the three regions concerned, they had never managed to establish a permanent settlement there—probably because of their lack of technological and economic resources to buttress such a settlement. The British missionaries, however, had behind them the superior medicines, weapons, trade goods, and financial support of an expanding technology fostered by the Industrial Revolution. This not only made it possible for them to persist where earlier Portuguese attempts had languished, but also made them acutely conscious of the cultural gap that separated them from their African flocks—a gap that later became the justification for the dominance of the whites, as a racial category, over the Africans.

The missionaries had come as strangers to these communities specifically to bring to them a new religion. Technically they had no power of coercion: they had to rely on their powers of persuasion only. Yet they could not avoid the roles that were thrust upon them, initially as representatives of a formidable foreign power whose reputation had frequently preceded them, and then later as a locus of power that held itself outside the jurisdiction of the chiefs and was able to flout their authority. Contact between the missionaries and local chiefs soon involved Britain indirectly, for missionaries called on the home government to support them, when, for example, they became involved in hostile relations with local potentates over harboring runaway slaves or when helping to protect villages from slave-raiders. Britain became involved with African peoples in terms of foreign relations sometimes, as in Nyasaland, formally through a Consul. This was the first, or "foreign relations," phase of race relations, as Barnes calls it (1955).

Prospectors, hunters, traders, concession-seekers, and plain adventurers were usually hard on the heels of the missionaries, so that by the 1880's there was a diverse group of whites who had visited Central Africa and knew something about its land and its peoples. At the same time the course of political and economic relationships among Belgium, Britain, Germany, and Portugal led to a new appreciation of the strategic significance of the possession of Central African colonies, and in the late 1880's all four powers directed considerable activity to establishing their claims to hegemony over different parts of Central Africa. As far as Central Africa was concerned, this was achieved largely through the mechanism of "protection," through which ostensibly responsible and independent chiefs signed treaties with British representatives whereby they agreed to allow the exploitation of mineral and other economic resources in return for being protected from other foreign powers. In fact the treaties were sought by the British South Africa Company operating under a Royal Charter, so that the protection offered was only indirectly that of the British government.[2] The upshot of these arrangements was, however, that the British South Africa Company could use them as a justification to establish political control over the African peoples. In Nyasaland protection implied, first of all, the suppression of the slave trade which was being conducted by Yao and Arab leadership. A series of primitive expeditions against these, financed partly by the British South Africa Company, continued until 1895 when the Arab slave trader Mlozi was defeated at Karonga at the northern tip of the Lake. European penetration continued by similar processes in other parts of the region.

Immediately after Lobengula had signed the Rudd Concession in 1888 and the British South Africa Company was able to obtain its Royal Charter on the strength of it, Rhodes, the founder of the company was able to gather a group of pioneers together to settle in Salisbury in 1890. In the same year a station was opened at Chuhgu on Lake Mweru, in 1892 one at Kalungwishi, and in 1893 at Abercorn. But it was clear that the erst-

2. Accounts of the concession hunters and the treaties they made with African chiefs are presented from different points of view, among others, by Gann, 1958, 1960, 1964; Hanna, 1956; Mason, 1958; Hall, 1965; Rotberg, 1965.

while autonomous chieftaincies were loath to give up their independence without demur, and between 1893 and 1898 a number of military actions took place which established without doubt the subservient position of the African peoples in the new political and social structure. Thus, for example, the Ndebele people were crushed in 1893 by a force of 670 settlers in Southern Rhodesia, following a dispute about a raid on a settlement near Fort Victoria. The Ndebele rose in rebellion in 1896, and the Shona-speaking peoples, among whom were a number of former payers of tribute to the Ndebele, followed suit a few months after. The rebels were subdued after many months of fighting by the superior organization and arms of the settlers supported with reinforcements from Britain and South Africa. In 1895 the Chewa Chief Mwase Kasungu resisted British administration and was forcibly made to yield by a punitive force. In the following year Gomani, the chief of the Ngoni in Central Nyasaland, was captured and shot following an action against him after his men had raided some mission stations. In 1898 the forces of Mpeseni, the Ngoni chief who had declined to make a treaty with company representatives, were routed by a British force near present-day Fort Jameson. In March 1899 a Bemba chief, Ponde, was attacked after he had advanced into a neighboring chief's territory to claim the chieftainship. Mporokoso, another Bemba chief, was also forced to submit (Gann, 1964:85). In October of the same year, company forces took action against the Lunda chief Kasembe on the Luapula after he had "received European traders in a hostile manner" (Rotberg, 1965:21).

The majority of the peoples, however, were incorporated into the new political structure without a show of force. Even tribes with warlike reputations accepted foreign domination without armed resistance. The Barotse kingdom, for example, had been incorporated by treaty and, although the Litunga may subsequently have regretted this decision, hostilities were avoided (Hall, 1965:61–80). Similarly the Ngoni kingdom under Mbelwa in northern Nyasaland had accepted British protection voluntarily. The eventual subjugation of all formerly independent groups in the region was inevitable, as Gann points out (1964:90), but there seems to be a good deal of evidence to suggest that economic interest was not far removed from the surface in these disputes. For example, the Europeans believed—falsely as it turned out—that the territories which the recalcitrant Ndebele and Ngoni people occupied contained rich gold deposits. Significantly the cattle which were taken from these peoples when they were conquered were referred to as "loot." The incidents that precipitated the war against the Ndebele and several of the Yao groups in Nyasaland and Gomani's people involved interference with the labor forces of European planters. As Gann points out, "White traders could not prosper as long as their potential customers were murdered by war bands. A wage-earning economy and a slave economy could not permanently exist side by side any more than a wage-earning and a raiding economy" (1960:66; see also Mason, 1958:163).

The cultural gap between the early European pioneers and their African subjects was wide, and this reinforced the dominance of the Europeans over them in the economic and political spheres. The early missionaries, administrators, planters, and traders, were men of their time, and they considered that the advancement of their own civilization, as against that of their African underlings, merely demonstrated natural superiority in an assumed evolutionary scale. They viewed their military, political, and economic dominance as a natural concomitant of their advanced evolutionary state as against that of the Africans, who in their view were a racial group at a lower stage in the scale, separated from them by an unbridgeable gap.

By 1912 when Rolin, a distinguished Belgian lawyer, visited Southern Rhodesia, he was able to describe what was later to be called a "plural society." He wrote:

> Society is composed, so to speak, of two societies, one superimposed upon the other, almost two castes: an aristocracy of white landowners and capitalists; a proletariat of black. . . . The whites conquered the country in 1893. They are established there as masters, with the overwhelming superiority given them by their intellectual and moral heritage from Greece and Rome, from the achievement of Europe in science and mechanical invention, in industry and the art of ruling, in accumulated skill and capital. Below the whites, the blacks. . . . one has to see them, in their sordid villages, half-naked . . . to appreciate the immense distance that divides the victors from the vanquished. (Quoted by Mason, 1958:245)

Fifteen years later the position was unchanged. Bishop May in 1929 said that "the average settler does not regard the native as an equal; . . . he repudiates them. To him the native is neither a fellow worker, a fellow-citizen, nor even . . . a fellow-man" (Rotberg, 1965:100–101). It should be appreciated that many of the planters and traders and some of the administrators, at least, had come from South Africa where a system of racial stratification had been established after two centuries of hostile contact between white and black. But an explanation of how a structure of social relationships of this sort comes into being does not explain why it persists. The Europeans' belief in their innate superiority over the Africans in terms of an evolutionary process was an important element in a myth which justified the social and economic privileges they enjoyed—a myth that has persisted to the present day.

The African people, however, did not accept their subservient position without demur. Dramatic and violent demonstrations of protest occurred in risings such as that of John Chilembwe in Nyasaland in 1915, and later in riots on the Copperbelt in 1935. But the position of the Europeans was maintained, in fact, by a discriminatory application of the law, by administering harsh punishments for infringements of it, and by practices and customs imposed by the Europeans which denied the marks of prestige to Africans in the mass.

The Orders in Council of 1894 and 1898 proscribed any legislation which did not apply equally to Europeans and Africans except insofar as the supply of arms and ammunition and of liquor was concerned, both of which matters were controlled by the Berlin Convention of 1885. But regulations were made, nevertheless, which on the surface of it may not have appeared to be discriminatory but were so in fact in their interpretation. For example, the death penalty was introduced for rape and attempted rape in 1903. The occasion for this appears to have been a number of "black peril" cases in which African men allegedly attacked European women (Rogers and Frantz, 1962:140). Although Africans were sentenced to death in 1908 and 1910 under this ordinance—in fact the sentences were not carried out—no European ever received a capital sentence (Mason, 1958:248). Similarly ordinances punished illicit sexual relations between African men and white women, but not those between white men and African women. As Mason comments: "A distinction had thus been made between the races in criminal law, the field in which a formal equality before the law is most often achieved" (Mason, 1958:247). Regulations under the Municipalities Ordinance of 1897 empowered local authorities to control the residence of Africans in towns. Some of the legislation was designed to protect Africans from exploitation, as, for example, the early laws establishing reserves for Africans, but these laws in time became devices for maintaining the status differential between Africans and Europeans. The course of events in Northern Rhodesia and Nyasaland was similar (see Rotberg, 1965; Hall, 1965).

Thus the law and the way in which it was administered insofar as the treatment of Africans was concerned, embodied the customs and practices of the dominant European group. From a sociological point of view we may look upon these practices as devices by means of which the Europeans stated and defined the status relationships between the two racial groups and thereby also maintained the differential between them.[3] The Europeans appreciated the relationship between themselves and the Africans in terms of the relationship between parents and children. The Attorney-General, for example, in a debate on the death penalty for rape or attempted rape in 1903 said that "the law did not recognise that the black man was the white man's equal," and quoting the example of the liquor laws,

3. Striking parallels are found in other situations where racial domination occurs (see Shibutani and Kwan, 1965, Chap. 12).

pointed out that the "native was put on the same footing as the white child," since he could not be supplied with intoxicating liquor (Mason, 1959:247). Consonant with this appreciation of their status vis-à-vis Africans, Europeans adopted the practice, followed also by whites in respect of Negroes in the American Southern States, of referring to all Africans as "boys"—a term of address which subsequently Africans came to resent deeply because of its connotation of menial status. Reciprocally Europeans expected Africans to call them "Bwana" (i.e., Swahili for "master") or "Baas" (i.e., Afrikaans for "master").

Newspapers of the time report many references to the behavior of Africans in terms of "cheeky Kaffirs." "Cheeky" here refers to the refusal of Africans to accept the status they had been allocated. We find resistance to educating the Africans or even of converting them to Christianity for fear they would not accept the role of manual worker to which the Europeans had ascribed them (Mason, 1959:252). Africans were expected to raise their hats to Europeans; Rogers and Frantz, referring to a *Rhodesian Herald* report in 1901, observe that "wearing a hat was like carrying a chip on the shoulder—an invitation to get it knocked off" (1962:210). Rotberg quotes the comment of a literate African (G. S. Mwase) about social relationships in Nyasaland in 1915. He wrote that any African "was oftentimes beaten by a whiteman if he did not take off his hat off his head some thousand yards away, even a mile away of a whiteman" (1965:79). Colonial Napier in 1904 introduced a motion in the Council that municipalities should be empowered to make bylaws "to restrain natives of Africa from making use of such parts of streets and roads as are set aside for public foot paths" (Mason, 1958:252). This somewhat bizarre denial of status equality still persisted in Northern Rhodesia in the 1930's when forty-three Africans were arrested in the town of Livingstone for loitering on the pavements (Hall, 1965:117).

Since the establishment of the social order in the last decade of the nineteenth century in which Europeans as a racial category occupied positions of authority and social ascendancy over Africans, the privileges of their status have been ensured by administrative practices, political arrangements, and legislation. The sanction of force has not been far behind the exercise of government. An efficient police force has been built up, especially in Rhodesia. There also a system of military national service has been in force since the establishment of the territory whereby each European youth undergoes military training. This training is directed more toward internal security than external and was used on many occasions in the fifties against African demonstrations of protest against their political disabilities. The situation is similar to that described for America in the slave-owning days where: "Behind the Southern slaveholder and his agents stood an elaborate system of military control—the police, the State militia and numerous voluntary associations that were well armed. These bodies, which were mobilised at the slightest hint of rebellion, periodically searched for and disbanded secret assemblies of slaves" (Shibutani and Kwan, 1965:322).

In the political sphere successive upward adjustments of the voting qualification have effectively excluded Africans from the common voters roll and have consequently ensured white rule.[4] Legislation has apportioned the land in Southern Rhodesia restricting the majority of it for use by the European minority, and in Northern Rhodesia the railway strip, some parts of the Eastern Province and the Copperbelt region were similarly reserved for European use for either farming or mining. In Nyasaland, rights to large tracts of land, particularly in the Shire Highlands, had been acquired at the turn of the century and remained subsequently a bone of contention between Africans and Europeans. In Southern Rhodesia Africans were excluded from the provisions of the laws that legalized strike action of trade unions. Similar provisions debarred Africans from being accepted as apprentices in skilled trades. In Northern Rhodesia a "closed shop" agreement between the European Mineworkers Union and the copper companies contracted during the war years, 1939–1945, excluded Africans from higher-paid posts until it was changed in 1956. Marketing regulations for agricultural produce in the same way protected European farmers against competition from African farmers.[5]

In the occupational field all higher administrative posts in the civil service and business—that is, those concerned with making the important decisions about the use of resources, the investment of capital, the allocations of rewards for labor, and the access to life chances—were filled by Europeans. There were a handful of African doctors and lawyers in the territories, but the overwhelming majority of the professional posts were occupied by Europeans. The only professional occupation in which substantial numbers of Africans were employed was teaching, and to a lesser extent in the church, but these African teachers and ministers served African pupils or congregations only. Access of most higher supervisory and skilled posts, and the majority of white-collar positions, were also European prerogatives. Correlatively very few Europeans were employed in occupations lower in status than supervisory, white-collar, or skilled.[6]

4. In Rhodesia this has been: 1898 Proclamation 17, £50 a year; 1914 Legislative Ordinance, £100 a year; 1951 Huggins Amendment, £240 a year; 1957 Home-Welensky Revision (Federal), £720 a year; 1961 Sandys-Whitehead Revision, £720 a year (Keatley, 1963:315).
5. The development and nature of discriminatory legislation and practices are set out in such works as Hall, 1965; Rotberg, 1965; Clegg, 1960; Leys, 1959; Gray, 1960. Keatley (1963: 358–84) summarizes the disabilities for Africans in the Army, the Railways Land, Agriculture, Public Services and Benefits, Industry taxation investments, education, local government, social relationships, and health at the time of the Federation, i.e., 1953–63.
6. In the towns line-of-rail of Northern Rhodesia between 1951 and 1954, according to an unpublished social survey, the percentage of adult males in occupational categories were

J. C. Mitchell: Race and Status in South Central Africa

In Southern Rhodesia, on the average, in 1961 a European employee earned £834 for every £100 that an African earned. In Northern Rhodesia the ratio was £1072 to £100. African workers, on the other hand, were overwhelmingly employed in unskilled manual occupations, as laborers, domestic servants, messengers, or in semiskilled jobs as truck drivers, tailor's assistants, machine operatives, factory hands, and so on. Some were employed as brick layers, carpenters, and mechanics, and fewer as teachers, clerks, hospital orderlies, nurses, and similar semiprofessional workers. The median income of Europeans in Southern Rhodesia in 1961 was £950 against an African median of £113.[7] The mean income in Northern Rhodesia was £1543 against £144.[8] The position is summarized by Rogers and Frantz when they write: "Opportunities for Africans to obtain positions with higher status have been resisted from the beginning by organized interest and pressure groups in all spheres of the economy" (1962:165).

In short, by the 1960's a system of racial stratification in Central Africa had been established in which the Europeans had secured for themselves a command over the allocations of resources and benefits of the economic system and over the life-chances for members of their own race as against other races—the Africans in particular—and had embattled their privileges in the political and legal systems in the three territories.

Two other groups are identified on racial grounds: the Asians and the "coloreds."[9] Asian immigration to Nyasaland had been encouraged during Sir Harry Johnston's administration, partly because of the use of Sikhs in the operations against the slave-raiders and partly because Johnston believed they could contribute to the economic development of the territory. From Nyasaland they migrated into Northern Rhodesia via the Eastern Province where they were not welcomed quite so warmly. In Southern Rhodesia immigrants came from South Africa, where they had been introduced in the 1860's as laborers on the Natal sugar plantations. Their role in Central Africa, however, was mainly in the field of petty trading and has remained so. The immigration of Indians into the territories has been very strictly controlled since 1951, so that the Asian

professional and white-collar, 4.5; supervisory and police, 6.6; skilled, 9.6; semi-skilled, 9.5; domestic and unskilled, 64.4; others, 5.5. According to Schwab (1961:130), the only data available for Rhodesia, the percentages in Gwelo were white-collar professional and commercial, 6.0; supervisory, 2.1; skilled, 12.9; domestic, 3.0; and unskilled, 73.6.

7. *Census of Southern Rhodesia.*
8. *Monthly Digest of Statistics, Republic of Zambia* (Vol. 11, No. 6, Table 4). Strictly speaking the mean earnings of £1543 refers to non-Africans. The economic effects of union pressures in maintaining the difference are described by Baldwin (1962).
9. There is very little systematic information available about the Asian and colored populations of Central Africa. The only published material available is Dotson, 1961, 1963. Mrs. P. Wheeldon is at present making a study in Rhodesia but has not yet published her findings.

community is growing by natural increase rather than by immigration. The majority today are locally born.

In terms of the color-caste system, both Africans and Europeans recognize the Asians as a separate race following a distinctive way of life. They constitute a "closed" community in that they confine marriages and other social relationships of an intimate kind almost entirely to their own kind. They nevertheless enjoy greater privileges than Africans in that housing is not so rigidly restricted for them, they are able to use public facilities to a greater extent than the Africans, and are more easily able to become voters on the common roll. Nevertheless they have had their trading rights restricted in some towns in Northern Rhodesia, and find it difficult if not impossible to obtain top-level posts in the civil services or to be appointed to important professional posts. For every £100 earned by Africans in Southern Rhodesia in 1961 Asians earned £540 as against the £834 earned by Europeans. Their status in the racial hierarchy is thus intermediate between the Europeans and Africans.

A fourth racial group identified and placed in the social structure of Central Africa is particularly interesting from a sociological point of view. These are the people of mixed racial descent commonly known as Eurafricans or "coloreds." A group of Cape coloreds came up to Southern Rhodesia with the pioneers in 1890. They are the progenitors of one section of the "colored" community. The majority, however, are the progeny of the sexual liaisons of European or Asian men with African women, largely though not entirely, in the early days of settlement. Most colored people today are the progeny of "colored" parents—i.e. they, like other racial groups, tend to form an endogamous stratum in the social structure but the community is increased by children still being born to African mothers by European or Asian fathers, usually outside marriage.

The official definition of "colored" people is partly racial and partly social. It is racial in that his African parentage excludes a "colored" person from membership to the superior racial stratum of his other parent, and it is social insofar as a person of mixed parentage is classified as African if he "lives according to the manner of Africans." Those who are "colored" or Eurafrican, therefore, by definition are those who follow a non-African way of life. Dotson, who has studied Asians and coloreds in Zambia, observed that "Insofar as one can speak meaningfully of a Coloured 'culture' that culture is European in origin and content. By the act of identifying oneself as 'Colored' one thereby sets a course which, as one makes the interminable series of choices and decisions which constitute living, moves one inevitably in the European direction culturally" (1963: 276). Not surprisingly, within the total social system the "colored" community is accorded a position intermediate between the Asians and the Africans, with the consequent advantages and disadvantages of this position.

J. C. Mitchell: Race and Status in South Central Africa

This implies that local authorities provide separate and somewhat better housing for "coloreds" than for Africans: "coloreds" may be placed on the common voters roll; they are provided with schools which are separate from those for Africans and for Europeans, but which sometimes they share with Asians; they have a wider range of occupations open to them than do Africans, but they are restricted as are the Asians from the highest administrative, professional, and managerial posts. For every £100 earned by Africans in Southern Rhodesia in 1961, "coloreds" on the average earned £375.

The social structure of these three Central African societies, therefore, has been characterized by the identification of these four racial categories. Table 1 shows the proportion of these racial groups in the three territories at the time of census in 1961. It will be seen that the Europeans were a tiny minority out of all proportion to the political power they have wielded in Malawi and Zambia and still wield in Rhodesia. The Asians and "colored" too were tiny minorities as against the Africans.

The groups had different degrees of control over production and the rewards that flowed from it. The Europeans exercised most control and enjoyed highest rewards from it, and the Africans, at the other end of the scale, least control and lowest rewards. This difference in access to economic power was reflected in the different levels of consumption and possession of property with consequent disparities in style of life among the racial groups. Each racial group tended to form a closed social group within which social intercourse, outside of economic or administrative matters, was normally confined. In particular they were almost entirely endogamous.

The racial categories, therefore, were "status groups" in the Weberian sense, since, apart from the physical features that identified them, they were seen to enjoy different levels of consumption, to follow distinct styles of life, and to confine social intercourse to themselves. These status groups at the same time were largely coincident with social classes in that they showed common interest in the "command over the possession of goods and the opportunities for income" (Weber, 1947:181), or alternatively in the lack of them. Lastly, power was also distributed in terms of racial

Table 1. Proportion of Racial Groups in Malawi, Rhodesia, and Zambia in 1961.

	Africans	Europeans	Asians	Coloreds	Total Pop.
Malawi	2,900,000	8,800	10,700	1,600	2,921,100
	(99.3)	(0.3)	(0.3)	(0.1)	(100.0)
Rhodesia	3,550,000	221,504	7,253	10,559	3,789,316
	(93.7)	(5.8)	(0.2)	(0.3)	(100.0)
Zambia	3,240,000	74,549	7,790	2,043	3,324,382
	(97.5)	(2.2)	(0.2)	(0.1)	(100.0)

Sources: Rhodesia: *Census of the European, Asian and Coloured Population*, p. 3.
Malawi: *Nyasaland: Report for the Year 1961* London H.M.S.O., p. 22.
Zambia: *Monthly Digest of Statistics.* No. xix (Oct. 1965), Table I.

principles—at least until the achievement of independence by Malawi and Zambia, so that the racial groups were also political interest groups or "parties" in Weber's sense.

Race was thus "pervasive" (Epstein, 1958:240) in the social structure in that it provided a primary basis or ordering social relations in nearly all social situations. This virtual identification of status group, social class, party, and race had a marked bearing on the course of social change in the three societies because there were so few situations in which status or class considerations, for example, could operate to modify political alignments.

DIFFERENTIATION AND STRATIFICATION WITHIN RACIAL GROUPS

The racial groups themselves, however, were internally differentiated, and the sectional interests of the component groups in turn sometimes combined and sometimes opposed in respect to relationships with other racial groups.

Status and role within racial groups were allocated primarily on principles of ethnicity, religion, and socioeconomic status. Within the European group, for example, the national origin of people influenced social alliances and cleavages. The distinction between those of South African and British origin and particularly between South African "Afrikaans" and British origin was politically and socially significant. These groups tended to be distinguished by cultural differences, especially by language, but also by occupation and by religion, the Afrikaners tending to concentrate on the mines and in farming and being predominantly members of the Dutch Reformed Church. Rogers and Frantz have shown that in general the Afrikaans group were less tolerant in their attitude toward African political aspirations (1960:303), and Gann has suggested that this division affected the voting in the referenda in Southern Rhodesia in 1923 and 1953 when the Afrikaans voted for union with South Africa in the first and against federation in the second (Gann, 1964:429). Other ethnic groups may be distinguished such as the Greeks and Portuguese but there is little information on how they fit in with other Europeans.

Religious differences partly coincided with ethnic differences. The virtual coincidence of Dutch Reformed Church membership with Afrikaner origin has already been mentioned. Similarly membership of the Greek Orthodox Church was patently limited to the Greeks. Among other Christians the major divisions were Anglicans, who were most numerous, Roman Catholics, and non-Conformists. In Southern Rhodesia, Rogers and Frantz have shown that in general Roman Catholics were more tolerant of African political advancement than other groups, but the effect of this on political alignment appears to have been negligible (Rogers and Frantz, 1962:303). The Jews, although few in number, were internally divided into Ashkenazi and Sephardic, but it is not clear to what extent intermarriage between these groups has taken place. The Jews were mainly business and professional men and tended thus to be concentrated in the higher socioeconomic categories. Rogers and Frantz show that on the whole in Southern Rhodesia they were slightly more liberal in their outlook toward race relations than Christians, except Roman Catholics, but the effect of socioeconomic status and length of residence must be taken into account here (Rogers and Frantz, 1962:303).

Of most significance as far as social and political action is concerned was socioeconomic stratification. The existence of a large population of Africans who have by convention nearly all been restricted to unskilled occupations and to a smaller extent to semiskilled occupations has meant that the incoming European population has been selected, both legally and economically, specifically to fill skilled, higher supervisory, managerial, and professional and higher administrative posts. Table 2 sets out the proportions of Europeans, Asians, and Eurafricans in broad occupational categories for the census of 1961.

Table 2. Broad European Distribution of European Asian and "Colored" Males, 1961.

	Rhodesia			Zambia		
	EURO.	ASIAN	COL.	EURO.	ASIAN	COL.
Professional, Technical and Related Workers	14.9	2.4	2.7	18.1	1.7	4.1
Administrative, Executive and Managerial	15.6	17.5	1.9	13.1	13.6	1.1
Clerical Workers	13.6	9.2	7.1	10.0	1.4	2.4
Sales Workers	7.0	49.4	3.2	3.4	77.7	4.1
Farmers, Fishermen, Hunters, Loggers and Related Workers	12.2	1.2	4.7	5.2	0.3	10.3
Miners, Quarrymen and Related Workers	1.5	—	1.6	11.2	—	—
Workers in Transport and Communication Occupations	4.7	3.6	10.9	5.1	0.2	7.3
Craftsmen, Production-process Workers and Labourers (not elsewhere classified)	26.3	13.2	60.9	28.9	4.4	69.6
Service, Sport and Recreation Workers	4.2	3.5	7.0	5.0	0.7	1.1
Total in Labor Force	62,914	1,726	1,708	23,316	2,020	369
Armed Forces and Not Elsewhere Classified	2,428	46	156	1,009	29	27
Total	65,342	1,772	1,864	24,327	2,049	396

Sources: Rhodesia: *1961 Census of the European, Asian and Coloured Population,* Table 22. Zambia: *1961 Census of the European, Asian and Coloured Population,* Table 9.

Differentiation and Stratification Within Racial Groups

Among the Europeans, approximately 25 percent of the males were managerial, administrative, and clerical workers; 14 percent were foremen and skilled workers, another 14 percent craftsmen and 12 percent professional and technical. The socioeconomic stratification associated with this occupational distribution is correlated with differences in political alignment. Rogers and Frantz point out that people at different levels of socioeconomic stratification had contrasting attitudes toward the advancement of Africans. The professional and technical workers were least rigid in their attitudes toward change in restrictive practices against Africans, followed in order by the managerial, administrative, and clerical workers; farmers, hunters, and lumbermen; sales workers, operating transport workers, foremen and skilled workers, service workers, and mine and quarry workers, and finally by the craftsmen, who were least willing to see changes (1962:Fig. 6, p. 303). At the referenda in Southern Rhodesia for self-government in 1922 and for federation with Northern Rhodesia and Nyasaland there was a cleavage between the colonial civil servants, especially those at the upper levels, and the miners, traders, and farmers. This led to a difference in political orientation reflected in the cleavage between "settler" and "official" representation in the Legislative Councils, a difference that turned particularly, as in Rhodesia, on the policy toward African advancement. There was, however, a recognized status equality between officials in the higher echelons of mining company bureaucracies, the higher officials of the administration, richer farmers, and leaders of the Anglican and major non-Conformist churches.

The correlation between socioeconomic status and race attitudes is not difficult to understand. The interests of professional workers, businessmen, and industrialists were not threatened in the same way by African competition as those of artisans, mine employees, and small farmers. Yet, on the other hand, these differences in alignment toward Africans as a category should be seen in context, for the opposition of Europeans as a whole to Africans as a whole tends to bridge the cleavages among them. No systematic information is available about the degree to which intermarriage, entertaining, and other forms of social intercourse take place across socioeconomic barriers, but the general impression is that, in the face of an African out-group, the distinctions among the Europeans who share special social economic and political privileges are diminished by common opposition to a racially defined group which challenges their right to these privileges.

It is for this reason that immigrants newly arrived from Britain and other European countries in which there are no clear-cut racial divisions very quickly assume the attitudes toward, and accept the stereotypes about, Africans which are common among Europeans in Central Africa. They move directly into a privileged position vis-à-vis Africans and are subjected to the intense personal pressures of a small minority group to conform to the norms of behavior which protect this position against challenge from Africans. The ranks are closed and internal differentiation in terms of ethnicity, religion, or socioeconomic status tends to become blurred.

The Asian communities are similarly divided by ethnic, religious, caste, and socio-economic status.[10] Asian immigrants have come into Central Africa from South Africa as well as from different parts of India and Pakistan. Thus, although the majority are Gujarati speaking, there are nevertheless some who speak Tamil or Hindi. Those at present in Central Africa appear to have been drawn from one or two castes of approximately the same status, though apparently marriages are still contracted within the appropriate caste. Until recently it has been customary for men to find wives from appropriate castes in India and Pakistan. A more important distinction is on religious grounds. In Southern Rhodesia, according to the most recent census, about one half of the Asians were Hindu, about one third Moslem, one sixth Roman Catholic, with small numbers of other Christian and other religions. The religious division relates to the political division between India and Pakistan, which correspondingly affects relationships within the Asian community. In Malawi there is a sizable Sikh community.

The majority of the Asians are involved in trading and commerce with smaller numbers in service (largely as waiters) and in skilled trades. The range of incomes is very wide, but the majority appear to live near poverty (see Dotson, 1961). Caste and religious proscriptions lead to a number of close-knit endogamous groups in the Asian community, but the effects of the internal divisions are not immediately discernible in social and political action as a whole.

The "colored" communities are internally differentiated by parental origin, by religion, and to a much lesser extent by socioeconomic stratification.[11] Some "colored" people came to Rhodesia with the pioneers in 1890 from the Cape where the "Cape Coloreds" have long been recognized as a distinct racial community. The descendants of these consider themselves an elite in the colored communities today. The Eurafricans are the progeny of mixed descent, either directly or by descent from parents themselves of mixed descent. The 1956 census showed that about 57 percent of colored people had both parents who themselves were colored. But a substantial number of others were the progeny of unions of European men with either colored or African women. A small minority were

10. There is a lack of systematic sociological data on the Asians in Central Africa. There appear to be only two papers available at present, i.e., Dotson, 1961, 1963. The material presented here is from these two papers supplemented by general impressions.
11. The data are derived primarily from Dotson (1963) and from private communications from Mrs. P. Wheeldon, whose assistance I gratefully acknowledge.

derived from unions with Indian men and African women. The social ranking of people of mixed parentage demonstrates the pervasive character of race. Colored persons whose parents were a white father and a colored mother were more highly ranked than those whose parents were both colored. Those whose parents were a white father and an African mother were ranked lower than those whose mother was not African, and those whose father was Asian and mother African were ranked lowest of all.

Religious and socioeconomic differentiation apparently do not play an important part in social interaction. Nearly half of the colored people in Southern Rhodesia are Roman Catholic and a quarter Anglican. Occupationally they fill mainly skilled, semiskilled, and supervisory posts, but on the whole they were relatively small populations of 10,600 in Rhodesia, 2000 in Zambia, and 1500 in Malawi in 1961. The communities in which they are settled—mainly in the towns—and within which virtually all their social contracts are confined, are small. Relationships among the coloreds, therefore, exist on a personal, face-to-face basis so that it is difficult for an outsider to perceive the social divisions among them. The community, hence, appears to be unstructured, but this is due in part also to uncertainty of identity and status inconsistency of the coloreds, whose social origins are in two racial groups of widely disparate social standing.

The Africans, constituting by far the largest proportion of the population, appear on the whole to be less differentiated internally than the other racial groups. Most significant divisions seem to have been on tribal, religious, and socioeconomic grounds. As already pointed out, Central Africa is ethnographically complex. The 150-odd distinguishable groups may be classified into 10 major ethnic categories and about 30 subsections within these groups representing clusters of groups with approximately similar linguistic and cultural characteristics (as discussed earlier). These divisions appear to have had little significance as distinct cultural groups before they were incorporated into a single political structure by the British at the close of the nineteenth century, when people of different backgrounds were confronted with one another in various labor centers. Here where workers from an extensive hinterland collected in towns or on plantations the distinctiveness of customs and languages became apparent and formed the basis of social differentiation. This differentiation was an essential process in the simplification of social relationships in novel circumstances, since ethnicity became a category of interaction defining appropriate modes of behavior between people in situations where the transitory nature of social contact entailed only superficial relationships. The process of categorization was taken to the extent that the wide range of tribes encountered in an urban situation, as on the Copperbelt, for example, could be compressed into five or six

J. C. Mitchell: Race and Status in South Central Africa

major ethnic types. The variation between persons from divisions within an ethnic category became imperceptible to a member from some other category, and the behavior adopted toward all people placed into one category was determined by one exemplar people. Thus a person from the Ngoni people could not discern the difference between Bemba-speaking people such as the Lungu, Tabwa, Mukulu, and Aushi and reacted to all of these as if they were Bemba. Similarly a person from these people could not perceive the differences between the Ngoni, Chewa, Nsenga, and Kunda and reacted to all of them as if they were Ngoni (Mitchell, 1956c, 1962). The hostility arising from military rivalry in precolonial times which has persisted into work situations, where these antagonisms must be suppressed, has been dissipated to some extent by institutionalized joking relationships between these broad "tribal" categories (Mitchell, 1956c).

The differentiation by ethnicity, however, does not *per se* imply superordination and subordination. It is primarily a matter of "social distance" in that people are prepared to accept members of some tribal groups into closer personal relationships with them than other tribal groups. The social distance, however, is perceived by each group separately in terms of superiority and inferiority by reason of the assumption that the people with whom one associates closely are more worthy than people with whom one does not associate. Consequently the public reputation of some groups influences their ratings in terms of social distance, and some "tribes" are relatively highly ranked by most groups and so carry high prestige in general. The Bemba and the Ndebele, for example, are highly ranked in general by groups which are both culturally similar to, and very different from, the two categories involved. They enjoy, therefore, a generally high prestige among all groups, a fact that is probably related to their military reputations in precolonial days. On the other hand, the people from the northwestern region of Zambia—that is, the Lovale, Luchaze, and Chokwe—seem to be ranked low in prestige by all groups except by themselves, a fact that is probably related to the common stereotype that these peoples habitually accepted jobs in towns involving the disposal of human feces. The important distinction here between the general principle of stratification by socioeconomic status and the rating in terms of ethnic social distance is that the evaluation by socioeconomic status is subscribed to by both those at the upper and those at the lower reaches of the system; "tribalism" or "ethnicity" in Central Africa, however, does not provide a mode of evaluation that is accepted by both the rankers and the ranked. Thus the Lovale people do not accept the low position they are accorded by, say, the Bemba.[12] It is a

12. Similar ranking of tribal groups occur among those people who were at one time incorporated into the kingdoms set up by dissident groups from the Zulu, such as the Ndebele and

Differentiation and Stratification Within Racial Groups

basis of social differentiation, therefore, which is likely to be the origin of disharmony unless it is counteracted by other bonds which render divisions nugatory.

Socioeconomic stratification provides one such basis for the bridging of the divisions among tribal groups. Although the sorts of occupation open to Africans have in general been severely curtailed by the color bar, at least until recently in Malawi and Zambia, and still in Rhodesia, nevertheless the Africans see the occupations they are able to fill as being differentiated in terms of a scale of general social prestige. This scale shares many features with those of occupational rating in other countries. This is illustrated in the ranking of occupations by 1455 African secondary school pupils in Rhodesia (Table 3). The occupations ranging from high to low prestige take up the following order in terms of a mean occupational prestige ranking:

Professional and white collar	1.32
Supervisory and police	1.66
Skilled	1.93
Semiskilled	2.01
Unskilled	2.74

As in all occupational prestige rankings, several different principles or dimensions lie behind these ratings: The usual factors of income, power, and community service underlie occupational prestige in Central Africa as elsewhere. But African respondents felt that high-ranking occupations were also "civilized" occupations. The significance of this factor in occupational prestige lies in the relationships of Africans to Europeans in the social structure as a whole. The Europeans occupying, as they have done, the economically, socially, and politically dominant positions have become exemplars of the values underlying the modern social system. One of the striking features of this system is its quality of "civilization" associated with life in towns in contrast to the "traditional" way of life of the rural areas. The occupations at the top of the prestige ranking, therefore, are distinguished by "civilization" which is also the characteristic of the Europeans in their socially superior position in the system of racial stratification. Those who fill the occupations at the top of the scale, by virtue of their higher salaries and better education, are able to follow a "civilized" or European style of life to a degree that those at the bottom of the scale are unable, because they lack the financial means and education.[13]

Ngoni. Little is known about intertribal relationships in Malawi or Rhodesia as a whole. Nowadays nationalist ideology abjures the recognition of tribal antipathies, which makes it difficult to assemble accurate data on this phenomenon.

13. See also Mitchell and Epstein, 1959; Mitchell, 1964; 1966; Mitchell and Irvine, 1966.

J. C. Mitchell: Race and Status in South Central Africa

Table 3. Prestige Ratings of Occupations.

(1,230 Boys and 255 Girls at Secondary Schools)

OCCUPA-TIONS	VERY HIGH	HIGH	NOT HIGH OR LOW	LOW	VERY LOW	TOTAL	DON'T KNOW	MEAN RATING	S.D.
Weights	(0.59)	(1.54)	(2.21)	(2.80)	(3.60)				
	i	ii	iii	iv	v	vi	vii	viii	ix
Lawyer	1,228	147	45	18	15	1,453	32	0.79	0.53
School Inspector	1,144	253	40	16	13	1,466	19	0.85	0.54
Sec. Sch. Teacher	1,009	426	36	7	3	1,481	4	0.92	0.51
Medical Officer	914	434	100	10	18	1,476	9	1.03	0.63
Headmaster	797	567	87	12	7	1,470	15	1.08	0.58
Priest	822	439	150	34	16	1,461	24	1.13	0.68
Afr. Min. of Rel.	776	491	153	33	20	1,473	12	1.17	0.69
Senior Clerk	610	720	124	22	2	1,478	7	1.23	0.58
Sergeant in Army	595	549	206	64	48	1,462	23	1.37	0.78
Radio Mechanic	501	618	296	41	3	1,459	26	1.39	0.66
Radio Announcer	483	683	271	27	11	1,475	10	1.39	0.64
Bus Owner	462	687	254	46	18	1,467	18	1.42	0.67
Afr. Police Insp.	528	611	218	55	58	1,470	15	1.43	0.78
Newspaper Editor	475	619	247	66	37	1,444	41	1.45	0.74
Medical Orderly	385	719	310	47	7	1,468	17	1.48	0.63
Afr. Welfare Officer	364	644	292	64	13	1,377	108	1.51	0.67
Hlth. Demonstrator	392	689	300	62	35	1,478	7	1.53	0.70
Typist	330	741	338	54	7	1,470	15	1.54	0.62
Prim. Sch. Teacher	327	751	318	63	16	1,475	10	1.55	0.64
Trade Union Br. Sec.	310	593	313	63	27	1,306	179	1.58	0.69
Garage Mechanic	326	647	397	83	14	1,467	18	1.60	0.67
Laboratory Asst.	263	651	373	65	19	1,371	114	1.63	0.65
Preacher	336	583	426	84	34	1,463	22	1.64	0.72
Carpenter	164	568	591	104	28	1,455	30	1.84	0.62
African Constable	238	548	414	145	117	1,462	23	1.86	0.81
Reporter	156	552	518	140	70	1,436	49	1.90	0.70
Bus Driver	156	468	650	159	27	1,460	25	1.91	0.64
Storekeeper	142	480	638	174	33	1,467	18	1.94	0.64
Taxi Driver	123	456	698	153	38	1,468	17	1.96	0.62
Diviner	292	306	407	210	225	1,440	45	2.04	0.97
Foreman	105	457	524	263	112	1,461	24	2.10	0.72
Painter	80	327	723	294	42	1,466	19	2.13	0.60
Plumber	137	366	531	274	134	1,442	43	2.13	0.77
Lorry Driver	79	341	699	285	62	1,466	19	2.14	0.62
Lift Operator	81	304	552	293	119	1,349	136	2.21	0.71
Office Messenger	60	257	668	371	99	1,455	30	2.27	0.63
Nat. Com. Messenger	94	309	517	334	209	1,463	22	2.30	0.78
Shoe Maker	49	185	713	411	100	1,458	27	2.33	0.60
Bricklayer	78	244	524	364	252	1,462	23	2.40	0.77

Table 3 (continued)

OCCUPA-TIONS	VERY HIGH	HIGH	NOT HIGH OR LOW	LOW	VERY LOW	TOTAL	DON'T KNOW	MEAN RATING	S.D.
Weights	(0.59)	(1.54)	(2.21)	(2.80)	(3.60)				
	i	ii	iii	iv	v	vi	vii	viii	ix
Station Boy (Rlys.)	48	192	562	443	201	1,446	39	2.44	0.68
Bus Conductor	30	152	630	472	179	1,463	22	2.47	0.62
Domestic Servant	53	193	471	444	295	1,456	29	2.52	0.74
Market Seller	18	112	612	484	244	1,470	15	2.56	0.61
Petrol Pump Boy	26	99	494	573	252	1,444	41	2.61	0.62
Hotel Waiter	23	104	463	595	277	1,462	23	2.64	0.63
Cook	58	92	394	534	383	1,461	24	2.68	0.73
Pedlar	16	60	420	434	377	1,307	178	2.76	0.65
Newspaper Boy	35	67	348	574	445	1,469	16	2.79	0.68
Road Repairer	87	91	206	305	790	1,479	6	2.94	0.87
Tea Boy	26	50	230	585	571	1,462	23	2.94	0.65
Wood Cutter	20	50	249	506	639	1,464	21	2.98	0.66
Lorry Boy	18	42	255	506	656	1,477	8	2.99	0.64
Garden Boy	40	52	164	414	801	1,471	14	3.07	0.71
Dagga Boy	29	51	154	342	898	1,474	11	3.14	0.68
Sweeper of San. Lanes	34	41	137	268	970	1,450	35	3.19	0.68
Scavenger	73	38	65	98	1,166	1,440	45	3.27	0.77

Religious differentiation among the African population tends to some extent to be correlated with both tribe and education. Flowing from the history of mission endeavor in Central Africa, certain regions have been proselytized mainly by particular mission societies. The people in those areas, usually of one particular tribal group, tend therefore to have been influenced by one particular religious denomination. Thus the Bemba are predominantly Roman Catholic, the Barotse, Protestants from the Paris Evangelical mission, the Ngoni members of the Dutch Reformed Church, the Lakeside Tonga of Malawi, the Church of Scotland. There is, therefore, a partial coincidence of religious with tribal differentiation.

Education had been almost entirely in the hands of the missionaries from the turn of the century until the 1940's, so that there tends also to be a partial coincidence of education with Christianity. Unfortunately there are no statistics available showing the proportion of Christians among Africans as a whole. The social survey of the line-of-rail towns in Northern Rhodesia between 1951 and 1954 showed that among adult male and females 32.8 percent were pagan; 23.7 percent Roman Catholic; 11.7 percent Watchtower; 10 percent Free Church; 6.3 percent Dutch Reformed; 2.5 percent Separatist sects; 1.3 percent Moslem and the rest other Christian sects.[14] In 1960 during the general budget survey of African families it was found that about one quarter of adult males were pagan, slightly more were Roman Catholic, about 15 percent were Free Church,

14. Unpublished results of Rhodes-Livingstone Urban Social Survey.

and 10 percent Jehovah's Witnesses, 17 percent Dutch Reformed, and the rest were of the Christian denominations and Moslems (Gann, 1964:456). The distribution of religions in the rural population is unknown.

It seems likely that in the first instance educated Christian Africans are distinguished from uneducated pagans, but that amongst educated Christians, in turn, members of Roman Catholic, Dutch Reformed, Anglicans, and Free Church congregations are drawn largely from the same tribal groups, so that tribe and religious denomination tend to coincide. At the same time the absolute number of Christians with secondary school education—that is, those among the educated elite—is so small that if they are to find fellows of commensurate educational status they need to look beyond the confines of their own religious denomination and tribal group. Among the less well educated, particularly in the towns, other religious movements have arisen, like the Jehovah's Witnesses (Watchtower), which unite people of different tribal backgrounds.

In the African population as a whole, therefore, there is an educated elite employed in the occupations at the top of the prestige scale all of whom are Christians of various denominations and all of whom have secondary school education. By virtue of their incomes and familiarity with Western culture, their dress, entertainments, interests, and patterns of consumption are like those of the Europeans insofar as their finances will allow. Ranking lower in prestige are those with less education in lower status occupations. Their patterns of consumption are partially traditional and partly Western. They are marked off from one another by tribal and religious differences, the majority of pagans being employed in the least prestigious occupations and following the least "civilized" way of life.

ELITES, REFERENCE GROUPS, AND
RELATIVE DEPRIVATION

An appreciation of the position of the intellectual elite within the underprivileged African population as a whole is crucial to the understanding of the social and political development that has affected the system of racial stratification in Central Africa. Skin color and other physical characteristics within a system of racial stratification, as Blumer points out, allow "an easy and repetitive 'pegging' of feelings, views and definitions."

> The sense of biological difference sustains and rivets given race relations in another and more important way, namely, in that whatever is ascribed to the group as part of its racial being is automatically regarded as a constant and as transmissable intact from generation to generation. Thus a

fixity is imported to the complex of views and feelings that grow up around a belief in biological difference, that is not found in the same degree in the case of other kinds of group difference. (Blumer, 1955:9)

From the European point of view, since they have a privileged position to defend, it has been convenient for them to assume that the way of life of racial groups is intrinsically linked to their physical characteristics, and to justify their political, economic, and social behavior in terms of beliefs of this sort. Thus beliefs about the inability of Africans to think abstractly and hence to be occupied in managerial or technical posts, to lay a line of bricks on the level or set the frame of a door square and hence to be employed as craftsmen, to understand the principles of democracy, to comprehend fully the tenets of Christianity, to appreciate art, music and literature, or to become civilized people in general, have been accepted by whites in Central Africa. These beliefs have become linked with a strangely outdated evolutionary point of view which holds that the Africans have not yet reached the developmental stage to be able to follow a civilized way of life and, as has been pointed out, constitute a part of the myth validating the Europeans' superior position in the social structure.

The missionaries, on the other hand, whose calling was to bring the Gospel to pagan Africa, saw the Christian way of life as implying a civilized way of life. Thus an eminent missionary saw the role of the first Free Church of Scotland mission at Livingstonia in Nyasaland as "an instruction at once industrial and educational, to teach the books of the Gospel and the arts of civilized life to the natives of the country" (quoted in Rotberg, 1965:6). As Rotberg observes: "The missionaries urged Africans to copy the White man's ways—to put on clothes, to purge themselves of sin and corruption, and accept the truths of the Gospel as a complete code of conduct." He concludes that in general "the missions and the overall impact of European experience contributed profoundly to the outward and inward Westernisation of the peoples of trans-Zambezia" (Rotberg, 1965:9).

From the African point of view, then, the superiority of the Europeans rested not upon their innate abilities, that is, their race, but rather upon their way of life, their skills, practices, customs, beliefs and values, seen as a whole and appreciated in terms of "civilization." Access, therefore, to the social, economic, and especially political privileges enjoyed by the whites from the point of view of the African depended upon acquisition of civilized behavior.

The standards of the dominant groups, therefore, became linked inevitably with the power they exercised. In terms of the social system as a whole, they became an elite but an elite into and out of which there was no circulation from the rest of the system. Members of other racial groups

J. C. Mitchell: Race and Status in South Central Africa

aspired to the standards set by the Europeans but could not themselves become members of the European community. The Europeans thus as a social group became a "reference group" for certain styles of person in the Asian "colored," and African communities in the sense that these people measured their behavior against what they perceived to be the pattern followed by the Europeans.[15]

Among Africans the process has already been described and is documented in several different places (Schwab, 1961; McCulloch, 1956; Mitchell, 1956b, 1956c, 1960b; Epstein, 1961). Among Asians the Dotsons report that "younger Indians are slowly beginning to take on the value system of the main consumption economy" (F. and L. Dotson, 1961:65). The colored community, on the other hand, as has been pointed out, follow a European way of life in any case and do not seem to be affected much by the cultural background of their part African parentage.

Therefore, although the social system as a whole was stratified by race, and each racial group in turn was divided internally in terms of varied principles, all forms of racial groups had a common reference in the idea of a "civilized way of life." The "civilized way of life" in these terms may be thought of as a major value in the Parsonian sense, but it becomes a source of conflict rather than the occasion for consensus, as Parsons argues.

The conflict arises on several different grounds. The orientation of the younger Asians toward a European way of life, for example, conflicts with the more traditional outlook of the older generation, so that different sections of the community justify their behavior and have their expectation of the behavior of others in different norms (F. and L. Dotson, 1961:65). The same process occurs among the African population where the orientation of the younger, urban, Christian, educated population toward the European way of life conflicts with that of the older, tribal, pagan, illiterate population.

But a radical conflict exists between the achievement-oriented value system upon which the bureaucratic industrial, commercial, and administrative organization is based and with which socioeconomic stratification is closely linked, and the ascriptive-oriented racial philosophy upon which the social and political structures have been based. This means that it was precisely the Africans, Asians, and coloreds who had responded to the challenge of achievement in terms of Western values who found that their aspirations were blocked by the "color bar." They suffered acute relative deprivation, and it is they who have been foremost in challenging

---

15. Goldthorpe (1961:157) and Jones (1962:40) object to this argument on the grounds that the adoption of "European" practices is simply because they are more convenient. My argument is that the adoption of the practices acquires an additional symbolic meaning within a system of racial stratification.

the system of racial stratification and in providing the leadership, especially among the Africans, of industrial, religious, and political protest movements.[16]

AUTHORITY, THE SOCIAL ORDER, AND CHANGE

Protest movements of these kinds were essentially rooted in the rejection of the assumed privilege of Europeans as a racial category to control—and therefore to restrict—the access of members of other races to life-chances. The African trade unions protested against the exclusion of Africans from posts carrying high authority and responsibility—and therefore high wages—and against the difference in wages of Europeans and Africans when they were employed in similar occupations. Rural Africans in overcrowded reserves resented the alienation of large tracts of land to Europeans and in defiance of countermanding legislation became squatters on soil which, in comparison with the land they were entitled to cultivate, was manifestly underutilized. Separatist churches broke away from mission churches, partly because the Gospels as interpreted by the European missionaries implied a more radical break with traditional customs than they were prepared to make, but also because authority within the churches was monopolized by Europeans. These disabilities, combined with the innumerable humiliations suffered by Africans in their day-to-day contact with Europeans, provided a fertile loam in which movements of political protest could strike deep roots.[17]

But paradoxically conflict can only arise out of common interests: it is only because the pursuit of their interests by one group (the Africans) had been frustrated by the other group (the Europeans), who were pursuing the same interests, that these protests arose. While European prospectors were interested only in rocks in which Africans were not, there was no cause for conflict between them. But when mining enterprises were established, which involved the alienation of land and control over the fate of people, in which the Africans were deeply interested, then conflicts were bound to arise.

The shift in the focus of conflict from the direct command over resources, such as land, labor, or cattle, which was apparent in the earliest

16. The leadership for such movements could hardly have come from the chiefs, who had a vested interest in a tribally oriented, traditional way of life. The involvement of the chiefs, either as supporters of nationalist movements or frequently as opponents to them, came when the movements were well established.

17. Descriptions of the rise of African nationalist movements in these terms can be found in Epstein, 1958; Rotberg, 1965; van Velsen, 1964b; Hall, 1965; Keatley, 1963.

J. C. Mitchell: Race and Status in South Central Africa

days of colonization, to the more indirect command through positions in authority and control in the new commercial, industrial and administrative structure, had to wait until the Africans were able to appreciate the significance and relevance of these positions. In other words, it was only when Africans began to accept the norms and values underlying the social order introduced by the Europeans that they began to compete with them in terms of the same interests. These interests were, of course, centered in the gaining of access to positions of authority through which the allocation of rewards and benefits could be controlled.

Thus Africans and Europeans involved in a single framework of political, social, and economic relations were bound to each other by interests in the same goals and to this extent shared the same set of values. There was consensus between Africans and Europeans about the desirability of the goals defined by these values, but it became the basis of their conflict, for the Africans did not concur with the status they had been allocated in respect to their access to these goals. The common interests became both the basis of cooperation and the source of conflict.

Gluckman, in describing the parallel situation of Africans in South Africa, makes this point. He shows how for a variety of reasons Africans have become dependent on wage labor for subsistence. He goes on to say that "the small groups of Whites in Zululand derive their control over the Africans from their technical superiority, but it was money rather than the Maxim gun or telephone which established social cohesion by creating common, if dissimilar, interests in a single economic and political system, though it is one with irreconcilable conflicts" (1958:43). In criticizing Malinowski, who had argued that the mines had provided a basis of cooperation between Europeans and Africans in South Africa, he points out that the industrial situation at the same time allowed their opposition to be expressed in a new form (1949:8). It is part of Gluckman's thesis that where a major cleavage does not divide a community into disparate parts —that is, when what Dahrendorf calls pluralism exists[18]—then people who are divided in some situations are united in others, and these counterbalancing cleavages prevent the bonds among them from tearing apart (1955a:24–26). But in Central African contexts the division of the races has tended to prevail in most social situations involving white and black. Although both white and black may belong to the same Christian denomination, their common interest in their religion does not obliterate the

18. Dahrendorf (1959:214). Dahrendorf's use of "pluralism" here implies exactly the opposite of what I imply by "the plural society." He implies by it that different groups exercise authority in different situations so that power is never concentrated in the hands of one single group. I imply by "the plural society" that the society is divided into two groups linked only by a minimum of functionally specific and affectively neutral bonds, which is what he implies by "superimposition," the opposite of "pluralism." See Mitchell, 1960c: 28, 1960b:294.

racial division. Although Africans and Europeans have common occupational interests, such as teaching, business, or farming, these interests do not impel them sufficiently to overcome the racial cleavages between them to allow common associations, such as teachers' associations, trade associations, or farmers' unions, through which they can further their interests together. Instead these associations are formed on racial grounds. Although white and black workers may both have joint interests in opposition to their common employers, this does not allow them to form a single trade union to prosecute their common interests—they form separate trade unions. In other words, the same people meet in different contexts but in identical relations of conflict (Dahrendorf, 1959:214).

Dahrendorf considers that real societies will fall somewhere along a continuum between the ideal types of extreme superimposition at one end to extreme pluralism at the other. The social orders in Malawi and Zambia in the period just before they gained independence, and in Rhodesia at the present time (1966), fall remarkably close to the hypothetical "ideal type" at the extreme "superimposition" end of this continuum. Dahrendorf describes this as follows:

> At the one extreme of the scale . . . we should find a society in which all patterns, issues and contexts of political conflict are superimposed and combined into two large camps. There is superimposition with respect to the structure of authority and of the scales of reward that make up social stratification. Whoever occupies a position of authority has wealth, prestige and other emoluments of social status at his disposal too: whoever is excluded from political authority has no hope of climbing very far on the scale of social status. Furthermore the conflicts arising from different associations are superimposed. Power is generalized in the sense that a homogeneous and interchangeable elite governs an identifiable subjected class in the state, in industry, in the army and in all other associations. Finally, such non-class conflicts as exist in society are congruent with the conflicts arising out of the unequal distributions of authority. Political class conflict, industrial class conflict, regional conflicts, conflicts between town and country, possibly racial and religious conflicts—all are superimposed so as to form a single and all embracing antagonism. (Dahrendorf, 1959:316)

Dahrendorf then comments: "Under these conditions the intensity of political conflict reaches its maximum," and it is when conflicts are most intense that structural change is likely to be most radical (Dahrendorf, 1959:234-35).

Dahrendorf here relates radical social change to the intensity of conflict, and the intensity of conflict in turn to the degree to which interest groups are congruent in the society. In effect he takes conflict and the type of change associated with it to be variables dependent on the struc-

J. C. Mitchell: Race and Status in South Central Africa

ture of social relationships in the society.[19] The evidence from Central Africa, however, suggests that the structure of social relationships may in turn be affected by the nature of conflict. Conditions for the development of "pluralism" in Dahrendorf's sense came into being when Africans began to adopt Western institutions and the value orientations associated with them. In fact the "pluralism" that might have reduced the conflict in the system never came into being. Where organizations arose which crosscut the black-white cleavage they tended to dissolve when black-white relationships deteriorated: the bonds between the two racial groups within the organizations have not been sufficiently strong to overcome their opposition outside them. It is no accident that no truly multiracial political party has survived in any of the three territories, although several have been launched (see van Velsen, 1964b: 151). Even multiracial social clubs have tended to founder. In other words, the opposition between the two racial groups has prevented the development of "plurality": the lack of plurality is the consequence of conflict. The conflict, in turn, is derived from the wish of the dominant group to retain its privileged access to the economic, social, and political benefits of racial stratification, while the subjected group wishes to secure for itself greater access to these benefits.

The political changes in Malawi and Zambia have been both radical and sudden in that they involved widespread substitution of incumbents of authority position, and these changes were effected within a few years—between 1960 and 1963 in Malawi and 1960 and 1964 in Zambia. These changes were preceded by violent demonstrations leading to the declaration of states of emergency and the consequent use of police forces and militia to suppress them. After independence in these two countries there has been what Dahrendorf would call a partial dissociation of authority and associations. Many important posts in government, particularly those of a technical nature, are still filled by Europeans. Europeans still operate the larger farms employing many Africans. The large industrial and commercial firms are still managed by Europeans, and the leaders of the main churches are not yet Africans. The salaries of such Europeans who have retained their positions are still high; and they still constitute a substantial part of the standard-setting group—the social and cultural elite. Yet Africans have taken over all the important political and administrative positions in the government, and it is they who control the allocation of public benefits and rewards, such as schooling, health, services, positions of authority in the state, and so on. In other words, some distribution of authority into disparate "associations" has taken place.

19. Note for example his proposition 4.1.1.3: "The intensity of class conflict decreases to the extent that class conflicts in different associations are dissociated (and not superimposed)" (1959:239).

Conflict has manifestly been reduced. The underprivileged class has gained political control but the Europeans have lost only a part of their privilege —that related to political authority—not their social and economic ascendancy.[20] It is therefore difficult to argue that the conflict has been reduced because of an increase in plurality. Both phenomena are derived from a common cause. In Rhodesia, on the other hand, the European oligarchy had felt it so important to suppress conflict that in November 1965 it assumed independence from Britain, whose policies were in the direction of greater African participation in government, and has continued to make laws even more stringent and draconian to suppress the challenge to its position of authority.

Dahrendorf argues that the suppression of conflict in this way in the long run is impossible and goes on to say:

> ... where an attempt is made to suppress conflict altogether, either of two consequences is likely to occur within at most a decade. Either suppression amounts to complete non-recognition and exclusion of opposition, in which case revolutionary changes of the Hungarian type are virtually bound to occur; or suppression of opposition is coupled with a careful and continuous scrutiny of the embryonic manifest interests of the potential opposition, and changes are introduced from time to time which incorporate some of these interests. In the latter case, suppression is not complete, and violent conflicts may simmer under the surface for a long time before they erupt; the ineffectiveness of the former type of suppression needs no comment. (Dahrendorf, 1959:224–25)

These are, by Dahrendorf's own admission, "gross assertions" and he clearly intended them to relate to circumstances in western Europe. Where, however, the opposing groups are identified easily by skin color, there is a marked disparity in the access to the instruments of power— in the last resort weapons and armaments; there is almost complete congruence of interest groups, and the dominant group ruthlessly suppresses all forms of organization through which opposition to it may be expressed. There seems no reason why, on the face of it, the dominant group cannot maintain its position indefinitely. The Europeans in South Africa and Rhodesia have done so for nearly eighty years, even though the measures they have had to adopt have become more and more severe to allow them to do so.

It is clear that many factors, some as yet unidentified and unanalyzed, play a part in determining the pace of change in the system of social

20. The struggle for independence was accompanied as in other African countries by an emphasis on "African" as against "European" cultural characteristics, such as the wearing of African traditional dress, the performance of African tribal dances, and a new interest in traditional African cultures. These features constitute a new element in social prestige, but they are concerned with relationships with other African states and with foreigners rather than with the internal social system.

J. C. Mitchell: Race and Status in South Central Africa

stratification based on racial criteria. In Africa, the ratio of one race to the other appears to be one important factor. The smaller the proportion of Europeans in the population as a whole, the sooner the Africans gain control.

In Central Africa, for example, in 1961 when independence was on the point of being achieved in Malawi and Zambia there were 3 and 22.5 Europeans respectively in every thousand of the population. In Rhodesia where the European minority still retains control, there were 59 Europeans in every thousand. At the crudest level there are more of the ruling racial class to bear arms to crush any violent expression of opposition. Furthermore where there are proportionately more of the dominant race available they are able to fill a greater proportion of the crucial economic and administrative posts through which the lives of the subject race are controlled.

But as the subordinate race becomes more and more dependent for its subsistence and welfare on the economic and administrative system manned by the dominant race, it becomes less and less inclined to destroy that system by violent protests. Progressive separation of Africans from dependence on land, especially because of the overcrowding and impoverishment of their rural homelands, with a correlated increasing dependence on wages, makes it more difficult for Africans to protest against the system. The pattern of distribution of Africans in industries and the effect of this on the organization of protests also affects the rate of political change. Where there is a concentration of Africans in one crucial industry, as in copper mining in Zambia, clearly the protest can be made more effective through solidary action in that industry than where the majority of workers are scattered in small enterprises, as on tobacco farms. This applies especially in Rhodesia where many of the workers are of foreign origin and have no involvement in seeing the social order changed: here it is much more difficult for concerted action to be organized. And, of course, if the ruling racial group impedes the development of organizations aiming to achieve the difficult task of coordinating actions across a wide variety of disparate interest groups—such as townsmen and countrymen, agricultural and industrial workers, foreign-born and home-born, people from different tribal and linguistic groups—by restricting the activities of all leaders and potential leaders, the change will obviously be delayed.

The timetable of change in any racially stratified society is determined by the interaction of such factors as the proportion of people in the dominant racial group and the involvement of the subordinate group in the economic enterprises controlled by the dominant race, as well as by unique historical factors which make it difficult to trap the flux of time in any net of sociological analysis.

BIBLIOGRAPHY

Adams, Bert N. 1966 Coercion and consensus theories: some unresolved issues. American Journal of Sociology, 71:714–17.

Baldwin, Robert E. 1962 Wage policy in a dual economy—the case of Northern Rhodesia. Race, 4:73–87.

Barnes, J. A. 1954 Politics in a Changing Society. Cape Town, Oxford University Press, for Rhodes-Livingstone Institute.

——— 1955 Race relations in the development of South Africa, in: Lind A. W. (ed.), Race Relations in World Perspective. Honolulu, University of Hawaii Press, pp. 167–86.

Brelsford, W. V. n.d. (circa 1956) The Tribes of Northern Rhodesia. Lusaka, Government Printer.

Blumer, Herbert G. 1955 Reflections on theory of race relations, in: Lind, A. W. (ed.), Race Relations in World Perspective. Honolulu, University of Hawaii Press, pp. 3–21.

Clegg, E. 1960 Race and Politics: Partnership in the Federation of Rhodesia and Nyasaland. London, Oxford University Press.

Colson, E. 1958 Marriage and the Family Among the Plateau Tonga of Northern Rhodesia. Manchester, Manchester University Press, for Rhodes-Livingstone Institute, Appendix III.

——— 1960 Social Organization of the Gwembe Tonga: Human Problems of Kariba, Vol. 1. Manchester, Manchester University Press, for Rhodes-Livingstone Institute.

——— 1962 The Plateau Tonga of Northern Rhodesia: Social and Religious Studies. Manchester, Manchester University Press.

——— and Gluckman, M. (eds.). 1951 Seven Tribes of British Central Africa. London, Oxford University Press, for Rhodes-Livingstone Institute.

Cunnison, I. G. 1959 The Luapula Peoples of Northern Rhodesia. Manchester University Press, for Rhodes-Livingstone Institute.

Dahrendorf, Ralf 1959 Class and Class Conflict in Industrial Society. Stanford, California, Stanford University Press.

Davis, K. 1948 Human Society. New York, The Macmillan Co.

——— and Moore, W. E. 1945 Some principles of stratification. American Sociological Review, 10:242–49.

Doke, C. 1931 The Lambas of Northern Rhodesia. London, George G. Harrap & Co.

Dotson, L. and F. 1961 Cultural values and housing needs, in: Apthorpe, R. (ed.), Social Research and Community Development. Based in the Fifteenth Conference of the Rhodes-Livingstone Institute for Social Research. Lusaka, Rhodes-Livingstone Institute, pp. 58–66.

——— 1963 Indians and coloureds in Rhodesia and Nyasaland. Race, 5:61–75. Reprinted in van den Berghe, P. (ed.), Africa: Social Problems of Change and Conflict (1965). San Francisco, Chandler Publishing, pp. 267–82.

341340

J. C. Mitchell: Race and Status in South Central Africa

Douglas, M. 1964 Matriliny and pawnship in Central Africa. Africa, *34*:301–13.

Epstein, A. L. 1958 Politics in an Urban African Community. Manchester, Manchester University Press, for Rhodes-Livingstone Institute.

—— 1961 The network and urban social organization. Rhodes-Livingstone Journal, *29*:29–62.

Fortune, G. 1959 The Bantu Languages of the Federation: A Preliminary Survey, Lusaka, Rhodes-Livingstone Institute.

Furnivall, J. S. 1948 Colonial Policy and Practice: A Comparative Study of Burma and Netherlands. Cambridge, Cambridge University Press.

Gann, L. H. 1958 The Birth of a Plural Society. Manchester, Manchester University Press, for Rhodes-Livingstone Institute.

—— 1960 History of Rhodesia and Nyasaland: 1889–1953, in: Brelsford, W. V. (ed.), Handbook to the Federation of Rhodesia and Nyasaland. London, Cassell & Co. pp. 57–116.

—— 1964 A History of Northern Rhodesia. London, Chatto & Windus.

Garbett, G. K. 1960 Growth and Change in a Shona Ward. Occasional paper No. 1, African Studies Dept. Salisbury, University College of Rhodesia and Nyasaland.

Gelfand, M. 1956 Medicine and Magic of the Mashona. Cape Town, Juta & Co.

—— 1959 Shona Ritual with Special Reference to the Chaminuka Cult. Cape Town, Juta & Co.

—— 1962 Shona Religion with Special Reference to the Makorekore. Cape Town, Juta & Co.

Gluckman, M. 1941 The Economy of the Central Barotse Plain. Rhodes-Livingstone Paper No. 7.

—— 1949 An Analysis of the Sociological Theories of Bronislaw Malinowski. Rhodes-Livingstone Paper No. 16. Cape Town: Oxford University Press, for Rhodes-Livingstone Institute.

—— 1955a Custom and Conflict in Africa. Oxford: Basil Blackwell.

—— 1955b The Judicial Process Among the Barotse of Northern Rhodesia. Manchester, Manchester University Press, for Rhodes-Livingstone Institute.

—— 1958 Analysis of a Social Situation in Modern Zululand. Rhodes-Livingstone Paper No. 29. Manchester, Manchester University Press.

Goldthorpe, J. E. 1961 Educated Africans: conceptual and terminological problems, in: Southall, A. (ed.), Social Change in Modern Africa. London. Oxford University Press, for International African Institute, pp. 144–58,

Gray, R. 1960 The Two Nations: Aspects of the Development of Race Relations in the Rhodesias and Nyasaland. London, Oxford University Press.

Hall, Richard 1965 Zambia. London, Pall Mall Press.

Hanna, A. J. 1956 The Beginnings of Rhodesia and North-Eastern Rhodesia 1859–95. Oxford, Clarendon Press.

Holleman, J. F. 1952 Shona Customary Law. Cape Town, Oxford University Press, for Beit Trust and Rhodes-Livingstone Institute.

Horton, John 1966 Order and conflict theories of social problems as competing ideologies. American Journal of Sociology, *71*:701–13.

Hughes, A. J. B. 1956 Kin Caste and Nation Among the Rhodesian Ndebele. Rhodes-Livingstone Paper No. 25. Manchester, Manchester University Press.

Jones, A. D. 1962 Two views of European influence of African behaviour, in: Dubb, A. A. (ed.), The Multiracial Society. Proceedings of the Sixteenth Conference of the Rhodes-Livingstone Institute. Lusaka, Rhodes-Livingstone Institute, pp. 39–48.

Kapferer, Bruce 1967 Cooperation, Leadership and Village Structure: A Preliminary Political and Economic Study of Ten Bisa Villages. Zambian Paper No. 1. Manchester, Manchester University Press.

Keatley, P. 1963 The Politics of Partnership. Penguin African Library AP2. Harmondsworth, Penguin Books.

Leys, C. 1959 European Politics in Southern Rhodesia. Oxford, Clarendon Press.

McCulloch, M. 1956 A Social Survey of the African Population of Livingstone, Rhodes-Livingstone Paper 26.

Marwick, M. G. 1965 Sorcery in Its Social Setting. New York, The Humanities Press.

Mason, P. 1958 The Birth of a Dilemma: The Conquest and Settlement of Rhodesia. London, Oxford University Press.

Miracle, M. 1960 Plateau Tonga entrepreneurs in historical inter-regional trade. Rhodes-Livingstone Journal, *26*:34–50.

Mitchell, J. C. 1956a The Yao Village. Manchester, Manchester University Press, for Rhodes-Livingstone Institute.

——— 1956b The African middle classes in British Central Africa, in: INCIDI, Development of a Middle Class in Tropical and Sub-Tropical Countries. Record of the 21st session held in London, September 13–16, 1955. Bruxelles: INCIDI: 222–232.

——— 1956c The Kalela Dance: Aspects of Social Relationships Among Urban Africans in Northern Rhodesia. Manchester, Manchester University Press, for Rhodes-Livingstone Institute. viii, 52 pp., Rhodes-Livingstone Paper 27.

——— 1960a The African Peoples, in: Brelsford, W. V. (ed.), Handbook of Rhodesia and Nyasaland. London: Cassell & Co., pp. 117–81.

——— 1960b White-collar workers and supervisors in a plural society. Civilizations, *10*:293–306.

——— 1960c Tribalism and the Plural Society: An Inaugural Lecture. London, Oxford University Press.

——— 1961 Chidzere's tree: a note on a Shona land-shrine and its significance. Nada, *38*:28–35.

——— 1962 Some aspects of tribal distance, in: Dubb, A. (ed.), The Multitribal Society: Proceedings of the Sixteenth Conference of the Rhodes-Livingstone Institute, pp. 1–38.

——— 1964 Occupational prestige and the social system: a problem in comparative sociology. International Journal of Comparative Sociology, 5:78–90.

────── 1966   Aspects of occupational prestige in a plural society, in: Lloyd, P. (ed.), The New Elites of Tropical Africa. London, Oxford University Press, for International African Institute, pp. 256–71.

────── and Epstein, A. L.   1959   Occupational prestige and social status among urban Africans in Northern Rhodesia. Africa, 29:22–40.

Mitchell, J. C. and Irvine, S. H.   1966   Social position and the grading of occupation. Rhodes-Livingstone Journal, 39:42–54.

Parsons, Talcott   1954   A revised analytical approach to the theory of social stratification, in Bendix, R., and Lipset, S. M. (eds.), Class, Status, and Power. London, Routledge & Kegan Paul, pp. 92–128.

Read, M.   1936   Traditions and prestige among the Ngoni. Africa.

────── 1956   The Ngoni of Nyasaland. New York, Oxford University Press.

Richards, A. I.   1939   Land, Labour and Diet in Northern Rhodesia. London, Oxford University Press, for International African Institute.

Rogers, Cyril A. and Frantz, C.   1962   Racial Themes in Southern Rhodesia: The Attitudes and Behavior of the White Population. New Haven, Yale University Press.

Rotberg, Robert I.   1965   The Rise of Nationalism in Central Africa: The Making of Malawi and Zambia 1873–1964. Cambridge, Mass., Harvard University Press.

Schwab, W.   1961   Social stratification in Gwelo, in: Southall, A. (ed.), Social Change in Modern Africa. London, Oxford University Press, for International African Institute, pp. 126–44.

Shibutani, Tamotsu and Kwan, Kian M.   1965   Ethnic Stratification: A Comparative Approach. New York and London, Macmillan.

Smith, E. W. and Dale, A.   1920   The Ila-Speaking Peoples of Northern Rhodesia, 2 vols, London, Macmillan.

Smith, M. G.   1960   Social and cultural pluralism. Annals of the New York Academy of Sciences, 83:763–77. Reprinted in van den Berghe, P. (ed.), Africa: Social Problems of Change and Conflict (1965). San Francisco, Chandler Publishing Co.

Stefaniszyn, B.   1964   Social and Ritual Life of the Ambo of Northern Rhodesia. London, Oxford University Press, for International African Institute.

Tuden, A.   1959   Ila slavery. Rhodes-Livingstone Journal, 24:68–78.

Turner, V. W.   1957   Schism and Continuity in an African Society. Manchester, Manchester University Press, for Rhodes-Livingstone Institute.

van den Berghe, Pierre   1963   Dialectic and functionalism: toward a theoretical synthesis. American Sociological Review, 28: 695–705.

van Velsen, J.   1964a   The Politics of Kinship. New York, The Humanities Press.

────── 1964b   Trends in African nationalism in Southern Rhodesia. Kroniek van Afrika, 139–57.

Veblen, T.   1954   The theory of the leisure class, in: Bendix, R., and Lipset, S. M. (eds.), Class, Status and Power. London, Routledge & Kegan Paul, pp. 35–45.

Watson, W.   1958   Tribal Cohesion in a Money Economy. Manchester, Manchester University Press, for Rhodes-Livingstone Institute.

Weber, Max   1947   Class, status, party, in: Gerth, H. H., and Mills, C. W. (eds.), From Max Weber: Essays in Sociology. London, Kegan Paul, Trench, Trubner & Co. pp. 180–95.

Werbner, R.   1967   Federal politics, rank and civil strife among the Bemba of Zambia. Africa, *37.*

White, C. M. N.   1957   Clan, chieftainship and slavery in Luvale Political Organization. Africa, *27.*

——   1959   A Preliminary Survey of Luvale Rural Economy. Rhodes-Livingstone Paper No. 29. Manchester, Manchester University Press.

——   1960   An Outline of the Luvale Social and Political Organization. Rhodes-Livingstone Paper No. 30.   Manchester, Manchester University Press.

Williams, Robin M., Jr.   1966   Some further comments on chronic controversies. American Journal of Sociology, *71*:717–21.

Wilson, G.   1939   The Constitution of the Ngonde. Rhodes-Livingstone Paper No. 3. Livingstone, Rhodes-Livingstone Institute.

—— and Wilson, M.   1945   The Analysis of Social Change. Cambridge, Cambridge University Press.

RACE, CLASS, AND ETHNICITY
IN SOUTH AFRICA

BY PIERRE L. VAN DEN BERGHE

The Hindu caste system, with its proliferation of status groups, its subtle complexity, and its elaborate religious and ideological superstructure, has exerted a strong fascination on Indian and Western sociologists, historians, and anthropologists. Yet the South African status system, which is as intrinsically deserving of scholarly interest, has not received a commensurate amount of attention from social scientists. To be sure, some aspects of white domination in South Africa, notably the political, economic, and legal ones, have been the object of numerous publications. But general sociological descriptions and analyses of South African stratification have been few.[1]

A terminological note is necessary at this point. The 1960 "racial"

1. See among recent studies of book length Leo Kuper, *An African Bourgeoisie*, New Haven, Yale University Press, 1965, which deals with the black middle class; Pierre L. van den Berghe, *Caneville, the Social Structure of a South African Town*, Middletown, Wesleyan University Press, 1964, a community study; and Pierre L. van den Berghe, *South Africa, A Study in Conflict*, Middletown, Wesleyan University Press, 1965, a more general work. There have been, however, a number of excellent nontechnical background works that help to understand contemporary South Africa. Among the best are Leo Marquard, *The Peoples and Policies of South Africa*, London, Oxford University Press, 1962; Sheila Patterson, *Colour and Culture in South Africa*, London, Routledge & Kegan Paul, 1953; Cornelis W. De Kiewiet, *A History of South Africa, Social and Economic*, Oxford, Clarendon Press, 1941; and Muriel Horrell, *A Survey of Race Relations in South Africa*, Johannesburg, South African Institute of Race Relations (annual).

Portions of the present text have appeared in slightly different form in my book, *South Africa, A Study in Conflict*, Middletown, Conn., Wesleyan University Press, 1965 composition of the South African population was as follows: Africans, 10.9 millions or 68.2 percent; Europeans, 3.1 million or 19.4 percent; "coloreds," 1.5 million or 9.4 percent; and Asians, 0.5 million or 3.0 percent. The Africans belong to various Bantu-speaking groups (Zulu, Xhosa, Sotho, Venda, Ndebele, Swazi, and others) indigenous to the continent. They usually identify themselves either as "Africans" or by ethnic group, but the Europeans have used several other terms in reference to them which have all become more or less distasteful to Africans. Until the nineteenth century, the Europeans referred to Africans as "Kaffirs" (literally "heathen" in Arabic). The word "Kaffir" is still used today, but only as a racial invective. More recently, the English-speaking whites have used and still use the term "Native," while the Nationalist government prefers the word "Bantu" (literally "men" in a large family of African languages called "Bantu languages" by linguists and anthropologists).

The Europeans, who also call themselves "whites," are the descendants of people of many nationalities, but principally of Dutch (some 60 percent) and English (some 40 percent) origin. Small minorities (like French Huguenots) have been generally absorbed by one of the two main ethnic groups. The English call themselves "English-speaking whites," but people of Dutch descent developed a dialect of their own, Afrikaans, which now has the status of one of the two official languages of South Africa, and are now referred to as "Afrikaners." The term "Boer" (literally "peasant" or "farmer") was most commonly used in the nineteenth and early twentieth centuries to designate Dutch settlers in the frontier districts of the Cape and in the Boer Republics of the Transvaal and the Orange Free State.

The Asians are overwhelmingly of East Indian or Pakistani origin, generally refer to themselves as "Indians," and are referred to by members of other groups as "Indians" or "Asiatics." In the nineteenth century, Indians were often called "coolies," a word that still survived as a racial epithet. Finally, the "coloreds" are a residual category including all people not classified in the other three groups. Nearly 90 percent of them are "Cape Coloreds," i.e., the descendants of imported slaves, and the product of miscegenation between whites, slaves, and Hottentots in the Western Cape. Some are also the offspring of whites and Africans. Bushmen have been exterminated on the territory of the Republic of South Africa, and Hottentots no longer survive in pure form. Cape Malays are a Muslim minority of Indonesian origin within the Cape Coloured group, and the term "Bastard" (historically not an insulting word) refers to a special type of colored, namely the offspring of whites and Hottentots.

In order to understand contemporary stratification in South Africa, one has to go back to the origin of the "white problem" in 1652, when the first Dutch settlement gained a foothold at the Cape of Good Hope. Within six years, the importation of a shipload of servile labor had transformed the infant European colony into a slaveholding society. Before long, the paternalistic master-slave model of social relations was established in Cape Town and the surrounding farms and towns of the Western Cape. The resulting status system was relatively complex. From the second half of the seventeenth century until the abolition of slavery in the 1830's, Western Cape society was clearly and rigidly stratified into three main status groups: Europeans, mostly of Dutch but also of French, English, German, and other descent; free people of color, namely Hottentots, political exiles from the Dutch East Indies, emancipated slaves, and, beyond the boundaries of white settlement, Bushmen; and slaves of East African, Malagasy, or Dutch East Indian origin.[2]

During the first two decades of European settlement, culture, or more particularly Christianity as conferred by baptism, appears to have been the primary criterion of membership in the dominant group; however, within a generation, racial prejudice developed, and the three groups had become crystallized into color castes or quasi-castes. Miscegenation was common, as in most slave regimes, but it was almost entirely the result of concubinage between women of color and white men, and people of mixed descent were not admitted to the dominant group, nor even in most cases emancipated if they were born of a slave mother. White "blood" led at best to a privileged status of house slave or of concubine. This great genetic melting pot of slaves, Hottentots, and whites gave rise to a largely Westernized Afrikaans-speaking group who became known as "coloreds" and who still constitute one of the four racial castes of modern South Africa.

The three main color castes of the Western Cape were themselves stratified into social classes. Thus, within the white group one could distinguish a well-to-do bourgeoisie consisting of high-ranking Dutch East India Company employees, merchants, professionals, and fruit farmers near Cape Town; a poorer but still respectable class of artisans, petty employees, and wheat, cattle and sheep farmers in more remote districts; and a lower class of transient sailors, soldiers, and farm laborers. The slaves were stratified into an "aristocracy" of house servants (who were often of partially European ancestry), a "middle class" of skilled craftsmen (such as smiths or carpenters), and the mass of unskilled field

2. Among the best secondary sources on Cape society in the seventeenth and eighteenth centuries are C. G. Botha, *Social Life in the Cape Colony in the 18th Century,* Cape Town and Johannesburg, Juta, 1926; Henri Dehérain, *Le Cap de Bonne-Espérance au 17e Siècle,* Paris, Hachette, 1909 Victor de Kock, *Those in Bondage,* London, Allen & Unwin, 1950; Nobel E. Edwards, *Towards Emancipation: A Study in South African Slavery,* Cardiff, Gomerian Press, 1942; and J. S. Marais, *The Cape Coloured People, 1652-1937,* London, New York and Toronto, Longmans, 1939.

Pierre L. van den Berghe : Ethnicity in South Africa

hands. Of lowest status of all were the slaves owned by the Dutch East India Company who were housed in a notorious "lodge" which served as a sailors' and soldiers' brothel in the evening.[3] Among the nominally free Hottentots, an aristocracy of "Bastards" arose. These people were the offspring of Dutch colonists and Hottentots who proudly called themselves "Bardards" to distinguish themselves from half-breeds of slave ancestry.

By the late seventeenth century, the color line had become quite rigid, although some surreptitious "passing" into the white group took place during the eighteenth and nineteenth centuries, and even later. As in most slave societies, there was little physical segregation by race. Masters and slaves (especially house servants) lived in close symbiosis, but *social* distance, as symbolized and enforced by an elaborate etiquette of race relations (terms of address, sumptuary regulations, etc.), was great. Emancipation was uncommon: between 1715 and 1792, only 893 persons were liberated out of a slave population increasing from 2000 to nearly 15,000.[4] Also, the lot of the legally and nominally free Hottentots (who constituted the bulk of the "free people of color" until they miscegenated out of existence and fused with the rest of the Cape Colored population) was less secure than that of slaves, and their status was scarcely any higher.

The boundaries of the white settlement expanded continuously in spite of attempts by the Dutch East India Company and later the British government to contain the immigration of the Boer pastoralists into the hinterland. Thus, beyond the settled districts of the Western Cape, there existed until the 1880's a vast frontier area inhabited by *trekboers* (as the nomadic Dutch settlers were named); by Hottentots who were gradually deprived of their cattle and pasture land and were forced into symbiotic serfdom, working as herdsmen and servants for the Boers; and by Bushmen who were hunted like wild beasts by the Boers and were wiped out in the present area of South Africa. The frontier area of the Northern and Eastern Cape had quite a different system of stratification from the settled districts of the Western Cape. The whites were, for the most part, poor sheep and cattle farmers who had only sporadic contacts with the market economy of Cape Town. Consequently, they were much less stratified among themselves and could afford to own fewer slaves than the Dutch in and around Cape Town. They fought endemic guerrillas against the aboriginal population on whose hunting and pasture land they encroached, and reduced the remnants of the Hottentots to serfdom under a paternalistic model of race relations. There too, physical segregation was minimal, but social distance was great. The farther one went from the Cape, the fewer the slaves became, and the more numerous the Hottentots.

3. O. F. Mentzel, *A Description of the African Cape of Good Hope, 1787*, Cape Town, The Van Riebeeck Society, 1944, Vol. II, p. 125.
4. H. P. Cruse, *Die Opheffing van die Kleurling-Bevolking*, Cape Town, Citadel Press, 1947, p. 253.

When the Boers encountered the Bantu-speaking peoples (who today call themselves "Africans") on the great Fish River in the 1770's, a new phase of South African history began. A new series of frontier wars (the so-called Kaffir Wars) opened, but the white advance eastward was greatly slowed down for over half a century. Unlike the Hottentots, the Africans were organized in large, politically centralized nations. Starting in 1836, the Great Trek marked a sudden expansion of the Boers into what are today the provinces of Natal, the Orange Free State, and the Transvaal. Repeating their treatment of Hottentots on a larger scale, the Boers forcibly pushed back most of the African nation states beyond the area of white occupation, and made serfs (or what they euphemistically called "apprentices") of the remaining African population. A new two-caste system along rigid master-and-servants lines was established. The white frontier population, thinly scattered over vast expanses of savannah, continued to exhibit, both in its ideology and in its social organization, the syndrome of what I have called "*Herrenvolk* egalitarianism." They were an individualistic people mistrustful of power and authority, who regarded each other as equals and ruled themselves democratically (or, indeed, not at all); but, at the same time, they were imbued with a feeling of moral, religious, and social superiority vis-à-vis the "Kaffirs." In part as a reaction against British policies at the Cape which had been among the immediate causes of the Great Trek, the color bar was enshrined in the 1858 Constitution of the South African (Transvaal) Republic: "The people will suffer no equality of whites and blacks in either state or church."

Meanwhile the British occupation of the Cape from 1795 to 1803, and then again more permanently from 1806 on, further complicated the South African scene. With the subsequent immigration of some 5000 British settlers in the Eastern Cape in 1820, the steady increase in British settlement in the Western Cape, and the extension of British power to Natal in 1843, a long history of conflict between English and Afrikaners was started which culminated in the Anglo-Boer Wars of 1880 and 1899–1902. Starting in 1860, the coming of indentured Indian laborers to work on the sugarcane plantations of Natal introduced the fourth major element into the South African kaleidoscope. Along with indentured workers came free "passenger" Indians of both Muslim and Hindu religion, who settled as a merchant class principally in Natal and on the Witwatersrand.

In 1867, the discovery of diamonds and, to a much greater degree, the 1886 openings of the Witwatersrand gold fields opened up the interior of the continent to outside influences. Railways were built; towns sprang up to rival with Cape Town; the pastoral Boer Republics of the Transvaal and the Orange Free State became embroiled in conflicts of interest with British imperialism which led to their downfall; servile African labor was

Pierre L. van den Berghe: Ethnicity in South Africa

gradually replaced by a highly mobile force of migratory contract workers; in time, secondary and service industries supplemented the mines to make the Johannesburg-Pretoria area the largest economic complex in Africa.

When the four territories of the Cape, Natal, the Transvaal, and the Orange Free State were united to form the white-settler dominated Union of South Africa in 1910, the basic structure of the country was largely established. South Africa was already an economically expanding nation undergoing rapid urbanization, industrialization, and Westernization, but saddled with an anachronistic system of racial castes and with a white minority ruling as a home-based colonial regime over 80 percent of the population. The two World Wars and the aftermath of the second one witnessed an acceleration of these processes, a constant deepening of these fundamental contradictions in the social structure, and a steady rise in the tensions which threaten to destroy the status quo.

Before turning to an analysis of the system of social stratification in contemporary South Africa, and at the risk of belaboring what is well known, let us review briefly some of the major ways in which the country differs from the rest of the continent.

1. While South African society is partially the result of the colonial expansion of Europe, as were other African territories, it also grew out of a slave society similar, on a smaller scale, to the antebellum southern United States, northeastern Brazil, or the West Indies. Thus, South Africa has at least as many similarities with, say, Alabama as it does with Nigeria or the Congo.

2. As a colonial country, South Africa has been largely ruled since the mid-nineteenth century not by the civil servants of a distant European power, but by the local white settlers through a "representative" government. As a result, the involvement of the ruling group has been not only economic and political but also emotional, and color policies have been more rigid and unadaptable than elsewhere in Africa. In fact, whatever change did take place in the legal and political status of the nonwhite groups has been reactionary: Africans and "coloreds" have lost most of the few rights they had in 1910.

3. Although South Africa only has the continent's fourth largest population and seventh largest land area (exclusive of South West Africa), it stands out as an economic and industrial giant by African standards. The three largest cities south of the Sahara are within its borders; nearly half (47 percent in 1960) of its population is urban; its gross national product accounts for approximately one fourth of the continental total; and its economy is well diversified in spite of the continued importance of gold mining. The contrast between this highly dynamic modern industrial economy and the preindustrial system of

ascribed castes is thus more pronounced than in any other former colonial territory.

4. With a white population of over three million, the European minority is several times larger, both absolutely and relatively, than that of any other African country. (Algeria with the second highest European population had a non-Muslim minority of about one million, or 10 percent of the total, before independence.) The size of the white population is not so important in itself as it is in its social consequences: greater monopolization of means of production, including land; more entrenched military and political power; greater internal stratification of the white group; lower occupational ceilings on Africans; and generally a more oppressive and exploitative regime for the subordinate groups.

5. South Africa is also the most Europeanized of African countries, particularly the Western Cape, which belongs culturally more to Europe than to Africa. Approximately one third of the population speak European languages in their homes (namely, all whites, virtually all "coloreds," numerous Indians and a small but growing minority of Africans). Over half of the population are literate, and over two thirds are Christians if one includes the African Separatist churches. Islam is practiced only by small nonindigenous minorities (Cape Malays and Indians). African traditions are steadily undermined, or at least profoundly modified in the urban environment.

In studying the modern South African system of stratification, we shall first describe its major characteristics and dimensions, then indicate the sources of strain and the dynamics of change within the system, and finally raise some of the theoretical problems involved in analyzing complex status systems such as that of South Africa.

As a first approximation, the South African system of stratification can be described in terms of caste and class, as Warner, Dollard, Myrdal, and other authors dealing with the United States have done.[5] It is not my intention here to reopen the debate on the use of the term *caste* in a racial context, for the discussion is largely one of definition.[6] I shall therefore adopt a minimum definition of *caste* as an endogamous group, hierarchically ranked in relation to other groups, and wherein membership is determined by birth and for life. To avoid equivocation with Hindu caste, I shall speak, where necessary, of *color castes* or *racial castes*.

In most general terms, South African society consists of four racial

5. See Gunnar Myrdal, *An American Dilemma*, New York, Harper & Row, 1944; John Dollard, *Caste and Class in a Southern Town*, New Haven, Yale University Press, 1937; Allison W. Davies, B. B. Gardner, and M. R. Gardner, *Deep South*, Chicago, University of Chicago Press, 1941.
6. Oliver C. Cox is one of the prominent opponents of the use of the term *caste* in the race context. See his *Caste, Class and Race*, Garden City, Doubleday, 1948.

Pierre L. van den Berghe: Ethnicity in South Africa

castes, and each of those is subdivided according to the usual criteria of a Western class system. Such a description is only approximate, however, insofar as many other lines of cleavage, some hierarchical, others not, further subdivide the population. Let us begin, nevertheless, with the most important criterion of status in South Africa, namely *race*. Although race gives rise to an extremely rigid division into four easily recognized color castes, its social definition is oddly vague. There exist numerous legal definitions of *race*, adopting differing combinations of physical appearance, ancestry, association with other people, and even "reputation" (e.g., the testimony of witnesses can be accepted as evidence concerning one's racial membership). Unlike statuses in the southern United States, which gave precise definitions of Negroes as any persons having more than a specified percentage of African "blood" (1/16, 1/32, etc.), no such precision exists in South Africa. This lack of formal precision about the most basic single principle on which the society is organized is only one of the many paradoxes of South Africa.

In practice, however, there is relatively little confusion as to who belongs to which group, except in the Cape, where a long history of miscegenation allows many light-skinned coloreds to "play white," and where many "whites" have "a touch of the tar brush." A number of lighter-skinned Africans can also successfully pass for colored, but, in the large majority of cases, physical appearance is a reliable indicator of race. The four racial groups satisfy the minimum definition of *caste* previously given. They are hierarchized, almost entirely endogamous, and mobility between groups is, with a few exceptions, impossible. Let us examine each of these three characteristics in turn.

The whites or Europeans, numbering 19.4 percent of the total population, are clearly at the top of the hierarchy. Not only do they enjoy a much higher standard of living, education, and health than the vast majority of the nonwhites, but they virtually monopolize all the occupations above the level of semiskilled workers; they are, for all practical purposes, the only group to have political rights, and they enjoy countless other legal and customary privileges. By comparison, all three nonwhite races occupy a much lower status, and the differences between the three nonwhite groups are smaller than those separating Europeans and non-Europeans. The "coloreds" (9.4 percent of the total population) are nearest to the whites insofar as they suffer under fewer vexations and legal disabilities than the other nonwhites, but, in terms of education and income, they stand perhaps a little lower, on the average, than the Indians, who constitute 3 percent of the population. Indians and coloreds occupy thus a nearly equal position in the hierarchy between the Europeans and the Africans, but nearer the latter than the former. The Africans, more commonly referred to by the whites as "Natives" or "Bantu,"

number 68.2 percent of the population and constitute the broad base of
the racial pyramid. Their standards of living, occupational status, and
education are the lowest, and they are the target of most discrimination.
The three lowest color castes are often referred to collectively as "nonwhites" or "non-Europeans" to mark the gulf that separates them from
the whites, so that it might be more appropriate to speak of two color
castes, the lower one subdivided into three subcastes. For purposes of
simplicity, however, I shall speak of four castes.

Not only is the socioeconomic gap between whites and nonwhites
wide and unbreachable, but, in some respects, the racial differential
increased until the mid-fifties, largely as a result of political restrictions.
In spite of a tendency toward equalization of wages in developing economies, Africans then got a diminishing share of the national income (less
than 20 percent), and were worse off in terms of purchasing power than
before the war. Educational statistics indicate that Africans are progressing
proportionately faster than whites, but since the passage of the Bantu
Education Act, the quality of African schooling is steadily decreasing.

Endogamy, the second essential characteristic of caste, is likewise
found in the four racial groups in South Africa.[7] Since 1949 marriage
between whites and all nonwhites is forbidden under the Prohibition of
Mixed Marriages Act. There is thus complete compulsory endogamy
between these two groups. Even miscegenation outside marriage is a
criminal offense under the Immorality Act of 1927 as amended in 1950
and 1957. Marriages between Indians, colored, and Africans are legally
permitted, but actually rare. The same was true of white-nonwhite
marriages before they were forbidden. In 1946, for example, only 1
European out of 714 married outside his racial group. The corresponding
figures for coloreds, Indians, and Africans were 1 in 20, 1 in 31, and 1 in
67 respectively. Of the total number of registered marriages in 1946, only
1.38 percent were racially exogamous.[8] Among the Europeans, there
exists now, contrary to the tolerant attitude in the old Cape, a strong
taboo against miscegenation, and even more so against intermarriage. In
the other groups, the racial taboo is not as strong as among whites, but
other factors such as religion, language, and education level effectively
hinder exogamy.

The four racial groups in South Africa also satisfy the minimum
definition of caste, in that membership in them is ascribed at birth, and
mobility is practically nonexistent, except through surreptitious passing.
The offspring of racially exogamous unions are defined at birth as "colored," regardless of the parent groups. In fact, a number of light-skinned

7. For a more detailed study of mixed marriages and miscegenation, see my article: "Mis-
    cegenation in South Africa," *Cahiers d'Etudes Africaines*, 4, 1960, pp. 69–84.
8. *Ibid.*

Pierre L. van den Berghe: Ethnicity in South Africa

coloreds manage to be accepted as whites, and brown-skinned Africans as coloreds. A number of first-generation coloreds also become assimilated in the African group. The extent of passing is, of course, impossible to determine accurately or even approximately, but while passing has probably become increasingly rare during the past decade, the racial groups today are certainly anything but "pure" after three hundred years of miscegenation. Since the genetic situation remained relatively fluid until at least the first third of the nineteenth century, one can safely estimate that anywhere from one tenth to one quarter of the persons classified as "white" in the Cape Province are of mixed descent, and that almost every "old family" in white Cape society has genealogical connections with colored families. The passage of the Population Registration Act in 1950, however, intended to eliminate passing and to make the four castes absolutely rigid. Indeed, the Act provides for the issue of identity cards where the race of the person will be indicated. Special boards are entrusted with the task of deciding once and for all the racial membership of marginal persons who contest their classification. While the task of these boards is still far from completed,[9] mobility between the color-castes has become virtually impossible.

Besides the properties of the racial castes already mentioned, membership in a given "race" entails many other crucial consequences. To be white entails full humanity and citizenship plus a number of special privileges restricted to the master race. All Europeans over eighteen years of age (except convicted criminals) have the franchise at all levels of government. White workers are protected from nonwhite competition, insofar as they retain a virtual monopoly of skilled manual jobs, as well as of higher clerical, managerial, civil service, and professional posts, at rates of pay from *five* to *fifteen* times those of unskilled nonwhite jobs. They have the right to organize in trade unions, to go on strike, to bear arms, to own land in freehold in most of the country (except in the Native Reserves and in the few areas declared for occupation of Indians and coloreds), to move freely in the entire country (except in certain African areas where they need permits), to change freely their place of residence, to buy and consume alcoholic beverages,[10] to stand for elective office, etc.

Technically, of course, the Europeans are subject to racial segregation, as are the non-Europeans, and a white person may not use facilities reserved for nonwhites or live in nonwhite areas. In practice, such restrictions are irksome only to a small minority of liberal whites who reject segregation in principle, and who resent the possession of racial privileges. For the vast majority of Europeans, these "restrictions" are, in

9. Some 21,000 borderline "Coloreds" have yet to be classified, according to a *Time* report of May 24, 1963.
10. Since 1962 this right has been extended to Africans.

fact, advantages, since the whites monopolize the lion's share of existing facilities and resources, in terms of both quantity and quality. Whites own and occupy, for example, 87 percent of the country's land. In many cases, a given facility (e.g., park bench, swimming pool, golf course, cinema, etc.) is *only* available for whites in a given community.

To be nonwhite means being deprived of most or all of the foregoing advantages and being treated as a helot and an unwelcome intruder in one's own country. Nonwhites are not only segregated but almost invariably given inferior service and facilities, or no facilities at all, in practically every sphere of life, except in most shops (which have become sensitive to the threat of nonwhite economic boycotts). Racial segregation is the rule in restaurants, hotels, cinemas, hospitals, schools, waiting rooms, park benches, beaches, cemeteries, residential areas, ambulances, taxis, trains, buses, picnic areas, airports, entrances to public buildings, swimming pools, sports grounds, post offices, elevators, banks, toilets, bars, national parks, and many other places. Nonwhite servants accompanying their masters are, however, tolerated in many of these places, provided their servile condition is unambiguous. Some of that segregation is "customary" (i.e., imposed by traditional white prejudices), while some is compulsory under law. To avoid any ambiguity as to whether segregated facilities must be physically equal, a special law, the Reservation of Separate Amenities Act, was passed in 1953, stating that facilities may be not only separate but also *unequal*.

All nonwhites (except foreign diplomats and the Japanese, who, for reasons of international trade, have been declared to be "white") are subject to the daily humiliations of segregation. No non-European may bear arms in the defense forces, stand as a candidate for Parliament, or live anywhere but in specially set aside "Group Areas." Beyond these restrictions, there are differences between Africans, Indians, and coloreds in the number and extent of disabilities and vexations. Africans are by far the most oppressed, and the coloreds are the least underprivileged of the nonwhites, although their condition is rapidly deteriorating.

The coloreds in the Cape Province still have a vestigial, though meaningless, franchise on a separate roll electing special white representatives to Parliament, whereas the Africans and the Indians have no franchise rights in the election of national, provincial, or municipal representatives.[11] The coloreds still retain an increasingly precarious foothold in some skilled trades from which Africans and Indians are excluded. Unlike Africans who have to carry a "reference book" limiting their spacial mobility, and unlike Indians who are forbidden to enter or

---

11. Since the establishment of the first Bantustan in the Transkei, Africans living in that area may elect a minority of the members of the Transkeian Assembly.

Pierre L. van den Berghe: Ethnicity in South Africa

to stop in certain areas of the country (such as the Transkei and the Orange Free State), the coloreds are relatively free to travel in South Africa. Coloreds have always had access to liquor, from which Africans, and to a lesser degree Indians, were debarred by law until 1962. Where there is segregation between the nonwhite groups, as in schools, the facilities for coloreds and Indians are generally better than for Africans, though considerably inferior to the white facilities. Coloreds and Indians still have a limited right to strike, which is completely denied to Africans. Similarly, coloreds and Indians have a right to own land in freehold in certain small areas legally set aside for their occupation. Africans, on the other hand, with a few insignificant exceptions, may possess land nowhere in their own country. Land tenure in practically all Native Reserves is communal, not personal; in practice this means that the right to use and occupy land can be granted and revoked at the whim of government-appointed chiefs.

As can be seen from the preceding, the Africans bear the brunt of white oppression in South Africa. Well-to-do Indians and coloreds can isolate themselves to a degree from much unpleasant contact with whites, and from daily humiliation from the officialdom. Africans, on the other hand, are constantly exposed to police intimidation, imprisonment for purely technical offenses under the pass regulations, arbitrary deportation and countless other indignities.

Although "race" is by far the most important criterion of status in South Africa, it is not the sole relevant factor in the system of social stratification, for each racial group is internally subdivided. We shall take in turn the whites, coloreds, Indians, and Africans. The whites are first segmented into three distinct subgroups along linguistic and religious lines—namely the Afrikaners, the "English-speaking South Africans," and the Jews, not to mention much smaller groups such as the Germans. These divisions are not directly hierarchical, but they are related to social status and to political and economic power.

The Afrikaners are the whites who speak Afrikaans. The vast majority of them also belong to one of the Dutch Reformed Churches. Afrikaans-speaking coloreds are, of course, excluded from the *Volk*. Afrikaners number approximately 57 percent of the whites; and under a practically all-white franchise, they have played a predominant role in the politics of the country. Since 1948 they have held a virtual monopoly of political power through the Nationalist Party, which represents the vast majority of them. In terms of education and economic status, however, they still lag behind the other whites, on the average, although these differences tend to disappear. Among Johannesburg whites in 1952, for example, only 1.5 percent of the Afrikaners compared to 10 percent of the English families earned more than £1000 a year.[12] In Durban in 1951 the mean *per capita* income was £299 a year for English-speaking whites and £187 for Afrikaans-speaking whites.[13]

The Afrikaners are less urbanized than the English and the Jews, and their representation in big business, mining, and banking is still small compared with that of the English whites. In 1949 it was estimated that Afrikaners were in control of 6 percent of South African industry and 25 to 30 percent of commerce. However, the number of Afrikaner-owned firms increased from 2428 to 9585 between 1939 and 1949, and Afrikaner gains have continued since.[14] Yet, in the mid-fifties, Afrikaner capital in all branches of mining controlled only 1 percent of total production.[15] The "poor whites," who continued to be numerous until the depression of the 1930's, were practically all Afrikaners, but through government subsidies and the so-called civilized labor policy, "poor whites" have disappeared as a class.[16] In spite of this, Afrikaners are more heavily represented than the English or the Jews in the lower white echelons of the occupational, income, and educational scales. In the medical and legal professions, however, the Afrikaners are rapidly increasing. The vast majority of civil service posts reserved for whites are held by Afrikaners, at all levels of administration. The 1957 civil service recruitment figures show that of 100 white entrants at the professional level, 81 were Afrikaners; at the clerical level, 89 percent were Afrikaans-speaking.[17]

The term *English-speaking South African* is doubly ambiguous, insofar as it is not only a linguistic label but also a racial and a religious one. English-speaking nonwhites are not included in this category, since, in the eyes of most whites, they are not citizens of the country. This label sometimes also implies membership in, or allegiance to, one of the Christian denominations. While most Jews are linguistically assimilated to the English whites, they generally consider themselves, and are considered by the Christians, as constituting a separate group. Altogether, some 39 percent of the whites speak English at home. The English and the Jews share many socioeconomic characteristics, as opposed to the Afrikaners. Both groups are predominantly urban, the Jews almost exclusively so, retain a virtual monopoly of large commercial, mining, and financial concerns, and are practically excluded from political power and the civil

12. Stanley Trapido, "Political Institutions and Afrikaner Social Structures in the Republic of South Africa," *American Political Science Review*, 57, 1963, pp. 75–97.
13. Heinz Hartmann, *Enterprise and Politics in South Africa*, Princeton, Princeton University Press, 1962.
14. Sheila Patterson, *The Last Trek*, London, Routledge & Kegan Paul, 1957.
15. Leo Kuper et al., *Durban, A Study in Racial Ecology*, London, Cape, 1958, p. 89.
16. Of course, improved economic conditions in the late 1930's and during the Second World War also contributed to the disappearance of "poor whites."
17. Hartmann, *op. cit.*, p. 62.

Pierre L. van den Berghe: Ethnicity in South Africa

service, except in the Natal Provincial Administration and in the large municipalities of the Transvaal and the Eastern Cape. Compared with the Afrikaners, the other two white groups are wealthier and more highly educated. This is even truer of the Jews than of the English. Politically, the majority of the English support the United Party, but in recent years the English upper class and many Jews have turned to the less conservative Progressive Party.

The three main white subgroups cannot be called "castes," as the divisions between them are not rigid. Intermarriage is fairly common; many persons of Afrikaner origin have become Anglicized; and conversely a few originally English families are Afrikanerized. The 1951 census classifies 73 percent of the whites as bilingual, though only 2 percent habitually speak both European languages at home. The main importance of the linguistic cleavage within the white caste is in the field of politics. This is particularly true since the Nationalist victory of 1948; there has been an increasing polarization of white party politics along ethnic lines.

The three white groups cannot be ranked hierarchically. While many Afrikaners have traditionally had a cultural inferiority complex vis-à-vis the English,[18] and while they are, on the whole, of a lower socioeconomic status than the English and the Jews, the social class system cuts across linguistic and religious distinctions, and must be analyzed independently.

In general, the white class system resembles that of the United States, Canada, or Australia, except for the virtual absence of a lower class. White artisans enjoy a legally protected position and a relatively high standard of living, and lack any consciousness of belonging to a proletariat opposed to the white bourgeoisie, or having any common interests with the nonwhite proletariat. To speak of class alignments in the Marxian sense of relationship to the means of production does not correspond to social reality in South Africa. This absence of a white proletarian class consciousness accounts for the weakness of the South African labor movement. The latter has always been tainted by racialism in South Africa and has always defined its function as that of protecting the white manual worker against nonwhite competition.

There is no clear-cut distinction between European artisans, smaller farmers, and petty civil servants or white-collar workers. Together they constitute what could be called a petty bourgeoisie or a lower middle class. Many white industrial workers come from a rural background, as a number of small farmers have been forced away from marginal land into the urban economy. The members of this bottom stratum of white society have, in general, primary and some secondary or technical education, and an income of £40 to £80 a month; they live in modest but

18. Cf. Patterson, *op. cit.*

comfortable houses, own a small motorcar, and employ one or two non-white servants. Politically, members of that stratum are as conservative as other whites, if not more so, and they distinguish themselves from the upper bourgeoisie mostly through lower income and education, and through taste and life-style differences which these imply. Rather than constituting a well-defined, corporate class in the Marxian sense, they are an amorphous stratum of individuals sharing roughly the same socioeconomic status in the sense of Warner's "lower middle class."

The white upper bourgeoisie is similarly ill-defined. It consists of persons having at least secondary education and occupying the higher echelons of the occupational scale. It includes as disparate groups as higher civil servants, managers, large farmers, small businessmen, and professionals. Its style of life is more luxurious than that of the petty bourgeoisie. Homes and motorcars are larger, newer, and more elegant, and the number of nonwhite servants often reaches three or four. Tastes in reading and entertainment become more "refined."

At the apex of white society, one finds small groups wielding considerable power. As in many other "new" societies, there is no entrenched aristocracy in South Africa, but rather a number of distinct and conflicting elites or oligarchies competing for power. Of these, the most important are the big-business and the political groups. The military is not a distinct power group in South Africa. The white intelligentsia is small, geographically scattered in the various universities and large urban centers, internally divided along political lines, largely excluded from direct participation in power, but nevertheless influential in certain spheres. Needless to say, these various white elites, while sharing a high socioeconomic status, differ widely in their tastes and modes of life, and do not, in any sense, constitute a unitary upper class.

In short, we see that the white class system is relatively fluid and open. The fact that South Africa is a fairly "young" country may account, in part, for this fluidity, but the color situation has also played an important role. South African whites view themselves, first and foremost, as members of the dominant racial group. Internal class differences become secondary, and the gulf that separates Europeans from non-Europeans serves to minimize class consciousness and the perception of objective class differences within the dominant white caste. As a corollary of the rigid system of racial castes, Europeans exhibit "*Herrenvolk* egalitarianism." Not only does color-consciousness create bonds of solidarity between all whites regardless of class, but it also prevents the establishment of class ties *across* racial barriers. Color overshadows and weakens class and class consciousness.

The "colored" group is stratified along lines similar to the whites, but at a much lower socioeconomic level. Whereas the lower class is

Pierre L. van den Berghe: Ethnicity in South Africa

almost nonexistent among the whites, the vast majority of the coloreds constitute an impoverished proletariat of agricultural workers, domestic servants, and unskilled or semiskilled factory workers. Above this lower class, one finds a much smaller but sizable lower middle class of artisans and petty clerks, and a tiny upper middle class of small businessmen and professionals, mostly schoolteachers. In economic terms, this colored elite live at about the same level as the white petty bourgeoisie, because coloreds earn much less than equally qualified whites doing the same work.

The colored stratification system is, however, qualitatively different from the white system in one important respect. Of the four racial groups, the colored group is the only one to be internally differentiated on the basis of physical traits. All other things being equal, the more closely a colored resembles a white person in skin color, hair texture, and facial features, the higher his status is. Coloreds are, on the average, at least as color-conscious as the majority of the Europeans. In recent years socio-economic criteria have become more important than physical traits in determining status within the colored group, but appearance still plays an important role among older and uneducated people.[19] Educated coloreds, for the most part, react strongly against status differences based on physical characteristics, and against the approval of concubinage with whites among some members of the colored lower class as a method of "improving" the race. In practice, the two sets of status criteria are difficult to dissociate, because there is still a fairly high correlation between physical traits and various indices of socioeconomic status within the colored group.

Racial consciousness among coloreds has also entailed other consequences. As an intermediate caste, the coloreds have traditionally been caught between their feelings of racial superiority vis-à-vis the Africans, and their constantly frustrated hope of acceptance by the whites. This has led to ambivalent attitudes toward the whites, to political passivity, and to a failure to identify with the Africans. The mass of the colored proletariat have, like the white manual workers, refused to identify with the African proletariat, which they view with feelings of superiority and hostility.

Of the four racial groups, the Indians are by far the most complexly stratified and segmented. They are first divided along religious and linguistic lines which are not hierarchical, but which are correlated with socioeconomic status. The most profound rift is between Muslims and Hindus. Religious intermarriage is extremely rare, and social intercourse is limited

19. Cf. W. van den Merwe, "Stratification in a Cape Coloured Community," *Sociology and Social Research, 46,* 1962, pp. 302–11; and Pierre L. van den Berghe, "Some Trends in Unpublished Social Science Research in South Africa," *International Social Science Journal, 14,* 1962, pp. 723–32.

to the fields of employment, education and politics. The few Christians who are almost all converts from Hinduism, interact rather freely with Hindus. Although there are some poor Muslims and a few rich Hindus, the Muslims are, on the average, considerably better off than the Hindus, and are overrepresented in the merchant class.

Each of the Indian religious groups is subdivided along linguistic lines. The Muslims are either Gujarati or Urdu, and the Hindus are divided among the Tamil, Hindi, Telugu, and Gujarati. The language groups are not as widely apart as the religious communities, but, except between Tamil and Telugu, intermarriage is rare. The Gujarati, whether Muslim or Hindi, almost all belong to the merchant class and constitute the conservative economic elite among Indians. Among Hindus there are profound cultural differences between the northern Indian groups (Hindi and Gujarati) and the southern groups (Tamil and Telugu). Each of the Hindu linguistic entities is itself subdivided into hierarchized *varnas* and castes, but these traditional cleavages are quickly losing in importance. *Varna* endogamy is still largely practiced, but the rules of caste (*jat*) endogamy are broken with increasing frequency. In other aspects of life such as religious practices, diet, commensality, and purification rituals, the Hindu caste system has practically ceased to operate.[20]

Yet another line of cleavage among Indians is the distinction between "indentured" and "passenger." The former are the descendants of indentured laborers who came to Natal to work in the sugarcane plantations, whereas the latter paid their own sea voyage from India and established themselves mostly as merchants and clerks. Although the distinction is losing in importance, the passengers, who are in the minority, consider themselves superior on the whole to people of indentured stock. Most passenger Indians were Gujarati, and to a lesser extent Hindi and Urdu. A far greater proportion of Muslims than of Hindus is of passenger origin. The passenger–indentured division is thus correlated with religion and language groups and is clearly hierarchical. Among the younger generation the distinction has, however, lost almost all of its meaning, as has the Hindu caste system. Religious barriers remain quite strong, but linguistic divisions progressively lose their rigidity, as English slowly supplants Indian languages in all spheres of life.

Western criteria of status, such as education, income, and occupation, on the other hand, are of growing importance, and stratify the Indian group along increasingly distinct class lines. Contrary to European belief, most Indians are poor and are either small farmers, agricultural

20. For more detailed descriptions of social stratification among Indians see H. Kuper, *Indian People in Natal*, Natal, University of Natal Press, 1960; Pierre L. van den Berghe, *Caneville*, *loc. cit.*; and Birbal Rambiritch and Pierre L. van den Berghe, "Caste in a Natal Hindu Community," *African Studies*, 20, 1961, pp. 217–25.

Pierre L. van den Berghe: Ethnicity in South Africa

laborers, or unskilled and semiskilled industrial workers. Above this poor working class, one finds a lower middle class of medium farmers, clerks, small shopkeepers, and skilled workers. The Indian upper middle class is divided into two distinct groups: a conservative, traditional elite of large merchants, some of whom are quite wealthy, and a Western-oriented, politically active intelligentsia consisting mostly of teachers, physicians, and lawyers. The white image of the Indian is largely based on the small merchant class, which is anything but typical of the Indian community.

The African "race" is both stratified into emerging social classes and segmented into ethnic groups, but the two types of division are in an antithetical relationship to one another. In short, one can say that ethnic affiliation recedes in importance as social classes emerge from the process of Westernization. This statement is too schematic, however, and covers a more complex reality. Since practically all Africans still speak a Bantu language as their mother tongue, and retain other African cultural characteristics, they almost all belong to a so-called tribe, in a formal sense. For most town dwellers and many rural inhabitants, this ethnic affiliation has become vague, however, and has ceased to be an important social reality. Such people are integrated into the Western economic system; they have lost all political, and sometimes even kinship, ties with traditional society; they are Christians, at least nominally so, and they live altogether outside of the traditional environment. They continue to speak their mother tongue at home, and they may preserve a sense of affiliation to their original national group, but many factors make for the rapid disappearance of "tribalism."

All urban centers are ethnic melting pots where Africans learn not only European languages, but also Bantu tongues other than their own, and common "pidgin" dialects. The disintegration of the traditional family through the migratory labor system favors interethnic unions, in the form of both marriage and concubinage. More and more Africans are thus of mixed stock. As members of Christian denominations, as neighbors in the "locations," as fellow workers in the mines or factories, Africans of various linguistic groups constantly mix with one another. Moreover, Africans are becoming increasingly conscious that they are subject to a common system of political oppression and economic exploitation. Political consciousness militates against ethnic particularism and leads people to think in terms of "we Africans."

All of these factors notwithstanding, a substantial segment of the rural population remains integrated, through kinship and local political ties, in the traditional way of life. This is particularly true of the Transkei and Zululand, the two principal remaining pockets of cultural conservatism in South Africa. These people, known among the whites as "raw

Natives" or "red-blanket Kaffirs," enter periodically into the Western economy in order to provide minimum means of subsistence to their families in the impoverished reserves, but remain often staunchly traditional and reject Christianity, Western education, and the other "white man's ways."[21] Even in these conservative rural areas, however, a segment of the population known as the "school" people have accepted missionary influence and are in the process of acculturation.

Traditional Southern Bantu society is unstratified in Western class terms, though there are, of course, wide differences in status between commoners and chiefs, and between various clans. Ownership of cattle, polygyny, and numerous descendants are important status symbols in traditional rural society, which has thus its own prestige system independent of the emerging class system of urbanized and Christianized Africans. Traditional Africans are on the margin of the class system which they do not accept, and in which they do not participate. At the same time they constitute a stratum at the bottom of the African community, insofar as status among Westernized urban people is largely a function of the degree of acculturation to the European way of life. The "raw" Africans are viewed by most educated urban Africans as backward, primitive, and ignorant pagans, or, at least, as naïve and unsophisticated countryfolk.

Among Africans at various stages of Westernization, class distinctions following Western lines are becoming increasingly sharp. Prestige is closely related with the extent to which a person has acquired European culture, and the urge toward Westernization is strong. This is not to say that urban or Christian Africans want to be "white," as many coloreds do, but rather that they have accepted the values of Western culture. The principal criteria of status among urban Africans are education, Christianity, occupation, clothing, and moral "respectability." Wealth does not play the role that it does in the white community, because the scope for capital accumulation among Africans is stringently limited. An African may not acquire land or open a business except in a few small areas, and discrimination debars him from practically all better-paid jobs, no matter how well qualified he is. The monotonous uniformity of municipal housing in the "Native locations" imposes a common mold and standard of living on Africans of all classes. Except in clothing and furniture, there is little scope for conspicuous consumption and for material symbols of wealth.

The majority of Africans live on or below the minimum standard for health, as domestic servants, mine workers, agricultural laborers, or unskilled workers in secondary and tertiary industry. Agriculture in the Native Reserves is almost invariably *sub*-subsistence, and must be supplemented by wage earnings. A small minority of petty white-collar workers

21. Cf. Philip Mayer, *Townsmen or Tribesmen*, Cape Town, Oxford University Press, 1961.

Pierre L. van den Berghe: Ethnicity in South Africa

live more or less precariously above the vital minimum as a *Lumpen-bourgeoisie*, and an even smaller class of teachers, students, ministers, nurses, and other professionals constitutes the elite of the emerging African middle class. In 1959 there were 49 African lawyers, 67 librarians, 81 medical doctors, 73 chartered accountants, 176 laboratory assistants, and 61 analytical chemists in the entire country.[22] Even this elite lives at a material level inferior to that of all but destitute "poor whites," in spite of the fact that many of its members have matriculated and hold university degrees. Literacy, knowledge of a European language, mostly English, membership in an established (i.e., non-"Zionist") church, and a certain standard of moral respectability are the minimum requirements for membership in the *Lumpenbourgeoisie*, and correspondingly higher requirements are necessary for membership in the tiny elite. It is largely from this last group that the political leadership of the liberatory movements is recruited.

Unlike among Indians, there is practically no African business class, partly for reasons just mentioned. The relative absence of an indigenous entrepreneur class is common to most African countries where commerce, finance, and industry have been monopolized by European and, secondarily, by Asian interests. But although the South African economy is considerably more developed than that of Ghana or Nigeria, the African entrepreneur class is even more embryonic than in these two countries. A survey of the South-Western Townships of Johannesburg (the large ghetto for Africans some 12 to 20 miles from the metropolis) reveals that only some 1200 African traders serve a population of approximately 400,000. By far the greatest majority of these traders are small businessmen, with net assets of under £1000, such as 400 general dealers, 243 butchers, 176 fresh produce dealers, 136 eating-house keepers, 95 wood and coal dealers, etc. By far the greatest handicaps mentioned by a sample of 47 African merchants are lack of capital and of police protection.[23] Rules of African hospitality (misleadingly termed *family parasitism* by Europeans), whereby a financially successful man is descended upon by numerous relatives who expect him to share his wealth, are of course another important hindrance to capital accumulation. This African system of familial social security, which had a definite function in a traditional rural milieu, thus becomes a liability in the urban environment, or at any rate in one that is dominated by a capitalist system of production.

In addition to this cultural limitation and to crippling apartheid restrictions on the purchase of real estate, African traders are granted

22. Hartmann, *op. cit.*, p. 43.
23. Lawrence Reyburn, *African Traders*, Johannesburg, South African Institute of Race Relations, 1960, pp. 2, 10–13. On the other hand, the government's policy of denying trade licenses to persons of a race different from that of the population living in a specific "group area" has protected to some extent African traders from competition from European or Indian merchants.

licenses only in African areas, and draw their clientele almost exclusively from their own racial group, as the government intends that they should. Not only do their customers have limited purchasing power, but African merchants have to compete with larger European and Indian merchants, who generally undersell them through volume of trade. Lacking real estate as guarantees for loans, the raising of capital for Africans is extremely difficult, except in small sums and at usurious rates of interest. On the other hand, in order to retain customers, African traders have to extend credit beyond their financial capacity. This leads to a relatively high rate of bankruptcies, and the latter, in turn, reinforce the European stereotype that Africans constitute bad risks, and make it even more difficult to raise capital. In view of such staggering handicaps, it is a wonder that any Africans at all have become successful businessmen, as indeed a few have.[24]

From the foregoing description it can be seen that the stratification system of South Africa is far too complex to conform in detail to the American "class and caste" schema of Warner and others. The only principle that pervades the whole society is that of "race," leading to a rigid, fourfold classification imposed by the whites, and rejected as illegitimate by the nonwhites. But each of the four color-castes is internally subdivided and stratified according to criteria that differ from one group to the other. While there is a general tendency in all groups to develop social classes along Western lines, numerous other traditional factors continue to play an important role. Even when status is distributed according to Western class criteria, the standards of achievement are proportionally lower according to the position of the racial group in the color-caste hierarchy. Furthermore, the relative emphasis placed on the various criteria (such as wealth, education, and occupation) differs from one "race" to the other. Not only are the objective characteristics of class widely divergent from one racial group to another, but such class consciousness as exists is largely limited to one's racial caste. Because of the all-pervading racial barrier, each "race" constitutes at once a separate reference group in the status system and an autonomous subsystem of status with its own criteria. At the same time, the significance of "race" and the acceptance of racial criteria of status vary widely, being greatest among whites and coloreds, and minimal among Africans and Indians. Racial barriers are objective realities, but the vast majority of the non-Europeans are not accommodated to their lower status, and deny any legitimacy to the racial hierarchy which is ultimately maintained through the might of the white-controlled state.

The South African stratification system not only exhibits great rigidity

24. For a more detailed treatment of the African urban middle class, see Leo Kuper, *An African Bourgeoisie*, New Haven, Yale University Press, 1965.

Pierre L. van den Berghe: Ethnicity in South Africa

and complexity, but also pervades virtually all other aspects of society. To speak of white supremacy in South Africa is to describe not only the country's status system, but also its economic and political organization, the value system of the dominant group, and processes of cultural change. To trace the ramifications of the color-caste system through the entire fabric of South African society is clearly beyond the scope of this chapter.[25] I should like, however, to go beyond the somewhat static picture presented so far, and to mention the most important strains which inevitably undermine the status quo.

One of the most basic sources of conflict in South Africa, besides the very existence of the color-caste system as such, is that the "races" no longer constitute ethnic groups, if indeed they ever have. The major racial cleavage between whites and nonwhites cuts across the cultural distinction between Westernized and non-Westernized. The coloreds are fully as Western in culture as American Negroes; but, like Negroes, they are denied admission to the dominant group, purely on the basis of "race." The same applies to increasing numbers of Westernized Africans and Indians. Thus, the government's argument that apartheid aims at separating peoples of different cultural backgrounds rests on less than a half-truth. Apartheid is nothing less than rigid *racial* segregation, irrespective of culture. The overlap between race and culture is not only partial; it is steadily decreasing as Westernization spreads through schooling, the mass media, the churches, urban employment, and other means. This results in mounting tensions as nonwhites increasingly attack white domination in terms of techniques, values, and concepts acquired in the process of Westernization. The government is so cognizant of the threat that Westernization poses to white domination that much of the apartheid program aims at reversing acculturation and at sponsoring a revivalism of pseudo-traditional "Bantu culture."

The rigidly ascribed color-caste system also conflicts with economic imperatives in a highly industrialized society such as South Africa. The anachronism of the caste system and of the government's racial policies in an economically dynamic country constitutes perhaps the most glaring source of strain in modern South Africa. The Nationalist government increasingly endeavors to restrict the urban migration of Africans, to compartmentalize the country into artificial racial ghettos, to quadruplicate racially based school systems, to restrict occupations by race regardless of competence, to create industries or urban centers where there is no economic basis for them, to build vast African townships far away from places of employment in the "white" cities, to perpetuate the wasteful "migratory labor system," to enforce artificially high wages for whites

25. Cf. Leo Marquard, *The Peoples and Policies of South Africa, loc. cit.*, and Pierre L. van den Berghe, *South Africa, A Study in Conflict, loc. cit.*

and low wages for nonwhites, and to impose countless other racially inspired restrictions on economic life.

The relationship between race and politics is so close that the "color problem" and "non-European policies" have become the central concern of both major white parties. As government policies have become increasingly reactionary, ideological polarization along racial lines took place: the nonwhite opposition turned reluctantly away from its tradition of *Satyagraha* and passive resistance, and the Afrikaner and English segments of the white population were drawn together against the "black menace." There is virtually complete agreement on basic color issues between the ruling Afrikaner Nationalists and the English opposition represented by the United Party. If anything, the United Party has recently moved to the right of the Nationalist Party. Conversely, there is almost no area of consensus between Africans and the overwhelming majority of the whites.

Not only have the South African status system and polity failed to adjust to the profound economic and cultural changes of the last half century, but whatever change did occur was in a reactionary direction. The color castes were made more rigid; miscegenation and intermarriage between whites and nonwhites were outlawed; attempts were made to legislate away or to minimize interracial contact except in the master-servant relationship; considerable resources were devoted to reversing trends toward acculturation and urbanization; white racism and nationalism called forth their black counterparts. In short, the internal contradictions within South Africa society are deepening, conflict has become endemic, the scope of white tyranny widens, and the vicious circle of racial prejudice and discrimination becomes less and less reversible.

In conclusion, I should like to raise some theoretical issues raised by the South African system of stratification. To the extent that the present case is a very special and extreme one, it highlights the inadequacy of certain simplifying assumptions which underlie much stratification or class theory. The functionalist model is perhaps most patently inadequate, but so are some conflict or elitist theories based on monocausal determinism and neat dichotomies such as the classical views of Marx and Mosca, or those of recent theorists such as Dahrendorf.[26] Perhaps a major source of limitations in the treatment of class has been the making of unnecessary of false assumptions concerning the presence of cultural homogeneity, value consensus, or the "objective" determinants of class.

A growing body of theory developed in recent years, mostly by anthropologists working in the African or West Indian field, has attempted

26Cf. Ralf Dahrendorf, *Class and Class Conflict in Industrial Society*, Stanford, California, Stanford University Press, 1959.

Pierre L. van den Berghe: Ethnicity in South Africa

to deal with stratification in plural societies.[27] South Africa is both *socially* pluralistic in that it is segmented into groups with parallel structures and sets of institutions, and *culturally* pluralistic in that several cultural traditions are represented which share no common system of values. Clearly pluralism and the resulting lack of consensus make for a different and much more complex stratification system than, for example, a culturally homogeneous class society.

In the preceding description of the South Africa status system I have used the "caste and class" model which Warner and others have utilized to deal with Negro-white relations in the United States. However, in South Africa (a considerably more pluralistic country than the United States), the "caste and class" model (which only deals with structural cleavages) is only a rough first approximation to a more complex reality. Let us examine briefly some complicating factors introduced by cultural and structural pluralism in the analysis of social stratification:

1. As a consequence of the multiplicity of criteria of status and of the lack of agreement on their relative weight, any description of "objective reality" becomes quite difficult. If one takes the position that the social reality of stratification is constituted by the composite and mutual evaluations of members of a society, one ends up not with a single system, but with many microsystems which are at best loosely integrated with each other. If one arbitrarily defines "class" as a resultant of some external "objective" condition (e.g., relationship to the means of production, or the exercise of power), the picture becomes much simpler, but the universe with which one endeavors to deal is grotesquely pulled out of shape or indeed eludes one altogether. It is doubtful that "objective" criteria of stratification or "class" are anything but arbitrary categories, the definition of which exhausts their content. On the other hand, the extreme relativistic and subjectivist approach almost precludes the very notion of system in a highly pluralistic society.

Fortunately, there is a partial escape from these difficulties: while, at the limit, every member's estimation of others defines the total situation, in fact, some members' evaluations are much more determining than others. Thus, the South African whites who have the power to translate their prejudices into coercive power have created and perpetuated a color-caste system, even though the latter is denied legitimacy by most non-whites. Much of our preceding description of castes has been made in terms of the subjective definition of the whites as translated by the latter's power into observable behavior.

27. Cf. M. G. Smith, "Social and Cultural Pluralism" and Lloyd Braithwaite, "Social Stratification and Cultural Pluralism," in *Annals of the New York Academy of Sciences, 83,* 1959–60; see also, Pierre L. van den Berghe, "Toward a Sociology of Africa," *Social Forces, 43,* 1964, in which I attempt to apply pluralist theory to the South African case, and Clyde Mitchell, *Tribalism and the Plural Society,* London, Oxford University Press, 1960.

Yet, the dominant group's definition of the situation is not the only relevant one. For example, the fact that many whites regard Indians as a fairly undifferentiated group does not make it so. Indeed, it may be cogently argued that South African Indians only constitute a group insofar as whites regard them as such and have imposed certain common disabilities on them.

2. Even in a relatively simple "caste and class" system such as that of the United States, i.e., in a system where there is some modicum of agreement on the criteria of social class stratification within the various castes, class status between castes is not convertible because the castes themselves are hierarchized. Furthermore, class and caste are not commensurate; there is no single continuum, but rather there are two somewhat overlapping ones. Thus, in the United States, one can say that Negroes (in general) rank lower than whites, but not that any Negro ranks lower than any white, nor for that matter that the average status of a middle-class Negro is equivalent to that of a middle class white. With four color-castes as in South Africa, these problems resulting from social or structural pluralism become even more complex. Does a working-class colored rank higher than a middle-class African, or a middle-class colored than a working-class white, or an African lawyer than a white bricklayer? There is simply no valid answer to that order of question.

3. In the process of cultural contact, millions of persons in South Africa are continuously shuttling back and forth between two or more cultural universes.[28] In terms of social status, this "cultural commuting" in time and space means that the same person is alternatingly incorporated in different systems of rank based on different criteria, and that consequently his statuses in the various systems may be quite discrepant. Thus, an African domestic servant who has a lowly status in the white hierarchy may in his traditional rural environment be the son of a chief, a polygynist, a cattle owner, and a paragon of filial piety, all factors making for high traditional status. Or a Hindu girl of Sudra origin may be the daughter of a physician and thus enjoy high socioeconomic status. Indeed the same criterion, e.g., age, may work in opposite directions in different systems: the respected elder in traditional society may become the unemployed beggar in the city. Such status discrepancies may or may not be accompanied by role conflicts, depending on how clearly the sphere of applicability or boundaries of each system are defined. But they are almost invariably accompanied by value conflicts (which often take an intergenerational form) as different persons within the same groups ascribe various weights or degrees of legitimacy to the status criteria involved.

28. These processes have been studied, among others, by Philip Mayer. See his *Townsmen or Tribesmen*, Cape Town, Oxford University Press, 1961; and "Migrancy and the Study of Africans in Towns," *American Anthropologist*, 64, 1962, pp. 576–92.

4. Another aspect of stratification raised by cultural pluralism is the extent to which conventional criteria such as life-style, income, occupation, education, etc., can in fact be regarded as indices of "class" or stratum as opposed to simply "status locators" for individuals. One of the essential conditions for the existence of an established class system as commonly defined is a strong anchorage in the kinship system. This anchorage can take many forms, but typically includes some mechanisms for the inheritance of wealth, status, and power between generations and some status transference between spouses and between parents and children. This has characterized most industrial as well as preindustrial stratified societies.

In pluralistic countries, however, where non-Western segments of the population are in the process of entering a Western-type class system, the transition situation is more complex. In the case of many first-generation urbanites, socioeconomic status characteristics describe individuals rather than families, and individual status differences appear long before the crystallization of any well-defined class system. Thus, an African professional, who is very much middle class or even "elite" by Western urban standards, will often have parents and siblings who are nonliterate peasants. His wife may have had little formal education, be quite traditionally oriented, and have few meaningful contacts with her husband's colleagues and associates. This cultural dualism may even be reflected in the household itself—e.g., traditional diet and eating customs may be followed within the family, and Western customs when outsiders are present; or the front parlor will be furnished with "prestige" Western items, while the kitchen and bedrooms will reflect a more traditional approach.

Clearly, this situation is not simply one of "upward mobility." Rather, it results from movement from one culture to another, one of the aspects of which is individual *entry* into a new status system. Equally clearly, one can only speak of an *incipient* class system in a situation where many basic ties of kinship, ethnicity, locality of origin, politics, etc., cut across emerging class barriers.

5. Highly pluralistic societies also raise the problem of *scope* of the status system. The sphere of applicability of a given criterion or rank may be wide or narrow, thereby establishing a rough scale of importance between criteria and subsystems. Thus, in South Africa, "race" as socially defined by the whites is clearly the most pervasive criterion, and the color-caste system has primacy over the other subsystems of rank. Social class in the Western sense, as determined by the usual educational and socioeconomic criteria, probably takes second place; and traditional non-Western status systems (such as the Hindu caste system) are increasingly relegated to a tertiary position.

6. Generally but not necessarily related to scope (in the sense of number of people affected) is the factor of *relevance* for a given individual or

group. For example, the Hindu caste system only affects some 2 percent of the South African population, but for a Hindu, *varna* membership is a factor determining such important events as marriage. Or, to take another illustration, when the rural African seeks employment in the "white" towns he becomes "objectively" a member of the urban *Lumpenproletariat*, and is generally regarded as such by both whites and settled urban Africans. Yet, if he is traditionally oriented and has his significant social ties in his home village, the urban status system may be so alien to his world view and so irrelevant to his self-image that he will exhibit no class consciousness. He may be aware that he is the butt of jokes and that other Africans regard him as a naive country bumpkin, an illiterate or a "pagan," but these categories have little if any subjective meaning to him if his significant reference group is his patrilineage, his patriclan or his village.

These considerations by no means exhaust the problems presented by the analysis of stratification in plural societies. I have left untouched a number of interesting complicating elements such as age and sex criteria of status as these differ from one cultural tradition to another and relate, for example, to changes in the status of urban African women. The role of orthodoxy, social conformity, and morality as criteria of status has been greatly neglected in the sociological literature, and I followed precedent on this score. For example, interesting forms of ostracism, somewhat analogous to outcasting and concepts of ritual defilement in India, affect whites who associate with nonwhites or express liberal views. Even white civil servants who, in the line of duty, come in close contact with Africans have lower status than their counterparts working with whites, as remarked by Kuper.[29] Some of the few Europeans who have married nonwhites before the Prohibition of Mixed Marriages Act (1949) or who have lived extramaritally with nonwhites have been legally outcasted and reclassified as coloreds. Similarly, I have not dealt with the elaborate South African etiquette of race relations, with the detailed implementation of racial segregation, and with other mechanisms of social control whereby the white minority maintains physical and social distance from nonwhites.[30] I have also barely touched upon the intricate superstructure of racial mythology and stereotyping, and the ideological excrescences of apartheid.

All these limitations are dictated by the nature of the case. Where ascribed status is so pervasive and so closely related to polity and economy, social stratification is probably the best analytical vantage point from which to survey the society as a whole; but this is obviously a bigger task than present space allows.

29. Leo Kuper, *An African Bourgeoisie*, New Haven, Yale University Press, 1965.
30. I do so at greater length in my community study, *Caneville, loc. cit.*

INDEX

373

Index

Index

378

Index

Index

Index

Index

Index

Index

Index